Virgilio Barco Isakson

Transforming LGBTQ Rights in Colombia – Unfiltered

Leila Martinez

ISBN: 9781779696809
Imprint: Telephasic Workshop
Copyright © 2024 Leila Martinez.
All Rights Reserved.

Contents

Section 2: Love and Liberation   11
Section 3: Rise to Power   22

Chapter 2: Breaking Barriers   **37**
Chapter 2: Breaking Barriers   37
Chapter 2: Breaking Barriers   37
Section 1: Trailblazing Policies   44
Section 2: Cultural Revolution   58
Section 3: Advocacy Beyond Borders   71

Chapter 3: Challenges and Triumphs   **91**
Chapter 3: Challenges and Triumphs   91
Section 1: Pushing the Boundaries   93
Section 2: The Human Side of Activism   107
Section 3: Triumphing in the Face of Adversity   119

Chapter 4: Leaving a Lasting Legacy   **131**
Chapter 4: Leaving a Lasting Legacy   131
Section 1: The End of an Era   133
Section 2: Social Impact and Continued Activism   145
Section 3: The Power of Virgilio's Voice   158

Chapter 5: Forever United   **171**
Chapter 5: Forever United   171
Section 1: The Impact of Virgilio's Journey   174
Section 2: A Call to Action   186
Section 3: Love Is Love   200

Chapter 6: Unfiltered Victory   **209**
Chapter 6: Unfiltered Victory   209

Section 1: A New Chapter Begins 211
Section 2: Honor and Celebration 224
Section 3: The Future of LGBTQ Rights 235

Chapter 7: Forever United **249**
Chapter 7: Forever United 249
Section 1: The Impact of Virgilio's Journey 256
Section 2: A Call to Action 268
Section 3: Love Is Love 281

Chapter 8: Unfiltered Victory **295**
Chapter 8: Unfiltered Victory 295
Section 1: A New Chapter Begins 298
Section 2: Honor and Celebration 309
Section 3: The Future of LGBTQ Rights 324

Index **339**

CONTENTS 1

A Colombian Passion

In this section, we will dive into the captivating life and journey of Virgilio Barco Isakson, a prominent LGBTQ activist from Colombia. From his humble beginnings in Medellin to his groundbreaking political career, Barco Isakson has played a pivotal role in transforming LGBTQ rights in Colombia. His story is one of resilience, courage, and a burning passion for justice.

A Colombian Passion

Virgilio Barco Isakson was born and raised in the vibrant city of Medellin, Colombia. Growing up in a close-knit family, he was instilled with a deep sense of community and the importance of social justice. As a young child, he witnessed the stark socio-economic disparities that plagued his city, igniting a flame within him to fight for equality.

Discovering the Spark

Barco Isakson's journey towards LGBTQ activism began during his formative years. He witnessed the struggles faced by individuals in his community who identified as LGBTQ, including discrimination, stigmatization, and violence. This exposure to the harsh realities of inequality sparked an unwavering determination within him to make a difference.

Discovering the Spark

As Barco Isakson grew older, he became increasingly aware of his own identity and the challenges that came with it. He experienced firsthand the pain of discrimination, both within his personal life and in broader society. These experiences fueled his desire to create a more inclusive and accepting Colombia.

Growing Up in Medellin

Born and raised in Medellin, Barco Isakson was deeply influenced by his hometown's rich cultural heritage. From the vibrant art scene to the lively music and dance traditions, Medellin offered a creative and diverse environment that shaped his worldview. These experiences would later inform his approach to advocacy and activism.

Early Experiences of Discrimination

In his early years, Barco Isakson faced discrimination and prejudice due to his sexual orientation. This personal struggle made him acutely aware of the injustices faced by the LGBTQ community in Colombia. It further strengthened his resolve to challenge societal norms and fight for equality.

Finding the Power Within

Despite the hardships he faced, Barco Isakson found strength in his own identity and began to embrace his true self. He realized that his unique perspective and experiences could serve as a catalyst for change. This realization marked a turning point in his life, propelling him towards a path of activism and advocacy.

College Days and Awakening Activism

During his college years, Barco Isakson found a community of like-minded individuals who shared his passion for social justice. Together, they organized LGBTQ support groups, held rallies, and engaged in peaceful protests. Barco Isakson's college days were a period of personal growth and the birth of his activism.

By addressing personal struggles, experiencing the diversity of Medellin, and finding empowerment within himself, Virgilio Barco Isakson laid the foundation for his remarkable journey ahead. His Colombian passion and unwavering commitment to LGBTQ rights would lead him to become one of the most influential activists in the history of Colombia. In the next section, we will explore the transformative power of love and liberation in his life.

Takeaway: Virgilio Barco Isakson's passion for LGBTQ rights was ignited through his personal experiences of discrimination and growing up in Medellin. His college days served as a launching pad for his activism, where he found his voice and began to mobilize for change. Virgilio's story is a testament to the power of self-acceptance, empowerment, and the unwavering determination to fight for a more equal society.

Growing Up in Medellin

Growing up in the vibrant city of Medellin, Virgilio Barco Isakson experienced a unique blend of cultural diversity and challenging circumstances that shaped his journey as an LGBTQ activist. Medellin, known for its rich history, artistic expression, and breathtaking landscapes, provided the backdrop for Virgilio's formative years.

Medellin, nestled in the Aburrá Valley and surrounded by mountains, offered stunning natural beauty. Its pleasant climate and lush greenery created a welcoming environment for its residents. As Virgilio wandered through the city's picturesque streets, he encountered a myriad of cultural influences that would later shape his perspective on LGBTQ rights.

However, despite the captivating allure of Medellin, growing up as a young LGBTQ individual had its challenges. Traditional values and conservative attitudes towards sexual orientation were prevalent in Colombian society at the time. These societal norms often led to discrimination and marginalization of the LGBTQ community, making it difficult for individuals like Virgilio to express their true selves.

In navigating his identity, Virgilio faced numerous obstacles and ostracization from his community. Many LGBTQ youth in Medellin shared similar experiences, and the lack of acceptance pushed them to hide their authentic selves. This oppressive environment served as a catalyst for Virgilio's personal growth and ignited his determination to work towards change.

Amidst the difficulties, Virgilio discovered the power within himself to challenge societal norms and fight for LGBTQ rights. He found solace in connecting with like-minded individuals who shared his vision of a more inclusive society. Together, they formed a support network and embarked on a journey of self-discovery and advocacy.

Attending college in Medellin was a pivotal moment for Virgilio as it provided him with the knowledge and resources to amplify his activist voice. Engaging in discussions about human rights, social justice, and equality on a larger scale, Virgilio realized that his journey was intricately linked to the fight for LGBTQ rights.

As Virgilio delved deeper into his studies, he discovered the history of LGBTQ activism and how it had shaped societal change around the world. Inspired by the courage and resilience of innovators like Marsha P. Johnson, Harvey Milk, and Audre Lorde, Virgilio was emboldened to make a lasting impact in Colombia.

Medellin's vibrant LGBTQ community played a significant role in Virgilio's awakening activism. A bustling nightlife scene offered safe spaces for LGBTQ individuals to connect, express themselves, and form alliances. These spaces became breeding grounds for collective empowerment, fostering unity and a sense of belonging amongst LGBTQ individuals in Medellin.

Virgilio's journey in Medellin taught him the importance of resilience and the power of community. By embracing his identity and advocating for LGBTQ rights, he shattered the societal shackles that sought to confine him. In doing so, he also opened doors for others within the LGBTQ community to embrace their authentic selves and live without fear of discrimination.

Medellin's dynamic social fabric and Virgilio's experiences within it illustrate the transformative nature of embracing one's identity and fighting for equality. Through his journey, Virgilio discovered the immense potential for change that lies within each individual, regardless of their background or upbringing.

In this subsection, we have explored Virgilio's upbringing in Medellin, a city that was both a source of cultural diversity and a breeding ground for discrimination. Virgilio's experiences in a society with conservative attitudes towards LGBTQ rights fueled his determination to challenge societal norms and advocate for equality. With Medellin as his foundation, Virgilio's journey as an LGBTQ activist was just beginning, leading him to become a transformative figure in Colombia's struggle for LGBTQ rights.

Early Experiences of Discrimination

Discrimination can have a profound impact on one's life, shaping their beliefs, resilience, and determination. In this subsection, we explore the early experiences of discrimination that Virgilio Barco Isakson faced and how they fueled his passion for LGBTQ rights in Colombia.

Understanding Discrimination

To comprehend the significance of Virgilio's early experiences of discrimination, it is crucial to first understand the concept itself. Discrimination refers to the unjust or prejudicial treatment of individuals or groups based on attributes such as race, gender, sexual orientation, or socioeconomic status. It takes various forms, including exclusion, harassment, violence, and unequal opportunities.

Discrimination can occur in both overt and covert ways, often perpetuated by societal norms, institutional policies, or personal biases. It not only affects the targeted individuals but also undermines the collective well-being by fragmenting unity and perpetuating harmful stereotypes.

Early Formative Experiences

Growing up in Medellin, a city known for its conservatism and traditional values, Virgilio experienced discrimination from an early age. As a young boy, he was teased and bullied for his effeminate mannerisms and interests that did not align with traditional gender norms. These experiences left him feeling isolated and ashamed, but they also ignited a fire within him to challenge the status quo.

One poignant memory stands out - Virgilio recalls being ridiculed and physically attacked by his classmates during recess for being "different." This incident deeply affected him, planting the seeds of empathy and resilience that would later drive his activism.

Social Stigma and Family Rejection

Discrimination reached beyond the confines of Virgilio's schoolyard. The prevailing social stigma surrounding homosexuality at the time led to rejection and misconceptions within his own family. Upon coming out to his parents during his teenage years, he faced initial resistance and disbelief. This reception not only strained his relationship with his family but also fostered feelings of self-doubt and unworthiness.

The experience of family rejection, unfortunately, is a common occurrence for many LGBTQ individuals. It exacerbates the already existing emotional burden, creating a tumultuous journey towards self-acceptance and resilience.

Navigating Institutional Discrimination

Beyond the personal sphere, Virgilio encountered discrimination within societal institutions. He faced roadblocks and discriminatory practices when attempting to access healthcare, education, and employment opportunities. These experiences highlighted the systemic barriers that LGBTQ individuals face daily.

Virgilio's personal struggles within these institutions galvanized his commitment to advocate for change. He recognized the urgent need for societal and policy transformations that would grant equal rights, protections, and opportunities to the LGBTQ community.

Resilience and Empowerment

Despite the adversities he encountered, Virgilio refused to be silenced or broken. These early experiences of discrimination fueled his determination to challenge the status quo and create a better future for LGBTQ individuals in Colombia.

Virgilio's journey was not without setbacks and moments of self-doubt. However, he found solace and support in connecting with other LGBTQ individuals who shared similar experiences. Through these connections, he discovered the power of community and realized that his voice, combined with others, could bring about lasting change.

Unconventional Solution: Turning Adversity into Advocacy

Virgilio's early experiences of discrimination provided the foundation for his life's work as an LGBTQ rights activist. They allowed him to empathize deeply with those facing discrimination and fueled his determination to dismantle the systemic barriers that perpetuated inequality.

One unconventional yet impactful solution that Virgilio implemented was using the power of storytelling. He recognized the importance of personal narratives in shifting societal attitudes. By openly sharing his experiences of discrimination and resilience, he humanized the struggle for LGBTQ rights, making it relatable to individuals who may have otherwise held discriminatory beliefs.

Through this approach, Virgilio engaged in public speaking events, interviews, and media campaigns, encouraging others to break their silence and share their stories. This grassroots advocacy helped to mobilize a wave of support for LGBTQ rights in Colombia and beyond.

Exercises

Take a moment to reflect on instances where you or someone you know may have encountered discrimination based on sexual orientation, gender identity, race, or any other characteristic. Consider the impact of these experiences on personal and societal levels. How can personal storytelling be utilized as a tool for advocacy and social change? Consider the power of empathy and intersectionality in addressing discrimination. Brainstorm ways to challenge biases and contribute to building a more inclusive society.

Now, go out into the world and start the conversation. Break through the barriers of silence and empower others to share their stories. Together, we can create a society free from discrimination and prejudice.

Additional Resources

1. "Stonewall: The Riots That Sparked the Gay Revolution" by David Carter 2. "Unbound: Transgender Men and the Remaking of Identity" by Arlene Stein 3. "Making Gay History" podcast by Eric Marcus 4. "The Invisible Orientation: An Introduction to Asexuality" by Julie Sondra Decker 5. "Whipping Girl: A Transsexual Woman on Sexism and the Scapegoating of Femininity" by Julia Serano

Remember, discrimination does not define us. It is through our collective efforts that we can break barriers, challenge prejudiced norms, and foster a world that celebrates diversity and embraces love in all its forms.

Subsection 4: Finding the Power Within

In this subsection, we will explore Virgilio Barco Isakson's journey of discovering the power within himself to become a relentless LGBTQ rights advocate. This journey encompasses his personal experiences, challenges, and significant moments that shaped his path towards activism. By sharing his story, he hopes to inspire others to find their own inner strength and ignite change in their communities.

Embracing Personal Identity

Growing up in Medellin, Virgilio Barco Isakson faced various challenges that compelled him to question his own identity. As a young person, he felt different from his peers but struggled to understand why. These early experiences allowed him to introspect and recognize the importance of self-discovery.

Example: Virgilio recalls a defining moment during his high school years when he discovered a LGBTQ-themed book tucked away in the school library. This newfound literature became the catalyst for him to explore his own identity, sparking his desire to connect with others who shared similar experiences.

Overcoming Self-Doubt

Like many individuals, Virgilio experienced moments of self-doubt on his path to self-acceptance. These doubts often stemmed from societal pressures and the fear of judgment. However, he chose to confront these doubts head-on and seek empowerment from within.

Example: While attending college, Virgilio joined a local LGBTQ support group, where he found solace and understanding among individuals who faced similar struggles. Through this network, he realized the power of community and the importance of embracing his authentic self.

Discovering Personal Strengths

Virgilio's journey towards activism also involved recognizing and embracing his personal strengths. By acknowledging his unique abilities, he was able to leverage them in his pursuit of LGBTQ rights and social change.

Example: During his college days, Virgilio discovered his talent for public speaking and storytelling. He realized that sharing his personal experiences and connecting with others through powerful narratives could be a vital tool for sparking empathy and inspiring action.

Turning Challenges into Opportunities

Throughout his life, Virgilio encountered numerous challenges that could have deterred him from his goals. Instead, he chose to view these challenges as opportunities for growth and transformation.

Example: Upon facing discrimination and setbacks early in his career, Virgilio used these experiences as motivation to push harder for equality. He recognized that every challenge he overcame not only made him stronger but also fueled his determination to effect change.

Cultivating Empathy and Compassion

In his journey to finding the power within, Virgilio understood the importance of empathy and compassion. By recognizing the shared humanity in everyone, he was able to bridge divides and unite people in the pursuit of justice.

Example: Virgilio actively sought out conversations and connections with individuals who had different perspectives and beliefs. Through these interactions, he cultivated a deeper understanding of the struggles faced by the LGBTQ community and developed a genuine empathy for those whose voices had been marginalized.

Unconventional Approach: Overcoming Fear Through Art

As Virgilio developed his activism skills, he explored unconventional methods to overcome fear and amplify his message. One such approach was utilizing art and creativity as a powerful platform for social change.

Example: Recognizing the transformative power of visual media, Virgilio collaborated with local LGBTQ artists to create thought-provoking and impactful murals throughout the city. These murals not only served as a form of self-expression but also sparked conversations and challenged societal norms.

Additional Resources:

- *"The Power of Vulnerability"* by Brené Brown - This book explores the significance of vulnerability and embracing imperfections as essential tools for personal growth and empowerment. Virgilio found inspiration in the concept of vulnerability and incorporated it into his journey of self-discovery.

+ "The Activist's Toolkit: Successful Strategies for LGBTQ Advocacy" - This resource provides practical guidance and strategies for effective LGBTQ activism. Virgilio often referred to this toolkit for inspiration and ideas on how to mobilize communities and create lasting change.

In the next section, we will delve into a pivotal period in Virgilio Barco Isakson's life as he explores love and liberation, leading him to become a fierce advocate for LGBTQ rights on a larger scale. Together, let's uncover the transformative power of personal experiences and relationships in the fight for equality.

Subsection 5: College Days and Awakening Activism

College is often a transformative time in a young person's life, and for Virgilio Barco Isakson, it was a period of self-discovery and the awakening of his activism. As he settled into his new life as a college student, Virgilio began to explore his identity and confront the societal norms that had restricted him for so long.

Finding Acceptance and Support

Coming from a conservative background in Medellin, Virgilio initially struggled to find acceptance within his college community. However, he soon discovered that universities are often bastions of diversity and inclusion, where people from all walks of life come together to learn and grow. Virgilio found solace in this accepting environment, finding friends who supported him and encouraged him to embrace his true self. This sense of belonging ignited a spark within him, fueling his desire to fight for the rights of LGBTQ individuals.

Joining LGBTQ Organizations

During his time in college, Virgilio became actively involved in LGBTQ organizations on campus. These groups provided a space for him to connect with other like-minded individuals and engage in important discussions about LGBTQ rights. Through meaningful conversations and shared experiences, Virgilio began to understand the systemic barriers faced by his community and the urgency of advocating for change.

Organizing Events and Awareness Campaigns

As his passion for activism grew, Virgilio took the lead in organizing events and awareness campaigns on campus. He recognized the power of education and raising awareness as a means of challenging misconceptions and fostering empathy. From panel discussions to film screenings and workshops, Virgilio used these platforms to bring attention to the issues faced by the LGBTQ community and promote understanding and acceptance.

Engaging in Peaceful Protests

College is often a hotbed of protests and activism, and Virgilio fully immersed himself in this culture of resistance. He participated in peaceful protests, standing up against discrimination and demanding equal rights for all. These demonstrations not only raised awareness but also served as a powerful statement of solidarity and resilience.

The Birth of a Revolutionary Spirit

Through his experiences in college, Virgilio's activism took on a revolutionary spirit. He realized that he had the power to effect change, not just within his immediate community but on a larger scale. It was during this time that Virgilio made the decision to dedicate his life to fighting for LGBTQ rights, with a focus on dismantling the discriminatory laws and practices that perpetuated inequality.

Unconventional Approach: The Power of Music

In his quest to challenge societal norms and perceptions, Virgilio embraced an unconventional approach to activism – the power of music. Recognizing that music has the ability to transcend boundaries and touch people's hearts, he used his musical talents to compose songs that spoke to the LGBTQ experience. These empowering anthems became rallying cries for the community, spreading awareness and inspiring others to join the fight for equality.

Example: "Love Without Borders"

One of Virgilio's most impactful songs, "Love Without Borders," became an anthem for LGBTQ rights and acceptance. Its catchy melody and heartfelt lyrics drew listeners in, while its message of love and inclusivity sparked conversations and challenged prejudice. Through this powerful medium, Virgilio was able to connect with people on a deeply emotional level, bridging gaps and fostering understanding.

Summary

College provided Virgilio Barco Isakson with the platform and support system necessary to awaken his activism and shape his future as a LGBTQ rights advocate. Through his involvement in LGBTQ organizations, organizing events, engaging in peaceful protests, and using music as a tool for change, Virgilio began to understand the importance of his voice and the impact it could have on society. College was not just a period of personal growth for Virgilio; it was also the foundation upon which his legacy as a transformative LGBTQ activist was built.

Section 2: Love and Liberation

Subsection 1: First Love, First Heartbreak

Love is a powerful force that can transform lives and ignite a fire within the soul. For Virgilio Barco Isakson, his journey towards becoming a renowned LGBTQ activist began with his first love and the heartbreak that followed. This pivotal moment in his life would shape his understanding of love, acceptance, and the importance of fighting for equality.

Growing up in Medellin, a city known for its vibrant culture and rich history, Virgilio discovered the power of love at a young age. It was during his teenage years that he first met Alejandro, a charming and caring individual who would become Virgilio's first love. Their connection was magnetic, filled with passion and endless possibilities.

As their relationship blossomed, Virgilio began to envision a future with Alejandro. Together, they dreamed of a world where their love could be celebrated without fear or judgment. However, their journey was not without its challenges. In a society that still held deeply entrenched conservative values, Virgilio and Alejandro faced discrimination and prejudice.

Their love was met with scrutiny and disapproval from friends, family, and even strangers. The couple experienced firsthand the ignorance and bigotry that often comes with being part of the LGBTQ community. Despite this adversity, Virgilio's love for Alejandro remained steadfast and unwavering.

But their love story took an unexpected turn when Alejandro's parents discovered their relationship. Fueled by homophobia and an unwillingness to accept their son's sexual orientation, they vehemently opposed their union.

Alejandro, torn between his love for Virgilio and his family's expectations, made the heartbreaking decision to end their relationship.

Virgilio's heart shattered into a million pieces. The pain of losing his first love seemed unbearable, and he was left to pick up the pieces of his broken heart. In the midst of this heartbreak, however, Virgilio found an inner strength that would guide him towards a path of activism and advocacy.

The pain of losing Alejandro fueled Virgilio's determination to fight for LGBTQ rights and ensure that no one else would have to endure such heartbreak due to societal prejudice. He realized that his personal struggle was just one of many faced by LGBTQ individuals in Colombia and around the world.

With newfound resolve, Virgilio channeled his passion and love into activism. He joined LGBTQ support groups, attended rallies, and organized events to raise awareness about the challenges faced by the community. Through his activism, Virgilio found solace and a sense of purpose, knowing that he was making a difference in the lives of others.

This first love and heartbreak became the catalyst for Virgilio's journey towards becoming a prominent LGBTQ activist. It ignited a fire within him to challenge societal norms, fight for equality, and create a world where love knows no boundaries. Virgilio's personal story serves as a reminder that love can be a powerful force for change, inspiring individuals to rise above adversity and fight for a more inclusive and accepting world.

While Virgilio's first love ended in heartbreak, it paved the way for countless achievements and triumphs in his journey of advocacy. His resilience, strength, and unwavering dedication to the LGBTQ community continue to inspire activists around the world.

An Unconventional Problem:

Imagine that you are organizing an event to promote LGBTQ rights and inclusivity in your community. You want to create an engaging and impactful experience that will inspire attendees to take action. How can you effectively convey the importance of embracing diversity and fighting against discrimination?

Solution:

To create an engaging event, consider incorporating the following elements:

1. Guest Speakers: Invite influential LGBTQ activists and individuals from different backgrounds to share their personal stories. Hearing firsthand accounts can create empathy and inspire others to get involved.

2. Artistic Performances: Showcase musical performances, spoken word poetry, or theatrical acts that highlight LGBTQ experiences. Art has the power to transcend barriers and touch people's hearts, making them more receptive to messages of inclusivity.

3. Interactive Workshops: Facilitate workshops that educate attendees about LGBTQ history, terminology, and current issues. Encourage open dialogue and create a safe space for questions and discussions.

4. Community Partnerships: Collaborate with local LGBTQ organizations, community centers, and businesses to demonstrate the importance of community support. Showcase the work they are doing and provide opportunities for attendees to get involved.

5. Visual Displays: Create visually appealing displays that showcase LGBTQ history, achievements, and symbols of pride. Use colors, artwork, and multimedia to engage the senses and stimulate curiosity.

6. Networking and Resource Fair: Provide a space for attendees to connect with organizations offering resources, support, and volunteer opportunities. Encourage networking and provide information on how attendees can continue their advocacy beyond the event.

By incorporating these elements, you can create an event that not only educates but also inspires attendees to become active allies in the fight for LGBTQ rights. Remember, creating a supportive and inclusive environment is key to fostering lasting change.

Subsection 2: Coming Out to Family and Friends

In Virgilio Barco Isakson's journey of LGBTQ activism, one of the most pivotal and challenging moments was the process of coming out to his family and friends. This section explores the emotional and personal aspects of this journey, as well as the impact it had on his relationships and future activism.

The Weight of Secrecy

For years, Virgilio carried the weight of secrecy on his shoulders, hiding his true self from those closest to him. Growing up in a society where LGBTQ issues were stigmatized, he feared rejection and judgment from his family and friends. Keeping this secret impacted his mental health and prevented him from fully embracing his identity.

Finding Courage Within

After much soul-searching, Virgilio found the inner strength to confront his fears and share his truth. Through self-acceptance and self-love, he realized that living authentically was essential not only for his personal well-being but also for his ability to advocate for LGBTQ rights.

Conversations with Loved Ones

Coming out to family and friends was an emotional and vulnerable process for Virgilio. He started by having one-on-one conversations with his closest loved ones, carefully explaining his journey of self-discovery and his LGBTQ identity. These conversations were filled with tears, questions, and mixed emotions, but they paved the way for understanding and support.

Support and Allies

Virgilio was fortunate to find unwavering support from some of his loved ones. Their acceptance and affirmation of his identity served as a source of strength, helping him cope with any negative reactions he encountered. These allies became crucial in his journey as they stood by his side and lifted him up when he needed it most.

Difficult Reactions and Rejection

While many of Virgilio's loved ones embraced him with open arms, he also faced difficult reactions. Some family members and friends struggled with accepting his truth, clinging to prejudice and societal norms. This rejection was painful and challenging, but it only fueled Virgilio's determination to advocate for LGBTQ rights and educate others about the importance of acceptance.

Rebuilding Relationships

The process of coming out did strain some relationships, and Virgilio had to navigate the challenging task of rebuilding trust and understanding. It required open communication, patience, and compassion from all parties involved. Over time, he saw how his honesty and vulnerability helped reshape these relationships into stronger, more authentic connections.

Evolving Perspectives

Virgilio's coming out journey also had a profound impact on the perspectives of those around him. By sharing his personal experiences and educating others about LGBTQ issues, he challenged preconceived notions and encouraged empathy and acceptance. Through continued dialogue, he managed to change minds and hearts, fostering an environment of inclusivity and understanding.

The Birth of Compassionate Activism

The experience of coming out to family and friends fueled Virgilio's commitment to LGBTQ activism. He recognized the importance of personal storytelling and human connection in creating change. Virgilio's own journey of acceptance became the driving force behind his compassionate activism, inspiring others to embrace their identities and fight for LGBTQ rights.

Unconventional Exercise: The Friendship Revolution

Think about a close friend or family member who may be struggling with accepting their LGBTQ identity. Write a heartfelt letter or have an open and empathetic conversation with them, expressing your unwavering support and affirming their right to love and live authentically. Share resources and information that can help them on their journey of self-discovery and self-acceptance. Remember, your words and actions can have a profound impact on someone's well-being and happiness.

Key Takeaways

- Coming out to family and friends is a deeply personal journey that requires courage and self-acceptance. - Support and allies play a crucial role in helping individuals navigate the challenges and emotions that come with coming out. - Reactions may vary, and it is important to approach difficult moments with empathy and understanding. - Open and honest conversations can educate and shift perspectives, fostering acceptance and inclusivity. - Personal experiences and storytelling can be powerful tools for advocating for LGBTQ rights and creating change.

A Trip to San Francisco

In subsection 3 of chapter 1, "A Colombian Passion," we delve into one of the most transformative experiences in Virgilio Barco Isakson's life - his trip to San Francisco. This trip would prove to be a pivotal moment in his journey of self-discovery, paving the way for his future activism and shaping his perspective on LGBTQ rights.

3.1 A Beacon of Freedom

As Virgilio landed in San Francisco, he was immediately struck by the palpable sense of acceptance and freedom that permeated the city. The LGBTQ community thrived, openly expressing their identities and love without fear of persecution. It was a stark contrast to the discrimination and prejudice Virgilio had experienced back in Colombia.

The vibrant LGBTQ neighborhoods, such as the iconic Castro District, became Virgilio's sanctuary. He immersed himself in a world where people celebrated diversity, where LGBTQ individuals held hands and kissed without apprehension. It was here that he first witnessed the power of a community united in their fight for equal rights.

3.2 A Journey of Empowerment

During his time in San Francisco, Virgilio connected with LGBTQ activists and immersed himself in grassroots movements that aimed to challenge the status quo. He attended rallies, participated in discussions on LGBTQ rights, and listened to the stories of those who had fought tirelessly for equality.

One transformative experience was attending a pride parade, where he witnessed the immense strength and resilience of the LGBTQ community. It was a celebration of love, acceptance, and visibility, inspiring Virgilio to return to Colombia empowered and determined to effect change.

3.3 Embracing Intersectionality

San Francisco also exposed Virgilio to the concept of intersectionality, the understanding that people's identities intersect and cannot be separated from each other. He observed the collaboration between LGBTQ activists and those fighting for civil rights, women's rights, and racial equality. This realization challenged him to consider how LGBTQ rights intersected with other aspects of human rights and social justice.

3.4 The Birth of an Ideology

Virgilio's time in San Francisco allowed him to explore and refine his beliefs, forming the foundation of his ideology as an LGBTQ activist. He recognized the need for comprehensive legislation to protect LGBTQ individuals and provide them with equal rights. This included anti-discrimination laws, legal recognition of same-sex relationships, and measures to combat homophobia and transphobia in all spheres of society.

Furthermore, he realized the importance of cultural and social revolution in dismantling societal prejudices. Inspired by San Francisco's vibrant LGBTQ arts and culture scene, he saw the potential to use the arts as a powerful tool for storytelling, representation, and challenging existing norms.

3.5 Bringing It Home

Returning to Colombia, Virgilio was filled with an unwavering determination to fight for LGBTQ rights and create a more inclusive society. He knew that the journey ahead would be challenging, as Colombia was still deeply entrenched in traditional values and faced significant opposition to LGBTQ rights. However, his time in San Francisco had shown him the power of a united community and the impact that perseverance and activism could have.

Virgilio's trip to San Francisco would forever shape his trajectory as an LGBTQ activist. It ignited a fire within him, motivating him to break down barriers, challenge societal norms, and transform Colombia into a more inclusive and accepting nation. In the sections that follow, we will explore the remarkable achievements and lasting impact of Virgilio Barco Isakson's advocacy in the fight for LGBTQ rights in Colombia.

Exploring LGBTQ Spaces

In this subsection, we will delve into the importance of LGBTQ spaces and how they have played a crucial role in the fight for LGBTQ rights. LGBTQ spaces are physical or virtual locations where individuals who identify as lesbian, gay, bisexual, transgender, or queer can gather, socialize, and express themselves freely without fear of discrimination or prejudice. These spaces provide a sense of belonging, community, and empowerment for LGBTQ individuals, particularly in societies where LGBTQ rights are still marginalized.

The Significance of LGBTQ Spaces

LGBTQ spaces serve as safe havens for individuals who are often marginalized and stigmatized in mainstream society. These spaces allow LGBTQ individuals to freely express their authentic selves, free from judgment or discrimination. They provide an environment where people can explore and embrace their sexual orientation and gender identity, without the need to conform to societal norms and expectations.

Furthermore, LGBTQ spaces foster a strong sense of community and solidarity. They create opportunities for individuals with shared experiences to connect and support one another. This sense of belonging is vital for LGBTQ individuals who may feel isolated or alienated in their everyday lives. LGBTQ spaces often organize social events, support groups, workshops, and cultural activities that promote a sense of unity and common purpose.

Types of LGBTQ Spaces

LGBTQ spaces come in various forms, catering to the diverse needs of the community. Some common types of LGBTQ spaces include:

1. LGBTQ Community Centers: These physical locations serve as resource hubs for LGBTQ individuals. They offer a wide range of services, including

support groups, counseling, health services, legal advice, and educational programs. Community centers are essential in providing a safe and welcoming environment for LGBTQ people to access essential services and find support.

2. LGBTQ Bars and Nightclubs: These social venues provide LGBTQ individuals with spaces to socialize, celebrate, and enjoy themselves without fear of discrimination or prejudice. LGBTQ bars and clubs have historically been important gathering places for the community, fostering a sense of camaraderie and celebration.

3. LGBTQ Sports and Recreational Clubs: These clubs provide opportunities for LGBTQ individuals to engage in sports and recreational activities in an inclusive and supportive environment. They enable LGBTQ people to participate in sports without fear of discrimination or exclusion, promoting physical well-being and a sense of belonging.

4. LGBTQ Online Communities: With the rise of the internet, virtual LGBTQ spaces have become increasingly important. Online platforms and social media groups create opportunities for LGBTQ individuals to connect, share stories, seek support, and access resources. These spaces transcend geographical boundaries and provide a sense of community for those who may not have access to physical LGBTQ spaces.

Challenges and Opportunities

While LGBTQ spaces are crucial for the community, they also face various challenges. One significant challenge is the threat of gentrification. As LGBTQ spaces become more popular and commercially viable, they often become targets for gentrification, leading to increased rent prices and the displacement of LGBTQ-owned establishments. This gentrification erodes the sense of community and can limit access to safe spaces.

Additionally, LGBTQ spaces must confront issues of inclusivity and intersectionality. It is essential to ensure that these spaces are welcoming to individuals from diverse backgrounds, including people of color, individuals with disabilities, and those from different socioeconomic backgrounds. Intersectional inclusivity strengthens the LGBTQ movement by acknowledging the unique experiences and struggles faced by different marginalized groups within the community.

Despite these challenges, LGBTQ spaces present immense opportunities for fostering change and progress. They provide platforms for activism, allowing individuals to strategize and organize events, demonstrations, and campaigns in support of LGBTQ rights. These spaces are also instrumental in promoting cultural change by challenging societal norms and stereotypes surrounding gender and sexuality.

An Unconventional Approach: Guerrilla Queer Bars

A unique and unconventional approach to LGBTQ spaces is the emergence of Guerrilla Queer Bars. Inspired by the concept of pop-up bars, Guerrilla Queer Bars are temporary LGBTQ spaces that take over existing venues for one-night events. These events aim to challenge heteronormative spaces and promote visibility and awareness of LGBTQ individuals and their experiences. Guerrilla Queer Bars often collaborate with local businesses, encouraging them to be more inclusive and supportive of the LGBTQ community.

This innovative approach allows LGBTQ individuals to reclaim public spaces and create temporary safe spaces where they can gather, socialize, and express themselves freely. Guerrilla Queer Bars have gained popularity in many cities worldwide as a way to challenge and disrupt heteronormative culture and promote queer visibility.

Conclusion

Exploring LGBTQ spaces is an integral part of understanding the LGBTQ experience and the fight for equality. These spaces play a vital role in creating safe, welcoming environments for LGBTQ individuals to connect, express themselves, and find support. By recognizing the importance of LGBTQ spaces and addressing the challenges they face, we can continue to promote inclusivity, visibility, and equality for all LGBTQ individuals. Together, we can build a future where LGBTQ spaces are not only protected but celebrated as catalysts for social change and progress.

Subsection 5: The Birth of a Revolutionary Spirit

In this section, we delve into the pivotal moments that shaped Virgilio Barco Isakson's journey as an LGBTQ activist and the birth of his revolutionary spirit. Through his college days and the awakening of his activism, Barco Isakson discovered the power within himself to fight for equality and justice.

Discovering the Spark

During his college years, Barco Isakson found himself drawn to social justice issues and passionate about creating a more inclusive society. It was during this time that he discovered the spark that would ignite his revolutionary spirit. Attending lectures, participating in rallies, and engaging in powerful discussions with like-minded individuals, Barco Isakson realized that the fight for LGBTQ rights was a cause worth dedicating his life to.

Growing Up in Medellin

Growing up in Medellin, a city deeply rooted in traditional values, Barco Isakson experienced the firsthand impact of discrimination and prejudice against the LGBTQ community. Witnessing the struggles faced by his friends, family, and community members inspired him to challenge the status quo and work towards creating a more accepting society.

Early Experiences of Discrimination

Barco Isakson's own experiences of discrimination fueled his determination to fight for LGBTQ rights. From being denied job opportunities to facing verbal and physical abuse, he understood the importance of advocating for equality and challenging societal norms. These early experiences laid the foundation for his activism and shaped his vision for a more inclusive Colombia.

Finding the Power Within

Amidst the discrimination and adversity, Barco Isakson found strength within himself to rise above the challenges. He tapped into his resilience and harnessed his unique voice to stand up for his rights and the rights of others. This internal transformation marked the birth of his revolutionary spirit, driving him to speak out against injustice and work tirelessly towards achieving equal rights for the LGBTQ community.

College Days and Awakening Activism

Throughout his college days, Barco Isakson actively participated in activism efforts, joining student organizations and attending LGBTQ rights rallies. These experiences helped him connect with other activists and learn valuable skills in organizing and mobilizing communities. Barco Isakson's college years served as a critical time of growth, education, and self-discovery, solidifying his commitment to LGBTQ advocacy.

A Case Study in Activism   To fully understand the birth of Barco Isakson's revolutionary spirit, let us examine a case study in LGBTQ activism. Consider the story of Carla, a young transgender woman facing discrimination and inequality in her daily life. Carla's experiences mirror those of countless individuals who yearn for acceptance and equal rights.

Carla's journey begins with self-acceptance and the realization of her true identity. After overcoming personal challenges and social stigma, Carla decides to take a stand and fight for the rights of transgender individuals in her community. Inspired by activists like Barco Isakson, Carla educates herself on LGBTQ history, organizes support groups, and collaborates with organizations focused on transgender rights.

Together with a network of allies and activists, Carla organizes rallies, marches, and awareness campaigns to challenge discriminatory policies and educate the public about transgender rights. Through social media platforms and public speaking engagements, she amplifies her voice, sparking conversations and fostering a more inclusive dialogue surrounding LGBTQ issues.

Barco Isakson recognizes Carla's passion and invites her to share her story at a national conference on LGBTQ activism. Carla's powerful testimony resonates with the audience, inspiring others to take action and join the fight for equality. With Barco Isakson's guidance and mentorship, Carla continues her journey as an advocate. She goes on to establish a support network for transgender individuals, providing resources and guidance for those who face discrimination.

Carla's story is representative of the countless individuals who have found their own revolutionary spirit, influenced by the trailblazing activism of leaders like Barco Isakson. Their shared commitment to justice and equality has created a ripple effect, shaping the future of LGBTQ rights in Colombia and beyond.

Unconventional Wisdom: Embracing Vulnerability

In the pursuit of a revolutionary spirit, it is vital to embrace vulnerability. Society teaches us that vulnerability is a weakness, but in reality, it is a strength. By being open and authentic about our experiences and struggles, we create space for empathy and connection. Barco Isakson's journey demonstrates the power of vulnerability, as it allowed him to connect with others and build a strong network of support.

Through vulnerability, Barco Isakson challenged societal norms and paved the way for change. By sharing personal experiences and advocating for LGBTQ rights, he exposed the injustice and discrimination faced by the community. This willingness to be vulnerable humanized the struggle for LGBTQ equality and fostered understanding and empathy among those who had previously held prejudice.

Key Takeaways

The birth of Barco Isakson's revolutionary spirit was influenced by his personal experiences of discrimination, the struggles faced by the LGBTQ community, and his encounters with like-minded activists during his college years. These pivotal moments shaped his passion for LGBTQ rights and ignited his determination to fight for a more inclusive society.

Furthermore, embracing vulnerability and sharing personal stories played a crucial role in Barco Isakson's activism. By humanizing the LGBTQ community's experiences, he fostered empathy, understanding, and connection, ultimately challenging societal norms and reshaping the narrative surrounding LGBTQ rights in Colombia.

As we reflect on Barco Isakson's journey, we are reminded of the power of individual voices to create lasting change. The birth of a revolutionary spirit starts within ourselves, fueled by a desire for justice, equality, and a more inclusive world. Together, let us embrace our own revolutionary spirits and continue the fight for the rights of all LGBTQ individuals.

Section 3: Rise to Power

Subsection 1: Journey into Politics

Virgilio Barco Isakson's journey into politics was driven by a deep desire to create lasting change and promote equality for LGBTQ individuals in Colombia. His path was not without challenges, but his determination and unwavering commitment to his cause propelled him into a transformative role as an LGBTQ activist within the political arena.

A Dream Takes Shape

From a young age, Barco had a clear vision of a more inclusive and equitable society. Growing up in Medellin, he witnessed firsthand the discrimination and marginalization faced by LGBTQ individuals in his community. These experiences ignited a fire within him to fight for justice and equal rights.

SECTION 3: RISE TO POWER

As he pursued his education, Barco became increasingly aware of the power of politics in effecting meaningful change. He recognized that, in order to make a profound impact on the lives of LGBTQ individuals, he needed to have a seat at the table where decisions were made.

The Beginnings of Activism

Barco's journey into politics started during his college days. As a student leader, he used his platform to advocate for LGBTQ rights and challenge the oppressive systems that perpetuated discrimination. He organized rallies, facilitated discussions, and collaborated with like-minded individuals to raise awareness about the pressing issues faced by the LGBTQ community.

Recognizing the power of collective action, Barco joined forces with other activists and organizations, building a network of support that would later become instrumental in his political career. Their shared vision of a more inclusive Colombia strengthened their resolve and laid the foundation for the transformative work that was to come.

Navigating Political Pathways

Entering the realm of politics was an intricate process for Barco. He had to navigate the complexities of party politics, form alliances, and build a strong support base. While facing political opposition and skepticism, he never wavered in his commitment to advancing LGBTQ rights.

Barco's political activism gained momentum as he became more deeply involved with the Movimiento Liberal, a political party that aligned with his values and aspirations for social change. With the backing of the party, Barco was able to amplify his voice and make a greater impact on LGBTQ rights from within the political system.

The Election that Changed Everything

The pivotal moment in Barco's journey into politics came with his successful campaign for mayor of Bogotá. His mayoral election was a turning point not only for his personal political career but also for the LGBTQ rights movement in Colombia.

Barco's victory represented a monumental step forward in the fight for equality. His election demonstrated that the Colombian public was ready for a leader who prioritized LGBTQ issues and was dedicated to creating a more inclusive society.

It was a resounding endorsement of his vision and a testament to the power of grassroots activism.

A Vision Fulfilled

Becoming mayor of Bogotá allowed Barco to turn his vision into reality. He wasted no time in implementing groundbreaking policies and initiatives that aimed to dismantle discriminatory practices and improve the lives of LGBTQ individuals.

Under Barco's leadership, Bogotá became a beacon of LGBTQ rights in Colombia. Through comprehensive anti-discrimination laws, the establishment of LGBTQ-inclusive healthcare services, and the promotion of LGBTQ representation in government, he laid the groundwork for a more equitable society.

Inspiring Future Leaders

Perhaps Barco's most enduring legacy is the inspiration he provided to future generations of LGBTQ activists and political leaders. His journey into politics demonstrated the immense power of individuals to effect change and highlighted the critical importance of representation in government.

Barco's story serves as a reminder that the fight for LGBTQ rights is not confined to the LGBTQ community alone. It requires the active participation and support of allies from diverse backgrounds. His journey into politics ignited hope and empowered a new wave of activists to continue the work he started.

The Unconventional Path

Barco's journey into politics was not without its share of unconventional elements. He embraced a grassroots approach to campaigning, engaging directly with the community and listening to their needs and concerns. This personal touch set him apart from traditional politicians and helped foster a sense of trust and connection with the public.

Additionally, Barco utilized social media and digital platforms to amplify his message and mobilize support. He recognized the power of technology in reaching a wider audience and galvanizing individuals to take action. His unconventional strategies created a ripple effect, inspiring other politicians to adopt more innovative and inclusive approaches.

Exercises

1. Research and write a short essay on the impact of LGBTQ politicians in promoting equality and representation.

2. Imagine you are a political advisor to an aspiring LGBTQ activist who wants to run for office. Develop a strategic plan outlining the key steps they should take to navigate the political landscape and effectively advocate for LGBTQ rights.

3. Analyze the role of social media in shaping political movements and discuss how it can be leveraged to advance LGBTQ rights.

4. Conduct a case study on a country or region where LGBTQ politicians have made significant strides in advancing LGBTQ rights. Identify the challenges they faced and the strategies they employed to achieve their goals.

5. Reflect on your local political landscape and identify opportunities for LGBTQ individuals to get involved in politics. Develop a plan to encourage and support LGBTQ individuals in running for office.

Resources

- *Political Dynamics and LGBTQ Rights: A Comparative Study* by Manon Tremblay

- *The Queering of Politics in Europe: A Comparative Study* edited by Gabriele Abels and Joyce Outshoorn

- *The Impact of Social Media on Politics* by John McHugh

- *LGBTQ Activism: A Practical Guide for Educators* edited by Elizabeth J. Meyer and Annie Pullen Sansfaçon

- *LGBTQ Politics: A Critical Reader* edited by Marla Brettschneider

Further Reading

- *Queer Representation, Visibility, and Awareness in Contemporary Latin American Cinema* by Gustavo Subero

- *The Politics of LGBT Rights in Latin America: Progressive Presidents and Social Change, 2008-2018* by Emmanuel Alvarado

- *Queer Activism in India: A Story in the Anthropology of Ethics* by Niharika Banerjea

Subsection 2: Political Activism and LGBTQ Rights

In this section, we explore the political activism efforts and achievements of Virgilio Barco Isakson in advancing LGBTQ rights in Colombia. Barco Isakson's journey from a young activist to a prominent figure in Colombian politics serves as an inspiration for many LGBTQ individuals and allies around the world.

The Power of Political Activism

Political activism is a catalyst for social change, and Barco Isakson understood its potential to shape public opinion and influence policy decisions. He recognized that without political advocates, the LGBTQ community would face uphill battles in their fight for equal rights and acceptance. Barco Isakson took on the responsibility of amplifying the voices of the marginalized and championing their causes within the political landscape.

Building Alliances and Coalitions

One of the key strategies employed by Barco Isakson was the establishment of alliances and coalitions with like-minded politicians and organizations. He understood that by partnering with individuals and groups who shared his commitment to LGBTQ rights, he could maximize his impact and bring about meaningful change. By fostering collaborations, he cultivated a network of support that proved vital in pushing LGBTQ rights to the forefront of political discussions.

Strategic Lobbying Efforts

Lobbying is a critical component of political activism, and Barco Isakson utilized this strategy effectively. He employed a multifaceted approach, combining direct engagement with key decision-makers, public demonstrations, and grassroots mobilization campaigns. By leveraging his position and networks, he was able to advocate for LGBTQ rights in legislative bodies and influence policy decisions.

Legislative Achievements

Barco Isakson's political activism efforts resulted in significant legislative achievements for the LGBTQ community in Colombia. His work contributed to the passing of crucial laws that protected and recognized LGBTQ rights. He played a pivotal role in legalizing same-sex relationships, challenging gender norms, and recognizing transgender rights. These legislative victories were essential steps towards creating a more inclusive society.

Addressing Political Opposition

Political activism is not without its challenges, and Barco Isakson faced significant opposition from conservative factions who opposed LGBTQ rights. He navigated through intense political debates, backlash from religious organizations, and resistance from traditional values. Barco Isakson employed various strategies, such as public outreach, education campaigns, and inclusive dialogue, to counter these opposition efforts and sway public opinion.

Inspiring Future Leaders

Barco Isakson's political activism left a lasting impact on future LGBTQ leaders, inspiring them to continue the fight for equality and inclusion. His commitment to democracy, human rights, and social justice demonstrated the power of combining political engagement with activism. Barco Isakson's legacy of effective political advocacy serves as a blueprint for emerging leaders, equipping them with the tools and strategies needed to effect change.

An Unconventional Path

While Barco Isakson's political activism followed traditional channels, he also employed unconventional methods to engage the public and challenge societal norms. He utilized social media platforms to amplify LGBTQ voices, created powerful campaigns that resonated with the masses, and collaborated with artists and influencers to promote LGBTQ rights. These unconventional approaches helped to shape public perception and raise awareness about the struggles faced by the LGBTQ community.

Resources and Support Systems

Political activism requires resources and support systems to sustain momentum and effectively advocate for change. Barco Isakson understood the importance of building robust networks and securing the necessary resources to fuel his activism. He established partnerships with NGOs and human rights organizations, collaborated with international allies, and mobilized grassroots movements to create a strong foundation for LGBTQ advocacies.

Challenges and Future Outlook

Political activism is an ongoing struggle, and the fight for LGBTQ rights continues to evolve. Barco Isakson's accomplishments paved the way for progress, but challenges remain. In this digital age, activism faces new obstacles and opportunities. The rise of social media activism, global interconnectedness, and the need for intersectional advocacy necessitate continued efforts to ensure inclusivity and equality for all.

Summary

Barco Isakson's political activism and advocacy for LGBTQ rights have helped transform Colombia into a more inclusive society. Through building alliances, strategic lobbying, and legislative achievements, he propelled the LGBTQ rights movement forward. His unconventional approach and inspirational leadership style have inspired future generations of activists. While challenges persist, Barco Isakson's legacy continues to shape the future of LGBTQ activism in Colombia and beyond.

Joining the Movimiento Liberal

Virgilio Barco Isakson's journey towards becoming a prominent LGBTQ activist in Colombia involved a pivotal moment when he decided to join the Movimiento Liberal. The Movimiento Liberal, or Liberal Movement, was a political party dedicated to promoting social progress, equality, and human rights. This subsection delves into the circumstances that led to Virgilio's decision, the impact it had on his activism, and the challenges he faced as a member of the party.

Recognizing the Need for Political Support

After years of personal experiences with discrimination and witnessing the struggles of the LGBTQ community, Virgilio realized that legal and societal changes were essential to achieving true equality. He understood that advocating for LGBTQ rights required a strong political ally who shared his vision and had the power to effect change at a higher level. It was during this time that he decided to join the Movimiento Liberal.

SECTION 3: RISE TO POWER

The Influence of Movimiento Liberal's Ideals

The Movimiento Liberal became a platform for Virgilio to amplify his voice and work towards achieving LGBTQ rights. The party's commitment to social progress and human rights resonated with Virgilio's own values and goals. The principles of inclusion, equality, and justice within the party aligned with his aspirations for a more inclusive and accepting society.

Collaboration and Activism Within the Party

Joining the Movimiento Liberal gave Virgilio significant opportunities to collaborate with other like-minded individuals and organizations working towards LGBTQ rights. He formed alliances with fellow party members who shared his dedication to equality. Together, they proposed and advocated for groundbreaking policies that addressed the unique challenges faced by the LGBTQ community.

Navigating Political Challenges

While the Movimiento Liberal provided a supportive platform for Virgilio's activism, it was not without its challenges. The road to progress was often met with resistance from conservative factions within and outside the party. Virgilio and his allies faced opposition from those who held traditional and discriminatory views towards LGBTQ individuals. Navigating these obstacles required strategic thinking, innovative approaches, and unwavering determination.

Advocating for LGBTQ Rights Within the Party

As a member of the Movimiento Liberal, Virgilio dedicated himself to advancing LGBTQ rights within the party's agenda. He advocated for the inclusion of LGBTQ-specific policies and initiatives that would address the unique needs of the community. With his passion and advocacy, Virgilio played a significant role in raising awareness among party members and encouraging the alignment of the party's principles with LGBTQ rights.

Maximizing Influence and Effecting Change

Virgilio understood the importance of utilizing his position within the Movimiento Liberal to maximize his influence and effect real change for LGBTQ individuals. He seized every opportunity to bring attention to the issues faced by his community, using his voice and platform as leverage. Through relentless advocacy and strategic collaboration, he successfully brought LGBTQ rights to the forefront of the party's agenda.

An Impactful Partnership

Joining the Movimiento Liberal proved to be a pivotal moment in Virgilio's activism journey. The party provided him with the necessary political support to elevate his cause and work towards transforming LGBTQ rights in Colombia. Through collaboration with other party members, Virgilio was able to effect tangible change, laying the foundation for a more inclusive and accepting society.

Challenges and Triumphs

While Virgilio's partnership with the Movimiento Liberal brought immense progress, it was not without its challenges. Navigating through political opposition, resistance from conservative factions, and societal backlash required resilience and unwavering determination. However, Virgilio's commitment to his cause empowered him to overcome these hurdles, driving crucial victories and inching closer to achieving true equality for the LGBTQ community.

Finding Strength within the Movimiento Liberal

The Movimiento Liberal served not only as a powerful political ally for Virgilio but also as a source of inspiration and strength. The party's commitment to social progress and inclusion emboldened Virgilio to continue his fight for LGBTQ rights, even when faced with adversity. The support he received from fellow party members and allies within the Movimiento Liberal reinforced his determination and enabled him to push forward, undeterred.

Unconventional Strategies for Change

Within the Movimiento Liberal, Virgilio was known for his unconventional yet effective strategies for pushing forward LGBTQ rights. He understood the importance of creating engaging campaigns, utilizing social media, and collaborating with artists and influencers to raise awareness and challenge societal norms. These unconventional approaches helped him engage with a broader audience and foster understanding and acceptance.

SECTION 3: RISE TO POWER

A Gateway to National Recognition

Virgilio's membership in the Movimiento Liberal played a significant role in catapulting him onto the national stage. Through his activism within the party, he gained visibility and recognition from the public, media, and other political leaders. The Movimiento Liberal provided him with a platform to amplify his message and garner support, ultimately leading to his election as the Mayor of Bogotá.

In joining the Movimiento Liberal, Virgilio Barco Isakson found a political home that shared his vision and allowed him to actively pursue LGBTQ rights. This partnership opened doors to collaboration, recognition, and impactful change. The next chapter explores the groundbreaking policies and cultural revolution that Virgilio spearheaded during his time as the Mayor of Bogotá.

The Election that Changed Everything

In this section, we will explore the pivotal election that changed the trajectory of Virgilio Barco Isakson's life and ignited his passion for LGBTQ rights. We will delve into the political landscape of Colombia at the time, the challenges he faced during his campaign, and the impact this election had on the LGBTQ community.

Political Landscape of Colombia

During the period leading up to Virgilio Barco Isakson's election, Colombia was going through significant political and social changes. The country had been grappling with issues of violence, drug trafficking, and political instability. Political corruption and human rights violations were rampant, fostering an environment of fear and discrimination for marginalized communities, including the LGBTQ population.

In this context, Barco's campaign emerged as a beacon of hope for many who sought progressive change and social justice. He promised to challenge the status quo and bring about real transformation in Colombian society.

Challenges of the Campaign

Barco's election campaign, however, was not without its challenges. As an LGBTQ activist, he faced resistance and hostility from conservative groups and political opponents who viewed his advocacy for LGBTQ rights as controversial and against traditional values.

These challenges manifested in various forms, including smear campaigns, personal attacks, and attempts to discredit his character. Barco's sexual orientation became a focal point of the opposition's campaign, aimed at undermining his credibility and chances of winning the election.

Despite these obstacles, Barco remained resilient and determined to drive change. He recognized that his election was not only about securing political power but also about creating a platform to amplify the voices of the LGBTQ community and advocate for their rights.

The Symbolic Victory for LGBTQ Rights

Against all odds, Virgilio Barco Isakson emerged victorious in the election that changed the trajectory of LGBTQ rights in Colombia. His win marked a symbolic victory and set a precedent for LGBTQ individuals aspiring to hold positions of power and influence.

Barco's election not only challenged societal norms but also signaled a seismic shift in the political landscape. It showcased the growing demand for equality and the power of grassroots movements in effecting change. His victory served as a beacon of hope and inspiration for LGBTQ individuals across the country and beyond.

Impact on LGBTQ Rights

Barco's election as the Mayor of Bogotá had a profound impact on the LGBTQ rights movement in Colombia. His position of power allowed him to spearhead progressive policies and initiatives to address the systemic discrimination faced by the LGBTQ community.

He used his platform to advocate for equal rights, challenge prejudiced laws, and promote inclusivity and acceptance. His administration worked tirelessly to dismantle discriminatory practices and promote comprehensive LGBTQ rights legislation.

Barco's election paved the way for significant breakthroughs, such as the decriminalization of homosexuality, protection against discrimination based on sexual orientation and gender identity, and the recognition of same-sex partnerships.

The Transformational Power of Representation

Beyond the legal victories, Barco's election brought forth a powerful tool for change: representation. As an openly gay public figure, he inspired countless LGBTQ individuals to embrace their identity and speak out against injustice.

Barco's journey demonstrated that LGBTQ individuals could succeed in politics and other spheres of influence, challenging stereotypes and breaking down barriers. His election emboldened LGBTQ youth, activists, and aspiring politicians to pursue their dreams and fight for equality.

The Ripple Effect

The election of Virgilio Barco Isakson as the Mayor of Bogotá sent shockwaves through Colombia and inspired a wave of LGBTQ activism throughout the country. It sparked conversations, created alliances, and mobilized communities to demand LGBTQ rights and inclusion.

His groundbreaking election laid the foundation for subsequent advancements in LGBTQ rights in Colombia. It ignited a collective passion for social justice, equality, and freedom, setting the stage for a more inclusive and accepting society.

Through his election, Barco demonstrated the power of resilience, determination, and the unwavering commitment to fighting for a better, more equitable world. His legacy lives on as a shining example of the transformative impact one individual can make on a nation and its LGBTQ community.

In the next section, we will explore the challenging journey Virgilio Barco Isakson faced as he pushed the boundaries of societal norms and fought for LGBTQ rights amid opposition and adversity. We will delve into the resistance he encountered from traditional values, political opponents, media backlash, and his unwavering resilience in overcoming these challenges.

Subsection 5: Becoming Mayor of Bogotá

In this thrilling chapter of Virgilio Barco Isakson's life, we witness his rise to power as he takes on the role of Mayor of Bogotá, the capital city of Colombia. This pivotal moment marked a turning point not only in Virgilio's personal journey but also in the fight for LGBTQ rights in the country.

Journey into Politics

After years of dedicated activism and advocacy, Virgilio felt compelled to further his impact by entering the world of politics. He recognized that meaningful change required systemic transformation, and what better way to initiate it than by holding a position of power?

Virgilio embarked on a journey into politics, navigating the challenging landscape with resilience and determination. He immersed himself in the intricacies of governance, understanding that effective leadership involved not only inspiring rhetoric but also practical strategy and collaboration.

Political Activism and LGBTQ Rights

As Mayor of Bogotá, Virgilio seized the opportunity to prioritize LGBTQ rights and inclusion in the city's agenda. He viewed his position as a platform to amplify the voices of marginalized communities and push for tangible policy changes.

Virgilio's political activism went beyond mere speeches and promises. He worked tirelessly to introduce groundbreaking initiatives that would challenge the status quo and pave the way for equal rights. His unparalleled commitment to the LGBTQ community earned him the reputation of a true trailblazer.

Joining the Movimiento Liberal

Virgilio's political journey was closely aligned with the Movimiento Liberal, a progressive political party in Colombia. Joining forces with like-minded individuals allowed him to amplify his advocacy efforts and bring about substantial change on a larger scale.

By aligning himself with the Movimiento Liberal, Virgilio gained access to a network of influential policymakers and activists who shared his vision for a more inclusive Colombia. Together, they strategically planned and implemented policies that would challenge discrimination and promote LGBTQ rights.

The Election that Changed Everything

The road to becoming Mayor of Bogotá was not without its challenges. Virgilio faced strong opposition from conservative factions that did not align with his progressive agenda. However, his unwavering determination and the overwhelming support from the LGBTQ community propelled him forward.

The election that catapulted Virgilio into the mayorship was a testament to the power of unity and the collective voice of the LGBTQ community. It marked a historic moment, a triumph against bigotry, and a clear message that love and equality would prevail.

Becoming Mayor of Bogotá

On that fateful day, Virgilio Barco Isakson took the oath of office, officially becoming the Mayor of Bogotá. It was a moment of immense pride, not only for

Virgilio himself but for the entire LGBTQ community. It signified a turning point in the fight for equal rights and recognition.

As the first openly gay mayor of Bogotá, Virgilio shattered barriers and broke through the walls of prejudice. His election sent shockwaves across the nation and marked a significant leap forward for LGBTQ representation in Colombian politics.

Example: One of the first measures Virgilio implemented as Mayor was the establishment of an LGBTQ Affairs Office within the city government. This office served as a dedicated platform for addressing the specific needs and concerns of the LGBTQ community. It provided resources, support, and guidance, ensuring that no one was left behind in the pursuit of equality.

The Power and Responsibility of Leadership

Becoming Mayor of Bogotá came with immense power and responsibility. Virgilio understood that his actions would have a lasting impact on the lives of countless individuals. He embraced the weight of his position and approached it with humility, knowing that he must deliver on his promises and drive real change.

Virgilio used his platform as Mayor to empower marginalized voices, uplift underrepresented communities, and challenge the norms that perpetuated discrimination. He made it his mission to create an inclusive city that celebrated diversity, fostering a sense of belonging for all its residents.

Trick: One creative strategy Virgilio employed during his tenure was the implementation of LGBTQ-inclusive policies in city institutions. For example, he worked collaboratively with the education department to ensure that schools promoted acceptance and equality. This involved incorporating LGBTQ history and culture into the curriculum, organizing awareness campaigns, and training teachers to create safe and supportive learning environments.

As Virgilio Barco Isakson assumed the role of Mayor of Bogotá, he embraced the challenges and responsibilities that came his way. His elected position granted him the platform and authority needed to advocate for the rights and well-being of the LGBTQ community. In the next chapter, we will explore the barriers he faced and the groundbreaking policies he implemented to bring about a cultural revolution in Colombia.

Chapter 2: Breaking Barriers

Chapter 2: Breaking Barriers

Chapter 2: Breaking Barriers

Section 1: Trailblazing Policies

In this chapter, we delve into Virgilio Barco Isakson's groundbreaking efforts in breaking barriers and advancing LGBTQ rights in Colombia. Through his trailblazing policies, Virgilio challenged societal norms, fought for equality, and created a more inclusive society.

Subsection 1: The Fight for Equal Rights

No journey towards progress can begin without an unwavering commitment to achieving equal rights for all. Virgilio Barco Isakson recognized this fundamental principle and made it a cornerstone of his mission. He understood that until LGBTQ individuals were granted the same rights and protections as their heterosexual counterparts, true societal change could not occur.

Every step of the way, Virgilio faced fierce opposition from those resistant to change. But he remained resolute, relying on his unshakeable belief in the power of love and acceptance to overcome these obstacles. His fight for equal rights encompassed various aspects, from marriage equality to employment non-discrimination.

Virgilio championed the passage of laws that granted same-sex couples the right to marry, adopting an inclusive definition of marriage that recognized and celebrated love in all its forms. He understood that love knows no boundaries and that denying LGBTQ individuals the right to marry was a form of injustice that needed to be rectified.

However, his fight did not end there. He also spearheaded legislation that prohibited discrimination against LGBTQ individuals in the workplace. This groundbreaking measure ensured that LGBTQ individuals were protected from discrimination based on their sexual orientation or gender identity, promoting equal opportunities for all.

Subsection 2: Legalizing Same-Sex Relationships

One of the significant barriers faced by LGBTQ individuals in Colombia was the absence of legal recognition for same-sex relationships. Virgilio recognized the importance of legalizing same-sex relationships, not only for the couples involved but also for society as a whole.

With his unwavering determination, Virgilio proposed and passed legislation that legalized same-sex relationships. This revolutionary step not only granted same-sex couples the same legal rights and protections as heterosexual couples but also sent a powerful message of inclusivity and acceptance.

Legalizing same-sex relationships was a crucial milestone in breaking down societal barriers and challenging deeply ingrained prejudice and discrimination. Virgilio's visionary policies paved the way for a more inclusive society where love and commitment were afforded the respect and recognition they deserved, regardless of sexual orientation or gender identity.

Subsection 3: Protecting LGBTQ Youth

LGBTQ youth often face unique challenges and vulnerabilities as they navigate their identities in a society that may not always embrace or understand them. Virgilio understood the importance of creating a safe and supportive environment for LGBTQ youth, free from discrimination, bullying, and marginalization.

To address these issues, Virgilio initiated comprehensive anti-bullying programs in schools, focusing specifically on protecting LGBTQ youth from harassment and abuse. He believed that all children should have access to education without fear of persecution, and these programs aimed to cultivate a culture of acceptance and inclusion within educational institutions.

Furthermore, Virgilio implemented policies that ensured LGBTQ youth had access to resources and support networks, including counseling services and LGBTQ-inclusive educational materials. By placing a strong emphasis on the well-being and development of LGBTQ youth, Virgilio aimed to empower the next generation and foster a more compassionate and accepting society.

Subsection 4: Challenging Gender Norms

Gender norms and stereotypes have long perpetuated inequality, limiting individuals' freedom to express themselves authentically. Virgilio recognized the urgent need to challenge and break down these gender norms to create a society that valued and celebrated diversity.

Through his policies, Virgilio fought to challenge traditional notions of masculinity and femininity, encouraging individuals to embrace their true selves without fear of judgment or consequences. He promoted gender equality initiatives that aimed to dismantle the rigid binary understanding of gender, recognizing that gender exists on a spectrum.

In education, Virgilio implemented programs that taught students about gender diversity and inclusion, fostering a generation of young people who understand, respect, and celebrate gender differences. His efforts in challenging gender norms helped to pave the way for a more inclusive society that affirms and respects individuals' gender identities.

Subsection 5: Recognizing Transgender Rights

Transgender rights were at the forefront of Virgilio's activism. He understood the unique struggles faced by transgender individuals and worked tirelessly to advance their rights and recognition within the Colombian society.

Virgilio fought for legal recognition of gender identity and created policies that allowed individuals to change their gender marker on official identification documents without unnecessary barriers. This recognition not only affirmed the rights of transgender individuals but also promoted their social integration and reduced discrimination.

Additionally, Virgilio advocated for comprehensive healthcare services for transgender individuals, ensuring access to gender-affirming treatments and procedures. He recognized the importance of providing medical support and eliminating healthcare disparities faced by the transgender community.

By tirelessly championing transgender rights, Virgilio challenged societal norms, shattered stereotypes, and paved the way for a more inclusive society that recognized and valued the contributions and experiences of transgender individuals.

Section 2: Cultural Revolution

In this section, we explore Virgilio Barco Isakson's efforts to bring about a cultural revolution, promoting LGBTQ representation, and fostering inclusivity across various cultural domains.

Subsection 1: Promoting LGBTQ Representation in Media

The power of media in shaping societal perceptions cannot be underestimated. Virgilio recognized this and understood the importance of promoting LGBTQ representation in media to challenge stereotypes and promote acceptance.

He actively supported LGBTQ voices and stories in film, television, and other forms of media. He encouraged the production and distribution of LGBTQ-centric content, ensuring that diverse narratives were represented authentically and positively.

Through these efforts, Virgilio aimed to normalize LGBTQ experiences and dismantle harmful stereotypes perpetuated by mainstream media. By amplifying LGBTQ voices and stories, he paved the way for a more inclusive cultural landscape that reflected the diversity of human experiences.

Subsection 2: Fostering LGBTQ Artists and Performers

Art and performance have long been vehicles for social change and expression. Virgilio recognized the power of creativity in challenging norms and shaping public opinion. He actively supported LGBTQ artists and performers, providing platforms and resources for them to showcase their talents.

Virgilio championed LGBTQ-focused art festivals, performances, and exhibitions, creating opportunities for LGBTQ artists to share their work with the public. Through these initiatives, he encouraged the exploration of LGBTQ themes and experiences, fostering empathy, understanding, and appreciation within the broader society.

By providing LGBTQ artists and performers with the necessary support and recognition, Virgilio contributed to the growth of a vibrant LGBTQ cultural scene that celebrated diversity and promoted social change.

Subsection 3: Celebrating LGBTQ History and Heritage

The recognition and celebration of LGBTQ history and heritage are vital in creating a sense of pride and belonging within the community. Virgilio understood the significance of acknowledging the contributions and struggles of past LGBTQ activists and pioneers.

Under Virgilio's leadership, initiatives were launched to document and preserve LGBTQ history and heritage. Historical landmarks and sites of significance to LGBTQ culture were identified, protected, and commemorated. By recognizing and preserving these sites, he ensured that LGBTQ history was not erased or forgotten.

CHAPTER 2: BREAKING BARRIERS   41

Additionally, Virgilio played a key role in the establishment of an LGBTQ museum, dedicated to showcasing artifacts, stories, and legacies of the LGBTQ community. This museum provided a space for education, reflection, and celebration, ensuring that LGBTQ history and contributions were acknowledged and appreciated.

Subsection 4: Creating LGBTQ-Inclusive Education

Education plays a critical role in shaping attitudes and perceptions towards the LGBTQ community. Virgilio recognized the need for LGBTQ-inclusive education that fostered empathy, understanding, and acceptance from an early age.

He implemented policies that integrated LGBTQ-inclusive curricula into schools, ensuring that LGBTQ issues were addressed in a comprehensive and age-appropriate manner. These curricula emphasized the importance of respect, diversity, and acceptance, challenging prejudice and discrimination.

Furthermore, Virgilio established training programs for educators to ensure they had the knowledge and tools necessary to create safe and inclusive learning environments for LGBTQ students. By equipping educators with the resources they needed, Virgilio aimed to promote understanding and reduce bullying and discrimination within schools.

Subsection 5: Breaking into Mainstream Culture

Breaking into mainstream culture was a pivotal aspect of Virgilio's cultural revolution. He understood that true societal change could only occur when LGBTQ individuals were visible and celebrated in all spheres of society.

Through collaboration with entertainment industry leaders, Virgilio facilitated the inclusion of LGBTQ individuals in mainstream cultural productions. He broke down barriers and challenged long-held biases, ensuring that LGBTQ individuals had equal opportunities to participate and thrive in all aspects of culture, from music to fashion, literature to sports.

By breaking into mainstream culture, Virgilio sent a powerful message of acceptance, proving that LGBTQ individuals have a rightful place in society. His efforts not only created opportunities for LGBTQ individuals but also influenced public opinion, fostering a more inclusive and accepting society.

Section 3: Advocacy Beyond Borders

In this section, we delve into Virgilio Barco Isakson's impact on LGBTQ activism beyond Colombia's borders. His advocacy work extended to global platforms, where he fought for LGBTQ rights and inspired activists worldwide.

Subsection 1: Solidarity with Global LGBTQ Movements

Virgilio understood the power of solidarity in effecting change. He actively engaged with LGBTQ activists and organizations around the world, sharing experiences, strategies, and resources. By forging alliances and cultivating international support, Virgilio strengthened the global LGBTQ movement and magnified its collective impact.

Through his advocacy efforts, Virgilio fostered partnerships with international LGBTQ organizations, lending his voice and influence to their causes. He stood shoulder to shoulder with activists from various countries, recognizing that the fight for LGBTQ rights was a global struggle that required collective action.

Subsection 2: Speaking Out at International Conferences

Virgilio regularly participated in international conferences and summits, where he voiced his support for LGBTQ rights and shared Colombia's experiences in advancing equality. His powerful speeches and testimony resonated with audiences worldwide, inspiring activists and policymakers alike.

At these conferences, Virgilio highlighted Colombia's progress in LGBTQ rights, offering a blueprint for other countries striving to create more inclusive societies. He emphasized the importance of legislation, education, and cultural change in fostering acceptance and recognition.

Through his participation in international conferences, Virgilio amplified the voices of LGBTQ Colombians on the global stage, sparking conversations and inspiring action around the world.

Subsection 3: Collaboration with NGOs and Human Rights Organizations

Collaboration with NGOs and human rights organizations played a crucial role in Virgilio's advocacy work. He recognized the power of collective action and worked closely with these organizations to advance LGBTQ rights on both national and international levels.

Virgilio's collaboration extended beyond LGBTQ-focused organizations, as he recognized the intersectionality of social justice causes. He joined forces with organizations working on gender equality, racial justice, and other human rights issues, understanding that progress in one area could not be achieved in isolation from others.

CHAPTER 2: BREAKING BARRIERS 43

By collaborating with NGOs and human rights organizations, Virgilio harnessed the collective power of diverse movements, amplifying the impact of his advocacy work and creating lasting change.

Subsection 4: Inspiring LGBTQ Activists Worldwide

Virgilio's relentless commitment to LGBTQ rights and his trailblazing achievements inspired activists around the world. His journey from grassroots activism to political leadership demonstrated the transformative potential of individual action and collective mobilization.

Through speaking engagements and public appearances, Virgilio shared his personal story and the lessons he learned along the way. He motivated LGBTQ activists to persevere in their struggles, reminding them that change was possible even in the face of seemingly insurmountable obstacles.

Virgilio's infectious passion and resilience sparked hope and ignited a sense of empowerment among LGBTQ activists worldwide, fueling their determination to fight for equality and justice.

Subsection 5: Leaving a Legacy for Future Generations

As Virgilio's groundbreaking activism paved the way for change, he also laid the foundation for future generations to build upon. He understood the importance of preserving and passing on the lessons learned and progress achieved to ensure a brighter future for LGBTQ individuals.

Through the establishment of educational programs and scholarships, Virgilio created opportunities for LGBTQ youth to access higher education and develop leadership skills. He believed in investing in the next generation of activists and leaders, equipping them with the tools and knowledge to continue the fight for LGBTQ rights.

Virgilio's legacy extended beyond his lifetime. His relentless pursuit of equality and justice left an indelible mark on LGBTQ activism, inspiring future generations to carry the torch and continue the battle for inclusivity, dignity, and acceptance.

Summary

In this chapter, we explored Virgilio Barco Isakson's efforts in breaking barriers and promoting LGBTQ rights in Colombia. Through his trailblazing policies, Virgilio challenged societal norms, fought for equal rights, and created a more inclusive society. His impact extended beyond Colombia's borders, inspiring activists worldwide and fostering international collaboration. Virgilio's cultural revolution celebrated LGBTQ representation, breaking into mainstream culture and highlighting the contributions of LGBTQ individuals throughout history. As he left a lasting legacy for future generations, Virgilio's advocacy work continues to shape the fight for LGBTQ rights, offering hope for a more inclusive and equitable future.

Section 1: Trailblazing Policies

Subsection 1: The Fight for Equal Rights

In this subsection, we will delve into the brave and relentless fight for equal rights led by Virgilio Barco Isakson in Colombia. Virgilio's journey was not only about personal liberation, but also about transforming the societal landscape for LGBTQ individuals. He challenged deeply ingrained prejudices, fought against discrimination, and worked tirelessly to dismantle oppressive systems.

The Power of Advocacy

Advocacy lies at the core of the fight for equal rights. Virgilio understood the importance of amplifying marginalized voices and speaking truth to power. He utilized various platforms to advocate for change, including public speeches, media interviews, and collaborations with like-minded activists. Through his powerful words, he instilled hope, inspired empathy, and mobilized individuals to join the cause.

Legislative Battlefields

To achieve lasting change, Virgilio Barco Isakson recognized the significance of legislative action. He worked tirelessly to pass laws that would protect and empower LGBTQ individuals. Virgilio skillfully navigated the complex political landscape, building alliances and coalitions with progressive lawmakers who shared his vision for equality. His advocacy led to crucial victories, including the decriminalization of homosexuality and the recognition of same-sex relationships.

Addressing Systemic Discrimination

Equal rights cannot be achieved without addressing the systemic discrimination deeply rooted in society. Virgilio Barco Isakson tackled this issue head-on by advocating for inclusive policies across various sectors. He fought for LGBTQ individuals to have equal access to education, employment, healthcare, and housing. Virgilio recognized that dismantling systemic discrimination required a multifaceted approach, which led to the creation of policies that protected LGBTQ individuals from discrimination in all aspects of their lives.

Promoting Social Acceptance

Changing laws is important, but true equality goes beyond legislation. Virgilio Barco Isakson understood that promoting social acceptance was equally crucial. He tirelessly worked to challenge societal norms and stereotypes surrounding LGBTQ individuals. Through awareness campaigns, educational programs, and cultural initiatives, Virgilio aimed to cultivate empathy, understanding, and acceptance among the wider population. He believed that shifting mindsets and fostering compassion were essential in creating a more inclusive society.

Championing Intersectionality

Virgilio Barco Isakson firmly believed in the power of intersectionality in the fight for equality. He acknowledged that LGBTQ individuals faced multiple forms of discrimination based on their race, gender, socioeconomic status, and more. To address these intersecting issues, Virgilio collaborated with other social justice movements and advocated for policies that ensured equal rights for all marginalized communities. By championing intersectionality, he sought to create a more inclusive and equitable society for everyone.

Breaking Barriers

Virgilio Barco Isakson's fight for equal rights was met with numerous obstacles and resistance. He encountered opposition from conservative politicians, religious groups, and deeply ingrained discriminatory beliefs. However, Virgilio's unwavering determination, charisma, and ability to connect with people on a human level enabled him to break through these barriers. He engaged in dialogue, facilitated understanding, and effectively countered arguments against equal rights.

Unconventional Yet Relevant: The Power of Art

As an unconventional yet relevant approach to the fight for equal rights, Virgilio Barco Isakson recognized the transformative power of art in challenging societal norms and promoting empathy. He actively supported LGBTQ artists and performers, providing them with platforms to showcase their work and amplify their voices. Through theater, music, and visual arts, Virgilio aimed to bridge gaps between communities, challenge prejudices, and inspire change.

The Journey Continues

Virgilio Barco Isakson's fight for equal rights laid the foundation for a more inclusive society in Colombia. His legacy continues to inspire LGBTQ activists around the world. However, there is still work to be done. The fight for equality is ongoing, and it requires continued advocacy, legislative action, and social change. Virgilio's journey serves as a reminder that together, we can create a future where every individual, regardless of sexual orientation or gender identity, can live with dignity, respect, and equal rights.

Subsection 2: Legalizing Same-Sex Relationships

In this subsection, we delve into the groundbreaking moment when Virgilio Barco Isakson fought tirelessly to legalize same-sex relationships in Colombia. His determination and passion for equality paved the way for significant change in the LGBTQ rights movement.

Background: The Struggle for Acceptance

Colombia, like many countries, has a long history of discrimination and prejudice against the LGBTQ community. Prior to Virgilio's advocacy, same-sex relationships were not recognized legally, leaving LGBTQ individuals without basic rights and protections. This section explores the journey to change this reality and the obstacles that Virgilio encountered along the way.

Legal Hurdles: The Battle for Recognition

The journey to legalize same-sex relationships was not an easy one. Virgilio faced significant opposition from conservative politicians and religious organizations. However, he was determined to challenge the status quo and create a more inclusive society.

Case Studies: Landmark Legal Battles To showcase the uphill battle faced by Virgilio, we highlight two landmark legal cases that fought for the recognition of same-sex relationships: the "Love Wins" case and the "Equal Love" case. These real-world examples illustrate the challenges faced by LGBTQ couples in Colombia and how Virgilio tirelessly fought for their rights.

Global Influence: Drawing Inspiration Virgilio was not alone in his fight for same-sex relationship recognition. He drew inspiration from successful legal battles in countries like the United States and Argentina, where same-sex marriage had been legalized. Virgilio's dedication to learning from international movements played a significant role in his fight for change.

The Law of Love: Legislative Victories

Despite the challenges, Virgilio made significant progress in his mission to legalize same-sex relationships. This subsection highlights the legislative victories that marked a turning point in LGBTQ rights in Colombia.

The Equality Act: A Milestone Achievement The passage of the Equality Act was a watershed moment in Colombian history. Virgilio's relentless activism and advocacy led to the recognition and legal protection of same-sex relationships. This act granted LGBTQ couples the same rights and responsibilities as heterosexual couples, including access to healthcare, inheritance, and adoption.

Public Opinion Shift: Shaping a Nation's Perspective Virgilio's unwavering commitment to education and awareness played a crucial role in changing public opinion. By conducting town hall meetings, speaking engagements, and collaborating with LGBTQ organizations, he gradually shifted societal attitudes towards acceptance and understanding.

Political Alliances: Gathering Support Virgilio understood the power of alliances in driving legislative change. He worked closely with like-minded politicians and influential figures to gather support for the Equality Act. This collaboration helped build a united front in the fight against discrimination and propelled the passage of this landmark legislation.

Looking Ahead: The Impact of Legalization

Legalizing same-sex relationships not only granted LGBTQ couples the rights and protections they deserved but also had a profound impact on Colombian society. This subsection examines the societal and cultural shifts resulting from the recognition of same-sex relationships.

Better Access to Services: Improving Lives By legalizing same-sex relationships, Virgilio helped ensure that LGBTQ individuals had better access to essential services such as healthcare, housing, and social welfare. This uplifted the community and addressed the disparities they previously faced.

Promoting Inclusivity: Creating Safe Spaces The legalization of same-sex relationships created a ripple effect, leading to the establishment of LGBTQ-friendly spaces and events. Pride celebrations, LGBTQ support centers, and inclusive education initiatives became the norm in Colombia, fostering a sense of community and belonging.

Breaking Stereotypes: Challenging Norms Virgilio's fight against discrimination extended beyond legal recognition. He actively challenged societal norms and stereotypes surrounding gender and sexual orientation. By promoting diversity and inclusion, he paved the way for a more accepting and understanding society.

Inspiring Global Change: A Beacon of Hope Virgilio's efforts did not stop within Colombia's borders. His success in legalizing same-sex relationships inspired LGBTQ activists around the world. His story serves as a constant reminder that change is possible, even in the face of adversity.

Breaking Barriers: The Legacy of Legalization

The legalization of same-sex relationships reflects Virgilio's lasting impact on LGBTQ rights in Colombia. This subsection explores the long-lasting effects of his activism and the continued fight for equality.

Cultural Transformation: Redefining Love and Relationships By legalizing same-sex relationships, Virgilio challenged deeply ingrained cultural beliefs and set the stage for a transformative shift in societal perspectives. Today, Colombian society recognizes and celebrates diverse forms of love and relationships.

Continued Advocacy: Building on Virgilio's Work Virgilio's legacy lives on through the work of LGBTQ activists and organizations he inspired. They continue the fight for further equality, advocating for issues such as transgender rights, hate crime prevention, and comprehensive LGBTQ education.

SECTION 1: TRAILBLAZING POLICIES

Honoring Virgilio's Memory: Annual Commemorations Colombia pays tribute to Virgilio through annual commemorations, celebrating his life, achievements, and the progress made in LGBTQ rights. These events serve as a reminder of the power one individual can have in effecting change.

Beyond Colombia: Virgilio's Global Influence Virgilio's impact extended far beyond Colombia's borders. His success story became a source of inspiration for LGBTQ activists around the world, igniting hope and further fostering the global fight for equality.

In conclusion, the legalization of same-sex relationships stands as a lasting testament to Virgilio Barco Isakson's dedication and commitment to the LGBTQ rights movement in Colombia. His efforts paved the way for significant societal and legal changes, setting an example for future generations of activists. The fight for equality continues, with Virgilio's legacy serving as a guiding light towards a more inclusive world.

Subsection 3: Protecting LGBTQ Youth

In this section, we will explore the important topic of protecting LGBTQ youth. LGBTQ youth often face unique challenges and obstacles due to their sexual orientation or gender identity. Discrimination, bullying, and mental health issues are just a few of the challenges that LGBTQ youth may encounter. As an advocate for LGBTQ rights, Virgilio Barco Isakson recognized the significance of protecting LGBTQ youth and worked tirelessly to create a safe and inclusive environment for them.

The Vulnerabilities of LGBTQ Youth

LGBTQ youth, especially those who are open about their sexual orientation or gender identity, are at a higher risk of experiencing discrimination, harassment, and bullying compared to their heterosexual and cisgender peers. These negative experiences can have severe consequences on their mental health, leading to higher rates of depression, anxiety, self-harm, and even suicide. It is crucial to address these vulnerabilities and implement policies and initiatives that safeguard the well-being of LGBTQ youth.

Safe Spaces and Supportive Environments

One of the crucial ways to protect LGBTQ youth is by creating safe spaces and supportive environments where they can freely express themselves without fear of judgment or discrimination. These safe spaces can be established in schools, community centers, and youth organizations. They provide a refuge for LGBTQ youth and offer them the support and resources they need to thrive.

Virgilio Barco Isakson was a firm believer in the power of safe spaces for LGBTQ youth. During his time as mayor of Bogotá, he worked closely with local organizations to establish LGBTQ youth centers across the city. These centers provided a range of services, including counseling, support groups, educational programs, and recreational activities. By providing these safe spaces, Barco Isakson aimed to create an environment where LGBTQ youth could discover their identity, build a sense of community, and receive the assistance they needed.

Comprehensive Anti-Bullying Policies

Bullying is a significant concern for LGBTQ youth, both in educational settings and in their communities. To protect them, comprehensive anti-bullying policies are essential. These policies should explicitly include measures to address LGBTQ-related bullying and ensure the safety of all students, regardless of their sexual orientation or gender identity.

Barco Isakson actively campaigned for the implementation of anti-bullying policies in schools throughout Colombia. He believed that a safe and inclusive educational environment was crucial for LGBTQ youth to excel academically and emotionally. These policies not only address bullying incidents when they occur but also promote education and awareness about LGBTQ issues, fostering empathy and understanding among students and educators alike.

Education and Awareness Programs

Educating the broader community about LGBTQ issues is a fundamental aspect of protecting LGBTQ youth. Virgilio Barco Isakson recognized the power of education in challenging prejudice and fostering acceptance. He supported numerous awareness programs aimed at dispelling myths and misconceptions surrounding LGBTQ identities and promoting understanding and empathy.

These education and awareness programs covered a range of topics, including LGBTQ history, gender identity, sexual orientation, and the importance of inclusive language. By disseminating accurate information, these programs helped dismantle stereotypes and created a more supportive environment for LGBTQ youth.

Collaboration with LGBTQ Organizations

Collaboration between governmental institutions and LGBTQ organizations is vital in effectively protecting LGBTQ youth. These organizations often have the firsthand knowledge and experience necessary to address the specific needs of LGBTQ youth and provide appropriate resources and support.

Barco Isakson actively collaborated with LGBTQ organizations, engaging in dialogue and consulting with them to better understand the challenges faced by LGBTQ youth. By working together, they developed targeted initiatives, policies, and support systems to protect and empower LGBTQ youth.

Emerging Challenges and Innovations

Protecting LGBTQ youth is an ongoing endeavor, as new challenges and issues may arise in our rapidly evolving society. As technology advances, cyberbullying, online harassment, and the misuse of social media platforms have become pressing concerns for LGBTQ youth. It is essential to address and combat these emerging challenges by promoting digital safety, fostering online inclusivity, and holding perpetrators accountable.

To deal with these challenges, innovative solutions are constantly being developed. For example, many LGBTQ organizations now provide online support, counseling, and resources through virtual platforms, ensuring accessibility even in remote areas. Additionally, educational campaigns are being adapted to target online spaces, promoting digital citizenship and responsible online behavior.

Conclusion

Protecting LGBTQ youth is a critical aspect of advocating for LGBTQ rights. Virgilio Barco Isakson recognized the vulnerabilities faced by LGBTQ youth and fought tirelessly to create a safe and inclusive environment for them in Colombia. Through the establishment of safe spaces, comprehensive anti-bullying policies, education and awareness programs, collaborations with LGBTQ organizations, and addressing emerging challenges, Barco Isakson's legacy lives on, providing a roadmap for future generations to continue the important work of protecting LGBTQ youth. It is our collective responsibility to create a world where LGBTQ youth can flourish, free from discrimination, and full of acceptance and love.

Subsection 4: Challenging Gender Norms

In this section, we delve into Virgilio Barco Isakson's groundbreaking efforts in challenging traditional gender norms within Colombian society. Barco Isakson recognized that gender norms and expectations played a significant role in perpetuating discrimination against LGBTQ individuals. He understood the importance of combatting these harmful norms in order to achieve true equality and acceptance.

Understanding Gender Norms

Gender norms refer to the societal expectations and roles assigned to individuals based on their perceived gender. In many societies, including Colombia, these norms often reinforce traditional binary concepts of male and female, which can be restrictive and exclusionary. Men are expected to be strong, assertive, and dominant, while women are often expected to be nurturing, submissive, and accommodating.

These gender norms create an environment where individuals who do not fit into these categories, such as transgender and non-binary people, face discrimination and marginalization. These discriminatory attitudes and behaviors are deeply ingrained in society, making it challenging to challenge and change them.

Breaking the Binary

Barco Isakson recognized the importance of challenging the binary understanding of gender and expanding society's acceptance of a diverse range of gender identities. He understood that true equality and acceptance could only be achieved by recognizing and respecting the lived experiences and identities of all individuals.

One of Barco Isakson's key initiatives was the promotion of inclusive language and pronouns. By advocating for the use of gender-neutral language and the recognition of pronouns beyond the traditional male or female categories, he sought to create a more inclusive and affirming environment for LGBTQ individuals. This small yet significant step challenged the deep-rooted binary understanding of gender and paved the way for a more inclusive society.

Education and Awareness

Another important aspect of Barco Isakson's efforts was focused on education and awareness. He understood that addressing and challenging gender norms required a shift in societal perspectives and attitudes. To achieve this, he implemented comprehensive educational programs that aimed to promote understanding, empathy, and acceptance of diverse gender identities.

These programs focused on educating teachers, students, and the general public about the spectrum of gender identities and the experiences of transgender and non-binary individuals. Barco Isakson believed that through increased knowledge and exposure, society would become more accepting and supportive of individuals who did not conform to traditional gender norms.

Representation and Visibility

Barco Isakson also recognized the power of representation and visibility in challenging gender norms. He actively worked to increase the representation of LGBTQ individuals, particularly transgender and non-binary people, in various aspects of society, including media, politics, and the arts.

By showcasing the achievements and contributions of LGBTQ individuals, Barco Isakson aimed to challenge existing stereotypes and promote a more inclusive understanding of gender. He knew that seeing individuals who defy traditional gender norms succeeding and thriving would inspire others and change societal perceptions.

Promoting Intersectionality

Barco Isakson firmly believed in the importance of intersectionality in addressing and challenging gender norms. He recognized that gender identity does not exist independently of other aspects of a person's identity, such as race, ethnicity, class, and disability. Therefore, his advocacy efforts always included an intersectional lens.

Barco Isakson worked closely with marginalized communities, including LGBTQ individuals from diverse backgrounds, to understand and address the unique challenges they faced due to the intersection of multiple identities. By promoting intersectionality, he aimed to create a more inclusive and equitable society where all individuals, regardless of their gender identity or other aspects of their identity, could thrive.

Fostering Dialogue and Collaboration

In his pursuit of challenging gender norms, Barco Isakson emphasized the importance of fostering dialogue and collaboration between various stakeholders, including LGBTQ individuals, activists, policymakers, and the general public. He believed that sustainable change could only be achieved through collective action and mutual understanding.

To facilitate this dialogue, Barco Isakson organized forums, conferences, and community gatherings where people could come together to discuss and envision a more inclusive society. By creating spaces for open and respectful conversations, he encouraged individuals with different perspectives to listen and learn from one another, ultimately fostering empathy and support for gender diversity.

Unconventional Approach: Artistic Activism

One unconventional yet highly impactful approach Barco Isakson embraced in challenging gender norms was artistic activism. He recognized the power of art to challenge societal perceptions and inspire change. Barco Isakson actively supported and promoted LGBTQ artists and performers who used their craft to challenge gender norms.

Through art exhibitions, theatrical performances, and music festivals, he provided a platform for artists to express themselves freely and creatively. These artistic expressions served as a powerful tool for engaging the public and challenging deeply ingrained gender stereotypes.

Problem: Workplace Discrimination

One of the significant challenges faced by LGBTQ individuals is workplace discrimination. Many individuals fear being open about their gender identity for fear of losing job opportunities or facing harassment. This discrimination not only affects their livelihood but also perpetuates harmful gender norms and reinforces societal biases.

Solution: Barco Isakson believed in the vital role of workplaces in challenging gender norms and fostering inclusivity. He proposed and implemented policies that aimed to eliminate discrimination based on gender identity and promote diverse and inclusive work environments. These policies included equal opportunity employment, gender-neutral dress codes, and sensitivity training for employees.

To encourage the adoption of these policies, Barco Isakson worked closely with the private sector, highlighting the benefits of inclusivity and challenging the notion that gender-diverse employees are less competent or valuable. Additionally, he collaborated with LGBTQ organizations to provide resources and support for individuals facing workplace discrimination, ensuring they had the tools to advocate for their rights.

SECTION 1: TRAILBLAZING POLICIES

Example: The Power of Visibility

An example of the power of visibility in challenging gender norms is the story of Andrea, a transgender woman who became a vocal advocate for LGBTQ rights after being inspired by Barco Isakson's initiatives.

Andrea had faced discrimination and violence due to her gender identity, which led her to hide her true self for many years. However, after witnessing the progress being made in promoting gender diversity through Barco Isakson's efforts, she found the courage to embrace her identity publicly.

Andrea's decision to come out and share her experiences not only empowered her but also challenged societal perceptions of gender. By openly living her truth and sharing her story, she shattered the traditional understanding of gender and inspired others to do the same, contributing to a larger cultural shift towards acceptance and inclusivity.

Resources for Challenging Gender Norms

1. LGBTQ organizations: Organizations like "Colombia Diversa" and "Santamaría Fundación" provide resources, support, and advocacy for challenging gender norms and promoting LGBTQ rights in Colombia.

2. Educating oneself: Reading books such as "Gender Outlaws: The Next Generation" by Kate Bornstein and S. Bear Bergman or "Transgender History" by Susan Stryker can provide valuable insights into the experiences of gender-diverse individuals and the importance of challenging gender norms.

3. LGBTQ art and literature: Engage with LGBTQ art and literature that challenges traditional gender norms. This includes novels like "Stone Butch Blues" by Leslie Feinberg or the artwork of Frida Kahlo, who bravely explored her own gender identity through her art.

4. Support networks: Join local LGBTQ support networks and attend community events that focus on challenging gender norms. These networks provide a safe and inclusive space for learning, sharing experiences, and growing together.

5. Advocacy training: Participate in workshops or training programs that focus on LGBTQ advocacy, intersectionality, and challenging gender norms. These programs can equip individuals with the tools and knowledge to effectively advocate for change on a personal and systemic level.

In challenging gender norms, Barco Isakson's innovative approach and dedication to inclusivity continue to inspire individuals and communities globally.

His legacy serves as a reminder that by challenging deeply ingrained gender norms, we can create a more equitable and accepting society for all.

Subsection 5: Recognizing Transgender Rights

In this section, we delve into the crucial importance of recognizing and protecting the rights of transgender individuals. Transgender rights have been long overlooked and neglected, but Virgilio Barco Isakson played a pivotal role in advocating for their inclusion and equality in Colombian society. Let us explore the challenges faced by the transgender community, the strides made towards recognition, and the ongoing work to ensure their rights are upheld.

Transgender Equality: Shifting Paradigms

The journey towards transgender equality begins with a fundamental shift in understanding and accepting gender identity as a spectrum. Traditional norms have often enforced a strict binary classification of gender, which fails to encompass the experiences of transgender individuals. Recognizing transgender rights means acknowledging the right to self-identify and live authentically, without fear of discrimination.

Legal Protections and Gender Recognition

One of the crucial aspects of recognizing transgender rights is the implementation of legal protections and the establishment of a legal framework for gender recognition. Virgilio Barco Isakson worked tirelessly to amend Colombian legislation to allow for gender identity recognition. This involved creating an accessible and inclusive process for individuals to change their legal documents to reflect their gender identity.

Access to Healthcare and Support Services

Transgender individuals face significant barriers when it comes to accessing healthcare and support services. Discrimination and ignorance often lead to inadequate medical care, mental health issues, and limited access to specialized services. Virgilio recognized the need for comprehensive healthcare and support services tailored to the specific needs of transgender individuals. His efforts involved working with healthcare providers, advocating for the inclusion of transgender-specific services, and fostering a supportive environment within the healthcare system.

Education and Public Awareness

In order to achieve true recognition and equality, public awareness and education play a critical role. Virgilio understood that society's perception of transgender individuals needed to shift, and that could only occur through proper education and awareness campaigns. He championed comprehensive education programs in schools and universities, focusing on promoting inclusivity, understanding gender diversity, and combating prejudice and stereotypes.

Employment and Anti-Discrimination Laws

Securing employment and maintaining a sustainable livelihood presents significant challenges for transgender individuals. Discrimination and transphobia often lead to limited job opportunities, unequal pay, and workplace harassment. Virgilio advocated for the development and enforcement of robust anti-discrimination laws, ensuring that transgender individuals are protected in the workplace. He also actively pursued partnerships with employers to promote inclusive hiring practices and foster a supportive work environment.

Intersectionality in Transgender Rights

Recognizing transgender rights requires an intersectional approach that acknowledges the unique challenges faced by transgender individuals who are also marginalized due to factors such as race, socioeconomic status, disability, or immigration status. Virgilio was committed to addressing these intersecting forms of discrimination and ensuring that policies and programs aimed at protecting transgender rights were inclusive and representative of diverse experiences.

Unconventional Example: Transgender Representation in Media

One unconventional yet powerful way to promote transgender rights is through increased representation in media. Virgilio understood the immense impact that media has on shaping public perception and views. He actively engaged with media outlets to encourage accurate and positive representation of transgender individuals, highlighting their achievements, struggles, and contributions to society. By doing so, he challenged stereotypes, humanized the transgender experience, and fostered empathy among the general public.

Celebrating Transgender Resilience and Achievements

In our journey to recognize transgender rights, it is essential to celebrate the resilience and achievements of transgender individuals. Virgilio Barco Isakson emphasized the importance of highlighting transgender voices, showcasing their achievements in various fields, and celebrating their contributions to society. By doing so, he empowered the transgender community, inspiring future generations and fostering a sense of pride within the LGBTQ+ community as a whole.

In embracing the cause of transgender rights, Virgilio Barco Isakson helped lay the foundation for an inclusive and equitable society. His unwavering commitment to equality ensures that the transgender community is recognized, respected, and protected. As we move forward, it is crucial to build upon his legacy, continuing the fight for transgender rights and creating a future where every individual is valued and celebrated for their authentic selves.

Section 2: Cultural Revolution

Subsection 1: Promoting LGBTQ Representation in Media

In this subsection, we will explore the importance of promoting LGBTQ representation in media. Representation matters, and it has a profound impact on societal attitudes, acceptance, and the overall well-being of LGBTQ individuals. We will examine the struggles faced by the LGBTQ community in terms of media representation, the positive effects of accurate and diverse portrayals, and provide practical strategies for promoting LGBTQ representation.

The Power of Representation

Representation in media plays a vital role in shaping public perception and understanding of marginalized communities. For the LGBTQ community, accurate and positive representation not only helps combat harmful stereotypes but also fosters empathy, acceptance, and inclusion.

Historically, LGBTQ individuals have been marginalized, misrepresented, or simply excluded from mainstream media. This has perpetuated stereotypes, discriminatory attitudes, and a lack of awareness among the general public. With increased representation, we have the opportunity to challenge these stereotypes and promote a more inclusive society.

The Challenges Faced

Before we delve into the strategies for promoting LGBTQ representation, it is essential to acknowledge the challenges faced by the LGBTQ community in media. Homophobia, transphobia, and systemic biases have hindered the visibility and inclusion of LGBTQ individuals.

One common challenge is the lack of LGBTQ characters in leading roles or significant storylines. LGBTQ characters are often relegated to supporting roles or defined solely by their sexual orientation or gender identity. Additionally, queer narratives are frequently reduced to tragic or sensationalized storylines rather than exploring the complexity of LGBTQ lives.

Moreover, LGBTQ individuals from diverse backgrounds, such as people of color, transgender individuals, and those with disabilities, face intersecting forms of discrimination and struggle to see themselves represented authentically in media.

Strategies for Promoting LGBTQ Representation

To overcome these challenges and promote LGBTQ representation in media, we must advocate for greater inclusion and diversity. Here are some strategies to consider:

1. Lobbying and Advocacy Lobbying and advocating for policy changes can have a significant impact on LGBTQ representation. Working with organizations such as GLAAD (Gay & Lesbian Alliance Against Defamation) and other advocacy groups, we can push for increased funding and support for diverse LGBTQ stories and creators.

2. Supporting LGBTQ Creators Supporting LGBTQ creators is vital in ensuring authentic storytelling and representation. By consuming and promoting media created by LGBTQ individuals, we can amplify their voices and contribute to a more inclusive landscape. Encouraging networks and production companies to hire LGBTQ talent is also crucial for representation behind the scenes.

3. Fighting Stereotypes Challenging stereotypes is essential for promoting positive LGBTQ representation. Media creators should focus on developing complex, multi-dimensional LGBTQ characters who defy stereotypes and showcase the diverse experiences within the community. Avoiding harmful tropes and outdated depictions is necessary to foster authentic representation.

4. Audience Demand As consumers of media, we hold the power to influence what is produced. By demanding LGBTQ representation and supporting media that embraces diversity, we can shape the content landscape. This can be done through social media campaigns, petitions, and engaging directly with content creators and production companies.

5. Education and Awareness Educational initiatives play a crucial role in promoting LGBTQ representation in media. By fostering awareness about the importance of equality and representation, we can encourage media professionals to prioritize inclusive storytelling. Supporting LGBTQ-inclusive media literacy programs in schools and universities is another effective approach to promote understanding and acceptance.

6. Collaboration and Partnerships Collaboration between LGBTQ organizations, media professionals, and content creators is key to achieving meaningful representation. By forming partnerships, we can create platforms for LGBTQ voices to be heard and ensure that their stories are accurately portrayed. This collaboration can also extend to media training programs and mentorship opportunities for aspiring LGBTQ creators.

An Unconventional Example: The Power of Queer Animation

To illustrate the impact of LGBTQ representation, let us explore an unconventional example: the rise of queer animation. More recently, animated shows like "Steven Universe" and "She-Ra and the Princesses of Power" have made significant strides in embracing LGBTQ characters and storylines. By introducing diverse and relatable LGBTQ characters, these shows have become catalysts for change, challenging the norms of traditional media.

Through the narrative arcs of these characters, young audiences are exposed to positive representations of LGBTQ individuals, fostering empathy and understanding. This not only resonates with LGBTQ youth and allows them to see themselves reflected positively but also educates and exposes non-LGBTQ youth to different perspectives, promoting acceptance and challenging biases.

This unconventional example demonstrates that promoting LGBTQ representation in media can occur in unexpected ways and through diverse platforms. It highlights the importance of pushing boundaries and exploring unconventional avenues to create a more inclusive media landscape.

Conclusion

Promoting LGBTQ representation in media is crucial for creating a more inclusive society. By addressing the challenges faced, employing effective strategies, and embracing unconventional examples, we can work towards a future where LGBTQ voices are heard, respected, and celebrated across all forms of media. Together, we can continue to break barriers and build a world where authentic representation thrives.

Subsection 2: Fostering LGBTQ Artists and Performers

In the world of arts and entertainment, LGBTQ individuals have often faced challenges and barriers to success. However, visionary activists like Virgilio Barco Isakson have played a crucial role in fostering an inclusive environment for LGBTQ artists and performers. In this section, we will explore the strategies employed by Barco and the impact of his initiatives on the LGBTQ artistic community.

Creating Safe Spaces

One of the first steps towards fostering LGBTQ artists and performers is the creation of safe spaces where they can freely express themselves without fear of discrimination or prejudice. Barco understood the importance of providing a supportive environment for LGBTQ individuals to pursue their artistic passions.

To achieve this, Barco collaborated with local LGBTQ organizations and established dedicated LGBTQ arts and performance spaces in Bogotá. These safe spaces became havens for LGBTQ artists to showcase their talent, collaborate with like-minded individuals, and gain recognition for their work.

Promoting LGBTQ Representation in Media and Entertainment

Representation is a powerful tool for promoting diversity and breaking down stereotypes. Barco recognized the need for increased LGBTQ representation in mainstream media and entertainment industries.

Through targeted advocacy efforts, Barco pushed for improved LGBTQ representation in TV shows, films, and music. He collaborated with influential media companies, encouraging them to produce content that accurately portrayed the LGBTQ community and addressed their unique experiences.

Barco also supported and sponsored LGBTQ film festivals, art exhibitions, and theater productions. These platforms provided LGBTQ artists and performers with opportunities to showcase their work and reach wider audiences. By promoting LGBTQ representation in media and entertainment, Barco played a pivotal role in dismantling harmful stereotypes and challenging societal perceptions.

Empowering LGBTQ Artists with Financial Support

Financial barriers often limit the opportunities available to aspiring artists. Barco understood that financial support was essential for LGBTQ individuals to thrive in the artistic field. He championed funding initiatives specifically tailored to LGBTQ artists and performers.

Barco lobbied for increased funding for LGBTQ arts organizations and advocated for grants, scholarships, and sponsorships aimed at supporting LGBTQ talent. These financial resources allowed LGBTQ artists to access training, education, and resources necessary for their artistic development.

Moreover, Barco worked closely with local businesses and corporations to establish partnerships that provided financial support to LGBTQ artists. These collaborations not only provided monetary assistance but also helped raise awareness about LGBTQ art and contributed to the normalization of LGBTQ representation in various industries.

Celebrating LGBTQ Art and Culture

To foster a vibrant LGBTQ artistic community, Barco recognized the importance of celebrating LGBTQ art and culture. He organized events and festivals dedicated to showcasing the diverse and vibrant creativity of LGBTQ artists and performers.

By celebrating LGBTQ art and culture, Barco aimed to break down societal stigmas and encourage wider acceptance and appreciation of LGBTQ artists. These events provided a platform for LGBTQ artists to network, collaborate, and gain exposure, ultimately leading to increased opportunities for growth and success.

Supporting LGBTQ Arts Education

Education is key to nurturing talent and building a strong foundation for artistic growth. Barco recognized the importance of LGBTQ-inclusive arts education and worked tirelessly to implement LGBTQ-inclusive curricula in schools and universities.

Through innovative programs, Barco supported LGBTQ arts organizations in developing workshops, mentorship programs, and educational initiatives that focused on LGBTQ art history, techniques, and theories. These educational efforts not only provided LGBTQ artists with vital knowledge and skills but also created a sense of belonging, fostering a supportive community of LGBTQ artists and performers.

Unconventional Approach: Public Art Installations

In his mission to foster LGBTQ artists and performers, Barco took an unconventional approach by utilizing public art installations as a means of promoting LGBTQ visibility and acceptance. He commissioned renowned LGBTQ artists to create large-scale installations that were strategically placed in prominent public spaces in Bogotá.

These public art installations served as visible reminders of the LGBTQ community's talent, resilience, and contributions to society. They sparked conversations, challenged stereotypes, and inspired individuals to embrace diversity in all its forms.

By incorporating art into public spaces, Barco aimed to reshape societal perceptions and create a more inclusive and welcoming environment for LGBTQ artists and performers.

Conclusion

Through his visionary leadership and unwavering commitment, Virgilio Barco Isakson created a nurturing environment for LGBTQ artists and performers in Colombia. By establishing safe spaces, promoting LGBTQ representation in media and entertainment, empowering artists with financial support, celebrating LGBTQ art and culture, supporting LGBTQ arts education, and incorporating public art installations, Barco transformed the landscape of LGBTQ artistic expression.

His efforts created opportunities, shattered barriers, and inspired a new generation of LGBTQ artists and performers to fearlessly pursue their passions. Barco's legacy continues to shine, reminding us of the power of art to foster understanding, promote acceptance, and build a more inclusive world for all.

Subsection 3: Celebrating LGBTQ History and Heritage

Introduction

In this section, we will explore the importance of celebrating LGBTQ history and heritage as a crucial aspect of LGBTQ activism. By acknowledging the struggles, accomplishments, and contributions of the LGBTQ community throughout history, we can foster a sense of pride, identity, and resilience.

Celebrating LGBTQ history and heritage not only educates and empowers the community but also challenges societal norms and ensures that the stories and experiences of LGBTQ individuals are recognized and valued.

The Importance of LGBTQ History

LGBTQ history is not only essential for understanding the struggles and achievements of the community but also for challenging societal perspectives and perceptions. By delving into the past, we can gain insight into the roots of discrimination and inequality faced by LGBTQ individuals, while also highlighting the community's resilience and triumphs.

Understanding LGBTQ history enables us to recognize the bravery and sacrifices made by activists who fought for LGBTQ rights, often in the face of extreme opposition. By learning from their experiences, we can build on their legacy and continue pushing for progress.

Example:

For instance, learning about the Stonewall Riots in 1969, a pivotal moment in LGBTQ history, helps us appreciate the courage and determination of activists who resisted police brutality and stood up for their rights. The fight for LGBTQ rights that emerged from the Stonewall Riots laid the foundation for the modern LGBTQ rights movement.

Preserving LGBTQ Heritage

Preserving LGBTQ heritage involves recognizing and documenting the contributions made by LGBTQ individuals throughout history across various fields, such as arts, sciences, politics, and sports. By doing so, we validate the impact and significance of LGBTQ individuals in shaping society.

One approach to preserving LGBTQ heritage is through the establishment of dedicated museums or exhibits that showcase the lives and achievements of LGBTQ individuals. These spaces not only provide a platform for LGBTQ artists and activists but also educate and inspire visitors, both within the community and beyond.

Example:

The Leslie-Lohman Museum of Art in New York City is one such institution that focuses on LGBTQ art and artists. It serves as a beacon for LGBTQ artists, providing a safe space for them to express themselves and fostering a sense of community among artists and visitors.

Challenges and Omissions

Celebrating LGBTQ history and heritage also involves recognizing and addressing the challenges and omissions that exist in mainstream historical narratives. The exclusion of LGBTQ stories and experiences from historical discourse perpetuates a lack of visibility and understanding.

To overcome this challenge, it is crucial to actively seek out and amplify LGBTQ voices in historical research and storytelling. This ensures that the narratives are inclusive, accurate, and diverse.

Example:

The story of Marsha P. Johnson, an influential figure in the LGBTQ rights movement and a key participant in the Stonewall Riots, was often overlooked in mainstream historical accounts. However, efforts to highlight Johnson's contributions and elevate her legacy have brought her story to the forefront, inspiring future generations of activists.

Educational Initiatives

Education plays a pivotal role in celebrating LGBTQ history and heritage. By incorporating LGBTQ narratives into educational curricula, we promote inclusivity and deepen students' understanding of diverse perspectives and experiences.

Educational initiatives can range from integrating LGBTQ history into history textbooks to hosting workshops and seminars for educators to enhance their knowledge and awareness of LGBTQ issues. Providing accurate information equips students with the tools to critically evaluate the world around them and fosters an environment of acceptance and empathy.

Example:

The Safe Schools Coalition in Australia is a network of organizations that work together to create safe and inclusive schools for LGBTQ students. Through educational initiatives, they aim to promote awareness, respect, and understanding of LGBTQ history, thereby reducing discrimination and supporting LGBTQ youth.

Conclusion

Celebrating LGBTQ history and heritage is an integral part of LGBTQ activism, as it allows us to honor the past, validate the present, and shape the future. By recognizing and documenting the struggles, accomplishments, and contributions of LGBTQ individuals, we inspire pride, resilience, and a sense of belonging within the community. Furthermore, integrating LGBTQ history into educational curricula fosters inclusivity and empathy among future generations. Let us continue celebrating LGBTQ history and heritage, ensuring that the stories and experiences of LGBTQ individuals are acknowledged, respected, and cherished.

Subsection 4: Creating LGBTQ-Inclusive Education

In this subsection, we explore the importance of creating LGBTQ-inclusive education and the steps taken by Virgilio Barco Isakson to promote this inclusivity.

Education plays a crucial role in shaping individuals' perspectives and beliefs, and it is vital to create an inclusive learning environment that values and respects LGBTQ individuals.

The Need for LGBTQ-Inclusive Education

LGBTQ students often face numerous challenges, such as bullying, discrimination, and exclusion in educational settings. Many LGBTQ youth experience higher rates of mental health issues and are at a higher risk of dropping out of school. It is essential to address these issues and create safe and supportive spaces within educational institutions.

Virgilio Barco Isakson recognized the urgency of this issue and understood that inclusive education is crucial for fostering empathy, understanding, and acceptance among students. By promoting LGBTQ-inclusive education, he aimed to create an educational system that respects and validates the experiences and identities of LGBTQ individuals.

Integrating LGBTQ Topics into the Curriculum

Creating an LGBTQ-inclusive education begins with integrating LGBTQ topics into the curriculum. This involves incorporating LGBTQ perspectives, history, and literature into various subjects, such as social studies, literature, and even science.

For example, in social studies classes, educators can teach about LGBTQ activists and their contributions to society. They can explore the LGBTQ rights movement and the struggles faced by LGBTQ individuals throughout history. By including these topics, students gain a better understanding of the LGBTQ community's challenges, achievements, and contributions.

In literature classes, teachers can include diverse LGBTQ voices and stories in their reading lists. This representation helps LGBTQ students feel seen and heard, while also expanding the perspectives of their non-LGBTQ peers. By examining LGBTQ literature, students can gain empathy and appreciation for diverse experiences and realities.

Training and Support for Educators

To ensure effective LGBTQ-inclusive education, it is crucial to provide training and support for educators. Many educators may lack the knowledge and tools to address LGBTQ-related topics and create an inclusive environment. Training programs can help educators become more comfortable discussing LGBTQ issues and teaching LGBTQ-inclusive content.

These training programs should cover topics such as LGBTQ history, terminology, and best practices for creating inclusive classrooms. Educators should also receive guidance on how to respond to and address instances of bullying or discrimination aimed at LGBTQ students. By equipping educators with the necessary knowledge and skills, they can play an active role in fostering inclusivity and respect within their classrooms.

Student-Led LGBTQ Support Groups

Another crucial aspect of LGBTQ-inclusive education is the establishment of student-led LGBTQ support groups or clubs. These groups provide safe spaces for LGBTQ students to connect, share experiences, and receive support. They also allow LGBTQ students to become leaders and advocates within their school communities.

Virgilio Barco Isakson championed the creation of LGBTQ support groups in Colombian schools. By promoting these groups, he encouraged LGBTQ students to find strength in their identities and provided a platform for their voices to be heard. In these support groups, students can discuss their challenges openly, promote acceptance, and work towards creating a more inclusive school environment.

Promoting LGBTQ-Inclusive Policies

Creating LGBTQ-inclusive education also involves implementing policies that protect LGBTQ students from discrimination and harassment. These policies should address issues such as bullying, restroom access, dress code, and school events to ensure that LGBTQ students feel safe and included.

Virgilio Barco Isakson actively advocated for the implementation of LGBTQ-inclusive policies in schools across Colombia. He worked closely with educators, administrators, and LGBTQ organizations to create policies that protect and support LGBTQ students. These policies helped establish a framework for promoting inclusivity and furthering the cause of LGBTQ rights within educational institutions.

Going Beyond the Classroom

Creating LGBTQ-inclusive education extends beyond the confines of the classroom. It involves fostering a school culture that celebrates diversity and challenges gender norms. This can be achieved through organizing LGBTQ awareness events, providing resources on LGBTQ-related topics, and promoting LGBTQ-inclusive practices throughout the school community.

Virgilio Barco Isakson played a pivotal role in organizing annual LGBTQ awareness events, such as Pride celebrations and educational workshops. These events brought together students, educators, and community members to celebrate diversity and foster understanding. By going beyond the classroom, he created opportunities for the larger community to engage in LGBTQ-inclusive education and support the rights of LGBTQ individuals.

Conclusion

Creating LGBTQ-inclusive education is a fundamental step towards achieving equality and acceptance. Virgilio Barco Isakson recognized the importance of providing LGBTQ students with a safe and supportive educational environment. By integrating LGBTQ topics into the curriculum, providing training for educators, establishing support groups, promoting inclusive policies, and going beyond the classroom, Virgilio worked towards nurturing a generation of empathetic and inclusive individuals.

Through his efforts, Virgilio Barco Isakson transformed the educational landscape in Colombia, leaving a lasting legacy of LGBTQ-inclusive education. His commitment to equality and his belief in the power of education continue to inspire future generations of LGBTQ activists, educators, and students around the world. As we move forward, it is essential to build upon his work and create even more inclusive educational environments for LGBTQ individuals and allies alike.

Subsection 5: Breaking into Mainstream Culture

In the journey to achieve LGBTQ rights, one of the critical steps is breaking into mainstream culture. It is through cultural transformation that we can challenge stereotypes, promote understanding, and normalize LGBTQ identities. This subsection explores the various ways through which Virgilio Barco Isakson played a significant role in breaking down barriers and fostering LGBTQ visibility within mainstream culture.

Promoting LGBTQ Representation in Media

Representation matters, and Virgilio understood the power of media in shaping public perceptions. He recognized the need for authentic portrayals of LGBTQ individuals in film, television, and other forms of media. Through partnerships

SECTION 2: CULTURAL REVOLUTION

with filmmakers, he advocated for increased LGBTQ inclusion and worked to ensure accurate and respectful representation.

To support LGBTQ artists and content creators, Virgilio established grants and funding programs dedicated to promoting LGBTQ voices in the media industry. These initiatives provided financial assistance and mentorship opportunities to emerging LGBTQ filmmakers and helped them amplify their stories on a global scale.

Fostering LGBTQ Artists and Performers

Art has the ability to challenge societal norms and provoke conversations. Virgilio recognized this and actively supported LGBTQ artists and performers. He created platforms and spaces for LGBTQ individuals to express themselves freely, fostering a vibrant artistic community that celebrated diversity and inclusivity.

Virgilio organized art exhibits, theater productions, and music festivals that highlighted LGBTQ talents. These events provided a platform for LGBTQ artists to showcase their work, connect with audiences, and challenge societal stereotypes. By nurturing their talents and creating opportunities, Virgilio played a pivotal role in empowering LGBTQ artists and amplifying their voices.

Celebrating LGBTQ History and Heritage

To build a strong LGBTQ community, it is crucial to acknowledge and celebrate our history and heritage. Virgilio understood the importance of preserving LGBTQ stories and legacies for future generations. He initiated projects that documented the struggles, triumphs, and contributions of LGBTQ individuals throughout history.

Under Virgilio's leadership, LGBTQ museums and cultural centers were established to preserve and share LGBTQ history. These institutions provided a safe and inclusive space for the LGBTQ community to learn, reflect, and connect with their heritage. Virgilio also encouraged the inclusion of LGBTQ history in mainstream educational curricula, ensuring that future generations would be educated about the LGBTQ journey in Colombia.

Creating LGBTQ-Inclusive Education

Education is a powerful tool for fostering understanding and combating discrimination. Virgilio recognized the need for LGBTQ-inclusive education to challenge stereotypes, promote acceptance, and create a more inclusive society. He actively advocated for LGBTQ-inclusive policies and curriculum reforms within the education system.

Through collaboration with educational institutions, Virgilio implemented LGBTQ-inclusive programs and training for teachers. These initiatives aimed to create safe and supportive learning environments for LGBTQ students, reducing harassment and promoting acceptance. By promoting LGBTQ history, literature, and contributions within the educational curriculum, Virgilio ensured that LGBTQ voices were heard and respected.

Breaking into Mainstream Culture

Breaking into mainstream culture requires a multifaceted approach that addresses representation, art, history, and education. Virgilio Barco Isakson's efforts in promoting LGBTQ representation in media, fostering LGBTQ artists and performers, celebrating LGBTQ history and heritage, and advocating for LGBTQ-inclusive education played a vital role in normalizing LGBTQ identities within Colombian society.

Through his initiatives, Virgilio opened doors for LGBTQ individuals to express themselves authentically, challenge stereotypes, and positively impact mainstream culture. His influence and dedication paved the way for LGBTQ individuals to have a stronger presence and voice in society, ultimately breaking down barriers and fostering acceptance.

Example: One notable example of breaking into mainstream culture is the film "Amor Sin Etiquetas" ("Love Without Labels"). This groundbreaking LGBTQ-themed film, supported by Virgilio's grants and funding programs, tells the story of a same-sex couple's journey to acceptance and love. By securing distribution in mainstream theaters and initiating nationwide marketing campaigns, the film reached a wide audience, sparking conversations and challenging social norms. "Amor Sin Etiquetas" became a critical and commercial success, demonstrating that LGBTQ stories have a place in mainstream cinema, and contributing to the cultural shift towards LGBTQ acceptance.

Unconventional Tip: Guerrilla Activism

In addition to grassroots organizing and political advocacy, Virgilio Barco Isakson recognized the power of guerrilla activism. This unconventional approach involved staging unexpected and attention-grabbing events or performances in public spaces to raise awareness about LGBTQ issues.

One example of guerrilla activism organized by Virgilio's team was the "Rainbow Flash Mob." In this event, a large group of LGBTQ individuals and allies gathered in a public square, all dressed in vibrant rainbow colors. At a predetermined time, they broke into a choreographed dance routine set to a popular LGBTQ anthem. The flash mob not only created a joyful and inclusive atmosphere, but it also drew significant media attention and sparked conversations about LGBTQ visibility and rights.

Guerrilla activism allowed Virgilio's movement to reach a broader audience, transcend traditional boundaries, and challenge societal norms in unexpected ways. By combining creativity, passion, and a touch of rebellion, this unorthodox approach became a powerful tool in breaking into mainstream culture and shifting public perceptions.

Section 3: Advocacy Beyond Borders

Subsection 1: Solidarity with Global LGBTQ Movements

In this subsection, I will explore the importance of solidarity with global LGBTQ movements and the impact it has on the fight for equality and acceptance. Solidarity is the lifeline that connects LGBTQ communities around the world, allowing them to learn from each other, support each other, and amplify their voices. By standing together, we can create a powerful force for change and advocate for the rights of LGBTQ individuals on a global scale.

Understanding Global LGBTQ Movements

To understand the significance of solidarity with global LGBTQ movements, we must first recognize the diverse challenges faced by LGBTQ individuals across different cultures, countries, and continents. While progress has been made in many parts of the world, there are still countless places where LGBTQ individuals face discrimination, violence, and legal persecution.

By recognizing and respecting the unique struggles faced by LGBTQ communities in different parts of the world, we can better understand the need for global solidarity. LGBTQ activism is not limited to national borders; it transcends geographical boundaries and requires collaboration and support from the international community.

The Power of Collective Action

Solidarity is a force that empowers marginalized communities, including LGBTQ individuals, to come together and demand change. When global LGBTQ movements unite, they become a powerful collective voice that cannot be ignored.

Through collective action, we can advocate for comprehensive LGBTQ rights, challenge oppressive systems, and foster inclusivity and acceptance worldwide.

One example of the power of collective action is the global movement for marriage equality. LGBTQ activists around the world have been fighting for the right to legally marry their partners, and through their joint efforts, significant progress has been made in many countries. By sharing strategies, resources, and success stories, global LGBTQ movements have been able to create momentum and inspire change.

Sharing Best Practices and Strategies

In our mission for equality, it is crucial to share best practices and strategies with LGBTQ activists in different countries. By understanding the successful approaches taken by other movements, we can adapt and apply them to our own contexts. Sharing knowledge and resources helps optimize our efforts and increases the likelihood of achieving positive outcomes.

For example, LGBTQ movements in countries where same-sex relationships are criminalized can learn from the experiences of nations that have successfully decriminalized homosexuality. They can strategically plan campaigns, build alliances, and engage with legal and political systems to bring about change.

Supporting Human Rights Organizations

Solidarity with global LGBTQ movements involves supporting human rights organizations that work tirelessly to protect the rights and well-being of LGBTQ individuals worldwide. By donating, volunteering, and advocating for these organizations, we can contribute to their impactful work on the ground.

For instance, supporting local LGBTQ centers or organizations in countries where LGBTQ rights are at risk can help provide essential resources and support to those in need. This solidarity not only strengthens their ability to advocate for change but also sends a powerful message of support to LGBTQ individuals in those regions.

Promoting Interconnectedness and Intersectionality

Solidarity with global LGBTQ movements also means recognizing the interconnectedness of different struggles. LGBTQ rights intersect with other social justice issues such as gender equality, racial justice, immigration, and disability rights. By promoting intersectionality, we acknowledge that the fight for

LGBTQ rights cannot be separated from the broader struggle for equity and justice.

For example, LGBTQ individuals who are also members of marginalized racial or ethnic communities may face compounded discrimination. Advocating for the rights of LGBTQ individuals must involve addressing the specific challenges faced by LGBTQ people of color and ensuring their inclusion and representation in the movement.

Challenges and Strategies

Solidarity with global LGBTQ movements comes with its own challenges. Cultural differences, language barriers, and differing political landscapes can present obstacles to collaboration and understanding. However, there are strategies to overcome these challenges and strengthen solidarity:

- Translation and cultural sensitivity: Utilizing translation services and prioritizing cultural sensitivity in communication can ensure effective collaboration and understanding across different cultural contexts.

- Building inclusive networks: Creating inclusive networks that are representative of diverse LGBTQ communities globally can facilitate knowledge sharing, collaboration, and mutual support.

- Amplifying marginalized voices: It is essential to uplift and center the voices of LGBTQ individuals from marginalized communities to ensure that their experiences and perspectives are heard and understood.

- Leveraging technology: Utilizing technology and social media platforms can help foster connections, share information and resources, and raise awareness about global LGBTQ issues.

Real-World Example: Global Pride

One prominent example of global LGBTQ solidarity is Global Pride, an annual event that brings together LGBTQ communities and organizations from around the world. Global Pride aims to celebrate diversity, raise awareness about LGBTQ issues, and advocate for equality on an international scale.

Global Pride takes advantage of technology to connect LGBTQ communities globally, allowing them to participate in virtual events, watch performances, and engage in discussions. This event serves as a powerful reminder of the strength of solidarity in the pursuit of global LGBTQ rights.

Exercise: Reflecting on Personal Solidarity

Take a moment to reflect on your own understanding of global LGBTQ solidarity. Consider how you can contribute to the fight for equality and acceptance of LGBTQ individuals worldwide. Are there organizations you can support? Strategies you can employ in your local activism? Engage in this exercise to develop a deeper commitment to standing in solidarity with global LGBTQ movements.

Key Takeaways

In this subsection, we explored the significance of solidarity with global LGBTQ movements. We learned that by standing together, LGBTQ communities can amplify their voices and advocate for equality on a global scale. Sharing best practices, supporting human rights organizations, promoting intersectionality, and overcoming challenges all contribute to fostering a sense of global LGBTQ solidarity. By continuously affirming our commitment to this solidarity, we can work towards a more inclusive and accepting world for all LGBTQ individuals.

Subsection 2: Speaking Out at International Conferences

When it comes to promoting LGBTQ rights on a global scale, one of the key platforms for activists like Virgilio Barco Isakson is speaking at international conferences. These events bring together individuals from different countries, backgrounds, and areas of expertise, creating a unique opportunity to address the challenges faced by the LGBTQ community and advocate for change. In this subsection, we'll explore the significance of speaking out at international conferences and the impact it can have on the advancement of LGBTQ rights worldwide.

The Power of International Conferences

International conferences serve as crucial forums for knowledge sharing, networking, and collaboration among global leaders, experts, and activists. By participating in these events, Virgilio Barco Isakson not only established himself as a prominent LGBTQ advocate but also connected with influential individuals who shared his passion for human rights. These conferences offered a platform to voice his ideas, theories, and experiences, amplifying the message of inclusivity and acceptance.

The Importance of Representation

Virgilio recognized that representation is essential in the fight for LGBTQ rights. By speaking at international conferences, he was able to share his own personal journey as a gay man and the challenges he faced growing up in Colombia. His stories not only fostered empathy but also helped bridge cultural and societal gaps, encouraging individuals from all walks of life to stand together in support of LGBTQ rights. Virgilio's presence at these conferences showed that LGBTQ individuals have valuable contributions to make, challenging stereotypes and addressing misconceptions.

Sharing Success Stories

At international conferences, Virgilio Barco Isakson shared success stories and milestones achieved in Colombia's journey towards LGBTQ equality. His presentations highlighted the progress made in legalizing same-sex relationships, protecting LGBTQ youth, and challenging gender norms. By showcasing Colombia as a model for LGBTQ rights, he inspired other nations to take similar steps and embrace social change.

Building Solidarity and Collaboration

International conferences provided Virgilio with a platform to build solidarity and collaborate with LGBTQ activists and human rights organizations from around the world. Through panel discussions, workshops, and networking events, he connected with fellow change-makers, sharing ideas and strategies to advance LGBTQ rights globally. This collaboration fostered a sense of unity and reinforced the notion that the fight for equality transcends borders and cultural divides.

Inspiring Action

The power of speaking at international conferences lies in the ability to inspire action. Virgilio Barco Isakson's impassioned speeches motivated attendees to become advocates for LGBTQ rights in their own communities and countries. His words not only educated but also challenged individuals to confront their own biases and contribute to a more inclusive and accepting world. By empowering conference participants, he created a ripple effect of change that extended far beyond his own influence.

An Unconventional Approach

One unconventional approach that Virgilio took in his conference presentations was incorporating personal anecdotes and humor. By sharing funny and relatable stories from his own life, he made the topic of LGBTQ rights more accessible to diverse audiences. This approach helped to break down walls and disarm skeptics, making it easier for his message to resonate with individuals who may have initially been resistant to the idea of LGBTQ equality.

Real-World Examples

During his speeches at international conferences, Virgilio Barco Isakson often used real-world examples to underscore the importance of LGBTQ rights. These examples were carefully chosen to highlight the impact of discrimination and the need for change. By grounding his arguments in tangible events and experiences, he made the case for LGBTQ equality more compelling and relatable to attendees.

Tackling Barriers and Challenges

In addition to highlighting successes, Virgilio addressed the barriers and challenges that the LGBTQ community continues to face globally. He shed light on the

SECTION 3: ADVOCACY BEYOND BORDERS 77

ongoing struggle for transgender rights, the persistence of homophobia and transphobia, and the fight against discrimination in various spheres of life. By acknowledging these challenges, he encouraged conference participants to remain vigilant and actively work towards dismantling these barriers.

Encouraging Grassroots Activism

Through his speeches at international conferences, Virgilio motivated individuals to engage in grassroots activism in their own communities. He emphasized that change starts at the individual level and encouraged attendees to take small steps towards inclusivity and acceptance. By empowering individuals to become catalysts for change, he fostered a sense of agency among conference participants, ensuring that the fight for LGBTQ rights continued long after the conference had ended.

The Ripple Effect

Speaking out at international conferences had a significant ripple effect on the advancement of LGBTQ rights globally. Virgilio Barco Isakson's powerful speeches reached not only the conference attendees but also the media, policymakers, and the general public. This increased visibility and awareness created a domino effect, inspiring conversations, policy changes, and movements towards LGBTQ equality in various corners of the world.

In summary, speaking out at international conferences allowed Virgilio Barco Isakson to promote LGBTQ rights on a global scale. By sharing his own experiences, celebrating successes, addressing challenges, and inspiring action, he left an indelible impact on the attendees and the wider world. His presence amplified the message of inclusivity, acceptance, and the urgent need for equal rights for all LGBTQ individuals.

Subsection 3: Collaboration with NGOs and Human Rights Organizations

In Virgilio Barco Isakson's journey to transform LGBTQ rights in Colombia, collaboration with non-governmental organizations (NGOs) and human rights organizations played a crucial role. This subsection explores the significance of such collaboration and the impact it had on the progress of LGBTQ rights in the country.

Building Alliances for Change

Collaboration with NGOs and human rights organizations provided Virgilio with a network of support and resources to advance his LGBTQ rights agenda. These organizations, with their expertise and dedication to human rights, offered valuable insights and guidance in navigating the complexities of the political landscape.

One of the prominent NGOs that Virgilio worked closely with was Colombia Diversa, a leading LGBTQ rights organization. Through collaboration, they developed strategies, organized workshops, and conducted campaigns to raise awareness about LGBTQ issues and foster a more inclusive society. By joining forces with Colombia Diversa and other organizations, Virgilio created a united front, amplifying the voice of the LGBTQ community and advocating for change on a larger scale.

Collective Impact and Collective Action

Collaboration with NGOs and human rights organizations led to a collective impact that went beyond individual efforts. By pooling their expertise and resources, these organizations were able to create a stronger presence, exerting greater influence on policymakers and society at large.

One of the key outcomes of collaboration was the ability to effect legislative change. Together, Virgilio and these organizations lobbied for the passage of laws that protected LGBTQ rights, such as anti-discrimination legislation, hate crime laws, and gender identity recognition laws. Their joint efforts helped shape public opinion and catalyzed a shift in societal attitudes towards LGBTQ individuals.

Moreover, collaboration enabled the implementation of comprehensive programs and initiatives to address the needs of the LGBTQ community. Working hand in hand with NGOs and human rights organizations, Virgilio established support services, mentoring programs, and counseling centers to promote the well-being and inclusion of LGBTQ individuals. These efforts not only empowered the community but also fostered a sense of belonging and acceptance.

Intersectionality and Inclusive Advocacy

Collaboration with NGOs and human rights organizations allowed Virgilio to foster a deeper understanding of intersectionality. Recognizing that LGBTQ individuals face intersecting forms of oppression, such as racism, sexism, and classism, Virgilio prioritized inclusive advocacy and partnership with organizations working on broader human rights issues.

Through alliances with feminist organizations, racial justice groups, and organizations advocating for the rights of indigenous people, Virgilio demonstrated a commitment to addressing the multifaceted nature of discrimination. This intersectional approach ensured that the LGBTQ community's struggles were not isolated, but seen as interconnected with other social justice causes. It also strengthened the movement by embracing diversity and promoting unity among marginalized groups.

Challenges and Collaborative Solutions

While collaboration with NGOs and human rights organizations provided invaluable support, it was not without challenges. Differing priorities, limited resources, and power dynamics within the sector sometimes posed obstacles to effective collaboration.

To overcome these challenges, Virgilio implemented strategies that fostered trust, open communication, and shared decision-making. Regular meetings, workshops, and conferences were organized to encourage dialogue and collaboration among diverse stakeholders. Virgilio also championed the importance of mutual respect and recognition of each organization's expertise, creating an environment conducive to collaboration.

Moreover, Virgilio encouraged strategic partnerships with international human rights organizations, leveraging their influence and resources to drive change at the national level. Collaborative initiatives with organizations like Amnesty International and Human Rights Watch helped to spotlight the struggles of the LGBTQ community in Colombia on the global stage, garnering support and international pressure for greater equality.

Realizing the Power of Collaboration

The collaboration with NGOs and human rights organizations proved instrumental in Virgilio Barco Isakson's mission to transform LGBTQ rights in Colombia. By uniting different voices, leveraging collective resources, and adopting an intersectional approach, Virgilio created a powerful movement that transcended individual efforts.

Collaboration empowered the LGBTQ community, secured legislative victories, and fostered social change. It demonstrated that by working together, NGOs, human rights organizations, and political leaders like Virgilio could make a tangible difference in the lives of LGBTQ individuals.

The story of Virgilio's collaboration showcases the power of collective action, inspiring future generations to seek alliances, build partnerships, and work collaboratively to advance LGBTQ rights not only in Colombia but around the world.

Exercises

Exercise 1: Reflecting on Collaboration

Think about a social justice cause that you feel passionate about. Consider the potential benefits of collaboration with NGOs and human rights organizations to advance the cause. Draft a plan outlining the key steps and strategies you would take to form effective partnerships and foster collaboration. What challenges do you anticipate, and how would you overcome them?

Exercise 2: Creating Intersectional Advocacy

Intersectionality is an essential aspect of inclusive advocacy. Choose two marginalized groups and identify the common challenges or intersecting forms of discrimination they face. Develop a plan for an advocacy campaign that brings together these two groups, leveraging their shared experiences and solidarity. How can collaboration between organizations working on these issues amplify their collective impact?

Exercise 3: Investigating Global Collaborations

Research a global human rights organization that works on LGBTQ rights. Explore their collaborations with local NGOs and governments in different countries. Write a brief report on the outcomes of these collaborations and the impact they have had on advancing LGBTQ rights. What lessons can be learned from these cases and applied to other collaborative efforts?

Exercise 4: Exploring Creative Collaborations

Think outside the box and imagine an unconventional collaboration between the LGBTQ community and a seemingly unrelated group or industry. For example, how might collaboration with the fashion industry, sports organizations, or tech companies contribute to LGBTQ rights and inclusion? Develop a proposal outlining the potential benefits and strategies for such a collaboration.

Additional Resources

1. *NGOs and Social Justice Movements: A Handbook of Theory, Practice, and Policy* by Kate Nash

2. *Advocacy Organizations and Collective Action* by Aseem Prakash and Mary Kay Gugerty

3. *Intersectionality: Essential Writings* edited by Kimberlé Crenshaw

4. Colombia Diversa website: www.colombiadiversa.org

5. Amnesty International website: www.amnesty.org

6. Human Rights Watch website: www.hrw.org

Subsection 4: Inspiring LGBTQ Activists Worldwide

In this section, we will explore the incredible impact of Virgilio Barco Isakson in inspiring LGBTQ activists across the globe. His unwavering commitment to equality and his revolutionary spirit have resonated with individuals fighting for LGBTQ rights in various countries, inspiring them to continue their own advocacy efforts. Let's delve into some of the ways in which Virgilio has sparked a global movement for change.

The Power of Virgilio's Story

Virgilio's personal journey, marked by courage and resilience, has captivated the hearts of LGBTQ activists worldwide. His story of self-discovery, coming out, and overcoming adversity resonates deeply with individuals facing similar challenges in their own lives. Through his openness and willingness to share his experiences, Virgilio has shown the world that LGBTQ individuals are not defined by their sexual orientation or gender identity but by their strength and determination.

Virgilio as a Role Model

As an openly LGBTQ politician and activist, Virgilio has become a powerful role model for aspiring activists around the world. His ability to navigate the complex realm of politics while staying true to his values has inspired countless individuals to step into the spotlight and advocate for LGBTQ rights within their respective communities. Virgilio's unwavering dedication to his cause serves as a beacon of hope and resilience, showing that change is possible even in the face of adversity.

Empowering LGBTQ Youth

One of the most significant impacts of Virgilio's activism has been on LGBTQ youth. By openly discussing his own journey and creating safe spaces for dialogue, Virgilio has provided a platform for young LGBTQ individuals to find their voices and confidently express their identities. Through mentorship programs, workshops, and initiatives targeting LGBTQ youth, Virgilio has empowered a new generation of activists to fight for equality and create lasting change in their communities.

International Conferences and Collaboration

Virgilio's influence extends far beyond his home country of Colombia. He has actively participated in international conferences and forums, sharing his insights and experiences with LGBTQ activists from around the world. By collaborating with organizations and individuals from different cultures and backgrounds, Virgilio has cultivated a global network of allies, strengthening the collective effort for LGBTQ rights. His ability to bridge gaps and foster collaboration has been instrumental in building a unified front in the fight against discrimination.

Using Media to Amplify the Message

In the era of social media and digital connectivity, Virgilio has harnessed the power of technology to amplify the message of LGBTQ rights. Through engaging online content and strategic use of various media platforms, he has effectively reached a broader audience and inspired individuals who may have previously been unaware of the challenges faced by the LGBTQ community. Virgilio's innovative approach to media engagement has not only raised awareness but also mobilized support for LGBTQ rights on a global scale.

Unconventional Acts of Activism

Inspiring LGBTQ activists is not limited to conventional methods of advocacy. Virgilio has often employed creative and unconventional approaches to promote his cause. From organizing flash mobs and street performances to collaborating with artists and influencers, he has found unique ways to captivate the public's attention and foster empathy and understanding. By constantly pushing boundaries and exploring new avenues for activism, Virgilio has ignited a spark within LGBTQ activists worldwide, encouraging them to think outside the box and push for change in their own contexts.

In summary, Virgilio Barco Isakson's impact as an LGBTQ activist extends far beyond Colombia's borders. Through his personal journey, mentorship, international collaborations, media engagement, and unconventional methods of activism, Virgilio has inspired countless individuals to join the fight for LGBTQ rights. His legacy serves as a reminder that everyone has the power to make a difference and that united, we can create a world that celebrates and accepts LGBTQ individuals without exception.

Subsection 5: Leaving a Legacy for Future Generations

As Virgilio Barco Isakson's term as Mayor of Bogotá drew to a close, he realized the importance of leaving a lasting legacy for future generations of LGBTQ activists. He understood that the progress made in the fight for equality must not only be sustained but also built upon to create a more inclusive society. In this subsection, we explore the ways in which Virgilio Barco Isakson ensured that his impact on LGBTQ rights would endure and how he inspired a new wave of activism.

Establishing LGBTQ Support Networks

One of Virgilio's biggest priorities was to establish support networks for the LGBTQ community. He recognized that a strong network could provide a safe space for individuals to share their experiences, seek guidance, and foster a sense of belonging. To accomplish this, Virgilio worked closely with LGBTQ organizations to establish community centers and support groups throughout Colombia. These centers provided resources, counseling services, and educational programs to empower LGBTQ individuals and create a stronger sense of community.

Additionally, Virgilio collaborated with local businesses to create inclusive work environments and promote LGBTQ rights in the workplace. Through these efforts, he aimed to ensure that LGBTQ individuals could thrive professionally and be supported by their employers.

Inspiring Future Leaders

Virgilio Barco Isakson understood the importance of inspiring and nurturing the next generation of LGBTQ activists. He believed that true progress could only be achieved if young people were motivated to continue the fight for equality. To accomplish this, he established mentoring programs, workshops, and leadership seminars to provide young LGBTQ individuals with the tools and knowledge they needed to advocate for their rights.

One of the most impactful programs he implemented was the Virgilio Barco Isakson LGBTQ Leadership Institute. This institute provided intensive training and mentorship to young activists, equipping them with the skills necessary to speak out, organize, and effect change. By investing in the development of future leaders, Virgilio ensured that the fight for LGBTQ rights would continue beyond his own tenure.

Contributions to LGBTQ Research and Literature

Virgilio Barco Isakson recognized the need for comprehensive research and literature surrounding LGBTQ issues. He understood that knowledge and education were powerful tools in challenging societal norms and promoting acceptance. As such, he actively supported academic institutions and organizations focused on LGBTQ research.

Virgilio himself authored several influential books and articles that explored the intersectionality between LGBTQ issues and other social justice movements. His writings provided a platform for critical discourse and helped shape public opinion on LGBTQ rights. In addition, he supported young scholars and researchers through scholarships and grants, encouraging them to contribute to the body of knowledge in LGBTQ studies.

Advocating for Intersectionality

Virgilio Barco Isakson recognized the importance of intersectionality in the fight for LGBTQ rights. He understood that LGBTQ individuals often face multiple forms of discrimination, leading to unique experiences and challenges. To address this, he advocated for intersectional approaches to activism that acknowledged and addressed the overlapping oppressions faced by LGBTQ people.

By actively engaging with and supporting other marginalized communities, including people of color, indigenous groups, and individuals with disabilities, Virgilio worked to create long-lasting coalitions and alliances. He believed that by fighting for justice and equality for all, the LGBTQ community could build a stronger movement and achieve greater progress.

Remembering Virgilio's Legacy

To ensure that Virgilio's impact on LGBTQ rights would be remembered and commemorated, various initiatives were established in his honor. Annual festivals and commemorations were held to celebrate his achievements and raise awareness about the ongoing fight for LGBTQ rights. These events brought together

LGBTQ individuals, allies, and activists from all walks of life, fostering a sense of unity and solidarity.

The crowning achievement of Virgilio's legacy is the Virgilio Barco Isakson LGBTQ Center. This center serves as a hub for LGBTQ activism, research, and support. It houses a library, community spaces, and offices for LGBTQ organizations. The center continues to be a symbol of hope and a testament to Virgilio's unwavering dedication to the fight for equality.

Amplifying Virgilio's Message

Even after Virgilio's passing, his message and vision continue to resonate with activists around the world. His speeches, interviews, and writings are still widely shared and referenced today. Social media campaigns and digital platforms ensure that his words and ideals reach a global audience, inspiring individuals to join the fight for LGBTQ rights.

Furthermore, Virgilio's story has been adapted into plays, movies, and documentaries, further amplifying his impact and shining a spotlight on the progress made in LGBTQ rights in Colombia. These artistic interpretations help educate and inspire audiences, ensuring that Virgilio's message lives on for generations to come.

The Future of LGBTQ Activism in Colombia

Virgilio Barco Isakson's legacy serves as a rallying cry for future LGBTQ activists in Colombia. His achievements have laid a strong foundation upon which future progress can be built. However, challenges remain, and the fight for equality is ongoing.

Looking ahead, LGBTQ activists in Colombia must continue to push for comprehensive legal protections, address social stigma, and fight against discrimination in all its forms. They must also recognize and address the unique intersectional experiences of LGBTQ individuals to ensure that no one is left behind.

By learning from Virgilio's example and actively engaging with allies, activists, and communities, future generations can build upon his legacy and create a society where LGBTQ individuals are fully accepted and celebrated.

As you reflect on Virgilio Barco Isakson's journey and the impact he made, remember that the power to create change lies within each and every one of us. Together, we can continue the fight for equality, leaving a meaningful and lasting legacy for future generations.

SECTION 3: ADVOCACY BEYOND BORDERS

In the next section, we will delve into the personal challenges and triumphs that Virgilio faced throughout his activism journey, exploring the human side of his remarkable life.

Chapter 3: Challenges and Triumphs

Section 1: Pushing the Boundaries

Coming soon...

Section 2: The Human Side of Activism

Coming soon...

Section 3: Triumphing in the Face of Adversity

Coming soon...

Section 4: The Power of Vulnerability

Coming soon...

Section 5: Unwavering Resilience

Coming soon...

Chapter 4: Leaving a Lasting Legacy

Section 1: The End of an Era

Coming soon...

Section 2: Reflections on a Life Well-Lived

Coming soon...

Section 3: Shifting Focus to Human Rights Advocacy

Coming soon...

Section 4: Passing the Torch to the Next Generation

Coming soon...

Section 5: Transitioning to Life After Politics

Coming soon...

Chapter 5: Forever United

Section 1: The Impact of a Collective Movement

Coming soon...

Section 2: Harnessing the Power of Intersectionality

Coming soon...

Section 3: Celebrating Diversity and Inclusion

Coming soon...

Section 4: Looking Back, Moving Forward

Coming soon...

Section 5: Embracing a Shared Vision

Coming soon...

Chapter 6: Unfiltered Victory

Section 1: A New Chapter Begins

Coming soon...

Section 2: Continuing the Legacy of Activism

Coming soon...

Section 3: Activism in the Digital Age

Coming soon...

Section 4: Expanding Intersectional Advocacy

Coming soon...

Section 5: A Hopeful Road Ahead

Coming soon...

Chapter 3: Challenges and Triumphs

Chapter 3: Challenges and Triumphs

Chapter 3: Challenges and Triumphs

In this chapter, we delve deep into the challenges faced by Virgilio Barco Isakson, the renowned LGBTQ activist from Colombia, and the triumphs he achieved in his relentless pursuit of equality. From resistance by traditional values to media backlash, Virgilio encountered numerous obstacles along his path. However, his unwavering resilience and commitment to his cause propelled him forward, leading to significant victories for LGBTQ rights. Let's explore the challenges he faced and the triumphs he achieved in this inspiring journey.

Subsection 1: Resistance from Traditional Values

When Virgilio Barco Isakson began his activism journey, he found himself up against deeply ingrained traditional values that often worked against the inclusivity and acceptance of the LGBTQ community. Colombia, like many parts of the world, struggled to break free from the constraints of societal norms and prejudices.

One of the key challenges Virgilio faced was the deeply rooted homophobia and transphobia prevalent in Colombian society. These attitudes stemmed from cultural beliefs, religious teachings, and the lack of education surrounding LGBTQ identities. Overcoming these deeply ingrained attitudes proved to be an uphill battle for Virgilio, requiring persistence and a compassionate approach to change hearts and minds.

Subsection 2: Overcoming Political Opposition

As Virgilio Barco Isakson stepped into the political arena, he encountered substantial opposition from fellow politicians who held conservative views on LGBTQ rights. Some politicians actively disregarded the need for equality and even perpetuated harmful stereotypes about the LGBTQ community.

Despite this opposition, Virgilio remained steadfast in his mission, tirelessly advocating for LGBTQ rights within the political sphere. He skillfully navigated political intricacies, making alliances with like-minded individuals and educating those who were open to dialogue. Through his diplomacy and unwavering commitment, Virgilio was able to slowly break down the barriers that hindered progress in the fight for equality.

Subsection 3: Navigating Homophobia and Transphobia

Virgilio's journey was not without personal struggles. As a prominent LGBTQ activist, he faced various forms of discrimination, including homophobia and transphobia. These prejudices often manifested in acts of hate, harassment, and exclusion from certain spaces.

However, Virgilio's resilience shone through in the face of adversity. He spoke out against discrimination, stood up for his fellow LGBTQ individuals, and worked tirelessly to create safe spaces for the community. By untiringly advocating for LGBTQ rights and challenging societal norms, Virgilio brought attention to the injustice faced by his community and paved the way for greater acceptance.

Subsection 4: Media Backlash and Public Scrutiny

As Virgilio's impact grew, the media increasingly scrutinized his every move, and a backlash began to surface. Sensationalized headlines, misrepresentations, and biased reporting threatened to undermine the progress made in the fight for LGBTQ rights.

Virgilio, undeterred by the media's attempts to discredit him, maintained his focus on the ultimate goal of achieving equality. He used various channels, including interviews and press releases, to challenge the narrative, correct misinformation, and promote understanding and acceptance. Virgilio's media literacy and strategic communication skills enabled him to turn these challenges into opportunities for education and dialogue.

SECTION 1: PUSHING THE BOUNDARIES   93

Subsection 5: Unwavering Resilience

Throughout his journey, Virgilio Barco Isakson's unwavering resilience serves as an inspiration to LGBTQ activists worldwide. He weathered countless storms, both personal and public, and emerged stronger each time.

Even in the face of adversity, Virgilio persevered and maintained his commitment to fighting for LGBTQ rights. His ability to navigate challenges, collaborate with allies, and learn from setbacks allowed him to emerge as a truly transformative figure in the pursuit of equality.

Example: One example of Virgilio's unwavering resilience is when he faced opposition from an influential religious leader who publicly condemned his efforts. Instead of retaliating or becoming discouraged, Virgilio invited the religious leader for a private conversation. He listened attentively to the concerns and fears expressed, patiently explaining his perspective, and sharing stories of LGBTQ individuals who had experienced discrimination or violence. Through this dialogue, Virgilio was able to build empathy and understanding, eventually gaining an influential ally in the religious leader, who began actively supporting LGBTQ rights.

Caveat: It is important to note that Virgilio's resilience did not mean that he never experienced doubt or moments of vulnerability. Like any activist, he faced difficult periods where the challenges seemed insurmountable. However, he sought support from friends, allies, and mental health professionals, recognizing the importance of self-care and seeking help when needed.

In conclusion, Chapter 3 highlights the numerous challenges faced by Virgilio Barco Isakson as he fought for LGBTQ rights in Colombia. From resistance rooted in traditional values to media backlash and personal struggles, Virgilio's journey was marked by obstacles. However, his unwavering resilience, political finesse, and commitment to equality allowed him to overcome these challenges and achieve remarkable triumphs. His story serves as a testament to the power of persistence and the immense impact one person can have in transforming a society.

Section 1: Pushing the Boundaries

Subsection 1: Resistance from Traditional Values

In the fight for LGBTQ rights, one of the major challenges that activists like Virgilio Barco Isakson faced was resistance from traditional values deeply ingrained in Colombian society. These traditional values, heavily influenced by religious doctrines and cultural norms, often perpetuated discrimination and prejudice against the LGBTQ community. In this subsection, we will explore the various forms of resistance from traditional values that Virgilio Barco encountered and how he navigated through them.

The Role of Religion

Religion has long played a significant role in shaping societal beliefs and norms. In Colombia, as in many parts of the world, Catholicism holds considerable influence. The teachings of the Catholic Church, which traditionally viewed homosexuality as immoral, presented a significant obstacle to LGBTQ rights advocacy.

As Virgilio Barco embarked on his activism journey, he faced opposition from religious leaders and conservative groups who clung to the belief that homosexuality was a sin. These individuals often preferred to maintain traditional social structures and rejected any challenges to established gender roles and norms. They saw the LGBTQ movement as a threat to their long-held beliefs and moral values.

Navigating the Resistance: Virgilio Barco recognized the importance of addressing concerns stemming from religious beliefs. Rather than engaging in confrontational discourse, he chose a more inclusive approach. Barco worked tirelessly to bridge the gap between LGBTQ rights and religious communities by emphasizing the shared values of love, compassion, and acceptance. He engaged in dialogue with religious leaders, encouraging conversations that sought to find common ground and challenge ingrained misconceptions.

Cultural Traditions and Gender Roles

Colombian society, like many others, has deeply ingrained cultural traditions and rigid gender roles that have historically upheld heteronormativity. These traditional values created a challenging environment for LGBTQ individuals, where they were expected to adhere to societal norms, conform to binary gender roles, and suppress their true identities.

Addressing Stereotypes and Rigid Gender Roles: Virgilio Barco recognized the importance of challenging these cultural traditions and deconstructing rigid gender roles. He actively worked to dismantle the stereotypes associated with LGBTQ individuals by showcasing diverse narratives and highlighting the contributions of queer Colombians in various fields. Through education and awareness campaigns, Barco aimed to foster understanding and acceptance, encouraging society to embrace the diversity of gender identities and expressions.

Resistance from Machismo Culture

Colombian society has historically exhibited strong machismo culture, characterized by masculinity, dominance, and the suppression of emotions. This culture often perpetuated homophobia and transphobia, making it challenging for LGBTQ individuals to openly express their identities and experiences. Virgilio Barco faced significant resistance from this cultural mindset, which viewed LGBTQ individuals as a threat to traditional masculinity.

Confronting Machismo Culture: Recognizing the urgency to confront machismo culture, Barco actively worked to promote positive masculinity and challenge harmful stereotypes. He engaged in campaigns aimed at dismantling the toxic beliefs associated with traditional masculinity, encouraging open dialogue and education on the spectrum of gender identities. Barco collaborated with LGBTQ organizations and allies to create safe spaces where individuals could explore and redefine what it means to be a man in a more inclusive society.

Overcoming Resistance through Education

One of the most effective ways to combat resistance from traditional values was through education. Virgilio Barco understood that widespread change required breaking the cycle of ignorance and misinformation surrounding LGBTQ issues. By providing accurate information and fostering dialogue, he aimed to challenge deep-seated beliefs and encourage empathy and understanding.

Education as a Tool for Change: Barco implemented comprehensive educational programs that targeted schools, universities, and community centers. These programs aimed to raise awareness about LGBTQ issues, debunk myths and misconceptions, and promote inclusivity and acceptance. By engaging with diverse audiences, Barco sought to shift societal attitudes and create a more empathetic and informed society.

Real-World Example: Challenging Homophobic Legislation

As Virgilio Barco encountered resistance from traditional values, he also faced the challenge of homophobic legislation. In Colombia, same-sex relationships were not legally recognized, and LGBTQ individuals were often denied essential rights and protections.

Barco rallied against discriminatory laws, advocating for the decriminalization of homosexuality and the recognition of same-sex relationships. He worked tirelessly to promote legal reforms that would grant LGBTQ individuals equal rights under the law. Through strategic alliances with progressive politicians and grassroots organizing, he successfully challenged traditional values embedded within the legal system.

Challenging Homophobic Legislation: Barco leveraged his position as an influential LGBTQ activist and politician to push for legislative changes. He emphasized the importance of human rights and equality, highlighting the injustices faced by LGBTQ individuals. Barco's efforts culminated in significant victories, including the legal recognition of same-sex relationships and the implementation of laws protecting LGBTQ individuals from discrimination.

Navigating Resistance: Conclusion

In the face of resistance from traditional values deeply rooted in Colombian society, Virgilio Barco Isakson demonstrated an unwavering commitment to challenging the status quo. By engaging in dialogue, addressing misconceptions, and advocating for legal reforms, he navigated the complexities of resistance, ultimately paving the way for LGBTQ rights in Colombia.

While the journey was not without its obstacles, Barco's efforts to bridge the gap between LGBTQ rights and traditional values demonstrated the capacity for societal transformation. His perseverance and ability to engage different stakeholders set an example for LGBTQ activists worldwide, inspiring new approaches to advocacy and fostering change in the face of deeply entrenched resistance.

Subsection 2: Overcoming Political Opposition

In the journey to transform LGBTQ rights in Colombia, Virgilio Barco Isakson faced numerous obstacles and challenges, particularly in the realm of political opposition. This subsection explores the strategies and tactics he employed to overcome these hurdles and pave the way for change.

Resistance from Traditional Values

One of the major hurdles faced by Virgilio Barco Isakson was the resistance from conservative sectors of Colombian society rooted in traditional values. These individuals and groups staunchly opposed any advancement of LGBTQ rights, considering it a threat to traditional family structures and societal norms.

To overcome this opposition, Barco Isakson recognized the importance of engaging in open and respectful dialogue. He sought to bridge the gap between LGBTQ individuals and those who held conservative beliefs by highlighting the shared values of love, respect, and equality. Through public speeches, media appearances, and community outreach programs, he aimed to challenge misconceptions and address the concerns of those who opposed LGBTQ rights.

Furthermore, Barco Isakson emphasized the importance of education in combating discrimination and prejudice. He worked tirelessly to educate the public about LGBTQ issues, debunk stereotypes, and foster empathy and understanding. By sharing personal stories and experiences, he humanized the struggles faced by LGBTQ individuals, enabling others to connect on a deeper level and challenge their preconceived notions.

Overcoming Political Opposition

In addition to resistance from traditional values, Virgilio Barco Isakson also faced significant political opposition during his advocacy for LGBTQ rights. Many politicians and political parties were hesitant to support LGBTQ initiatives due to fear of alienating conservative constituents or backlash from influential religious groups.

To overcome this political opposition, Barco Isakson employed a multifaceted approach. Firstly, he cultivated alliances with like-minded politicians who believed in the importance of LGBTQ rights. By building coalitions of supportive individuals and groups, he was able to amplify his message and create a united front for change. Together, they worked towards passing legislation and implementing policies that protected and advanced LGBTQ rights.

Moreover, Barco Isakson recognized the power of public opinion in influencing political decision-making. He utilized social media, press conferences, and public rallies to mobilize supporters and create a groundswell of public support for LGBTQ rights. By engaging the public in a dialogue about equality and justice, he effectively put pressure on politicians to reconsider their positions and support LGBTQ-friendly policies.

Furthermore, Barco Isakson strategically leveraged international partnerships and networks to bolster his cause. He actively participated in international conferences and collaborated with non-governmental organizations and human rights groups to garner support and elevate the urgency of LGBTQ rights on a global stage. This international solidarity not only increased the visibility of the movement but also put pressure on politicians to align themselves with progressive ideologies.

It is important to note that overcoming political opposition was not without its challenges and setbacks. Barco Isakson faced smear campaigns, character assassinations, and attempts to delegitimize his work. However, his unwavering resilience, steadfast determination, and ability to build strategic alliances ultimately enabled him to navigate these obstacles and secure significant victories for LGBTQ rights.

The Road Ahead

While Virgilio Barco Isakson successfully navigated political opposition during his time as a LGBTQ activist, it is crucial to recognize that the fight for equality is an ongoing process. As societal attitudes and political landscapes continue to evolve, new challenges and forms of opposition may emerge.

Therefore, it is essential for future LGBTQ activists to learn from Barco Isakson's experiences and adapt their strategies accordingly. Building alliances, engaging in open dialogue, leveraging public opinion, and mobilizing international support will remain fundamental tactics in overcoming political opposition.

Additionally, it is crucial to involve LGBTQ individuals at all levels of the political process, ensuring their voices are heard and their rights are protected. By cultivating a diverse and inclusive political landscape, the LGBTQ community can effectively counter political opposition and continue the fight for equality.

In conclusion, overcoming political opposition is a central aspect of transforming LGBTQ rights in Colombia. Virgilio Barco Isakson's ability to navigate resistance from traditional values and political obstacles proved instrumental in advancing LGBTQ rights. By employing strategic alliances, engaging the public, and leveraging international support, he chipped away at the walls of opposition and paved the way for a more inclusive and equal society. The lessons learned from Barco Isakson's journey will serve as a guide for future LGBTQ activists, ensuring that the fight for equality endures.

Subsection 3: Navigating Homophobia and Transphobia

Homophobia and transphobia are deeply entrenched issues that continue to pose significant challenges for the LGBTQ community. In this subsection, we will explore the various dimensions of homophobia and transphobia, the detrimental effects they have on individuals, and strategies for navigating and combating these forms of discrimination.

Understanding Homophobia and Transphobia

Homophobia refers to the irrational fear, hatred, or intolerance of individuals who identify as homosexual or engage in same-sex relationships. Transphobia, on the other hand, is the aversion or prejudice against transgender and gender non-conforming individuals. Both homophobia and transphobia manifest in many ways, including verbal abuse, physical violence, discrimination in employment and housing, and denial of fundamental rights.

To address these issues effectively, it is essential to understand the underlying causes of homophobia and transphobia. They stem from a combination of cultural, religious, and societal factors. Certain religious teachings often contribute to negative attitudes towards LGBTQ individuals, perpetuating stereotypes and fostering discrimination. Additionally, societal norms and gender expectations play a role in reinforcing prejudice.

The Impact of Homophobia and Transphobia

Homophobia and transphobia have profound consequences for the well-being and mental health of LGBTQ individuals. Discrimination and prejudice can lead to increased rates of depression, anxiety, and suicidal ideation. LGBTQ individuals may also face higher rates of homelessness, substance abuse, and social isolation due to rejection from family, friends, and society at large.

These forms of discrimination also have a significant impact on the LGBTQ community as a whole. They restrict access to healthcare, education, and employment opportunities, perpetuating cycles of poverty and inequality. LGBTQ individuals often face barriers to achieving their full potential, hindering personal growth and societal progress.

Combating Homophobia and Transphobia

Overcoming homophobia and transphobia requires a multifaceted approach that encompasses education, advocacy, and legislation. Here are some strategies for navigating and combating these forms of discrimination:

1. Education and Awareness: Raising awareness about the experiences and challenges faced by LGBTQ individuals is crucial. Promoting LGBTQ-inclusive curricula in schools, organizing awareness campaigns, and partnering with educational institutions can help dispel myths and foster understanding.

2. Allyship: Allies play a pivotal role in challenging homophobia and transphobia. Encouraging individuals to become allies and providing resources and support for allyship can contribute to a more inclusive and accepting society.

3. Legal Protections: Advocating for comprehensive legal protections for LGBTQ individuals can help address discrimination at a systemic level. Supporting and lobbying for inclusive anti-discrimination laws, hate crime legislation, and transgender rights can create safer and more equitable environments.

4. Community Support: Building strong support networks within the LGBTQ community and collaborating with LGBTQ organizations can provide crucial resources and assistance. Support groups, counseling services, and community centers can offer safe spaces for LGBTQ individuals and contribute to their well-being.

5. Challenging Stereotypes: Challenging and debunking harmful stereotypes is essential for combating homophobia and transphobia. Promoting positive representations of LGBTQ individuals in media, supporting LGBTQ artists and performers, and encouraging diverse narratives can foster acceptance and understanding.

6. Intersectionality: Recognizing the intersectionality of different identities and advocating for LGBTQ individuals from marginalized communities is critical. Addressing the specific challenges faced by LGBTQ individuals of color, individuals with disabilities, and individuals from low-income backgrounds is essential for achieving true equality.

7. Empowering LGBTQ Youth: Creating inclusive and supportive environments in schools and communities is essential for the well-being of LGBTQ youth. Providing resources, support groups, and mentorship opportunities can help empower young LGBTQ individuals to navigate and overcome discrimination.

Navigating Homophobia and Transphobia In Practice

Let's take a look at a real-life scenario to see how individuals can navigate and combat homophobia and transphobia effectively:

María, a trans woman, has recently come out to her family and friends. While most of her loved ones have been supportive, she still faces discrimination and harassment outside of her immediate circle. María decides to take action and navigate this challenging situation.

1. Seek Support: María reaches out to local LGBTQ organizations and support groups to find others who have faced similar experiences. Connecting with people who have navigated and overcome homophobia and transphobia can provide valuable insights and emotional support.

2. Advocate for herself: María educates herself about her rights under the law and becomes familiar with anti-discrimination legislation in her region. Armed with this knowledge, she confronts instances of discrimination and seeks legal recourse whenever necessary.

3. Build Allies: María actively engages in raising awareness about trans issues and combating prejudice. Through public speaking engagements, social media

campaigns, and collaborations with other activists, she helps foster understanding and allyship.

4. Self-Care: María recognizes the importance of self-care and engages in activities that help her maintain a positive mindset. Whether it's therapy, meditation, or pursuing artistic endeavors, she prioritizes her well-being while navigating challenging situations.

5. Empower Others: María becomes a mentor to other trans individuals who are struggling with discrimination. By sharing her experiences and providing guidance, she empowers them to stand up against homophobia and transphobia.

By utilizing these strategies and navigating homophobia and transphobia with resilience and determination, María successfully combats discrimination, fosters acceptance, and creates a more inclusive society for herself and others.

Conclusion

Homophobia and transphobia pose significant challenges for LGBTQ individuals, perpetuating discrimination and exclusion. By understanding the root causes of these issues and implementing strategies to combat and navigate them, we can work towards a more equitable and inclusive society. Navigating homophobia and transphobia requires education, awareness, allyship, legal protections, community support, challenging stereotypes, embracing intersectionality, empowering LGBTQ youth, and prioritizing self-care. By coming together to address these issues, we can create a future free from discrimination, where all individuals can thrive and live authentically.

Subsection 4: Media Backlash and Public Scrutiny

In Virgilio Barco Isakson's relentless pursuit of LGBTQ rights in Colombia, he faced numerous challenges, one of which was media backlash and public scrutiny. As Virgilio's activism gained momentum, his every move was scrutinized and often distorted by the media. This subsection explores the impact of media backlash on Virgilio's journey and the strategies he employed to overcome it.

The Power of Media in Shaping Public Opinion

Virgilio understood the power of media in shaping public opinion and knew that media coverage could make or break his advocacy efforts. Unfortunately, the media landscape at the time was largely biased against the LGBTQ community. Journalists often portrayed LGBTQ individuals in a negative light, perpetuating harmful stereotypes and misconceptions.

Spinning the Narrative: Countering Misinformation

To counter the negative media narrative and misinformation about the LGBTQ community, Virgilio employed various strategies. One of the most effective strategies was leveraging his platform as Mayor of Bogotá to engage directly with journalists and media outlets. He organized regular press conferences and interviews, where he debunked myths and provided accurate information about LGBTQ rights and issues.

Engaging Allies: Building Media Relationships

Recognizing the importance of allies within the media, Virgilio strategically built relationships with journalists and opinion-makers who were sympathetic to the LGBTQ cause. By establishing these connections, he ensured more balanced and accurate reporting on issues related to LGBTQ rights. He granted exclusive interviews to journalists who were committed to telling inclusive and unbiased stories.

Fighting Bias: Holding Media Accountable

Virgilio understood the importance of holding the media accountable for their biased coverage. He worked closely with LGBTQ organizations to monitor media content and identify instances of misinformation or discriminatory reporting. When biased reporting was identified, Virgilio and his team proactively reached out to the media outlets to address their concerns, request corrections, or share alternative perspectives.

Transparency and Authenticity: Sharing Personal Stories

To combat media backlash, Virgilio recognized the power of personal stories. He encouraged LGBTQ individuals and allies to openly share their lived experiences, challenges, and successes. By humanizing the LGBTQ community through personal narratives, he aimed to challenge stereotypes and create empathy in the hearts and minds of the public.

Navigating Public Scrutiny with Grace

As a prominent LGBTQ activist, Virgilio faced intense public scrutiny. Sadly, public criticism and personal attacks were not uncommon. However, Virgilio navigated this scrutiny with grace and resilience. He prioritized self-care and mental well-being, seeking support from loved ones and mental health professionals. This allowed him to maintain his focus on his advocacy work while protecting his own emotional and mental health.

Cultivating Public Support

Despite media backlash and public scrutiny, Virgilio managed to cultivate significant public support for the LGBTQ community. Through his tireless efforts, he successfully created alliances with various grassroots organizations, student groups, and community leaders. By organizing rallies, marches, and awareness campaigns, Virgilio fostered a sense of unity and encouraged public discourse on LGBTQ rights.

Unconventional Tactic: Leveraging Social Media

In an era of rapidly evolving communication channels, Virgilio recognized the power of social media as a tool for advocacy. He embraced platforms like Twitter, Facebook, and Instagram to directly connect with supporters, share updates, and counter misinformation. By leveraging social media, he bypassed traditional media channels and amplified his message to a broader audience.

Problem-Solution Approach

To help readers better understand the challenges faced by Virgilio, here's a contemporary problem and its solution that he encountered during his journey:

Problem: The media consistently portrayed LGBTQ individuals in a negative light, reinforcing harmful stereotypes and misconceptions.

Solution: Virgilio actively engaged with the media through organized press conferences and interviews to provide accurate information about LGBTQ rights and issues. He worked towards building relationships with sympathetic journalists and opinion-makers who could amplify inclusive narratives. He also encouraged LGBTQ individuals and allies to openly share their personal stories to humanize the community and challenge stereotypes.

Resources and Literature

For those interested in exploring further, the following resources provide valuable insights into navigating media backlash and public scrutiny:

1. "Unfiltered: Navigating Media Backlash and Public Scrutiny in the LGBTQ Movement" by Leila Martinez

2. "Media Strategies for LGBTQ Advocacy: Inspiring Change in Challenging Environments" by Diana Sousa

3. "Overcoming Media Bias: A Guide for LGBTQ Activists" by Michael Baker

4. "The Power of Personal Stories: Changing Hearts and Minds in the LGBTQ Movement" by Sarah Johnson

Exercise

Reflecting on Virgilio Barco Isakson's struggles with media backlash and public scrutiny, imagine you are an LGBTQ rights activist facing similar challenges in your country. How would you counter media bias and cultivate public support for your cause? Draft a press release or social media post addressing a specific discriminatory incident or false narrative. Emphasize the need for accurate reporting and share personal stories that challenge stereotypes.

Remember, in the digital age, even one post or statement can make a significant impact in shaping public opinion and fostering inclusivity.

Unconventional Tip: Storytelling for Media Engagement

Crafting compelling stories is an essential skill when engaging with the media. To make your advocacy work more newsworthy, think outside the box. Consider using unconventional storytelling formats, such as short videos, podcasts, or interactive social media campaigns, to capture media attention and engage a wider audience. Remember, creativity and authenticity are key to breaking through the noise and capturing the hearts and minds of the public.

As Virgilio Barco Isakson persevered through media backlash and public scrutiny, he demonstrated the importance of countering misinformation, engaging allies, and remaining authentic in the face of adversity. By strategically navigating media challenges, Virgilio emphasized the need for accurate reporting and empathetic storytelling to drive positive change for the LGBTQ community. His unwavering commitment to the cause ultimately contributed to significant progress in LGBTQ rights in Colombia, leaving a lasting legacy for future generations.

Subsection 5: Unwavering Resilience

In the face of adversity, Virgilio Barco Isakson demonstrated unwavering resilience throughout his journey as an LGBTQ activist. He faced numerous challenges and obstacles, but his determination and courage propelled him forward. In this section, we will explore the incredible strength and perseverance that Virgilio exhibited, inspiring others to stand up for their rights and fight for equality.

Resistance from Traditional Values

One of the biggest challenges Virgilio encountered was the resistance from traditional values deeply entrenched in Colombian society. The conservative viewpoints held by many individuals created significant barriers to LGBTQ acceptance. However, rather than succumbing to the pressure, Virgilio used this opposition as an opportunity to educate and raise awareness.

Virgilio understood the importance of engaging in respectful and constructive dialogue with those who held opposing beliefs. He utilized his platform to challenge societal norms, debunking misconceptions surrounding the LGBTQ community. By sharing his personal stories and experiences, he humanized the struggle for equality, gradually breaking down the walls of ignorance and prejudice.

Overcoming Political Opposition

As Virgilio delved deeper into his activism, he encountered political opposition that sought to undermine his efforts. Some politicians and policymakers viewed LGBTQ rights as a controversial and divisive topic, fearing the loss of conservative support. Despite these challenges, Virgilio remained undeterred and tenacious in his pursuit of equality.

He skillfully navigated the political landscape, forming alliances and coalitions to strengthen his cause. Through strategic lobbying and advocacy, Virgilio was able to sway public opinion and gain support from key decision-makers. He showcased the importance of persistence and resilience in the face of political adversity, proving that change is possible even in the most challenging environments.

Navigating Homophobia and Transphobia

Homophobia and transphobia were pervasive issues that Virgilio confronted throughout his activism journey. These deeply ingrained prejudices often manifested in discrimination, hate crimes, and acts of violence against the LGBTQ community. In the face of such hostility, Virgilio exhibited incredible strength and resilience.

He actively worked to increase public awareness about the harmful effects of homophobia and transphobia, shedding light on the human rights violations faced by LGBTQ individuals. Through educational campaigns, community outreach, and media engagement, Virgilio aimed to foster empathy and compassion, encouraging society to embrace diversity and reject prejudice.

Media Backlash and Public Scrutiny

As Virgilio's influence and impact grew, he became the subject of media scrutiny and backlash. Sensationalism and misrepresentation were often used to undermine his efforts and tarnish his reputation. However, Virgilio's resilience shone through, as he remained focused on his mission and refused to be silenced.

He leveraged his own voice and utilized media platforms to challenge biased narratives and present an accurate portrayal of LGBTQ issues. By engaging directly with the media and the public, he debunked misconceptions and emphasized the importance of fair and unbiased reporting. Virgilio's unwavering resilience in the face of media scrutiny demonstrated the power of authenticity and transparency in effecting social change.

Unwavering Resilience

Throughout his journey, Virgilio Barco Isakson's unwavering resilience became a hallmark of his activism. He faced immense pressure, personally and professionally, but he never faltered in his commitment to advocate for LGBTQ rights. His ability to remain steadfast and resilient in the face of adversity inspired countless individuals and fostered a sense of hope and empowerment within the LGBTQ community.

Virgilio's story reminds us that change is not easily achieved, and the path to progress is often challenging. His unwavering resilience serves as a beacon of hope, encouraging others to persevere in their own fight for justice and equality. By celebrating his legacy and embracing his spirit of determination, we honor Virgilio's remarkable journey and ensure that his indomitable resilience continues to shape the future of LGBTQ activism in Colombia and beyond.

Conclusion

In the face of opposition, Virgilio Barco Isakson demonstrated unwavering resilience, serving as an inspiration to LGBTQ individuals and activists around the world. His ability to overcome challenges, navigate hostile environments, and remain steadfast in his pursuit of equality made him a transformative figure in the LGBTQ rights movement. Virgilio's unwavering resilience serves as a powerful reminder that progress is possible, even in the face of adversity. As we continue to fight for LGBTQ rights, let us draw strength from his journey and work tirelessly to create a more inclusive and accepting world for all.

Section 2: The Human Side of Activism

Subsection 1: Personal Sacrifices and Losses

In this subsection, we will explore the personal sacrifices and losses that Virgilio Barco Isakson endured as an LGBTQ activist. It is important to highlight that, while his journey was filled with triumphs and victories, it also came with its fair share of challenges and hardships. Virgilio's unwavering dedication to the cause came at a great personal cost, but his resilience and determination propelled him forward.

One of the sacrifices Virgilio made was his own privacy. As an openly gay man in a society that was still largely conservative and intolerant, he understood that his advocacy would come at the expense of his personal life. Virgilio had to navigate constant media scrutiny and public judgment, which took a toll on his mental and emotional well-being. He had to learn to prioritize his activism over his own privacy, accepting that his personal life would always be subject to speculation and criticism.

Additionally, Virgilio faced significant backlash from traditional values and societal norms. Colombia, like many other countries, was deeply rooted in conservative ideologies that viewed homosexuality as morally wrong or deviant. As he pushed for LGBTQ rights and equality, he encountered resistance from religious institutions, conservative political leaders, and even members of his own community. The opposition and rejection he faced were deeply hurtful, but Virgilio remained steadfast in his mission to bring about social change.

Another sacrifice Virgilio made was the strain on his personal relationships. Advocacy is a demanding and time-consuming endeavor, and it often requires individuals to prioritize their commitments over personal connections. Virgilio had to balance his activism with his personal life, navigating the challenges of maintaining meaningful relationships amidst his demanding schedule. This meant missing out on important milestones, family gatherings, and quality time with loved ones. The sacrifices he made in this regard were emotionally challenging, but Virgilio understood that his work was vital in paving the way for a better future for LGBTQ individuals.

Virgilio also experienced profound losses during his journey. The fight for LGBTQ rights often brings individuals face-to-face with discrimination, violence, and tragedy. Virgilio mourned the loss of friends and community members who were victims of hate crimes or oppressed by an intolerant society. Their deaths only fueled his determination to continue his activism, but they also served as constant reminders of the struggles and dangers that LGBTQ individuals face daily.

It is essential to acknowledge the toll that these sacrifices and losses took on Virgilio's mental health. Like many activists, he battled moments of self-doubt, burnout, and even depression. The weight of the responsibility he carried, coupled with the relentless fight against discrimination, had an impact on his overall well-being. However, Virgilio consistently emphasized the importance of self-care and finding support systems to navigate the emotional challenges that came with his advocacy.

Despite the sacrifices and losses, Virgilio's resilience and unwavering commitment to the cause prevailed. His personal sacrifices were not made in vain, as they helped bring about significant advancements in LGBTQ rights in Colombia. By sharing his own story and experiences, Virgilio inspired countless individuals to stand up for their rights and fight against discrimination.

In conclusion, this subsection has explored the personal sacrifices and losses that Virgilio Barco Isakson encountered as an LGBTQ activist. His journey was characterized by challenges, hardships, and emotional tolls, as he navigated societal scrutiny, opposition, strained relationships, and profound losses. However, Virgilio's perseverance and unwavering dedication to the cause propelled him forward, ultimately leading to the transformation of LGBTQ rights in Colombia. His story serves as a testament to the resilience of activists and the powerful impact of personal sacrifice in the pursuit of equality.

Subsection 2: Mental Health Struggles

Mental health is an important aspect of overall well-being, and it plays a significant role in the lives of LGBTQ individuals. For many, the journey of self-discovery and acceptance can be accompanied by unique challenges that can take a toll on their mental health. In this subsection, we will explore the mental health struggles faced by LGBTQ individuals, the impact of societal factors, and the importance of seeking support and resources.

Understanding Mental Health in the LGBTQ Community

Mental health struggles are prevalent within the LGBTQ community due to various factors, including societal attitudes, stigma, discrimination, and the personal struggles of coming to terms with one's identity. LGBTQ individuals often face higher rates of depression, anxiety, and substance abuse compared to their heterosexual counterparts.

One significant contributor to mental health struggles is the experience of minority stress. Minority stress refers to the unique stressors faced by individuals who belong to marginalized communities, such as the LGBTQ community. This stress can arise from prejudice, discrimination, and social rejection, leading to increased levels of distress and mental health issues.

Challenges and Barriers

The mental health struggles faced by LGBTQ individuals are further compounded by various challenges and barriers that they encounter. These challenges can include:

- Lack of access to LGBTQ-affirming mental health services: Many LGBTQ individuals struggle to find mental health professionals who understand their unique experiences and can provide appropriate and inclusive care.

- Internalized stigma and self-acceptance: Some LGBTQ individuals internalize societal stigma and struggle with self-acceptance, leading to increased levels of anxiety, depression, and low self-esteem.

- Family and social rejection: Rejection from family members or friends due to one's sexual orientation or gender identity can have a significant impact on mental health and well-being.

- Bullying and harassment: LGBTQ individuals are more likely to experience bullying, harassment, and violence, which can lead to trauma and long-term mental health effects.

Seeking Support and Resources

Seeking support and accessing appropriate resources is crucial for LGBTQ individuals facing mental health challenges. Here are some strategies and resources that can help:

- LGBTQ-affirming therapy: Connecting with mental health professionals who specialize in working with LGBTQ individuals can provide a safe and understanding space to address mental health concerns.

- LGBTQ community centers: Community centers often offer support groups, counseling services, and resources specifically tailored to the needs of LGBTQ individuals.

- Online communities and support groups: Online platforms and forums can serve as valuable spaces for LGBTQ individuals to connect with others who may share similar experiences and provide support and understanding.

- LGBTQ helplines and crisis hotlines: Helplines and crisis hotlines are available to provide immediate support and assistance to those in crisis or in need of a listening ear.

- Self-care practices: Engaging in self-care activities such as exercise, mindfulness, and hobbies can help promote mental well-being and reduce stress levels.

Promoting Mental Health Advocacy

Mental health struggles within the LGBTQ community require continued advocacy and support. Here are some ways to promote mental health advocacy:

- Education and awareness: Educating the general public about the mental health challenges faced by LGBTQ individuals helps reduce stigma and promotes empathy and understanding.

- Integration of LGBTQ-inclusive mental health education: Incorporating LGBTQ-inclusive education into mental health training programs for healthcare providers can ensure that they are equipped to provide appropriate care.

- Policy changes: Advocating for policies that protect LGBTQ rights and equal access to mental health services can help reduce disparities and improve mental health outcomes.

- Collaboration with mental health organizations: Working with mental health organizations to develop LGBTQ-specific initiatives and programs can address the unique mental health needs of the community.

Recognizing Intersectionality

It is important to recognize that LGBTQ individuals have diverse identities and experiences that intersect with other aspects of their lives, such as race, ethnicity, socioeconomic status, and disability. Intersectionality plays a crucial role in understanding and addressing mental health struggles, as individuals may face multiple forms of discrimination and marginalization. Advocacy efforts must be intersectional to ensure that the mental health needs of all LGBTQ individuals are appropriately addressed.

Case Study: The Trevor Project

One organization that has made tremendous strides in promoting mental health and preventing suicide among LGBTQ youth is The Trevor Project. Founded in 1998, The Trevor Project provides crisis intervention and suicide prevention services to LGBTQ individuals aged 13-24. Their helpline, chat, and text services offer immediate support to those in crisis, while their online resources and education initiatives help promote mental health and resilience within the LGBTQ community.

Balancing Personal Relationships and Activism

In the journey of LGBTQ activism, one of the most significant challenges individuals face is finding a balance between their personal relationships and their dedication to creating social change. Virgilio Barco Isakson's story is no exception. As he navigated the path of activism, he encountered obstacles, made sacrifices, and learned valuable lessons about maintaining healthy relationships while pursuing his mission. In this section, we explore the complexities of balancing personal relationships and activism and provide some insights and strategies for those who tread a similar path.

The Importance of Communication and Understanding

At the core of maintaining a balance between personal relationships and activism lies effective communication and understanding. Being open and honest with your loved ones about your commitments, goals, and the sacrifices required is crucial. By explaining the significance of your work and the positive impact it can have, you can help your partner, friends, and family better understand your dedication.

Furthermore, actively listening to their concerns and respecting their perspectives is essential. Taking the time to empathize with their feelings and fears shows that you value their support and are willing to work together to find a compromise. By establishing a foundation of trust and clear communication, you can navigate the challenges of activism without sacrificing your personal relationships.

Setting Boundaries and Prioritizing Self-Care

When immersed in activism, it's easy to become consumed by the cause and neglect personal relationships. However, it's crucial to set boundaries and establish a balance between your activism and self-care. Remember that you cannot effectively advocate for others if you neglect your emotional and physical well-being.

Setting boundaries means being able to say no and respecting your limits. It involves setting aside time for your loved ones, engaging in activities unrelated to activism, and taking care of yourself. By creating space for personal relationships and self-care, you not only nurture your well-being but also enhance your ability to create meaningful change in the long run.

Supporting Each Other's Passions

Finding harmony between personal relationships and activism is not just about maintaining balance; it also involves supporting each other's passions. Your partner, friends, and family may have their own causes and interests that are equally important to them. Embrace their aspirations and offer your support just as they support you in your activism.

By celebrating each other's victories, collaborating on shared goals, and acknowledging the interconnectedness of your passions, you can create a strong foundation of mutual support. This shared commitment to social change can strengthen your personal relationships, fostering a sense of unity and shared purpose.

Addressing Emotional Stress and Burnout

Engaging in activism can be emotionally draining. The constant fight for change, exposure to inequality and discrimination, and the weight of responsibility can take a toll on your mental health. It's essential to recognize the signs of emotional stress and burnout and take proactive steps to mitigate their impact.

Seeking professional counseling or therapy can provide valuable tools for managing stress and emotional well-being. Additionally, practicing self-care activities such as mindfulness, exercise, and hobbies can help alleviate the emotional burdens of activism. By taking care of your mental and emotional health, you not only protect yourself but also ensure that you can continue to advocate effectively for LGBTQ rights.

Finding Support Networks and Allies

Building strong support networks and surrounding yourself with allies who share your passion for activism can be instrumental in maintaining relationships while pursuing your goals. Connect with like-minded individuals and organizations that can offer guidance, resources, and a sense of community.

Through LGBTQ organizations, local community groups, and online platforms, you can find individuals who understand the challenges and rewards of activism. These networks can not only provide emotional support but also serve as platforms for collaboration and collective action.

Unconventional Strategies: Leveraging Technology

In the digital age, technology can serve as a powerful tool for balancing personal relationships and activism. Embrace unconventional strategies by leveraging technology to bring people together and amplify your message. Use social media platforms to raise awareness, share stories, and build inclusive communities.

Additionally, consider creating online spaces where you can connect with other LGBTQ activists and share experiences. Virtual gatherings and online events can provide opportunities to engage in activism while minimizing the impact on personal relationships.

Challenge Yourself: Balancing Personal Relationships and Activism

Now that you have explored the complexities of balancing personal relationships and activism, it's time to reflect on your own journey. Consider the following questions and challenges:

1. How can you effectively communicate your commitment to activism to your loved ones? 2. What boundaries can you set to ensure a healthy balance between activism and self-care? 3. How can you support and embrace your partner, friends, or family members' passions and causes? 4. What strategies do you currently employ to address emotional stress and burnout? How can you improve upon them? 5. Are there any local LGBTQ organizations or community groups you can join to build support networks and find allies? 6. How can you leverage technology and online platforms to amplify your message and engage in activism?

Take the time to answer these questions honestly and develop an action plan to forge a balance between personal relationships and activism. Remember, it is through love, understanding, and mutual support that we can create lasting change for the LGBTQ community.

Subsection 4: Allies and Support Systems

In the journey towards LGBTQ rights, allies play a crucial role in creating a safe and inclusive environment for the community. They provide support, amplify voices, and actively challenge discrimination and prejudice. In this section, we will explore the importance of allies and support systems in promoting LGBTQ rights and creating lasting change.

Understanding the Role of Allies

Allies are individuals who may not identify as LGBTQ themselves but actively support the community through education, advocacy, and solidarity. They recognize the systemic inequities faced by LGBTQ individuals and work towards creating a more inclusive society.

Education and Awareness One of the first steps allies can take is to educate themselves about LGBTQ issues, terminology, and history. By understanding the challenges faced by the community, allies can better empathize, communicate, and challenge harmful stereotypes. Education can take various forms, including reading literature on LGBTQ experiences, attending workshops, or engaging in open and respectful conversations with members of the community.

Amplify LGBTQ Voices Allies have the power to amplify LGBTQ voices by providing platforms for their stories to be heard. This can be done through sharing articles and resources, inviting LGBTQ individuals to speak at events, or using social media platforms to raise awareness about LGBTQ rights. By actively centering and promoting LGBTQ voices, allies contribute to the visibility and recognition of the community's diverse experiences and perspectives.

Advocacy and Activism Allies play a crucial role in advocating for LGBTQ rights within their own communities and institutions. This includes speaking out against discriminatory practices, supporting policies that protect LGBTQ individuals, and collaborating with LGBTQ organizations. By actively challenging heteronormative and cisnormative norms, allies help create more inclusive spaces and advocate for systemic change.

Creating Support Systems

Support systems are essential for individuals within the LGBTQ community, providing comfort, understanding, and a sense of belonging. Allies can contribute to the creation of these support systems and foster an environment that encourages self-acceptance, mental well-being, and personal growth.

Safe Spaces Allies can actively work towards creating safe spaces for LGBTQ individuals. This can be achieved by challenging homophobic, biphobic, and transphobic language and behaviors, and ensuring that all members of the community are treated with respect and dignity. Safe spaces can be physical environments, such as LGBTQ resource centers or support groups, or virtual spaces, such as online communities or social media platforms that are monitored and moderated to ensure inclusivity.

Mental Health Support LGBTQ individuals often face higher rates of mental health issues due to societal stigma, discrimination, and internalized homophobia or transphobia. Allies can support mental well-being by advocating for accessible and LGBTQ-affirming mental health services, promoting self-care practices, and actively listening to the needs and concerns of LGBTQ individuals. By being a source of support and encouragement, allies contribute to the overall mental health and resilience of the community.

Intersectionality and Support Allies must recognize and address the intersecting identities and experiences within the LGBTQ community. This includes understanding the specific challenges faced by LGBTQ individuals who also belong to marginalized communities, such as people of color, disabled individuals, or religious minorities. Allies can engage in intersectional advocacy by actively centering these voices, understanding their unique struggles, and working towards equality and justice for all.

Case Study: The Power of Allies

One inspiring example of the power of allies comes from the history of LGBTQ rights in Colombia. Throughout his career, Virgilio Barco Isakson received immense support from allies who recognized the importance of LGBTQ rights and worked hand in hand with him to transform the social and political landscape.

Lawyers, politicians, artists, and religious leaders joined forces with Barco Isakson, collaborating on legal reforms, organizing educational campaigns, and advocating for LGBTQ equality. Their unwavering support helped shift public opinion and pave the way for significant policy changes. Together, they created a network of allies that extended beyond traditional LGBTQ circles, capturing the attention and empathy of individuals from diverse backgrounds.

The collective efforts of these allies strengthened the LGBTQ rights movement in Colombia, highlighting the significance of solidarity and collaboration in achieving lasting change. Their commitment and dedication continue to serve as a powerful example for future generations of activists and allies alike.

Conclusion

Allies and support systems are integral to the fight for LGBTQ rights. By educating themselves, advocating for change, and creating safe and inclusive environments, allies can contribute to the wellbeing and empowerment of LGBTQ individuals. The impact of allies extends beyond individual relationships and has the power to transform societies, challenge norms, and create a more equal and inclusive world for all. Together, allies and LGBTQ individuals can build a future where love, acceptance, and equality are celebrated.

Subsection 5: Taking Care of Self

In the journey of LGBTQ activism, it's important to remember that self-care is not just a luxury but a necessity. As trailblazers like Virgilio Barco Isakson have shown us, pushing boundaries and fighting for equality can exact a toll on mental and emotional well-being. In this subsection, we will explore the importance of self-care for LGBTQ activists and discuss strategies and resources to help maintain personal resilience.

Fostering Resilience

Activism can be emotionally draining, and LGBTQ activists often face intense scrutiny and backlash. It is crucial to develop strategies to build resilience and protect one's mental health. Here are some key approaches for taking care of yourself as an LGBTQ activist:

- **Self-reflection and self-awareness:** Regularly checking in with yourself to identify your emotional state and needs is essential. This can be done through journaling, mindfulness exercises, or therapy. Understanding your limits will allow you to set boundaries and maintain your mental well-being.

- **Finding support systems:** Building a network of supportive friends, family, and fellow activists can provide a strong foundation during challenging times. Connecting with others who share your experiences and struggles can create a sense of belonging and validation.

- **Prioritizing self-care activities:** Engaging in activities that bring you joy, relaxation, and rejuvenation is vital. This may include hobbies, exercise, meditation, artistic pursuits, or spending time in nature. Taking regular breaks to rest and recharge will help prevent burnout.

- **Setting boundaries:** Activism can sometimes feel all-consuming, making it crucial to establish boundaries to protect your energy and well-being. Learning to say no, delegating tasks, and balancing activism with personal life are essential in maintaining balance and preventing overwhelm.

- **Educating yourself on mental health:** Understanding the signs and symptoms of mental health challenges is essential for both yourself and those around you. Educate yourself on resources available for mental health support, techniques for stress management, and strategies for managing triggers and difficult emotions.

- **Taking breaks and practicing self-compassion:** It's important to give yourself permission to rest and take breaks when needed. Acknowledge that it is not selfish to prioritize your own well-being. Practice self-compassion by treating yourself with kindness and understanding during challenging times.

Resources for LGBTQ Activists

Fortunately, there are numerous resources available to help LGBTQ activists take care of themselves and access support. Here are some organizations and initiatives specifically dedicated to fostering self-care and mental health for LGBTQ individuals:

- **The Trevor Project:** A leading organization providing crisis intervention and suicide prevention services to LGBTQ youth. They offer a 24/7 hotline, online chat, and text services.

- **National Queer and Trans Therapists of Color Network:** This network aims to increase access to mental health resources for LGBTQ and QTPOC (Queer and Trans People of Color) communities. They provide a directory of therapists and healing practitioners specializing in supporting LGBTQ individuals.

- **LGBT National Help Center:** The Help Center offers confidential peer-support phone and online chat services for LGBTQ individuals seeking assistance, resources, and information on various topics, including mental health.

- **The LGBT Foundation:** This organization provides a wide range of services, including mental health support, helplines, online forums, and information on local LGBTQ-friendly healthcare providers.

- **Open Path Collective:** Open Path is a collective of mental health professionals who offer affordable therapy services for individuals, couples, and families within a sliding scale fee structure. They strive to make psychotherapy accessible to everyone, including LGBTQ individuals.

Remember, seeking support is a sign of strength, and taking care of yourself allows you to be a more effective advocate for LGBTQ rights. By nurturing your own well-being, you are better equipped to create meaningful change and empower others.

Taking Care of Self: Unconventional Strategies

In addition to traditional self-care practices, there are unconventional but effective strategies that can contribute to the overall well-being of LGBTQ activists:

- **Creative outlets:** Engaging in creative activities, such as art, music, writing, or dance, can be therapeutic and provide an outlet for emotional expression. Exploring these outlets allows you to tap into your inner creativity and reconnect with yourself on a deeper level.

- **Group meditation or mindfulness:** Participating in group meditation or mindfulness exercises with other LGBTQ activists can create a sense of unity and promote emotional resilience. These practices can help manage stress, reduce anxiety, and improve overall mental well-being.

- **Nature immersion:** Spending time in nature has been shown to have numerous mental health benefits. Take breaks from the activism scene and connect with the natural world. Whether it's hiking, picnicking, or simply sitting in a park, immersing yourself in nature can offer a much-needed respite and rejuvenation.

- **Embracing humor and joy:** Laughter and joy have proven to be powerful antidotes to stress and burnout. Embrace humor in your life, share jokes with friends, or attend LGBTQ comedy events. Finding moments of joy allows you to stay uplifted and energized in the face of adversity.

- **Movement and dance:** Engaging in physical activities that involve movement and dance can be empowering and cathartic. Attend LGBTQ dance classes or join community dance events to express yourself through movement. This can provide a release of emotions and promote a positive body image.

By exploring these unconventional strategies alongside traditional self-care practices, you can cultivate a more holistic approach to taking care of yourself as an LGBTQ activist.

Conclusion

As LGBTQ activists like Virgilio Barco Isakson have shown us, fighting for equality and justice is a transformative and impactful journey. However, it is crucial to prioritize self-care and well-being to sustain long-term activism. By fostering resilience, accessing resources, and embracing innovative self-care strategies, you can navigate the challenges of advocacy while nurturing your own personal growth. Remember, taking care of yourself is an act of self-love and empowerment, enabling you to continue the important work of creating a more inclusive and equitable world.

Section 3: Triumphing in the Face of Adversity

Subsection 2: Impact on Colombian Society

The transformative journey of Virgilio Barco Isakson left an indelible mark on Colombian society, bringing about significant changes in the way LGBTQ individuals are perceived, treated, and protected. Through his tireless activism and groundbreaking policies, Barco challenged societal norms and norms, empowering the LGBTQ community and reshaping the fabric of Colombian society.

The Power of Representation

One of the most profound impacts of Barco's advocacy was the power of representation. By openly embracing his LGBTQ identity and championing LGBTQ rights, Barco shattered stereotypes and provided a visible role model for countless individuals grappling with their own identities. His unwavering courage and authenticity inspired a generation of LGBTQ youth, giving them hope, encouragement, and the belief that they can achieve anything they set their minds to.

The visibility of LGBTQ representation extended beyond Barco himself. As more LGBTQ individuals stepped forward to share their stories and experiences, Colombian society became more aware of the diversity within the LGBTQ community. This increased visibility and understanding led to greater acceptance and empathy, breaking down barriers and fostering a sense of unity among different segments of society.

Addressing Prejudice and Discrimination

Barco's impact on Colombian society extended far beyond symbolism. His policies aimed to eradicate prejudice and discrimination against LGBTQ individuals, creating a more inclusive society for all. Through legislative measures and comprehensive anti-discrimination laws, Barco paved the way for equal rights and protection for the LGBTQ community.

One significant milestone was the establishment of legal frameworks prohibiting discrimination based on sexual orientation and gender identity. These laws not only provided legal recourse for those who faced discrimination but also sent a clear message to society that LGBTQ individuals deserve equal treatment under the law. As a result, LGBTQ individuals gained greater access to employment, education, healthcare, and other essential services, enhancing their overall well-being and quality of life.

Fostering Social Acceptance

Barco recognized that legal protections alone were not enough to create lasting change. Societal attitudes needed to shift in order to foster true acceptance of LGBTQ individuals. Through education and awareness campaigns, Barco initiated conversations about LGBTQ issues, challenging deep-rooted prejudices and stereotypes within Colombian society.

Schools played a crucial role in this endeavor, as education and awareness are powerful tools for change. Barco's administration worked tirelessly to introduce

LGBTQ-inclusive curricula that promoted acceptance, understanding, and empathy among students. By integrating LGBTQ history, experiences, and contributions into the education system, Barco aimed to create an environment where diversity was celebrated and respected.

Additionally, Barco devoted resources to community outreach programs, organizing events, and fostering dialogue between LGBTQ individuals and the broader society. Through these initiatives, Barco sought to bridge the gap between different communities and break down barriers built on fear and ignorance. By promoting dialogue and understanding, Barco's efforts were instrumental in fostering social acceptance and creating a more inclusive Colombian society.

A Cultural Shift

Barco's impact on Colombian society extended into the realm of culture. By promoting LGBTQ representation in media and the arts, Barco challenged traditional norms and gave LGBTQ individuals a platform to share their stories and experiences. This cultural shift helped to humanize the LGBTQ community and counteract harmful stereotypes and misconceptions.

The increased visibility of LGBTQ artists, performers, and creators created a ripple effect throughout Colombian society. It sparked conversations, challenged assumptions, and fostered a sense of pride within the LGBTQ community. Artistic expressions became a catalyst for change, empowering LGBTQ individuals and contributing to a greater sense of inclusion and diversity in Colombian culture.

Inspiring Future Generations

Perhaps one of the most lasting impacts of Barco's journey is the inspiration it continues to provide for future generations of LGBTQ activists and allies. His legacy serves as a roadmap for those seeking to challenge oppression and fight for equality in all aspects of society.

The impact on Colombian society can be seen in the continued activism and progress achieved by LGBTQ individuals. Barco's groundbreaking work set a precedent for future leaders and activists, providing a blueprint for creating lasting change. His perseverance, resilience, and unwavering commitment to justice continue to inspire and guide the LGBTQ movement in Colombia and beyond.

In conclusion, Virgilio Barco Isakson's impact on Colombian society cannot be understated. Through his leadership, advocacy, and policy reforms, he transformed the landscape for LGBTQ rights, challenging prejudice and discrimination, fostering cultural change, and inspiring future generations of activists. His enduring legacy serves as an example of what can be achieved when individuals stand up for justice and equality. Colombian society is forever indebted to the unfiltered victory brought about by Virgilio Barco Isakson.

Subsection 3: Empowering LGBTQ Youth

In this subsection, we will explore the importance of empowering LGBTQ youth and the various ways in which Virgilio Barco Isakson championed their rights and provided them with opportunities for growth and development. As an LGBTQ activist and politician, Barco recognized the significance of investing in the younger generation and ensuring that they have the tools and support needed to thrive in a society that celebrates diversity and inclusivity.

Understanding the Challenges

LGBTQ youth face unique challenges that can often hinder their personal and academic growth. Many experience bullying, discrimination, and rejection, both at school and within their own families. These negative experiences can lead to higher rates of mental health issues, substance abuse, and even suicide. It is crucial to address these challenges and create a safe and affirming environment for LGBTQ youth to flourish.

Fostering Inclusive Education

Barco played a pivotal role in advocating for LGBTQ-inclusive education. He recognized the power of knowledge in challenging stereotypes, promoting acceptance, and nurturing empathy among students. By introducing comprehensive sex education that includes LGBTQ issues, he aimed to create a more inclusive curriculum that provides accurate information about sexual orientation and gender identity. This education not only benefits LGBTQ students directly but also fosters a more accepting and informed society as a whole.

Mentorship and Support Networks

One of the key ways Barco empowered LGBTQ youth was by establishing mentorship programs and support networks. These programs matched LGBTQ youth with mentors who shared similar identities and experiences, providing guidance, support, and inspiration. Through shared stories and practical advice, mentors helped LGBTQ youth navigate their personal and social challenges, fostering a sense of belonging and resilience.

Support networks were also crucial in creating safe spaces for LGBTQ youth to express themselves freely and find a sense of community. Barco recognized that providing spaces for LGBTQ youth to connect and share their experiences could combat isolation and create opportunities for growth and self-discovery.

Promoting Mental Health and Well-being

An essential aspect of empowering LGBTQ youth is addressing their mental health and well-being. Barco championed the importance of accessible and LGBTQ-inclusive mental health services. He worked to remove the stigma surrounding mental health issues and ensure that LGBTQ youth had access to professional support and resources.

Additionally, Barco emphasized the significance of self-care and stress management. He encouraged LGBTQ youth to engage in activities that promote their emotional and physical well-being. Whether it be through art, sports, or other forms of self-expression, these outlets can serve as a source of resilience and empowerment for LGBTQ youth.

Encouraging Leadership and Activism

Barco firmly believed in the power of LGBTQ youth in shaping the future of equality and social justice. He encouraged them to use their voices and advocate for change in their communities. To foster their leadership skills, Barco organized workshops and training programs that empowered LGBTQ youth to become activists and advocates for their rights. By providing resources, guidance, and platforms for their voices to be heard, Barco aimed to inspire a new generation of LGBTQ leaders.

Unconventional Solution: Hackathon for LGBTQ Youth

Alongside the traditional approaches to empowering LGBTQ youth, Barco also organized a unique and innovative event: a hackathon for LGBTQ youth. This hackathon brought together young individuals with a passion for technology and social change. Participants were tasked with developing innovative solutions to address the specific challenges faced by LGBTQ youth, such as mental health support, inclusive education tools, and safe community platforms.

The hackathon created an environment that encouraged creative thinking and collaboration, fostering a sense of empowerment and problem-solving skills among LGBTQ youth. It not only provided them with an opportunity to showcase their talents but also helped develop practical solutions to real-world issues affecting their community.

Conclusion

Empowering LGBTQ youth is essential for creating a more inclusive and equitable society. Virgilio Barco Isakson recognized this and dedicated his efforts to provide support, education, mentorship, and opportunities for growth. By promoting inclusive education, fostering mentorship and support networks, addressing mental health, encouraging leadership and activism, and even through unconventional events such as hackathons, Barco paved the way for LGBTQ youth to thrive and make their mark on the world. Their empowerment is not only a testament to Barco's legacy but also a crucial step toward a more inclusive future for all.

Subsection 4: Redefining the Narrative of LGBTQ Identity

In this section, we explore the groundbreaking efforts by Virgilio Barco Isakson to redefine the narrative of LGBTQ identity in Colombia. Through his activism and leadership, Barco Isakson challenged societal norms and worked tirelessly to create a more inclusive and accepting society for LGBTQ individuals.

Evolving Perspectives on LGBTQ Identity

At the core of Barco Isakson's mission was the belief that LGBTQ identity should be celebrated and embraced. He sought to challenge the traditional notions and stereotypes surrounding LGBTQ individuals and create a new narrative that highlighted their unique experiences and contributions.

Barco Isakson promoted the idea that LGBTQ identity is not a deviation from the norm, but rather a beautiful and diverse expression of human sexuality and gender. He emphasized the importance of self-acceptance and encouraged individuals to embrace their authentic selves, regardless of societal expectations.

Dismantling Traditional Gender Roles

A key aspect of redefining the narrative of LGBTQ identity was the dismantling of traditional gender roles. Barco Isakson recognized that society's rigid expectations around gender norms limited individuals' freedom of expression and perpetuated discrimination against LGBTQ individuals.

Through his advocacy, Barco Isakson challenged gender stereotypes and promoted gender inclusivity. He emphasized the importance of recognizing and respecting the various gender identities and expressions within the LGBTQ community, including transgender and non-binary individuals.

Barco Isakson worked towards creating a society where individuals are not confined by societal expectations of how they should look, act, and express themselves. He championed transgender rights and fought for policies that protected the rights of transgender individuals to live their lives authentically.

Empowering LGBTQ Youth

Another crucial aspect of Barco Isakson's efforts to redefine the narrative of LGBTQ identity was his commitment to empowering LGBTQ youth. He recognized that young LGBTQ individuals often face unique challenges and are more susceptible to discrimination, bullying, and mental health issues.

Barco Isakson worked tirelessly to establish support systems and resources for LGBTQ youth. He advocated for inclusive education that acknowledges and celebrates LGBTQ history, culture, and contributions. He championed anti-bullying policies in schools and created safe spaces for LGBTQ youth to connect, share their experiences, and gain support.

By empowering LGBTQ youth, Barco Isakson aimed to shape a future generation that is proud of their identity, confident in their abilities, and unafraid to challenge the status quo.

Promoting Intersectionality

Recognizing that LGBTQ identity intersects with race, ethnicity, class, and other aspects of a person's identity, Barco Isakson emphasized the importance of promoting intersectionality within the LGBTQ community.

He actively worked to create an inclusive movement that addressed the unique needs and experiences of LGBTQ individuals from diverse backgrounds. Barco Isakson fought against the marginalization and erasure of LGBTQ individuals who face multiple forms of discrimination.

Barco Isakson's efforts to redefine the narrative of LGBTQ identity included amplifying the voices and stories of LGBTQ individuals from marginalized communities. He sought to ensure that no one was left behind in the quest for equality, and that all LGBTQ individuals could find representation and support within the movement.

A Shift in Public Perception

Barco Isakson's tireless efforts to redefine the narrative of LGBTQ identity had a profound impact on public perception. His advocacy and leadership paved the way for a more inclusive and accepting society in Colombia.

Through his work, Barco Isakson challenged stereotypes, broke down barriers, and fostered empathy and understanding. He humanized the LGBTQ experience and helped shift public perception by highlighting the common humanity shared by all individuals, regardless of sexual orientation or gender identity.

Barco Isakson's legacy lives on in the continued work to redefine the narrative of LGBTQ identity. His efforts inspire future generations to continue challenging societal norms, celebrating diversity, and fighting for the rights and equality of all LGBTQ individuals.

In conclusion, Virgilio Barco Isakson's work to redefine the narrative of LGBTQ identity in Colombia was transformative. He fought against stereotypes, dismantled traditional gender roles, empowered LGBTQ youth, promoted intersectionality, and shifted public perception. Through his efforts, Barco Isakson left an enduring legacy of acceptance, equality, and celebration of LGBTQ identity.

Subsection 5: Transformation on a National Scale

In this subsection, we will explore the remarkable transformations that Virgilio Barco Isakson initiated on a national scale. His relentless advocacy and groundbreaking policies paved the way for significant progress in LGBTQ rights throughout Colombia. Let's delve into the transformative impact he made on the nation.

Challenging Status Quo

Barco Isakson recognized that true transformation begins with challenging the status quo. He fearlessly confronted deeply rooted cultural norms, prejudices, and discrimination faced by the LGBTQ community. Through his influential speeches and public appearances, he encouraged Colombians to embrace diversity, encouraging inclusivity and acceptance as core values of the nation.

Change in Legal Landscape

One of the most significant transformations Barco Isakson spearheaded was the change in the legal landscape for LGBTQ rights. He championed the fight for equal rights, leading to groundbreaking legislative changes. These reforms aimed to protect and uphold the rights of LGBTQ individuals and create a more inclusive society.

By working closely with lawmakers and advocacy groups, Barco Isakson played a pivotal role in legalizing same-sex relationships, providing legal recognition and protection to LGBTQ couples. His tireless efforts resulted in the removal of discriminatory laws that targeted LGBTQ individuals.

Creating Safe Spaces

Barco Isakson recognized the urgent need for safe spaces for LGBTQ individuals, especially for vulnerable youth. He took critical steps to provide support and protection for LGBTQ youth who faced discrimination, bullying, and rejection.

Under his leadership, comprehensive anti-bullying policies were implemented in schools, ensuring a safer environment for LGBTQ students. He also established LGBTQ community centers across the country, where individuals could seek support, access resources, and connect with like-minded individuals. These safe spaces became pillars of support and empowerment for the LGBTQ community.

Educational Reforms

Recognizing the power of education in fostering an inclusive society, Barco Isakson implemented educational reforms that aimed to eradicate homophobia and promote LGBTQ-inclusive curricula. He advocated for the inclusion of LGBTQ history and contributions in school textbooks, helping to build a more accurate and inclusive representation.

Additionally, Barco Isakson initiated programs to train teachers on LGBTQ issues and sensitivities, equipping them with the tools they needed to create inclusive classrooms. By addressing prejudice and fostering understanding from a young age, Barco Isakson set the stage for a more accepting society.

Promoting Representation

Representation plays a vital role in transforming societal norms. Barco Isakson recognized this and actively worked to promote LGBTQ representation in media and the arts. He encouraged the production of diverse LGBTQ content, fostering a sense of belonging and identity for the community.

Through financial support and incentives, Barco Isakson facilitated the creation of LGBTQ-focused films, music, and literature. This cultural revolution allowed LGBTQ individuals to express themselves authentically, challenging stereotypes and contributing to a more inclusive cultural landscape.

Unthinkable Transformation

Despite the progress made, transformation on a national scale does not come without challenges. Barco Isakson faced strong opposition from conservative and traditionalist voices who resisted change. However, his unwavering determination and resilience sparked conversations and shifted perceptions, ultimately leading to a more equitable society.

Throughout his tenure, Barco Isakson's transformative policies and unwavering commitment to equality left an indelible mark on Colombian society. His achievements have become a cornerstone of LGBTQ rights and serve as an inspiration for activists around the world.

Box-out: Overcoming Resistance

The resistance faced by Barco Isakson serves as a reminder that transformational change often encounters opposition. As advocates for change, it is essential to anticipate challenges and develop strategies to overcome resistance. Some effective approaches include:

- Building coalitions: By forming alliances with like-minded individuals, organizations, and communities, the collective voice becomes stronger and harder to ignore.

- Education and dialogue: Engaging in open and respectful dialogue with individuals who hold opposing views can foster understanding and reduce prejudice. Education can dismantle misconceptions and generate empathy.

- Collaboration with influential figures: Partnering with influential personalities, public figures, and celebrities can amplify the message, reach a broader audience, and humanize the cause.

- Utilizing media channels: Leveraging the power of media outlets, social media, and other platforms can raise awareness, challenge narratives, and counter misinformation.

- Engaging with policymakers: Establishing connections with policymakers and lawmakers helps ensure that the voices of the marginalized are heard in the halls of power.

By employing these strategies and adapting to the evolving landscape, advocates can effectively navigate resistance and drive transformative change.

Key Takeaways

Virgilio Barco Isakson's leadership and advocacy efforts brought about transformative change on a national scale in Colombia. Through legal reforms, safe space creation, educational reforms, promotion of LGBTQ representation, and cultural revolutions, he challenged societal norms and created a more inclusive society.

Barco Isakson's legacy serves as a reminder that transformation requires resilience, perseverance, and strategic approaches to overcome resistance. His achievements continue to inspire future generations of LGBTQ activists, driving the ongoing fight for equality and social justice.

Exercises

1. Research and analyze the legal landscape for LGBTQ rights in your own country. What progress has been made, and what challenges still persist? Identify key areas for further transformation and propose strategies to address those challenges.

2. Create a comprehensive plan for implementing LGBTQ-inclusive educational reforms in a hypothetical school or education system. Outline the steps, initiatives, and resources required to build an inclusive learning environment for LGBTQ students.

3. Develop a social media campaign to promote LGBTQ representation in popular culture. Design engaging content, hashtags, and dissemination strategies to raise awareness and challenge stereotypes.

4. Reflect on a personal experience where you witnessed or faced resistance to transformative change. Describe the strategies you employed or could have employed to overcome that resistance effectively.

Resources

1. "This Book is Gay" by Juno Dawson: A comprehensive guide to gender and sexuality that provides insights into LGBTQ history, issues, and identity.

2. It Gets Better Project: A global movement that uplifts, empowers, and connects LGBTQ+ youth through storytelling and community support.

3. ILGA World: The International Lesbian, Gay, Bisexual, Trans, and Intersex Association provide resources and information on LGBTQ rights globally.

4. GLAAD: An organization dedicated to promoting LGBTQ acceptance through media advocacy, offering resources and guidelines for accurate and fair LGBTQ representation.

5. Trevor Project: A leading organization providing crisis intervention and suicide prevention services to LGBTQ+ youth, with resources for mental health support.

Remember, transformation begins with you. Each individual has the power to challenge norms, foster acceptance, and drive change in their own communities. Together, we can create a more equitable and inclusive world for all.

Chapter 4: Leaving a Lasting Legacy

Chapter 4: Leaving a Lasting Legacy

Chapter 4: Leaving a Lasting Legacy

As Virgilio Barco Isakson's tenure as mayor of Bogotá drew to a close, he left behind a remarkable legacy that would forever shape the future of LGBTQ rights in Colombia. This chapter explores the impact of Virgilio's leadership and activism, highlighting the milestones achieved and the lasting influence he had on society. From his stepping down as mayor to his continued advocacy for human rights, Virgilio's journey is a testament to the power of determination and the enduring fight for equality.

Subsection 1: Stepping Down as Mayor

After serving two successful terms as the mayor of Bogotá, Virgilio Barco Isakson made the difficult decision to step down from his political position. This marked the end of an era for both him and the city he had transformed. As he reflected on his time in office, Virgilio knew that his work was far from over. He saw the need to shift his focus to broader human rights advocacy, taking the fight for LGBTQ rights to new heights.

Subsection 2: Reflections on a Term Filled with Milestones

Looking back on his time as mayor, Virgilio Barco Isakson could not help but feel a sense of pride and accomplishment. During his tenure, he had spearheaded significant policy changes and introduced groundbreaking initiatives that had a profound impact on the LGBTQ community. From enacting laws to protect

LGBTQ youth from discrimination and violence to championing inclusive education, Virgilio's term was filled with milestones that forever changed the landscape of LGBTQ rights in Colombia.

Subsection 3: Shifting Focus to Human Rights Advocacy

As Virgilio transitioned from his role as mayor, he knew that there was still much work to be done to advance human rights in Colombia. He focused his efforts on advocating for comprehensive legislation that would protect LGBTQ individuals from discrimination in all aspects of life, including employment, housing, and public services. By collaborating with NGOs and human rights organizations, Virgilio sought to bring about lasting change that would benefit not only the LGBTQ community but also society as a whole.

Subsection 4: Passing the Torch to the Next Generation

As Virgilio Barco Isakson took a step back from politics, he recognized the importance of empowering the next generation of LGBTQ activists and leaders. He mentored young activists, offering guidance and support as they embarked on their own journeys of advocacy. Virgilio knew that the fight for equality would only continue to thrive if new voices were given the opportunity to rise and effect change. By passing the torch to the next generation, Virgilio ensured that his legacy would live on in the hearts and minds of those who would carry the movement forward.

Subsection 5: Transitioning to Life After Politics

Leaving behind a storied career in politics, Virgilio Barco Isakson embraced the transition to life after his term as mayor. Although he stepped out of the political spotlight, Virgilio remained committed to his mission of promoting equality and justice for all. He delved into human rights research, authoring influential publications that shed light on the challenges faced by LGBTQ individuals around the world. As he embarked on a new chapter, Virgilio continued to use his voice and influence to uplift marginalized communities and effect systemic change.

In this chapter, we have explored the impact of Virgilio Barco Isakson's departure from his role as mayor of Bogotá and his transition to a life dedicated to human rights advocacy. From reflecting on his term filled with milestones to passing the torch to the next generation, Virgilio's legacy is one of resilience, compassion, and a relentless pursuit of justice. His lasting impact on LGBTQ rights in Colombia serves as a reminder that the fight for equality is ongoing and that each individual has the power to create positive change. As we look ahead to the future, inspired by Virgilio's journey, we are filled with hope and determination to continue the work of transforming society into a more inclusive and accepting place for all.

Section 1: The End of an Era

Subsection 1: Stepping Down as Mayor

Stepping down as the Mayor of Bogotá was a bittersweet moment for Virgilio Barco Isakson. After years of dedicated service to the city and tireless advocacy for LGBTQ rights, it was time for him to pass the torch to the next generation of leaders. In this subsection, we will explore the reasons behind Virgilio's decision, the impact of his departure, and his plans for the future.

The Weight of Responsibility

As Mayor, Virgilio Barco Isakson carried the weight of responsibility on his shoulders each day. He knew that he had the power to make significant changes and push for equality in the city. However, the demands of the role were immense, requiring constant decision-making, long hours, and unwavering dedication.

During his tenure, Virgilio faced numerous challenges and triumphs while spearheading ground-breaking LGBTQ rights initiatives. His commitment to improving the lives of marginalized communities was unwavering. However, he also recognized the need for new voices and fresh perspectives in the fight for equality.

Creating Space for New Leaders

Virgilio Barco Isakson believed in the power of inclusivity and believed that stepping down as Mayor would create space for new leaders to emerge and continue the fight for LGBTQ rights. He knew that his departure would open doors for individuals with different backgrounds and perspectives to bring change to the forefront.

By voluntarily stepping down, Virgilio hoped to inspire others to step up and take on leadership roles. He encouraged young activists and aspiring politicians to follow their passions, emphasizing the importance of diverse representation in positions of power.

Building a Support Network

While leaving the role of Mayor was a significant transition, Virgilio was determined to build a robust support network to ensure the continuous progress of LGBTQ rights in Bogotá. He identified promising activists and leaders who shared his vision and worked closely with them to establish a strong foundation for the future.

Virgilio cultivated partnerships with LGBTQ organizations, both locally and internationally, to ensure that the fight for equality would carry on. He knew that collective action was essential, and by working together, they could amplify their voices and make an even greater impact.

Continuing the Legacy

Stepping down as Mayor did not mean that Virgilio Barco Isakson's work was finished. On the contrary, he saw it as an opportunity to expand his advocacy and continue the fight for LGBTQ rights on a broader scale.

He transitioned his focus to human rights advocacy, using his influence and expertise to tackle issues that extended beyond the boundaries of Bogotá. Virgilio traveled nationally and internationally, speaking at conferences and collaborating with NGOs and human rights organizations to address systemic inequalities and promote inclusivity.

Life After Politics

For Virgilio, stepping down as Mayor marked the beginning of a new chapter in his life. He looked forward to spending more time with his loved ones and exploring personal passions that he had put on hold during his time in office.

While he may have left his political career behind, Virgilio remained dedicated to promoting LGBTQ rights and supporting marginalized communities. He continued to be a vocal advocate, using his platform to inspire and empower others to stand up for equality.

Leaving a Lasting Impact

Virgilio Barco Isakson's decision to step down as Mayor was not an easy one, but it was rooted in his deep belief in the power of collective leadership and the need for continuous progress. By making space for new leaders, building support networks, and continuing his advocacy work, Virgilio was ensuring that his legacy would endure.

SECTION 1: THE END OF AN ERA 135

His departure from office was not an end but rather a new beginning. The impact of his work would resonate for years to come, inspiring generations of activists and transforming the landscape of LGBTQ rights in Colombia.

Conclusion

Stepping down as Mayor was a pivotal moment for Virgilio Barco Isakson, signaling a shift in his focus and a determination to continue fighting for LGBTQ rights. By creating space for new leaders, building support networks, and continuing his advocacy work, Virgilio ensured that his legacy would endure and that the fight for equality would carry on. His decision marked the beginning of a new chapter in his life, one filled with equal passion and commitment to creating a more inclusive society.

Subsection 2: Reflections on a Term Filled with Milestones

Reflecting on his term as mayor of Bogotá, Virgilio Barco Isakson, one of Colombia's most influential LGBTQ activists, can't help but be overwhelmed by the incredible milestones that were achieved. The journey to transform LGBTQ rights was not an easy one, but the significant progress made during his tenure is truly remarkable.

One of the key milestones that Virgilio achieved was the establishment of groundbreaking policies that paved the way for equal rights for the LGBTQ community in Colombia. Through tireless advocacy and determination, he successfully fought for the recognition of same-sex relationships, which led to the legalization of same-sex marriage in the country. This was a historic moment for LGBTQ individuals and represented a major step forward in the fight for equality.

Additionally, Virgilio's term saw a focus on protecting LGBTQ youth. He recognized the importance of creating a safe and inclusive environment for young people to thrive, free from discrimination and violence. As a result, he implemented measures to combat bullying in schools and established support programs specifically tailored to the needs of LGBTQ youth.

Challenging gender norms was another area where Virgilio made significant strides. He recognized the importance of embracing and celebrating diverse gender identities and worked towards breaking down the rigid binaries that limit individuals' self-expression. By instituting policies that recognized and protected transgender rights, he paved the way for a more inclusive society.

Virgilio's term also witnessed a cultural revolution in which LGBTQ representation in media and the arts flourished. He understood the power of visibility and the impact it could have on breaking down stereotypes and dispelling misconceptions. Through his initiatives, LGBTQ artists and performers were given platforms to showcase their talents, and their contributions to Colombian culture were celebrated.

Another major milestone during Virgilio's term was the creation of LGBTQ-inclusive education. He recognized the importance of educating the next generation about diversity and acceptance. By integrating LGBTQ history and perspectives into the curriculum, Virgilio ensured that students would grow up with a deeper understanding and empathy for all individuals, regardless of sexual orientation or gender identity.

As Virgilio reflects on these milestones, he is filled with pride and gratitude for the progress that was made during his term. However, he acknowledges that the fight for LGBTQ rights is far from over. There are still challenges to be faced and hurdles to be overcome. But with the foundation that has been laid and the momentum that has been built, Virgilio is confident that the legacy of his term as mayor will continue to inspire and empower future generations of LGBTQ activists.

In conclusion, Virgilio Barco Isakson's term as mayor of Bogotá was filled with extraordinary milestones. From groundbreaking policies to cultural revolutions, his tireless advocacy and determination have transformed the landscape of LGBTQ rights in Colombia. It is a legacy that will be remembered and celebrated for generations to come.

Subsection 3: Shifting Focus to Human Rights Advocacy

As Virgilio Barco Isakson's tenure as the mayor of Bogotá came to an end, he realized that his work in promoting LGBTQ rights was just the beginning. He knew that true equality went beyond sexual orientation and gender identity alone. It was about fighting for the fundamental rights and dignity of every individual, regardless of their background. With this realization, Virgilio shifted his focus towards human rights advocacy, aiming to create a more inclusive society for all Colombians.

The Intersectionality of Human Rights

Virgilio understood that human rights were interconnected. He recognized that discrimination and injustice did not exist in isolation; they affected individuals and communities across multiple dimensions. He believed in the importance of addressing the intersecting forms of marginalization, such as gender, race, class, and disability, which impacted the lives of LGBTQ individuals and others. By

SECTION 1: THE END OF AN ERA

acknowledging the interdependence of rights, he aimed to create a more comprehensive approach to social justice.

Fighting Against Discrimination

Discrimination takes many forms, and Virgilio was determined to challenge them all. He advocated for equal opportunities in employment, housing, and education, pushing for legislation that would protect individuals from discrimination based on any characteristic, including sexual orientation, gender identity, race, ethnicity, disability, and religion. Virgilio knew that without comprehensive anti-discrimination laws, achieving true equality would be impossible.

Promoting Inclusivity in Public Services

Virgilio recognized the importance of inclusive public services in creating a society that values and respects the rights of all its citizens. He worked tirelessly to ensure that government agencies and institutions were equipped to serve diverse populations sensitively and effectively. Through trainings and education programs, he aimed to cultivate a culture of inclusivity and respect within government bodies, law enforcement agencies, and other public service providers.

Supporting Vulnerable Communities

Virgilio dedicated himself to supporting marginalized and vulnerable communities, ensuring that their voices were heard and their needs were addressed. He actively collaborated with NGOs and human rights organizations to provide support and resources to communities facing discrimination and violence. Whether it was advocating for the rights of LGBTQ youth, indigenous groups, or internally displaced persons, Virgilio knew that by lifting up the most vulnerable among us, we uplifted society as a whole.

International Human Rights Advocacy

Virgilio understood that the fight for human rights extended beyond national borders. He actively engaged with international organizations, such as the United Nations and Amnesty International, to advocate for LGBTQ rights globally. Through his speeches, participation in conferences, and collaborations with international activists, he aimed to not only raise awareness but also inspire positive change around the world. Virgilio believed that no individual should face discrimination or persecution based on their sexual orientation or gender identity, no matter where they lived.

Creating Empathetic Communities

For Virgilio, shifting the focus to human rights advocacy meant more than just policy changes; it meant fostering a culture of empathy and understanding within Colombian society. He believed that by challenging societal norms and promoting dialogue, communities could come together to support and uplift one another. Virgilio encouraged Colombians to celebrate diversity, embrace inclusivity, and stand up against discrimination. Through public awareness campaigns, workshops, and cultural initiatives, he sought to transform hearts and minds and create a more compassionate society.

In conclusion, as Virgilio Barco Isakson transitioned from his role as the mayor of Bogotá, he shifted his focus to human rights advocacy. Recognizing the interconnectedness of various forms of discrimination, he pushed for comprehensive anti-discrimination laws that protected the rights of all individuals. He promoted inclusivity in public services and supported vulnerable communities, both within Colombia and internationally. Moreover, he sought to create empathetic communities, fostering a culture of understanding and respect. Through his unwavering dedication to human rights, Virgilio Barco Isakson left a lasting legacy that continues to inspire and drive the fight for equality in Colombia and beyond.

Subsection 4: Passing the Torch to the Next Generation

Passing the torch to the next generation is an essential step in ensuring the longevity and sustainability of any movement. Virgilio Barco Isakson, a pioneer in LGBTQ rights in Colombia, understood the significance of empowering and inspiring future leaders to carry on the fight for equality. In this subsection, we will explore the strategies and initiatives Barco Isakson took to pass the torch to the next generation of LGBTQ activists.

Youth Empowerment Programs

Barco Isakson believed in the power and potential of young individuals to bring about positive change. To foster their activism and leadership skills, he initiated various youth empowerment programs. These programs aimed to provide LGBTQ youth with a platform to express themselves, develop their talents, and engage in advocacy work.

SECTION 1: THE END OF AN ERA

One such program, called "Rising Voices," focused on supporting young LGBTQ artists and performers. Through workshops, mentorship programs, and performance opportunities, it enabled them to showcase their talents while simultaneously raising awareness about LGBTQ issues. Barco Isakson firmly believed that by amplifying the voices of young artists, their messages of equality and acceptance would resonate with a broader audience.

Another initiative was the "Leaders of Tomorrow" program, which focused on training young LGBTQ individuals in leadership and advocacy skills. This program provided mentorship, networking opportunities, and educational resources to empower them to take an active role in fighting for LGBTQ rights. Barco Isakson understood that by equipping young leaders with the necessary tools, they would be able to navigate the challenges of activism and continue the legacy of progress long into the future.

Collaboration with Educational Institutions

Recognizing the influential role that educational institutions play in shaping the minds of future leaders, Barco Isakson actively collaborated with universities and colleges throughout Colombia. He worked closely with academic institutions to incorporate LGBTQ-inclusive education into their curriculum, ensuring that young students gained a comprehensive understanding of LGBTQ history, rights, and experiences.

By normalizing discussions around LGBTQ topics within academia, Barco Isakson aimed to challenge societal norms and create a culture of acceptance and respect. He believed that education was a powerful tool for dismantling stereotypes, reducing prejudice, and fostering empathy. Through these collaborations, he encouraged a new generation of students to embrace diversity and advocate for equality.

Mentorship and Networking Opportunities

Barco Isakson understood the importance of mentorship and networking in nurturing young activists and preparing them for the challenges they would face. As part of his commitment to passing the torch, he established mentorship programs that connected experienced LGBTQ activists with aspiring ones.

These mentorship relationships provided guidance, support, and encouragement to young activists, helping them navigate the complexities of advocacy work. Through their mentors' experiences and wisdom, they gained valuable insights into effective strategies, learned from past mistakes, and developed their own unique approaches to activism.

In addition to mentorship programs, Barco Isakson organized networking events that brought together LGBTQ activists from different generations. These events served as platforms for intergenerational dialogue, allowing experienced activists to share their wisdom and younger activists to learn from their predecessors' experiences. By creating spaces for these connections, Barco Isakson aimed to strengthen the LGBTQ community and foster a sense of unity and solidarity among activists of all ages.

Inspiring Through Personal Stories

Barco Isakson recognized that personal stories have the power to inspire and create lasting change. He actively shared his own journey as an LGBTQ activist, emphasizing the challenges he faced and the victories he achieved. By openly discussing his experiences, he aimed to inspire and empower young individuals who were navigating their own paths of self-discovery and activism.

Barco Isakson also encouraged other LGBTQ individuals to share their stories. He believed that by amplifying diverse narratives, the broader society would develop a deeper understanding of the LGBTQ community's struggles, triumphs, and aspirations. Through platforms such as social media, storytelling events, and publications, he created opportunities for LGBTQ individuals to tell their stories and raise awareness about the issues they faced.

Championing Intersectionality

Barco Isakson recognized that the fight for LGBTQ rights intersected with other social justice movements. He actively advocated for intersectionality and encouraged young activists to engage with issues beyond LGBTQ rights. By acknowledging and addressing the interconnectedness of various forms of oppression, he believed that progress in one area would benefit marginalized communities as a whole.

To pass the torch to the next generation, Barco Isakson ensured that young activists understood the importance of coalition-building and solidarity. He organized workshops and conferences that facilitated dialogue between LGBTQ activists and those working on issues such as racial justice, gender equality, and economic empowerment. Through these initiatives, he encouraged a holistic approach to activism and empowered young individuals to work towards a more just and inclusive society.

SECTION 1: THE END OF AN ERA 141

In conclusion, passing the torch to the next generation was a central focus of Virgilio Barco Isakson's advocacy work. Through youth empowerment programs, collaboration with educational institutions, mentorship and networking opportunities, sharing personal stories, and championing intersectionality, he ensured that future LGBTQ activists were equipped with the knowledge, skills, and inspiration needed to continue the fight for equality. Barco Isakson's commitment to nurturing the next generation of leaders serves as a testament to his enduring legacy and the ongoing progress of LGBTQ activism in Colombia.

Subsection 5: Transitioning to Life After Politics

After a remarkable career in politics, Virgilio Barco Isakson faced a pivotal moment in his life - transitioning to life after politics. Stepping down as the Mayor of Bogotá marked both an end and a new beginning. This subsection explores the challenges, reflections, and future endeavors that awaited Virgilio in his post-political journey.

Stepping Down as Mayor

Leaving behind a role he had dedicated so much of his life to was not an easy decision for Virgilio Barco Isakson. The decision to step down as Mayor of Bogotá was met with mixed emotions. While he knew it was time to pass the torch, he couldn't deny feeling a sense of loss. The city had become his home, and the people his family. However, Virgilio recognized that there were other ways he could continue his impactful work.

Reflections on a Term Filled with Milestones

During his term as mayor, Virgilio Barco Isakson achieved numerous milestones for the LGBTQ community and the city of Bogotá. As he transitioned to life after politics, he took time to reflect on the progress made and the challenges yet to overcome. With a deep sense of accomplishment, Virgilio saw the transformation he had initiated, but also recognized that the fight for LGBTQ rights was far from over.

In this period of reflection, Virgilio started to lay the foundation for his ongoing advocacy work. This introspection guided his decisions and renewed his focus on human rights advocacy as a whole. He took stock of the lessons learned, the successes achieved, and the opportunities for growth.

Shifting Focus to Human Rights Advocacy

Virgilio's exit from politics did not mean his voice would go silent. On the contrary, he embraced the opportunity to shift his focus to a broader range of human rights issues. Virgilio became an avid supporter of organizations and initiatives dedicated to fighting for equality, education, healthcare, and social justice.

Recognizing the interconnections between various marginalized communities, he joined forces with NGOs and human rights organizations around the globe. Virgilio understood that change required collaboration and unity. By leveraging his platform and influence, he aimed to amplify the voices of those fighting for justice and equality.

Passing the Torch to the Next Generation

While Virgilio Barco Isakson transitioned out of politics, he knew that the fight for LGBTQ rights must continue. With a deep commitment to ensuring the momentum he had built would not fade, he focused on inspiring and empowering the next generation of leaders. Virgilio actively mentored young activists, providing guidance, support, and wisdom gained from his years in public service.

By nurturing future leaders, Virgilio aimed to create a sustainable movement that would persist long after his time in the political arena. He encouraged LGBTQ youth to find their voices, follow their passions, and actively engage in advocacy work. Virgilio firmly believed that the torch of change must always be passed to ensure progress.

Transitioning to Life After Politics

Transitioning from a career in politics to life after politics required not only adjustments but also rediscovering a sense of self. Virgilio Barco Isakson found solace in spending time with his loved ones, reconnecting with his passions for art and music, and engaging in the beauty of nature. He dedicated time to travel, explore different cultures, and broaden his horizons.

Moreover, Virgilio used his experience and knowledge to contribute to LGBTQ research and literature. He authored several influential books, sharing his insights and advocating for intersectionality within the LGBTQ movement. He became a sought-after speaker, captivating audiences with his powerful storytelling and inspiring others to embrace their own journeys of activism and self-discovery.

In his post-political life, Virgilio Barco Isakson embraced the power of self-care. He recognized the importance of balance and mental well-being, habits he had cultivated throughout his career. Virgilio understood that in order to

SECTION 1: THE END OF AN ERA 143

continue advocating effectively, he needed to take care of himself physically, mentally, and emotionally.

Leaving a Lasting Legacy

Through his transition to life after politics, Virgilio Barco Isakson left a lasting legacy. His dedication to LGBTQ rights, human rights advocacy, and the empowerment of future leaders ensured that his impact would transcend time. The Virgilio Barco Isakson LGBTQ Center was established to honor his memory and facilitate ongoing support for the community he fought tirelessly for.

The center serves as a space for community gatherings, workshops, and resources, offering support and guidance to LGBTQ individuals in need. Additionally, annual festivals and commemorations celebrate Virgilio's achievements, reminding future generations of the progress made and the work yet to be done.

Virgilio's voice continues to be heard through the ongoing influence he has on LGBTQ rights. His unwavering commitment to equality inspires activists worldwide, fueling the fire of change. The future of LGBTQ rights in Colombia is brighter because of his contributions, and the world at large continues to benefit from the lessons he taught through his activism and legacy.

The Power of Virgilio's Voice

Virgilio Barco Isakson's journey transcends his time in office. His voice remains a powerful force, serving as a guiding light for future generations. Through his ongoing influence, his ideas continue to shape the fight for LGBTQ rights.

Virgilio's legacy serves as a reminder that change begins with individuals who dare to speak up and challenge the status quo. His life story encourages everyone to embrace their unique journey, raise their voices, and fight for a more inclusive and accepting world.

With each person inspired by Virgilio's story, the collective strength of the LGBTQ community grows. The power of his voice lies not only in his achievements but in the spirit of hope and resilience he instills in those who continue the battle for equality.

Continuing the Fight for Equality

As the baton is passed from one generation to the next, the fight for LGBTQ equality goes on. Inspired by Virgilio Barco Isakson's legacy, activists and allies continue to champion equal rights across the globe. The struggle against discrimination and prejudice remains, both within Colombia and in countless communities around the world.

Through Virgilio's leadership and the cultural shift he spearheaded, the groundwork has been laid for ongoing progress. However, activists must remain vigilant, challenging systemic barriers and advocating for the rights of marginalized communities. By amplifying the voices of those who have been silenced, the fight for equality will persist.

Honoring Virgilio's Memory

The memory and impact of Virgilio Barco Isakson live on long after his time in politics. His unwavering dedication to human rights, inclusive legislation, and LGBTQ rights will forever be etched in the hearts of those he fought for.

From annual commemorations to educational initiatives, Virgilio's memory is honored through ongoing efforts to create a more equitable and inclusive society. The fight for justice and equality continues, fueled by the example of Virgilio's life and achievements.

Amplifying Virgilio's Message

To ensure Virgilio's legacy endures, it is crucial to amplify his message. This can be achieved through various means, such as documentaries, biographies, and educational programs that delve into the lessons learned from his activism. By sharing his experiences and insights, future generations can draw inspiration and continue the work he started.

Moreover, incorporating Virgilio's story into school curricula enables young minds to learn about the importance of LGBTQ rights and the impact of activism. By educating the next generation, we can foster a more accepting and inclusive society.

The Future of LGBTQ Activism in Colombia

As Virgilio Barco Isakson transitioned to life after politics, he left behind a legacy that continues to shape LGBTQ activism in Colombia. The future of the LGBTQ movement in the country holds immense potential, but it also faces challenges that demand ongoing perseverance.

Activists must remain mindful of the progress achieved while pushing back against setbacks and fighting for additional rights. Building bridges across diverse communities, reaching out to allies, and fostering dialogue are crucial components in creating lasting change.

SECTION 2: SOCIAL IMPACT AND CONTINUED ACTIVISM

The future of LGBTQ activism in Colombia relies on the tireless dedication of individuals who follow in Virgilio's footsteps. By standing united, the LGBTQ community and its allies can continue the fight for equality, ensuring that Virgilio's legacy is not only remembered but celebrated through tangible progress.

Acknowledging the Journey

Virgilio Barco Isakson's journey, as depicted in this biography, symbolizes the struggles, triumphs, and aspirations of LGBTQ activists in Colombia and beyond. It serves as a reminder of the power of perseverance, solidarity, and the unwavering pursuit of justice.

While the challenges faced by the LGBTQ community persist, the story of Virgilio Barco Isakson offers hope and encouragement. It reminds us that change is possible and that the fight for equality is an ongoing process that requires dedication, resilience, and a shared commitment to love and acceptance.

Through his transition to life after politics, Virgilio continued to make a difference, inspiring future generations to rise up and create a world where equality knows no boundaries. As readers, we are called to embrace the message of his life, amplify his voice, and work towards a future where discrimination and prejudice are but distant memories.

Forever united, we will continue to break barriers, celebrate diverse identities, and forge a path towards greater acceptance and inclusion. Virgilio Barco Isakson's story is one of unfiltered victory, and it is now our collective responsibility to carry that legacy forward, building a brighter future for LGBTQ individuals worldwide.

Section 2: Social Impact and Continued Activism

Subsection 1: Establishing LGBTQ Support Networks

Establishing LGBTQ support networks is a crucial step toward building a strong foundation for the LGBTQ community. These support networks serve as safe spaces where individuals can find understanding, acceptance, and resources to navigate the challenges they face. In this subsection, we will explore the importance of establishing LGBTQ support networks, the key elements they should include, and how they can be created and sustained.

The Importance of LGBTQ Support Networks

LGBTQ individuals often experience unique challenges, including discrimination, stigmatization, and lack of acceptance within society. Support networks provide a vital platform to address these issues and create a sense of belonging for LGBTQ individuals. These networks offer a range of benefits, including:

- Emotional support: LGBTQ support networks provide a space for individuals to share their experiences, feelings, and struggles with others who can relate and empathize. This emotional support can help alleviate feelings of isolation and promote mental well-being.

- Information and resources: Support networks serve as a valuable source of information about LGBTQ-specific issues, such as legal rights, healthcare resources, and community events. They can also connect individuals to relevant support services, organizations, and initiatives.

- Advocacy and empowerment: By establishing LGBTQ support networks, individuals are encouraged to become advocates for their rights and the rights of others. These networks empower individuals to challenge societal norms, advocate for policy changes, and promote inclusivity.

- Community building: Support networks foster a sense of community among LGBTQ individuals, creating opportunities for socializing, networking, and personal growth. Building strong connections within the community is essential for combating isolation and building resilience.

Key Elements of LGBTQ Support Networks

To establish effective LGBTQ support networks, it is essential to consider the following key elements:

1. Safe and inclusive spaces: LGBTQ support networks should prioritize creating safe and inclusive spaces that are free from discrimination, judgment, and harassment. It is crucial to establish guidelines and policies that promote respect, confidentiality, and equal participation for all members.

2. Education and awareness: Support networks should provide educational resources and workshops to raise awareness about LGBTQ issues, including sexual orientation, gender identity, and LGBTQ history. By enhancing

SECTION 2: SOCIAL IMPACT AND CONTINUED ACTIVISM   147

understanding, these networks encourage acceptance and allyship within wider communities.

3. Mental health support: LGBTQ individuals often face higher rates of mental health challenges, including depression and anxiety. Support networks should collaborate with mental health professionals to offer accessible counseling services and support groups tailored to the specific needs of LGBTQ individuals.

4. Intersectionality: LGBTQ support networks should recognize and address the intersectionality of identities and experiences within the community. This includes acknowledging the diverse backgrounds, cultures, and lived experiences of LGBTQ individuals, ensuring that support networks are inclusive and responsive to the needs of all individuals.

5. Collaboration and partnerships: To maximize impact and resources, LGBTQ support networks should collaborate with other community organizations, human rights advocates, and healthcare providers. These partnerships can facilitate information exchange, program development, and advocacy efforts.

Creating and Sustaining LGBTQ Support Networks

Establishing and sustaining LGBTQ support networks requires a collective effort from individuals, community organizations, and policymakers. Here are some steps to consider:

1. Needs assessment: Conduct a needs assessment within the LGBTQ community to identify the specific challenges and areas where support is lacking. This can involve surveys, focus groups, and consultations with community members and experts.

2. Community engagement: Engage with LGBTQ individuals and community organizations to raise awareness about the importance of support networks. Encourage participation and seek input to ensure the networks are responsive to the needs of the community.

3. Resource mobilization: Garner support from community organizations, philanthropic foundations, and government agencies to secure financial and logistical resources. Funding can be used to establish physical spaces, hire staff, and develop programs and services.

4. Training and capacity building: Provide training to support network staff and volunteers on LGBTQ issues, empathy, active listening, and mental health support. This ensures that individuals serving in these roles have the necessary skills and knowledge to effectively contribute to the support network.

5. Collaboration and networking: Foster collaboration with other LGBTQ support networks and community organizations to share resources, best practices, and advocacy efforts. This collaboration amplifies the impact of the support networks and promotes a unified front in fighting for LGBTQ rights and well-being.

Examples of LGBTQ Support Networks

Numerous successful LGBTQ support networks exist worldwide, each with its own unique approach. Here are a few notable examples:

- The Trevor Project (United States): Founded in 1998, this organization provides crisis intervention and suicide prevention services for LGBTQ youth. They offer a 24/7 helpline, online chat support, and educational resources to promote mental health and well-being.

- The Kaleidoscope Trust (United Kingdom): This organization works globally to uphold the rights of LGBTQ individuals, focusing on regions where LGBTQ rights are most at risk. They collaborate with local activists and organizations to provide advocacy, capacity building, and support for legal reform.

- Sangama (India): Sangama is an LGBTQ support network that focuses on the rights and well-being of LGBTQ individuals in India. They provide legal aid, healthcare services, community outreach, and conduct advocacy campaigns to challenge societal norms and promote inclusivity.

Tricks of the Trade

Building and sustaining LGBTQ support networks can be a challenging endeavor, but here are a few tricks to help make the process smoother:

- Utilize technology: Leverage social media platforms, websites, and online forums to facilitate communication, resource sharing, and community engagement. Online spaces can provide LGBTQ individuals with a sense of

SECTION 2: SOCIAL IMPACT AND CONTINUED ACTIVISM 149

support and connection, particularly in areas where physical support networks are limited.

- Engage allies: Encourage the involvement of allies, such as family members, friends, and community leaders. Allies play a crucial role in supporting LGBTQ individuals and can help amplify the impact of support networks by broadening their reach and influence.

- Empower youth leadership: Recognize the unique perspectives and strengths of LGBTQ youth and provide them with opportunities to take on leadership roles within support networks. Youth leadership ensures the longevity and relevance of support networks by incorporating evolving needs and perspectives.

Establishing LGBTQ support networks is an ongoing process that requires dedication, collaboration, and a commitment to inclusivity. By providing safe spaces, resources, and advocacy, these networks empower LGBTQ individuals, promote societal acceptance, and contribute to the overall well-being of the LGBTQ community.

Subsection 2: Inspiring Future Leaders

In this section, we explore the importance of inspiring future leaders in the LGBTQ movement. It is not enough to fight for rights and bring about change in the present; we must also ensure that there is a new generation of vibrant activists who will continue the fight for equality and justice. We will delve into the strategies and initiatives that can inspire and empower young individuals to become leaders in the LGBTQ community.

Empowering LGBTQ Youth

One of the key aspects of inspiring future leaders is empowering LGBTQ youth. Young people are the driving force behind social change, and it is crucial to provide them with the tools and resources they need to become leaders in their own right. This starts with creating safe spaces where young LGBTQ individuals can express themselves and connect with others who share their experiences. LGBTQ youth organizations and support networks play a vital role in fostering empowerment and leadership skills among young members of the community.

Additionally, mentorship programs can play a significant role in inspiring and empowering future leaders. Matching young individuals with experienced mentors who have made significant contributions to the LGBTQ movement can provide guidance, support, and valuable insights. Mentorship allows young people to learn from the experiences of those who have pioneered change and helps them develop their own unique leadership qualities.

Educational Initiatives

Education plays a fundamental role in shaping the mindset of future leaders. Incorporating LGBTQ-related topics into school curricula is a powerful way to normalize the experiences of LGBTQ individuals and foster acceptance among young people. By promoting LGBTQ-inclusive education, we can create a more empathetic and knowledgeable society.

Additionally, promoting LGBTQ history and heritage is a powerful way to inspire future leaders. By highlighting the contributions of LGBTQ activists, artists, and thinkers throughout history, we can show young individuals that their experiences are part of a rich and vibrant legacy. This can help young LGBTQ individuals feel a sense of pride in their identities and encourage them to make their mark on the world.

Leadership Development Programs

To inspire future leaders, it is crucial to provide opportunities for skill development and leadership training. Leadership development programs specifically designed for LGBTQ individuals can equip them with the necessary tools and knowledge to effect change in their communities.

These programs can focus on fostering essential leadership skills such as communication, collaboration, and problem-solving. They can also provide training in areas like advocacy, public speaking, and community organizing. By imparting these skills, we empower young leaders to take action and make a difference in the LGBTQ movement.

Representation and Visibility

Representation matters. To inspire future leaders, it is essential to provide them with role models who reflect their identities and experiences. LGBTQ individuals in positions of power and influence serve as powerful symbols of possibility, showing young people that they too can achieve great things.

Promoting LGBTQ representation across various fields and industries, including politics, media, arts, and sciences, is crucial. By showcasing successful

LGBTQ voices and stories, we inspire young individuals to aspire to leadership positions and realize their full potential.

The Power of Storytelling

Finally, storytelling plays a vital role in inspiring future leaders. Personal narratives have the power to humanize the LGBTQ experience and create empathy among listeners. Sharing personal stories of triumph and resilience can inspire young people to embrace their identities and pursue leadership roles.

Encouraging individuals to share their stories through writing, art, or public speaking empowers them to become agents of change. These narratives not only help others understand the LGBTQ experience but also provide guidance and inspiration for those who may be struggling with their own identities.

In conclusion, inspiring future leaders in the LGBTQ movement requires a multi-faceted approach. By empowering LGBTQ youth, providing inclusive education, offering leadership development programs, promoting representation, and embracing the power of storytelling, we can ignite a new generation of passionate leaders who will continue the fight for equality and justice. It is our collective responsibility to nurture and support these emerging leaders, ensuring that the flame of activism burns brightly for generations to come.

Subsection 3: Contributions to LGBTQ Research and Literature

In this subsection, we will explore the significant contributions made by Virgilio Barco Isakson to LGBTQ research and literature. His work in this area has been instrumental in advancing our understanding of LGBTQ issues and promoting awareness in the broader community. Through his groundbreaking research and compelling literary works, Barco Isakson has left an indelible mark on the LGBTQ community and the world.

Understanding LGBTQ History and Heritage

Barco Isakson's contributions to LGBTQ research include extensive studies on the history and heritage of the community. He dedicated himself to uncovering the hidden narratives of LGBTQ individuals throughout history, shedding light on the triumphs and struggles they faced. Through comprehensive archival research and oral history interviews, Barco Isakson brought forth stories that had long been silenced, forging a connection between past and present LGBTQ experiences.

By showcasing the rich heritage of LGBTQ individuals, Barco Isakson's research aimed to challenge societal norms and prejudices. He highlighted the

LGBTQ community's contributions to various fields, emphasizing their valuable presence in history and culture. Barco Isakson's work not only celebrated the resilience of LGBTQ individuals but also fostered pride and self-acceptance among present-day LGBTQ generations.

Literature as a Tool for Change

As an accomplished writer, Barco Isakson utilized literature as a powerful tool for change and advocacy. Through his novels, essays, and poetry, he amplified LGBTQ voices and experiences, offering diverse perspectives on the community's struggles and aspirations. Barco Isakson's literary works were known for their authenticity and emotional resonance, captivating readers from all walks of life.

One of his most renowned literary contributions was the groundbreaking novel "Shades of Love." This poignant and introspective work delved into the complexities of LGBTQ relationships, exploring themes of love, acceptance, and societal expectations. Through vivid character development and a compelling storyline, Barco Isakson challenged traditional notions of love and helped foster empathy and understanding of LGBTQ experiences.

Moreover, Barco Isakson's literary works served as a platform for raising awareness about LGBTQ issues and changing public perception. He fearlessly tackled taboo subjects and opened dialogue on topics such as discrimination, homophobia, and transgender rights. By bringing these issues to the forefront of literary discourse, Barco Isakson encouraged critical thinking and social change.

Advancing LGBTQ Studies and Scholarship

Barco Isakson also played a significant role in advancing LGBTQ studies as an academic discipline. He established scholarships and research grants to support LGBTQ scholars and their research endeavors. These initiatives not only provided financial assistance but also created spaces for LGBTQ academics to flourish and contribute to the body of knowledge surrounding LGBTQ issues.

Barco Isakson's commitment to LGBTQ studies extended beyond financial support. He actively promoted the inclusion of LGBTQ perspectives and theories in academic curricula, advocating for comprehensive LGBTQ education in schools and universities. By integrating LGBTQ research into mainstream academia, Barco Isakson dismantled barriers to knowledge and fostered a greater understanding of LGBTQ experiences among students and scholars alike.

Tackling Intersectionality in LGBTQ Research

An essential aspect of Barco Isakson's LGBTQ research was his emphasis on intersectionality. He recognized the interconnectedness of various forms of discrimination and oppression, collaborating with scholars from diverse backgrounds to explore the intersections of race, gender, class, and sexual orientation. Barco Isakson's work highlighted the unique challenges faced by LGBTQ individuals who exist at the intersections of multiple marginalized identities.

Through his research, Barco Isakson brought attention to the experiences of LGBTQ individuals who faced compounded forms of discrimination. By addressing these intersecting identities, he advocated for more inclusive and comprehensive approaches to LGBTQ research and activism. Barco Isakson's work paved the way for broader discussions on the diverse experiences of LGBTQ individuals and the need for intersectional advocacy.

Challenges and the Way Forward

While Barco Isakson's contributions to LGBTQ research and literature have brought about significant advancements, challenges remain. Limited funding for LGBTQ research, ongoing prejudices, and social barriers continue to impede progress in understanding LGBTQ experiences fully. It is crucial for future generations of researchers, activists, and scholars to build upon Barco Isakson's legacy, continuing to push the boundaries of knowledge and understanding.

To overcome these challenges, increased support for LGBTQ research, greater LGBTQ representation in academia, and ongoing collaboration across disciplines are necessary. By investing in LGBTQ studies and amplifying marginalized voices, we can continue transforming our understanding of LGBTQ issues and fostering positive change in society.

As we move forward, it is essential to remember and celebrate Barco Isakson's contributions to LGBTQ research and literature. By honoring his legacy, we can inspire future generations to push the boundaries of knowledge, challenge societal norms, and work relentlessly towards a more inclusive and accepting world for all LGBTQ individuals.

Subsection 4: Advocating for Intersectionality

Advocating for intersectionality is a crucial aspect of Virgilio Barco Isakson's LGBTQ activism. Intersectionality recognizes that individuals can experience different forms of oppression and discrimination based on the intersection of various social identities such as gender, race, sexuality, and class. In this subsection, we will explore the importance of intersectionality in the fight for LGBTQ rights and how Virgilio Barco Isakson championed this concept throughout his activism.

Understanding Intersectionality

Intersectionality is not just a theoretical framework, but a lived reality for many individuals. It acknowledges that identities and systems of oppression cannot be viewed in isolation, but rather, they intersect and interact with one another in complex ways. For example, LGBTQ individuals who also belong to marginalized racial or ethnic groups may face compounded discrimination and barriers to their rights.

Intersectionality emphasizes the need to address the overlapping systems of power and privilege that affect different communities. It challenges the notion of a single-issue struggle by recognizing that individuals may face multiple forms of oppression simultaneously. Recognizing and addressing intersectionality is essential to creating inclusive and effective LGBTQ activism.

Recognizing the Influence of Other Social Movements

Advocating for intersectionality means acknowledging and standing in solidarity with other social justice movements. Virgilio Barco Isakson recognized that struggles for LGBTQ rights cannot be separated from broader movements for racial justice, gender equality, economic equity, and other important causes. He actively collaborated with activists from diverse backgrounds to create a united front against all forms of discrimination.

By integrating intersectionality into his activism, Virgilio Barco Isakson was able to amplify the voices of marginalized communities and build coalitions that fought for justice on multiple fronts. This approach not only strengthened the LGBTQ movement, but also helped create a more inclusive and intersectional society.

Ensuring Inclusive Policies

Intersectionality demands the implementation of policies that address the specific needs and experiences of marginalized communities. Virgilio Barco Isakson understood the importance of inclusive policies that consider intersectional identities. He advocated for laws and regulations that protected not just LGBTQ individuals as a whole, but also recognized the unique challenges faced by LGBTQ individuals who are also racial minorities, socioeconomically disadvantaged, or disabled.

One example of Virgilio Barco Isakson's commitment to intersectionality was his campaign for affordable housing programs tailored to the needs of LGBTQ individuals from low-income backgrounds. By addressing the intersection between poverty and LGBTQ discrimination, he aimed to create meaningful change for individuals who face compounding disadvantages.

Educational Initiatives on Intersectionality

Education plays a vital role in advancing intersectional understanding and promoting inclusivity. Virgilio Barco Isakson advocated for the integration of intersectional perspectives into educational curricula at all levels. He understood that empowering future generations with knowledge about intersecting identities and systems of oppression was essential for building a more equitable society.

In collaboration with educational institutions, Virgilio Barco Isakson supported the development of inclusive teaching materials and programs that addressed intersectionality. He encouraged dialogue and debate on issues of power, privilege, and discrimination. By fostering an understanding of intersectionality from a young age, he aimed to promote empathy, tolerance, and active citizenship.

Overcoming Challenges and Building Alliances

Promoting intersectionality in activism also comes with challenges. It requires acknowledging and addressing the biases and blind spots that may exist within the LGBTQ community itself. Virgilio Barco Isakson recognized the need for introspection and constant learning within the movement. He worked to create spaces for dialogue and collaboration, where activists from different backgrounds could come together, learn from one another, and build stronger alliances.

To overcome challenges, Virgilio Barco Isakson emphasized the importance of building bridges between different social justice movements. By forging alliances with feminist organizations, racial justice groups, and disability rights advocates, he fostered a movement that recognized the interconnected nature of oppression and fought for justice on all fronts.

Conclusion

Advocating for intersectionality was a cornerstone of Virgilio Barco Isakson's LGBTQ activism. By recognizing the impact of intersecting identities and systems of oppression, he brought attention to the unique challenges faced by marginalized communities within the LGBTQ movement. Through his efforts, he emphasized the importance of unity, solidarity, and inclusive policy-making.

Intersectionality remains a critical aspect of LGBTQ activism today. By recognizing and addressing the ways in which different aspects of identity and power intersect, we can create more inclusive and effective movements for social change. As we continue the fight for LGBTQ rights, let us remember Virgilio Barco Isakson's legacy of advocating for intersectionality and work towards building a future where all individuals are valued and embraced.

Subsection 5: Remembering Virgilio's Legacy

In the wake of Virgilio Barco Isakson's groundbreaking activism and tireless dedication to the LGBTQ community, it is crucial to reflect on his enduring legacy. Virgilio's impact on Colombia and the world at large has been profound, forever shaping the landscape of LGBTQ rights and inspiring future generations of activists. Let us explore the ways in which Virgilio's legacy continues to shape the fight for equality and acceptance.

Honoring Virgilio's Memory

It is important to remember Virgilio as not just a political figure, but as a trailblazer who fearlessly championed LGBTQ rights in a time when they were severely marginalized. To honor his memory, several initiatives have been established to commemorate his legacy and ensure his work is never forgotten.

The Virgilio Barco Isakson LGBTQ Center stands as a testament to his enduring impact. This vibrant hub serves as a safe space for LGBTQ individuals, offering counseling services, support groups, and educational programs. It provides a platform for activists to gather, exchange ideas, and continue the fight for equality.

Furthermore, annual festivals and commemorations celebrate Virgilio's life and achievements. These events bring together LGBTQ individuals, allies, and activists to remember his courage and dedication. Through music, art, and various performances, they serve as a reminder of the progress made and the work that remains.

Virgilio's Ongoing Influence

Virgilio's influence on LGBTQ rights extends far beyond his term as Mayor of Bogotá. His groundbreaking policies and unwavering determination have inspired

… countless individuals and paved the way for significant progress. His work is particularly evident in the ongoing battle for equal rights in Colombia and globally.

Many current LGBTQ activists credit Virgilio as the catalyst for their involvement in advocacy. His unapologetic stance on equality and acceptance serves as a beacon of hope for those fighting for their rights. Through his persistent efforts, Virgilio has inspired a new generation of activists to carry on his legacy and fight for a more inclusive future.

Recognizing Virgilio's Achievements

Virgilio's achievements in the realm of LGBTQ rights are noteworthy and have transformed the landscape of Colombian society. He spearheaded significant policy changes that have had a lasting impact on the lives of LGBTQ individuals.

One of his most prominent achievements was the legalization of same-sex relationships. With Virgilio's unwavering support, Colombia became a trailblazer in South America by recognizing and protecting the rights of same-sex couples. This landmark decision provided a foundation for further progress in areas such as adoption and marriage equality.

Additionally, Virgilio's commitment to challenging gender norms and promoting LGBTQ inclusivity in education has had a profound impact. By advocating for inclusive curricula and LGBTQ-inclusive spaces in schools, he helped foster a more supportive environment for LGBTQ youth and promoted understanding and acceptance among students.

Annual Festivals and Commemorations

To ensure Virgilio's enduring memory and impact, annual festivals and commemorations are held to celebrate his life and achievements. These events serve as important reminders of the progress that has been made in LGBTQ rights and the work that remains to be done.

The Virgilio Barco Isakson LGBTQ Festival is a vibrant celebration that brings together people from all walks of life to honor Virgilio's accomplishments. It showcases the talents and achievements of LGBTQ individuals through music, art, performances, and community events. The festival not only fosters a sense of pride and unity but also serves as a platform to raise awareness about the challenges still faced by the LGBTQ community.

Remembering and Uplifting LGBTQ Activism

Remembering Virgilio's legacy goes beyond celebrating his achievements; it also involves uplifting and supporting current LGBTQ activism. By recognizing and amplifying the voices of LGBTQ activists, their work can continue to make a difference in society.

One way to achieve this is by establishing scholarships and grants in Virgilio's name. These initiatives provide financial support to aspiring LGBTQ activists, enabling them to further their education and continue their advocacy work. By investing in the next generation of activists, Virgilio's legacy can be perpetuated and strengthened.

Furthermore, supporting LGBTQ organizations and grassroots movements ensures that Virgilio's work lives on. Donating time, resources, or funds to these organizations helps sustain their efforts and push for further progress in LGBTQ rights.

Building a Brighter Future for LGBTQ Individuals

Ultimately, remembering Virgilio's legacy means actively working towards a brighter and more inclusive future for LGBTQ individuals. By continuing to fight for equal rights, challenging societal norms, and fostering acceptance, we can honor Virgilio's memory and solidify his impact.

Education is a powerful tool in this journey. By promoting LGBTQ-inclusive curricula and offering educational programs that raise awareness and foster understanding, we can break down barriers and combat prejudice. Educating future generations about the struggles and achievements of LGBTQ individuals ensures a more empathetic and accepting society.

In conclusion, Virgilio Barco Isakson's legacy transcends his time in office and continues to shape the fight for LGBTQ rights. Through initiatives that honor his memory, recognize his achievements, and uplift LGBTQ activism, we can ensure that his impact endures. By building upon his foundation and working towards a more inclusive future, we can celebrate Virgilio's enduring legacy and honor his commitment to love, acceptance, and equality.

Section 3: The Power of Virgilio's Voice

As a famous LGBTQ activist, Virgilio Barco Isakson had a profound and evolving influence on LGBTQ rights in Colombia. His tireless efforts and unwavering commitment to equality and justice helped shape the landscape of LGBTQ rights in the country, leaving a lasting legacy for future generations to build upon. In this subsection, we will explore the pivotal moments and strategies that contributed to Virgilio's evolving influence on LGBTQ rights.

1. A Voice for the Marginalized

Virgilio Barco Isakson recognized the importance of giving a voice to the marginalized and often ignored members of the LGBTQ community. He understood that true progress could only be achieved by amplifying the voices of those who had been silenced for far too long. Through his advocacy, Virgilio shed light on the challenges and struggles faced by LGBTQ individuals in Colombia, fostering compassion and understanding among the general public.

2. A Catalyst for Legal Change

Virgilio Barco Isakson played a crucial role in effecting legal change by pushing for progressive LGBTQ policies and legislation. He collaborated with like-minded lawmakers and activists to draft and advocate for bills that sought to protect LGBTQ rights. Virgilio's ability to navigate the political landscape and build coalitions allowed him to gain support for his initiatives and ultimately achieve tangible results.

3. Collaborations and Alliances

Recognizing the need for solidarity and unity, Virgilio Barco Isakson actively sought collaborations and alliances with other LGBTQ activists and organizations both within Colombia and on a global scale. By forging connections and sharing resources, ideas, and strategies, Virgilio contributed to the growing LGBTQ rights movement, showcasing the power of diverse voices united in a common cause.

4. Shifting Public Perceptions

Virgilio understood the importance of shifting public perceptions to create a more inclusive and accepting society for LGBTQ individuals. He utilized various platforms and media to challenge stereotypes and promote understanding, showcasing the diversity and strength of the LGBTQ community. Through public speaking engagements, interviews, and educational campaigns, Virgilio worked tirelessly to dismantle harmful myths and stereotypes, paving the way for greater acceptance and equality.

5. Holistic Approach to Activism

Virgilio Barco Isakson recognized that LGBTQ rights were intertwined with other social justice issues. He championed intersectionality, understanding that the struggle for LGBTQ rights intersected with issues such as gender equality, racial justice, and economic empowerment. By taking a holistic approach to activism, Virgilio broadened the scope of the LGBTQ rights movement and helped create spaces for collaboration with other marginalized communities.

6. Empowering LGBTQ Youth

One of Virgilio's key focuses was empowering LGBTQ youth. He understood the importance of providing support, resources, and safe spaces for young LGBTQ individuals to be their authentic selves. Through mentorship programs, awareness campaigns, and educational initiatives, Virgilio worked to ensure that LGBTQ youth had access to the tools and opportunities needed to thrive.

7. Challenging Discrimination and Violence

Virgilio Barco Isakson actively advocated for policies and initiatives aimed at challenging discrimination and violence against LGBTQ individuals. He raised awareness about hate crimes and pushed for the implementation of robust anti-discrimination laws. By shining a light on the experiences and vulnerabilities faced by LGBTQ individuals, Virgilio fueled conversations and action to create a safer and more equitable society.

In conclusion, Virgilio Barco Isakson's evolving influence on LGBTQ rights in Colombia can be attributed to his ability to give a voice to the marginalized, effect legal change, build collaborations and alliances, shift public perceptions, embrace intersectionality, empower LGBTQ youth, and challenge discrimination and violence. His legacy serves as a constant reminder of the power of activism and the importance of fighting for equality and justice for all. As we continue the fight for LGBTQ rights, we honor Virgilio's contributions and draw inspiration from his relentless pursuit of a more inclusive and accepting society.

Subsection 2: Continuing the Fight for Equality

In this section, we delve into Virgilio Barco Isakson's unwavering commitment to the ongoing fight for equality. Even after leaving office, Virgilio remained actively involved in advocating for LGBTQ rights and ensuring that the progress made during his tenure as mayor of Bogotá was not undone. This subsection explores the various ways he continued to make a difference and inspire change.

The Power of Education

Virgilio understood that education is a key element in achieving lasting change. He recognized the need for comprehensive and inclusive LGBTQ education in schools and universities. Through his foundation, Virgilio worked tirelessly to develop educational resources that promote acceptance, respect, and understanding of diverse gender and sexual identities.

One of his initiatives was the creation of the LGBTQ-inclusive curriculum, which aimed to raise awareness among students and teachers about the struggles and contributions of LGBTQ individuals throughout history. This curriculum emphasized the importance of empathy and solidarity, challenging societal norms and fostering a supportive environment for LGBTQ students.

Additionally, Virgilio advocated for the implementation of LGBTQ support groups in schools and universities, providing a safe space for students to share their experiences, seek guidance, and offer support to one another. By actively engaging with educational institutions, Virgilio aimed to ensure that future generations are equipped with the knowledge and tools to continue the fight for equality.

Empowering LGBTQ Youth

Recognizing the unique challenges faced by LGBTQ youth, Virgilio dedicated himself to empowering and uplifting this marginalized group. Through his foundation, he organized mentorship programs, leadership workshops, and skills development initiatives specifically tailored to LGBTQ youth.

These programs aimed to provide support and guidance to LGBTQ individuals as they navigated their identities and sought to forge a path towards success. By connecting them with successful LGBTQ role models and providing resources and opportunities, Virgilio enabled LGBTQ youth to dream big and overcome barriers that stood in their way.

Furthermore, Virgilio was a vocal advocate for mental health awareness within the LGBTQ community, recognizing the often disproportionate rates of mental health issues among queer individuals. He strived to destigmatize mental health discussions and pushed for accessible and LGBTQ-friendly mental health services across the country.

Collaboration and Solidarity

Virgilio firmly believed in the power of collaboration and solidarity in achieving meaningful change. He actively sought partnerships with local LGBTQ organizations, human rights NGOs, and other social justice movements to amplify their collective impact.

Through these collaborations, Virgilio aimed to share resources, knowledge, and strategies to enhance the progress of LGBTQ rights both locally and globally. He recognized that true change could only be achieved by addressing the interconnected nature of various forms of oppression and discrimination.

Virgilio also encouraged LGBTQ activists and organizations in other countries to share their experiences and strategies, fostering a sense of global solidarity in the fight for equality. He regularly participated in international conferences and spoke out about the importance of cross-border collaboration and learning from one another's successes and challenges.

Inspiring Future Activists

As an influential LGBTQ activist, Virgilio recognized the need to inspire and support the next generation of activists. He actively mentored young individuals passionate about LGBTQ rights, nurturing their potential and providing guidance and resources to amplify their voices.

Through public speaking engagements, workshops, and the publication of his memoir, Virgilio shared his personal journey and the lessons he learned along the way. He emphasized the importance of resilience, perseverance, and the power of collective action in effecting change.

Virgilio's legacy continues to inspire individuals, fostering a new wave of LGBTQ activists dedicated to advocating for equality and justice. His story serves as a reminder that activism is not limited to one person or one moment in time but is a continuous fight that requires the commitment and collective effort of many.

Remembering Virgilio's Legacy

To honor Virgilio's contributions and ensure that his legacy lives on, several commemorative events and initiatives have been established. Every year, on the anniversary of his passing, LGBTQ communities gather to celebrate his life and achievements, remembering the impact he had on their lives.

The Virgilio Barco Isakson LGBTQ Center was established in Bogotá, serving as a hub for LGBTQ activism, education, and support. This center provides resources, counseling services, and a physical space for community members to come together and continue the fight for equality.

Moreover, Virgilio's memoir, "Unfiltered Victory," serves as an enduring source of inspiration for LGBTQ individuals and activists worldwide. It chronicles his remarkable journey and offers valuable insights into the challenges and triumphs of LGBTQ activism.

Through these initiatives, Virgilio's memory lives on, ensuring that his fight for equality continues to inspire future generations, and his impact on LGBTQ rights in Colombia and beyond is never forgotten.

A Hopeful Road Ahead

While Virgilio's legacy is a testament to the progress made in LGBTQ rights, there is still much work to be done. In this final subsection of the book, we explore the ongoing challenges faced by LGBTQ communities globally and the promising avenues for future activism.

We examine the progress and setbacks in LGBTQ rights globally, highlighting the importance of intersectional advocacy and the need to address the intersecting forms of discrimination faced by LGBTQ individuals. We delve into the opportunities and risks presented by the digital age, exploring how online platforms can be harnessed for activism while navigating the dangers they pose.

Furthermore, we discuss the importance of sustaining equality movements and the role that allies play in creating an inclusive society. We provide practical tools and resources for individuals to engage in activism and education in their own communities.

In this hopeful conclusion to the book, we emphasize that the fight for LGBTQ rights is far from over. We encourage readers to join the ongoing struggle for equality, building upon Virgilio's legacy and ensuring a future where love is truly love, and acceptance knows no bounds.

Subsection 3: Honoring Virgilio's Memory

In this subsection, we will explore the various ways in which Virgilio Barco Isakson's memory and legacy continue to be honored. From annual commemorations to the establishment of institutions that uphold his vision, the impact of his work lives on in the hearts and minds of people around the world.

Annual Commemorations

To celebrate Virgilio Barco Isakson's life and contributions, an annual commemoration is held on the anniversary of his passing. This event brings together LGBTQ activists, allies, and community members to honor his memory and recommit to the ongoing fight for LGBTQ rights. The commemoration includes guest speakers, performances, and a reflection on the progress made since Virgilio's time as mayor. It serves as a reminder of the importance of his work and the continued effort needed to achieve full equality for all.

The Virgilio Barco Isakson LGBTQ Center

In order to ensure that Virgilio's legacy endures, the Virgilio Barco Isakson LGBTQ Center was established. Located in the heart of Bogotá, this center serves as a hub for LGBTQ activism, advocacy, and support. Open to all members of the LGBTQ community, it provides a safe space for people to gather, engage in dialogue, and access resources. The center offers a wide range of services, including counseling, legal assistance, and educational workshops. By providing these vital resources, the center continues to uplift Virgilio's memory and empower LGBTQ individuals to live authentically and fearlessly.

Virgilio Barco Isakson Scholarships

In recognition of Virgilio's commitment to education and the empowerment of marginalized communities, the Virgilio Barco Isakson Scholarships were established. These scholarships aim to support LGBTQ students from low-income backgrounds who demonstrate academic excellence and a passion for social justice. By providing financial assistance, mentorship, and networking opportunities, the scholarships aim to remove barriers to higher education and empower young LGBTQ individuals to become future change-makers. The recipients of these scholarships carry Virgilio's spirit forward, embodying his dedication to equality, education, and activism.

Virgilio Barco Isakson Memorial Park

To celebrate Virgilio's love for the environment and his belief in the importance of public spaces, the Virgilio Barco Isakson Memorial Park was created. This park is a sprawling green oasis in the heart of Bogotá, providing a sanctuary for both locals and visitors to connect with nature. It features walking paths, picnic areas, and beautiful gardens. The park also includes a memorial statue of Virgilio, honoring his contributions to LGBTQ rights and serving as a reminder of the continued fight for equality.

A Living Legacy

While these physical tributes serve as reminders of Virgilio's legacy, it is important to remember that his impact extends far beyond their boundaries. His influence continues to inspire LGBTQ activists and allies across the globe, and his message of love, acceptance, and equality lives on in the hearts and minds of those who are dedicated to creating a more inclusive world. The true honor to Virgilio's memory lies in the actions we take, the conversations we spark, and the progress we make in the ongoing fight for LGBTQ rights.

Beyond Memorials: Taking Action

It is not enough to simply honor Virgilio's memory through memorials and ceremonies. The most meaningful way to pay tribute to his legacy is by taking action and continuing the work that he started. This means advocating for LGBTQ rights in our communities, challenging discriminatory practices, and supporting organizations that fight for equality. It means having difficult conversations with family members, friends, and colleagues to educate and promote acceptance. It means amplifying LGBTQ voices and experiences, and working towards a future where everyone is treated with dignity and respect, regardless of their sexual orientation or gender identity.

A Lasting Impact

Virgilio's memory will forever be associated with monumental advancements in LGBTQ rights in Colombia. His dedication, resilience, and unwavering activism have made a lasting impact on the lives of countless individuals. By honoring his memory, we acknowledge the progress made and the work that still lies ahead. By carrying his torch, we ensure that his legacy of love, acceptance, and equality continues to shine brightly, guiding us towards a future where LGBTQ rights are fully realized and celebrated.

Remembering Virgilio

As we reflect on Virgilio Barco Isakson's life and work, let us remember his unwavering commitment to justice, his courage in the face of adversity, and his relentless pursuit of equality. Let us honor his memory not only through ceremonies and monuments but through continued action, advocacy, and love. By doing so, we can ensure that his transformative impact on LGBTQ rights in Colombia and beyond is never forgotten. Together, we will continue to build a future where love is love, and where all individuals are treated with the dignity and respect they deserve.

Subsection 4: Amplifying Virgilio's Message

In this subsection, we delve into the various strategies and methods Virgilio Barco Isakson employed to amplify his message and create a lasting impact on LGBTQ rights in Colombia. Virgilio recognized that in order to effect change, he needed to reach a wide audience and inspire others to join the fight for equality. Through his innovative approach to advocacy and his ability to connect with people from all walks of life, Virgilio made waves in Colombian society and beyond.

Engaging the Power of Media

Media has the potential to shape public opinion and challenge societal norms. Virgilio understood this, and he utilized various media platforms to amplify his message. He engaged with journalists, writers, and filmmakers to ensure accurate representation of LGBTQ individuals in the media. He promoted documentaries and films that highlighted the struggles and triumphs of the LGBTQ community, humanizing their experiences and fostering empathy and understanding.

To further amplify his message, Virgilio hosted radio and TV shows dedicated to LGBTQ issues. These platforms provided a space for open dialogue, allowing LGBTQ individuals to share their stories and experiences. Through these mediums, Virgilio was able to reach millions of people, challenging stereotypes and sparking national conversations about equality.

Harnessing the Power of Social Media

As technology advanced, Virgilio recognized the potential of social media in amplifying his message. He embraced platforms like Twitter, Instagram, and Facebook to engage directly with the public, sharing informative content, inspiring stories, and calls to action. With a strong online presence, Virgilio was able to reach individuals beyond the borders of Colombia, inspiring a global audience to join the fight for LGBTQ rights.

Virgilio also utilized social media to build online communities and foster dialogue. He encouraged LGBTQ individuals to share their experiences, creating an online support system that empowered individuals to embrace their authentic selves. Through social media, Virgilio fostered a sense of unity and mobilized people to take action in their own communities.

Collaborating with Influencers and Celebrities

Virgilio understood the power of influential voices in mobilizing public support. He collaborated with both local and international influencers, celebrities, and public figures who shared his passion for LGBTQ rights. By partnering with individuals who had large platforms and significant followings, Virgilio was able to reach diverse audiences and gain widespread support.

These collaborations took various forms. Virgilio enlisted the help of artists and musicians in producing catchy and powerful anthems that spoke to the struggles faced by the LGBTQ community. He organized concerts and performances to raise awareness and funds for LGBTQ organizations. By leveraging the popularity and influence of these individuals, Virgilio successfully brought LGBTQ issues to the mainstream and generated widespread support.

Using Art and Culture as Tools for Advocacy

Art has the power to challenge norms, spark conversations, and change hearts and minds. Virgilio recognized the transformative potential of art and culture, and he actively supported and promoted LGBTQ artists and performers. He organized art showcases, theater productions, and cultural events that celebrated LGBTQ identities and experiences, effectively challenging stereotypes and fostering acceptance.

In addition, Virgilio collaborated with artists to create compelling visual campaigns that highlighted the diversity of the LGBTQ community. These campaigns aimed to shatter misconceptions and promote inclusivity. By merging art and activism, Virgilio ignited conversations, shifted perspectives, and fostered a greater sense of understanding and empathy.

Educational Programs and Workshops

Education is vital in creating lasting change. Virgilio recognized the need for LGBTQ-inclusive education to challenge discriminatory attitudes and promote acceptance. He spearheaded the development of educational programs and workshops that focused on LGBTQ history, rights, and experiences. These programs were implemented in schools and universities, empowering students with knowledge and promoting a culture of respect and inclusivity.

Furthermore, Virgilio collaborated with educators and experts to develop comprehensive resources for teaching LGBTQ-inclusive curricula. These resources provided guidance and tools for educators to address LGBTQ issues in an age-appropriate and sensitive manner. By embedding LGBTQ education in the curriculum, Virgilio ensured that future generations would be more accepting and supportive of LGBTQ rights.

Unconventional Approach: LGBTQ Pride Carnival

As part of his mission to foster unity and celebration within the LGBTQ community, Virgilio organized an extravagant LGBTQ Pride Carnival. This event brought together people from all walks of life, LGBTQ individuals and allies alike, to celebrate love, diversity, and acceptance. The Carnival featured vibrant parades, music, dance, and cultural performances that showcased the rich LGBTQ heritage.

The Pride Carnival served as a powerful platform for visibility and empowerment. It not only provided a space for the LGBTQ community to express themselves freely but also attracted international attention. The impact of the Carnival went beyond the celebration itself, allowing Virgilio to engage with a wider audience and make the LGBTQ rights movement more visible and accessible to all.

Summary

Virgilio Barco Isakson's ability to amplify his message was essential in driving change and transforming LGBTQ rights in Colombia. Through media engagement, social media utilization, collaborations with influential voices, art and culture advocacy, educational programs, and the creation of the LGBTQ Pride Carnival, Virgilio effectively broadened his reach and garnered support on both a national and international scale. By employing these innovative strategies, Virgilio left an indelible mark on LGBTQ activism and paved the way for progress and equality in Colombia and beyond.

Subsection 5: The Future of LGBTQ Activism in Colombia

In this final subsection, we explore the future of LGBTQ activism in Colombia and the challenges and opportunities that lie ahead. As we look to build a more inclusive and equitable society, the fight for LGBTQ rights continues to evolve and expand. While significant progress has been made, there is still much work to be done to ensure full equality for all.

Creating Lasting Change

The future of LGBTQ activism in Colombia hinges on the creation of lasting change that goes beyond legislation and policy. It requires shifting societal attitudes and beliefs to foster true acceptance and inclusivity. This starts with education at all levels, from schools to workplaces, promoting sensitivity and understanding of LGBTQ issues. It also involves breaking down stereotypes and challenging harmful narratives that perpetuate discrimination.

One key aspect of creating lasting change is through allyship. It is not enough for the LGBTQ community to fight for their rights alone; they need strong allies who understand the importance of equality and are willing to stand up against injustice. Through education and awareness, we can cultivate a society where everyone, regardless of their sexual orientation or gender identity, feels supported and safe.

Intersectionality and Inclusivity

As we look to the future, it is essential to recognize the intersections of LGBTQ rights with other social justice movements. LGBTQ individuals exist within diverse communities with varying experiences of privilege and marginalization. Therefore, advocating for LGBTQ rights must be intersectional, encompassing the struggles faced by LGBTQ people of color, individuals with disabilities, and other marginalized groups.

By embracing intersectionality, we can strengthen the LGBTQ movement and create a more inclusive framework for activism. This entails amplifying the voices and experiences of underrepresented LGBTQ individuals and working in collaboration with other social justice movements. Recognizing and addressing the unique challenges faced by different communities will lead to more comprehensive and effective advocacy.

Leveraging Technology and Social Media

In the digital age, technology and social media play a crucial role in shaping public opinion and facilitating activism. The future of LGBTQ activism in Colombia must harness the power of these platforms to raise awareness and mobilize support. Social media campaigns can reach vast audiences, sharing stories of LGBTQ individuals and their struggles for equality.

Online platforms also provide spaces for organizing and connecting with like-minded individuals. Online support networks and communities can be invaluable resources for LGBTQ individuals in Colombia, offering a sense of belonging and solidarity. By leveraging technology and social media, activists can create virtual safe spaces, organize events, and disseminate vital information to promote and advance LGBTQ rights.

Addressing Mental Health and Well-being

The future of LGBTQ activism in Colombia must prioritize the mental health and well-being of LGBTQ individuals. Discrimination, violence, and societal pressures can significantly impact mental health outcomes for LGBTQ individuals. Advocacy efforts need to be holistic, addressing not only legal and policy changes but also providing resources and support structures for mental health services.

This involves working collaboratively with healthcare providers to develop LGBTQ-inclusive mental healthcare services. It also includes creating safe spaces and support networks where LGBTQ individuals can find community and access the resources they need. By addressing mental health, activists can ensure that the fight for LGBTQ rights encompasses the overall well-being of individuals.

A Hopeful Road Ahead

As we conclude this section on the future of LGBTQ activism in Colombia, we are filled with hope and determination. While challenges persist, the progress made thus far provides a strong foundation for continued advocacy and change. By embracing education, intersectionality, technology, mental health support, and allyship, we can work towards a future where LGBTQ individuals in Colombia can live their lives authentically and without fear of discrimination.

The road ahead may be long, but with unwavering commitment and collective action, we can create a society that celebrates and upholds the rights of every individual, regardless of their sexual orientation or gender identity. Let us come together, united in our pursuit of equality and justice, to ensure that the future of LGBTQ activism in Colombia is brighter than ever before.

Remember, love is love, and together, we will make history.

Chapter 5: Forever United

Chapter 5: Forever United

Chapter 5: Forever United

In this chapter, we delve into the lasting impact of Virgilio Barco Isakson's journey and the united front that continues to fight for LGBTQ rights. From personal testimonies to societal transformations, we explore how Virgilio's activism has shaped the landscape of equality and love. With a call to action and a focus on a brighter future, we celebrate his enduring legacy.

Subsection 1: Personal Testimonies of Lives Changed

Virgilio Barco Isakson's unwavering dedication to LGBTQ rights has touched countless lives, and personal testimonies stand as powerful testaments to his impact. In this subsection, we hear from individuals whose lives have been changed by Virgilio's activism.

One such testimony comes from María, a transgender woman who had struggled with discrimination and marginalization. Through Virgilio's efforts, she found hope and empowerment. "Virgilio's fight for transgender rights gave me the courage to embrace my true self and live my life authentically," María shares. "His unwavering support and advocacy helped create a more inclusive society where LGBTQ individuals can thrive."

Additionally, we hear from Carlos, a gay man who faced rejection and isolation from his family. Virgilio's work in promoting acceptance and love within families inspired Carlos to approach his loved ones again. "Because of Virgilio's message of unity and understanding, my family and I were able to bridge the divide. We now celebrate our love and support one another unconditionally," Carlos proclaims.

These personal testimonies highlight how Virgilio's activism has not only transformed individuals' lives but also strengthened relationships and fostered acceptance within families and communities.

Subsection 2: Virgilio's Influence on LGBTQ Icons

Virgilio Barco Isakson's impact extends beyond his direct advocacy work, influencing LGBTQ icons who have continued the fight for equality. In this subsection, we explore the profound influence Virgilio has had on renowned figures within the LGBTQ community.

One of these icons is Rosa, a prominent LGBTQ activist and artist. Inspired by Virgilio's fearless leadership, Rosa has used her platform to amplify LGBTQ voices and challenge societal norms. "Virgilio's courage and determination showed me the importance of using art as a tool for change. His activism paved the way for artists like me to express ourselves authentically and unapologetically," Rosa explains.

Another influential figure shaped by Virgilio's advocacy is Mateo, a transgender actor who has become a symbol of representation and visibility. Mateo credits Virgilio for paving the way for transgender individuals in the entertainment industry. "Virgilio's fight for transgender rights opened doors for us. He showed me that I could pursue my dreams and be proud of my authentic self," Mateo declares.

Through the stories of Rosa, Mateo, and many other LGBTQ icons, we witness the enduring legacy of Virgilio Barco Isakson and his ongoing influence on the fight for equality.

Subsection 3: Cultural and Social Transformations

Virgilio Barco Isakson's activism has sparked significant cultural and social transformations in Colombia. In this subsection, we explore the societal shifts that his fight for LGBTQ rights has brought about.

One notable transformation is the increased visibility and representation of LGBTQ individuals in media and popular culture. LGBTQ characters are now portrayed more authentically and positively, breaking stereotypes and challenging societal norms. Audiences are engaging with diverse narratives that promote understanding and acceptance, thanks to Virgilio's advocacy for LGBTQ representation.

Furthermore, societal attitudes toward LGBTQ individuals have markedly shifted. Discrimination and prejudice have been met with growing resistance and intolerance. As a result of Virgilio's tireless work, Colombian society has become more inclusive and accepting, embracing the diversity and human rights of the LGBTQ community.

These cultural and social transformations highlight the profound impact of Virgilio's activism, creating a society that celebrates and values the contributions of all its members.

Subsection 4: Looking Back on Virgilio's Achievements

In this subsection, we reflect on the achievements of Virgilio Barco Isakson throughout his remarkable journey. From groundbreaking policies to historic milestones, Virgilio's legacy is one of significant progress and lasting impact.

One of Virgilio's most notable achievements was the fight for equal rights, breaking down the barriers that inhibited LGBTQ individuals from fully participating in society. Through his advocacy, discriminatory laws and practices were challenged and repealed, laying the foundation for a more just and inclusive Colombia.

Virgilio also played a pivotal role in legalizing same-sex relationships, ensuring that love and commitment were recognized and protected by the law. This monumental achievement created a sense of validation and belonging for LGBTQ couples, fostering a society that rejects discrimination based on sexual orientation.

Additionally, Virgilio's relentless efforts to protect LGBTQ youth have transformed the landscape of education and support systems. Anti-bullying initiatives, inclusive curriculums, and safe spaces have been established, providing a nurturing environment for LGBTQ youth to grow and thrive.

By redefining the narrative of LGBTQ identity and challenging gender norms, Virgilio shattered societal expectations and championed the right to self-expression. This reshaping of cultural norms has ushered in an era of greater acceptance and diversity, empowering individuals to embrace their true selves without fear of judgment.

Subsection 5: Celebrating Virgilio's Enduring Legacy

In this final subsection, we celebrate the enduring legacy of Virgilio Barco Isakson and the everlasting impact of his activism. His unwavering dedication, vision, and determination have paved the way for a future where LGBTQ rights are not just acknowledged, but celebrated.

To honor his memory and ensure his work continues, organizations and activists have established annual festivals and commemorations. These events serve as a reminder of Virgilio's unwavering commitment to equality and as platforms to further advance the fight for LGBTQ rights.

In recognition of Virgilio's achievements, the Virgilio Barco Isakson LGBTQ Center was established as a hub for resources, support, and education. The center serves as a testament to Virgilio's vision of a united community that supports one another, and it continues to inspire future generations of activists.

Through ongoing advocacy and the amplification of Virgilio's message, his enduring legacy lives on. The fight for LGBTQ rights carries forward in the work of activists, researchers, and policy-makers who strive to build a society that is truly equal and inclusive.

As we look to the future, we acknowledge the challenges that lie ahead. However, inspired by Virgilio's example, we are driven to continue the fight, to uplift the voices of the marginalized, and to create a world where love, acceptance, and equality prevail.

Together, we can make history.

Section 1: The Impact of Virgilio's Journey

Subsection 1: Personal Testimonies of Lives Changed

In this subsection, we will dive into the personal testimonies of individuals whose lives were transformed by the LGBTQ activism of Virgilio Barco Isakson. These stories highlight the powerful impact of his work and serve as a testament to the importance of fighting for LGBTQ rights. Through these personal accounts, we gain a deeper understanding of the challenges faced by the LGBTQ community and the lasting legacy of Virgilio's activism.

Story 1: Carmen's Journey to Self-Acceptance

Carmen, a young transgender woman, recounts her experiences growing up in a small town on the outskirts of Bogotá. From an early age, she struggled with her gender identity, feeling trapped in a body that didn't align with her true self. The fear of rejection and discrimination forced her to hide her true identity, leading to a spiral of self-doubt and mental health struggles.

However, everything changed when Carmen discovered Virgilio Barco Isakson's activism. Through his advocacy for transgender rights and his relentless fight against discrimination, Carmen found hope and inspiration. She learned about the support available to LGBTQ individuals and realized that she was not alone in her journey.

Virgilio's dedication to creating inclusive spaces and promoting acceptance propelled Carmen to come out to her family and friends. While she faced initial

SECTION 1: THE IMPACT OF VIRGILIO'S JOURNEY

resistance and misunderstanding, Virgilio's influence provided her with the strength to persevere. With time, Carmen's loved ones began to understand and accept her for who she truly was, and she found a sense of belonging within her community.

Today, Carmen is a proud and confident advocate for transgender rights. She works closely with local LGBTQ organizations, striving to create a more inclusive society where every individual can live authentically and without fear.

Story 2: Luis' Escape from Homophobia

Luis, a young gay man, shares his story of growing up in a conservative neighborhood in Medellin. He vividly recalls the pervasive homophobia that dominated the community, making him feel like an outsider and forcing him to hide his true identity.

Virgilio Barco Isakson's activism became a beacon of hope for Luis, showing him that change was possible. Virgilio's unwavering commitment to fighting discrimination and championing LGBTQ rights inspired Luis to advocate for himself and his community.

Encouraged by Virgilio's efforts to challenge societal norms, Luis joined LGBTQ support groups and began organizing community events to promote understanding and acceptance. With each small step, he witnessed the transformation of his neighborhood, as attitudes gradually shifted towards a more inclusive and compassionate outlook.

Through his courage and determination, Luis eventually established an LGBTQ youth center in Medellin, providing a safe space for young individuals to celebrate their identities and access support services. His story is a testament to the profound impact that Virgilio's activism had on the lives of LGBTQ individuals, empowering them to overcome adversity and create a brighter future.

Story 3: Sofia's Triumph Against Discrimination

Sofia, a bisexual woman, bravely shares her experience of navigating discrimination within her family and the broader society. Growing up, Sofia struggled with her sexual orientation, feeling an immense pressure to conform to societal expectations.

It was through Virgilio Barco Isakson's advocacy for equal rights that Sofia found the strength and courage to embrace her true self. She learned about the importance of self-acceptance and self-love, regardless of societal judgments.

Buoyed by Virgilio's message of inclusivity, Sofia became an outspoken advocate for the LGBTQ community. She founded an LGBTQ support group in her local community, providing a nurturing environment for individuals like her to share their stories and find solace.

Sofia's journey wasn't without its challenges, as she faced resistance from her family and encountered discrimination in her workplace. However, the transformative power of Virgilio's activism and the sense of community she found within the LGBTQ movement fueled her determination to fight for acceptance and inclusivity.

Today, Sofia continues to champion LGBTQ rights, working with local policymakers and organizations to create legislation that protects and empowers the community. Her story is a testament to the profound impact Virgilio had in empowering individuals to rise above adversity and fight for their rights.

These personal testimonies are just a glimpse into the numerous lives that were transformed by Virgilio Barco Isakson's activism. They illustrate the power of resilience, acceptance, and the unwavering determination to fight for a more inclusive society. Through his work, Virgilio inspired a generation of activists and created a lasting legacy that continues to shape the future of LGBTQ rights in Colombia and beyond.

Subsection 2: Virgilio's Influence on LGBTQ Icons

Virgilio Barco Isakson's impact on the LGBTQ community extended far beyond legislation and policy. His leadership, bravery, and commitment to equality inspired a new generation of LGBTQ icons who continue his fight for inclusion and acceptance. In this subsection, we will explore the transformative influence Virgilio had on LGBTQ individuals who have become powerful advocates for their respective communities.

The Power of Visibility

One of the most significant ways Virgilio influenced LGBTQ icons was by creating a platform for visibility and representation. His groundbreaking policies and initiatives allowed LGBTQ individuals to come out of the shadows and celebrate their identities openly. As a result, the world witnessed a flourishing of LGBTQ artists, actors, musicians, and activists who found inspiration in Virgilio's leadership.

Antonella Rodriguez Antonella Rodriguez, a talented transgender actress and activist, found the courage to pursue her dreams and advocate for transgender rights in Colombia. Inspired by Virgilio's unwavering commitment to equality, Antonella became a prominent figure in the entertainment industry, using her platform to raise awareness about the struggles faced by transgender individuals.

SECTION 1: THE IMPACT OF VIRGILIO'S JOURNEY   177

Her fearless performances challenged societal norms and contributed to a more inclusive representation of transgender people in the media.

Santiago Gomez   Santiago Gomez, an acclaimed fashion designer, drew inspiration from Virgilio's push for gender inclusivity. Gomez's runway shows became platforms for self-expression, blurring the boundaries of traditional gender norms. By incorporating LGBTQ models and showcasing diverse identities, Gomez challenged the fashion industry to embrace inclusivity and prioritize authenticity. His designs celebrated the beauty in all forms and reinforced Virgilio's message of acceptance.

Carolina Ruiz   Carolina Ruiz, a renowned LGBTQ rights activist, credited Virgilio as the driving force behind her advocacy work. She established support networks for LGBTQ youth and provided a safe space where they could express themselves freely. Through educational programs and workshops, Carolina empowered LGBTQ individuals with the tools to navigate a world that often invalidated their identities. Her commitment to uplifting the community mirrored Virgilio's vision of a more inclusive society.

A Ripple Effect

Virgilio's influence on LGBTQ icons was not limited to Colombia alone. His impact resonated globally, inspiring activists and individuals from diverse backgrounds to fight for equality.

Marcelo Lima   Marcelo Lima, a transgender rights advocate from Brazil, drew strength from the progress Virgilio achieved in Colombia. Inspired by his example, Marcelo dedicated his life to combating discrimination and securing legal rights for transgender individuals in his own country. By creating empowering social media campaigns and organizing protests, Marcelo amplified Virgilio's message of inclusivity and acceptance, sparking conversations about transgender rights in Brazil and beyond.

Alice Chen   Alice Chen, a trailblazing LGBTQ advocate from Taiwan, found inspiration in Virgilio's political journey. Armed with Virgilio's wisdom and accomplishments, Alice campaigned tirelessly for marriage equality in Taiwan. Her activism united communities, challenged traditional beliefs, and contributed to the historic legalization of same-sex marriage in 2019. Just as Virgilio's leadership transformed Colombia, Alice's efforts reshaped Taiwanese society, demonstrating the ripple effect of Virgilio's influence.

Nadir Rahman Nadir Rahman, an LGBTQ youth activist from Bangladesh, faced immense adversity and violence due to his sexual orientation. However, Virgilio's story of resilience and triumph gave Nadir the strength to stand up for his rights and the rights of others. Through his advocacy work, Nadir promoted LGBTQ-inclusive education and fought against discriminatory laws and practices. Virgilio's impact reached even the most challenging corners of the world, inspiring individuals like Nadir to create change in their communities.

Continuing the Legacy

The influence of Virgilio Barco Isakson on LGBTQ icons continues to shape a new generation of activists and advocates. The torch he lit burns brightly in the hearts of those dedicated to realizing his vision of a more inclusive and accepting society.

You As a reader of this biography, you have the power to carry Virgilio's legacy forward. By educating yourself about LGBTQ issues, supporting LGBTQ individuals and organizations, and using your voice to advocate for equality, you become an icon in your own right. Your actions, no matter how small, contribute to the ongoing fight for LGBTQ rights and ensure Virgilio's influence endures.

Conclusion Virgilio Barco Isakson's impact on LGBTQ icons was profound and far-reaching. By creating spaces for visibility, representation, and empowerment, he inspired a new wave of activists, artists, and advocates who continue to push for progress. Through their collective efforts, the legacy of Virgilio lives on, creating a more inclusive and accepting world for LGBTQ individuals everywhere.

Subsection 3: Cultural and Social Transformations

In this subsection, we will explore the incredible cultural and social transformations that occurred as a result of Virgilio Barco Isakson's activism and the recognition of LGBTQ rights in Colombia. The impact of these transformations on society as a whole cannot be overstated, as they brought about a shift in the perception of LGBTQ individuals and challenged long-standing norms and prejudices.

SECTION 1: THE IMPACT OF VIRGILIO'S JOURNEY

Cultural Blurring of Gender and Sexuality

One of the most profound cultural transformations resulting from Virgilio Barco Isakson's activism was the blurring of traditional gender and sexuality concepts. Through his advocacy, he helped break down social barriers and challenge the rigidity of traditional gender roles.

Colombian society began to embrace the spectrum of gender identities and sexual orientations, leading to a more inclusive and diverse environment. This cultural shift fostered a sense of acceptance and openness, where individuals felt empowered to express their true selves without fear of judgment or discrimination.

As a result, artists and performers started exploring themes of gender fluidity, non-conformity, and alternative sexualities in their work, reflecting the changing cultural landscape. Colombian music, art, and literature showcased a vibrant mix of identities, challenging societal norms and promoting a culture of acceptance and respect.

Example:

One prominent example is a renowned Colombian artist, Isabel Jimenez, who became a symbol of gender fluidity and self-expression. Through her provocative artwork, Isabel challenged societal norms, questioning the traditional definitions of masculinity and femininity. Her powerful pieces challenged viewers to reimagine and celebrate the complexity of human identity, ultimately reshaping the national artistic landscape.

Increased LGBTQ Visibility in Media

Another significant cultural transformation brought about by Virgilio Barco Isakson's activism was the increased visibility of LGBTQ individuals in media. As society became more accepting of different sexual orientations and gender identities, mainstream media outlets began to represent LGBTQ characters and stories more authentically and positively.

Television shows, movies, and advertising campaigns started featuring LGBTQ characters and storylines, breaking the heteronormative mold that had dominated the media landscape for years. This increased representation helped foster empathy and understanding among the general population, challenging stereotypes and promoting acceptance.

Additionally, the rise of social media platforms provided a platform for LGBTQ voices to be heard. Virgilio Barco Isakson utilized these platforms to amplify his message and advocate for equal rights. The embracing of social media as a tool for activism led to a wave of LGBTQ youth finding support and inspiration, sparking a new generation of activists.

Example:

One groundbreaking Colombian television series, "Out and Proud," followed the lives of a diverse group of LGBTQ individuals navigating their personal and professional lives. The show received critical acclaim for its authentic representation and complex storytelling, helping to redefine societal perceptions of the LGBTQ community.

Promoting LGBTQ History and Heritage

Recognizing the importance of preserving LGBTQ history and heritage, Virgilio Barco Isakson advocated for the inclusion of LGBTQ narratives in educational curricula and public discourse. This push for historical recognition aimed to combat erasure and ensure that the contributions of LGBTQ individuals were acknowledged and celebrated.

By integrating LGBTQ history into education, Colombia began to raise awareness and promote understanding of the struggles and triumphs of the LGBTQ community. This inclusive approach not only empowered LGBTQ individuals with a sense of pride in their heritage but also promoted empathy and unity among all Colombians.

Furthermore, museums and cultural institutions began hosting exhibitions that highlighted LGBTQ art, history, and achievements. These initiatives aimed to erase the stigmatization of LGBTQ individuals while educating the public and fostering a sense of collective history.

Example:

The National Museum of Colombia launched an exhibition titled "Queering the Narrative: Embracing LGBTQ History." This groundbreaking exhibition showcased the untold stories of LGBTQ individuals throughout Colombian history, shedding light on their contributions to art, culture, politics, and science. By exhibiting these stories, the museum challenged societal perceptions and honored the LGBTQ community's resilience.

Creating LGBTQ-Inclusive Spaces

Virgilio Barco Isakson's activism led to the creation of LGBTQ-inclusive spaces across Colombia. These safe and inclusive environments served as gathering places for LGBTQ individuals, fostering a sense of belonging and community.

SECTION 1: THE IMPACT OF VIRGILIO'S JOURNEY

Public spaces, such as parks and plazas, were reimagined as LGBTQ-friendly zones where individuals could express their identities openly and without fear. This transformation not only provided physical safe spaces but also challenged societal biases and normalized LGBTQ presence within the broader community.

Moreover, LGBTQ centers and organizations flourished, providing support services and resources to the community. These centers were vital in promoting mental health, offering counseling, and providing educational workshops. They also played a crucial role in advocating for LGBTQ rights and social equality.

Example:

The "Open Hearts Center" in Bogotá became a hub for LGBTQ individuals seeking support and community. The center offered a range of services, including mental health counseling, job placement assistance, and educational programs. Its welcoming atmosphere and inclusive approach created a safe space where individuals could explore their identities and connect with others who shared similar experiences.

Challenging Prejudices through Art and Performance

Art and performance played a transformative role in challenging prejudices and sparking critical conversations about LGBTQ rights. Virgilio Barco Isakson recognized the power of artistic expression as a catalyst for change, and he actively supported LGBTQ artists and performers.

Through theater, dance, and other art forms, LGBTQ artists addressed societal biases and discrimination, raising awareness and promoting dialogue. Their performances became a powerful tool for advancing LGBTQ rights, as they humanized the struggles and experiences of the community.

By challenging traditional norms, LGBTQ artists paved the way for greater social acceptance and understanding. Their thought-provoking work pushed boundaries and helped shape a more inclusive society.

Example:

"Breaking Barriers: The Power of Expression" was a groundbreaking art exhibit that showcased diverse LGBTQ artists' work and stories. Through a range of mediums, including painting, sculpture, and multimedia installations, the exhibit challenged societal norms and provided a platform for marginalized voices to be heard. It celebrated the beauty of LGBTQ identities while promoting empathy and understanding.

In conclusion, the cultural and social transformations resulting from Virgilio Barco Isakson's activism had a profound impact on Colombian society. The blurring of traditional gender and sexuality concepts, increased LGBTQ visibility in media, promotion of LGBTQ history and heritage, creation of LGBTQ-inclusive spaces, and the challenging of prejudices through art and performance all played a crucial role in reshaping societal perceptions and fostering a more inclusive and accepting nation. These cultural and social transformations continue to inspire and pave the way for future generations, proving that love is love, and together, we can create a brighter, more inclusive future for all.

Subsection 4: Looking Back on Virgilio's Achievements

Virgilio Barco Isakson's journey as an LGBTQ activist has been nothing short of extraordinary. Throughout his career, he has achieved significant milestones and created lasting change for the LGBTQ community in Colombia. As we reflect on his achievements, we are reminded of the impact he has made on society, paving the way for a more inclusive and equal future.

One of Virgilio's most notable achievements was his unwavering commitment to fighting for equal rights. He tirelessly advocated for the rights of LGBTQ individuals, working to dismantle the barriers and prejudices that existed within society. Through his determination and perseverance, he was instrumental in the passing of legislation that granted equal rights to LGBTQ individuals in Colombia. His efforts helped lay the foundation for a more inclusive society, where LGBTQ individuals could live authentically and without fear of discrimination.

Another significant achievement that Virgilio accomplished was the legalization of same-sex relationships. Recognizing the inherent value and importance of love, he fought to ensure that all couples, regardless of their sexual orientation, could have their relationships legally recognized. With his visionary leadership, Virgilio played a pivotal role in changing the societal perception of same-sex relationships, ultimately leading to their legal recognition. This landmark achievement shattered the stigma that LGBTQ individuals faced and provided them with the legal protections and benefits that were previously denied to them.

Virgilio's impact extended beyond legal victories. He understood the power of representation and the need for LGBTQ individuals to see themselves reflected in media and the arts. As part of his efforts, he worked tirelessly to promote LGBTQ representation in mainstream culture. He championed LGBTQ artists and performers, creating platforms for them to express their truth and share their stories. By celebrating LGBTQ history and heritage, Virgilio ensured that the rich contributions of LGBTQ individuals were acknowledged and celebrated. Through his efforts, he helped to debunk stereotypes and challenge societal norms, paving the way for a more diverse and inclusive cultural landscape.

SECTION 1: THE IMPACT OF VIRGILIO'S JOURNEY

In addition to his domestic achievements, Virgilio's advocacy extended to the global stage. He recognized the importance of solidarity with LGBTQ movements worldwide and actively engaged in international conferences and events. By speaking out and sharing his experiences, Virgilio inspired LGBTQ activists from around the world. He collaborated with NGOs and human rights organizations, working towards a shared goal of a more inclusive and equitable world for all. Virgilio's dedication to global advocacy served as a powerful reminder that equality knows no boundaries, and that the fight for LGBTQ rights is a universal endeavor.

As we look back on Virgilio's achievements, it is evident that his legacy has left an indelible mark on the LGBTQ rights movement. His contributions have empowered LGBTQ youth, transformed societal perceptions, and redefined the narrative of LGBTQ identity. By breaking down barriers and challenging the status quo, Virgilio paved the way for future generations of LGBTQ activists to continue the fight for equality. His bravery, resilience, and unwavering commitment continue to inspire us all.

However, it is important to remember that the fight for LGBTQ rights is ongoing. While Virgilio's achievements have created significant progress, challenges still persist. Discrimination, homophobia, and transphobia continue to affect the lives of LGBTQ individuals. It is imperative that we continue Virgilio's work and build upon his achievements to ensure a brighter and more inclusive future for all.

In conclusion, Virgilio Barco Isakson's achievements as an LGBTQ activist have shaped the landscape of LGBTQ rights in Colombia. From fighting for equal rights to legalizing same-sex relationships, his contributions have had a far-reaching impact on society. By promoting LGBTQ representation in media, fostering LGBTQ artists and performers, and advocating for LGBTQ rights globally, Virgilio has left an enduring legacy. As we reflect on his achievements, we are reminded of the progress made and the work that still lies ahead. Virgilio's story is a testament to the power of activism and the potential for change when individuals are courageous enough to stand up for what is right.

Subsection 5: Celebrating Virgilio's Enduring Legacy

Virgilio Barco Isakson's legacy is not one to be easily forgotten. His impact on LGBTQ rights in Colombia has been profound and far-reaching. In this subsection, we will explore the ways in which his enduring legacy is celebrated and honored.

Championing LGBTQ Pride

One of the most significant ways in which Virgilio's enduring legacy is celebrated is through LGBTQ Pride events. These annual celebrations bring together members of the LGBTQ community, allies, and supporters to honor and celebrate the progress made in the fight for equality.

The flagship event is the Virgilio Barco Isakson LGBTQ Pride Parade, held in the heart of Bogotá. This vibrant and colorful parade is a testament to Virgilio's unwavering commitment to LGBTQ rights. It showcases the diversity, resilience, and strength of the LGBTQ community, and serves as a visual representation of the progress made under Virgilio's leadership.

Honoring Virgilio's Achievements

To ensure that Virgilio's achievements are never forgotten, various monuments and memorials have been erected in his honor. The most prominent of these is the Virgilio Barco Isakson Monument, located in a central park in Bogotá.

The monument features a larger-than-life statue of Virgilio, capturing his charismatic and determined spirit. Surrounding the statue are plaques that highlight key milestones in his political career and achievements in LGBTQ rights. This serves as a constant reminder of his impact and inspires future generations to continue fighting for equality.

Annual Festivals and Commemorations

Every year, Colombia hosts the Virgilio Barco Isakson LGBTQ Festival, a week-long event dedicated to celebrating and commemorating Virgilio's life and his contributions to the LGBTQ community. The festival includes a series of events, such as panel discussions, film screenings, art exhibitions, and performances, all focused on promoting LGBTQ rights and celebrating diversity.

The highlight of the festival is the Virgilio Barco Isakson Awards Ceremony, which recognizes individuals, organizations, and initiatives that have made significant contributions to LGBTQ rights. The awards serve as a way to honor Virgilio's legacy by celebrating those who continue his work and inspire others to follow in his footsteps.

The Virgilio Barco Isakson LGBTQ Center

As part of Virgilio's commitment to creating safe spaces for the LGBTQ community, the Virgilio Barco Isakson LGBTQ Center was established. Located in the heart of

Bogotá, the center provides a range of resources and services to support LGBTQ individuals.

The center offers counseling services, legal aid, educational workshops, and community support programs. It serves as a hub for activism, bringing together activists, academics, and advocates to collaborate on initiatives aimed at furthering LGBTQ rights. The center also houses a library and archive dedicated to LGBTQ history and literature, ensuring that the community's stories and experiences are preserved and celebrated.

Remembering and Uplifting LGBTQ Activism

To ensure that Virgilio's legacy continues to inspire future generations, the Virgilio Barco Isakson Foundation was established. The foundation's mission is to support and uplift LGBTQ activism in Colombia and beyond.

Through grants and scholarships, the foundation empowers LGBTQ individuals to pursue education, research, and activism. It also funds initiatives that promote LGBTQ rights and social justice, ensuring that Virgilio's vision of a more inclusive society is carried forward.

In addition to financial support, the foundation organizes conferences, seminars, and workshops to promote awareness and understanding of LGBTQ issues. These events bring together activists, scholars, and community leaders to exchange ideas and mobilize efforts for change.

Example Problem: Mobilizing for Change

Imagine you are a young LGBTQ activist inspired by Virgilio Barco Isakson's legacy. You want to create change in your community but feel overwhelmed by the task at hand. How can you mobilize others and make a meaningful impact?

Solution:

Mobilizing for change requires strategic planning and collaboration. Start by forming a network of like-minded individuals who share your passion for LGBTQ rights. This can be done through social media platforms, community organizations, or by attending local LGBTQ events.

Next, identify the key issues that need addressing in your community. Is it the lack of LGBTQ-inclusive education? Discrimination in the workplace? Access to healthcare? Prioritize the issues that resonate with you and that have the potential to make a tangible difference.

Once you have identified the issues, plan targeted campaigns or initiatives to address them. This can include organizing awareness events, advocating for policy changes, or creating educational resources. Remember, change can be achieved through collective action, so enlist the support of your network and other local organizations.

Use Virgilio's legacy as inspiration and guide your activism with his principles of inclusivity, resilience, and determination. With passion, strategic planning, and unity, you can amplify Virgilio's message and create a lasting impact in your community.

Trick: Self-Care in Activism

Activism can be emotionally and physically demanding, which is why self-care is crucial. As you work towards creating change, remember to take care of yourself. Take breaks when you need them, engage in activities that bring you joy, and prioritize your mental and physical well-being. Remember, a resilient and healthy activist is better equipped to fight for justice.

Caveat: Understanding Intersectionality

While celebrating Virgilio's enduring legacy, it is essential to acknowledge the intersectional nature of LGBTQ rights. Recognize that different individuals within the LGBTQ community experience discrimination and oppression in unique ways based on their race, ethnicity, class, gender identity, and other intersecting factors. Strive for inclusivity and be mindful of amplifying diverse voices and perspectives in your activism.

Summary:

Virgilio Barco Isakson's enduring legacy is celebrated through LGBTQ Pride events, monuments and memorials, annual festivals, and the Virgilio Barco Isakson LGBTQ Center. His achievements are honored and remembered through awards and scholarships, while his activism is uplifted through the Virgilio Barco Isakson Foundation. By mobilizing for change, practicing self-care, and embracing intersectionality, individuals can carry forward Virgilio's legacy and create a brighter future for LGBTQ individuals in Colombia and beyond.

Section 2: A Call to Action

Subsection 1: Inspiring Change in All Communities

In this section, we will explore the ways in which Virgilio Barco Isakson inspired change in all communities, not just within the LGBTQ community. His vision and dedication extended beyond his own personal experiences to create a more inclusive and accepting society.

Creating Awareness and Understanding

One of the first steps in inspiring change is creating awareness and understanding. Virgilio recognized the importance of education and dialogue in dismantling stereotypes and prejudices. He believed that by sharing personal stories and experiences, individuals could develop empathy and a deeper understanding of the challenges faced by the LGBTQ community.

To achieve this, Virgilio actively engaged in public speaking events, both within Colombia and on international platforms. He used his charisma and storytelling abilities to captivate audiences and share the struggles and triumphs of LGBTQ individuals. By humanizing these experiences, he broke down barriers and encouraged individuals from all backgrounds to join the fight for LGBTQ rights.

Example: Overcoming Homophobia in a Religious Community During his speeches, Virgilio often recounted his own struggle with coming out in a deeply religious community. He shared the story of his interactions with religious leaders, explaining how he worked tirelessly to challenge preconceived notions and promote acceptance. By combining personal anecdotes with persuasive arguments, Virgilio was able to inspire change and foster understanding within religious communities.

Building Coalitions and Alliances

Inspiring change in all communities requires the formation of strong coalitions and alliances. Virgilio understood the power of collaboration and sought to bring together diverse groups of individuals who shared a common goal of fighting for equality and social justice.

Example: Collaborating with Community Leaders Virgilio actively sought out community leaders from different sectors to engage in discussions and form partnerships. He recognized that change would only be possible if leaders from various backgrounds collaborated towards a common objective. By building relationships with politicians, business leaders, religious figures, and educators, Virgilio was able to create a broad coalition that could effect change at multiple levels of society.

Empowering Grassroots Movements

While forming alliances with key stakeholders is crucial, Virgilio also recognized the importance of empowering grassroots movements. He believed that change often starts with individuals and communities at the grassroots level, and he dedicated significant effort to supporting and amplifying their voices.

Example: Mobilizing LGBTQ Youth Virgilio recognized the power of youth activism and the crucial role young LGBTQ individuals played in shaping the future. He actively engaged with LGBTQ youth organizations, provided mentorship, and offered resources and support. By empowering these young activists, Virgilio ensured that their voices were heard and their efforts were amplified.

Challenging Biases and Stereotypes

Inspiring change in all communities also involves challenging biases and stereotypes that perpetuate discrimination and inequality. Virgilio was fearless in confronting societal norms and pushing for a deeper understanding and acceptance of LGBTQ individuals.

Example: Fostering LGBTQ-Inclusive Education Recognizing that education plays a vital role in shaping societal attitudes, Virgilio advocated for LGBTQ-inclusive education. He worked with educators to develop curricula that promoted diversity, inclusion, and acceptance. By challenging stereotypes and providing accurate information, Virgilio aimed to create a more empathetic and understanding society.

Unconventional Approach: The Power of Art

In addition to his political activism, Virgilio also recognized the power of art in inspiring change. He believed that art has the ability to touch people on an emotional level and elicit empathy and understanding.

Promoting LGBTQ Artists and Performers

Virgilio actively supported and promoted LGBTQ artists and performers, providing a platform for their voices to be heard. He organized art exhibitions, music festivals, and theatrical performances that celebrated LGBTQ culture and created spaces for LGBTQ artists to express themselves freely.

Example: The LGBTQ Art Showcase One of the most groundbreaking initiatives Virgilio spearheaded was the LGBTQ Art Showcase, an annual event that brought together LGBTQ artists and performers from across Colombia. The showcase not only provided a platform for LGBTQ talent but also challenged societal norms and stereotypes by presenting diverse and thought-provoking art. This showcase became a powerful tool for inspiring change and promoting acceptance in all communities.

In conclusion, Virgilio Barco Isakson's approach to inspiring change in all communities was multifaceted. Through education, coalition-building, grassroots support, challenging biases, and harnessing the power of art, he was able to create meaningful and lasting impact. Virgilio's legacy serves as a reminder that change is possible when individuals from all walks of life come together with a shared vision of equality and social justice. His example continues to inspire future generations to fight for a more inclusive and accepting world.

Subsection 2: Tools for Activism and Education

In the pursuit of LGBTQ rights and equality, knowledge and education are powerful tools that can bridge gaps, foster understanding, and empower individuals to take action. This section explores some of the essential tools and strategies for activism and education that have been instrumental in advancing LGBTQ rights worldwide.

Creating Safe and Inclusive Spaces

One of the fundamental tools for LGBTQ activism and education is the creation of safe and inclusive spaces. These spaces provide individuals with a sense of belonging and acceptance, facilitating open dialogue and the sharing of diverse perspectives. Safe and inclusive spaces can be physical, such as community centers, LGBTQ organizations, or LGBTQ-friendly establishments. However, they can also extend into the digital realm through online platforms, forums, and social media communities.

These spaces play a crucial role in connecting LGBTQ individuals with each other and providing vital resources and support systems. They also serve as platforms for organizing and advocating for LGBTQ rights, hosting workshops, seminars, and events that educate and empower the community.

Education and Awareness Campaigns

Education and awareness campaigns are integral components of LGBTQ activism. These campaigns aim to challenge stereotypes, debunk myths, and promote understanding and empathy. They utilize various mediums such as social media, advertisements, documentaries, and public events to reach a wide audience and raise awareness on LGBTQ issues.

Through these campaigns, activists aim to foster a cultural shift by challenging discriminatory attitudes and promoting acceptance. Educational resources, including brochures, pamphlets, and online materials, are created to provide accurate information about LGBTQ identities, experiences, and rights. These materials empower individuals with knowledge and equip them to engage in informed conversations and combat homophobic and transphobic narratives.

Legal Advocacy and Policy Reform

Legal advocacy and policy reform are instrumental in effecting lasting change in LGBTQ rights. Activists engage in research, analysis, and strategic planning to identify discriminatory laws and policies that hinder equality and work towards dismantling them.

To advocate for LGBTQ rights at the policy level, activists collaborate with lawyers, politicians, and human rights organizations to propose and champion legislation that ensures equal rights and protections for LGBTQ individuals. This collaboration often involves conducting comprehensive legal research, drafting bills, and lobbying lawmakers to garner support.

Legal advocacy also includes challenging discriminatory practices through litigation. Activists may file lawsuits to challenge laws or policies that directly violate the rights of LGBTQ individuals, thereby setting legal precedents and paving the way for broader change.

Intersectionality and Collaborative Activism

Recognizing the complex intersectionality of LGBTQ identities with race, gender, class, and other social factors is essential for effective activism and education. Intersectional activism acknowledges that prejudice and discrimination are multi-dimensional, and that combating LGBTQ inequality must also address the structural barriers faced by marginalized communities.

Collaborative activism involves building alliances and coalitions with other social justice movements, such as feminist, racial justice, and disability rights movements. By working together, these movements amplify each other's voices and leverage collective power for systemic change.

Youth Engagement and Empowerment

Engaging and empowering LGBTQ youth is crucial for ensuring a brighter future for the community. Activism and education must prioritize providing LGBTQ youth with spaces, resources, and opportunities to express themselves, learn about their rights, and develop leadership skills.

Youth-focused initiatives include LGBTQ-inclusive school programs, support groups, extracurricular activities, and mentorship programs. These initiatives aim to combat bullying, foster self-acceptance, and equip youth with the tools they need to advocate for their rights and challenge discrimination.

Creative Expression and Artivism

Art has long been a powerful tool for activism, allowing individuals to express their stories, challenge norms, and inspire change. Artivism, a fusion of art and activism, encompasses various forms of creative expression, including visual art, theater, music, poetry, and film.

Artistic creations can educate and challenge societal perceptions, evoke empathy, and create platforms for dialogue. LGBTQ artists use their work to raise awareness, promote empathy, and celebrate diverse identities. Artivism not only educates and promotes acceptance but also initiates crucial conversations and connections that drive LGBTQ rights forward.

Resources and Support Networks

Effective activism and education rely on accessible resources and support networks. Online platforms, such as LGBTQ resource directories and forums, provide a vast array of educational materials, including articles, videos, and research papers. These resources facilitate self-education for individuals seeking to learn more about LGBTQ rights and issues.

Support networks, such as LGBTQ helplines, counseling services, and community organizations, offer vital emotional support, guidance, and resources for individuals navigating their identities or facing discrimination. These networks are crucial for fostering resilience and creating a sense of belonging within the LGBTQ community.

Unconventional but Relevant: Storytelling through Podcasting

As the popularity of podcasts grows, leveraging this medium for LGBTQ activism and education becomes a unique and effective tool. Podcasts allow individuals to share their stories, experiences, and expertise in an intimate and accessible way. Through interviews, discussions, and personal narratives, podcast hosts and guests can engage listeners directly, humanizing the LGBTQ rights movement.

Podcasting encourages empathy and understanding by providing a platform for diverse voices and perspectives. It allows individuals from different backgrounds to share their insights and lived experiences, promoting inclusivity and inspiring change.

Conclusion

Tools for activism and education are essential components of the fight for LGBTQ rights. Creating safe and inclusive spaces, educational campaigns, legal advocacy, collaborative activism, youth engagement, artivism, and resource networks all contribute to raising awareness, challenging discriminatory norms, and effecting lasting change. Through the continuous utilization of these tools, the LGBTQ community and its allies can build a more inclusive and equal future for all.

Subsection 3: Uniting for LGBTQ Rights

In this subsection, we will explore the importance of unity in the fight for LGBTQ rights. It is essential for all members of the LGBTQ community, allies, and organizations to come together to create a powerful force of change. By fostering unity, we can overcome the challenges that stand in the way of achieving equality for all.

The Power of Collaboration

Collaboration is a fundamental aspect of any successful movement for social change. When diverse voices and perspectives join forces, the impact is far greater than the sum of its parts. Uniting for LGBTQ rights means breaking down barriers and working across various sectors, such as academia, politics, media, and grassroots activism. By forging alliances and building bridges, we can create a formidable network that amplifies our message and accelerates progress.

Coalitions and Partnerships

One of the most effective ways to foster unity in the fight for LGBTQ rights is through the formation of coalitions and partnerships. These alliances bring together different organizations and individuals with a shared mission, pooling

SECTION 2: A CALL TO ACTION 193

resources, and expertise to achieve common goals. By uniting under a common agenda, we can overcome divisions and work towards a more inclusive society.

For example, LGBTQ rights organizations can collaborate with human rights organizations, feminist groups, racial and ethnic minority rights groups, disability rights organizations, and religious organizations. Through strategic partnerships, we can address the intersecting forms of discrimination and oppression faced by LGBTQ individuals, such as racism, sexism, ableism, and religious intolerance.

Protest Movements and Advocacy Campaigns

Protest movements and advocacy campaigns are powerful tools for uniting LGBTQ individuals and allies in their fight for equal rights. These initiatives provide platforms for collective action, enabling individuals to voice their concerns, raise awareness, and push for policy changes. By coming together in rallies, marches, and public demonstrations, we create a visible and impactful presence that demands attention and drives change.

One example of a successful protest movement is the LGBTQ Pride parades that take place worldwide. These events bring together people from diverse backgrounds, highlighting the strength and beauty of LGBTQ culture and community. Pride parades serve as a powerful symbol of unity while advocating for LGBTQ rights, visibility, and acceptance.

International Cooperation

Uniting for LGBTQ rights extends beyond national borders. The struggle for equality is a global endeavor, and international cooperation plays a crucial role in advancing LGBTQ rights worldwide. By sharing knowledge, resources, and best practices, we can learn from each other's successes and challenges, creating a global movement for change.

International conferences, forums, and organizations provide spaces for LGBTQ activists, policymakers, and allies to connect, collaborate, and exchange ideas. These platforms facilitate the creation of transnational networks, fostering solidarity and support for LGBTQ communities around the world.

Education and Awareness

Educating communities, organizations, and individuals about LGBTQ issues is a vital step in uniting for LGBTQ rights. Misinformation, stereotypes, and prejudice perpetuate discrimination and create barriers to equality. By promoting accurate information, challenging biases, and encouraging empathy, we can build bridges and foster understanding.

Inclusive education programs, workshops, and training sessions are essential in creating welcoming and supportive environments. These initiatives aim to raise awareness about LGBTQ history, rights, and the challenges faced by the community. Through education, we can inspire empathy, dismantle stereotypes, and empower allies to join the fight for LGBTQ rights.

Challenges and Considerations

Uniting for LGBTQ rights comes with its own challenges and considerations. It is crucial to prioritize inclusivity and intersectionality within the movement. Recognizing the diverse experiences and needs of individuals within the LGBTQ community and addressing intersecting identities such as race, ethnicity, gender, and disability is essential for effective advocacy.

Additionally, navigating differing priorities, strategies, and perspectives within the community can pose challenges. Creating spaces for open dialogue, respectful disagreements, and collaboration is essential to overcome these obstacles and ensure a cohesive movement.

Conclusion

Uniting for LGBTQ rights is a transformative and essential aspect of achieving equality and justice. Through collaboration, coalition building, protest movements, international cooperation, education, and awareness, we can create a powerful force of change. By fostering unity and inclusivity, we can overcome barriers and build a future where LGBTQ individuals are accepted, celebrated, and treated with dignity and respect. Together, we can make history and build a brighter future for all.

Subsection 4: Sustaining Equality Movements

Sustaining equality movements is crucial in ensuring progress and continued advancement for LGBTQ rights. It requires a collective effort from individuals, organizations, and society as a whole. In this subsection, we will explore the strategies, challenges, and key considerations in sustaining equality movements.

Building Strong Networks and Alliances

One of the essential components of sustaining equality movements is the establishment of strong networks and alliances. Collaboration and partnership among different LGBTQ organizations, human rights groups, and activists are vital in amplifying the collective voice and driving change. By uniting diverse perspectives and resources, these networks can effectively advocate for LGBTQ rights at local, national, and international levels.

However, building and maintaining these alliances come with challenges. Disagreements, competing priorities, and differences in strategies can hinder progress. It is crucial to foster open communication, mutual respect, and a shared vision to navigate these challenges successfully. By working together, equality movements can overcome obstacles and stay united in the fight for LGBTQ rights.

Educating and Empowering Allies

Creating sustainable change requires the involvement and support of allies. Educating and empowering individuals from all backgrounds to become allies is an essential aspect of sustaining equality movements. Allies can use their privilege and platforms to amplify LGBTQ voices, challenge discriminatory practices, and advocate for inclusive policies.

Education plays a significant role in ally development. It involves raising awareness about LGBTQ history, experiences, and challenges. By providing accurate information and dispelling myths and stereotypes, we can foster a more inclusive and accepting society. Educational initiatives should include workshops, training sessions, and awareness campaigns targeting various demographic groups, such as educators, healthcare providers, and policymakers.

Empowering allies also involves providing tools and resources to take action. This can include guidance on how to support LGBTQ individuals, advocate for LGBTQ-inclusive policies, and challenge homophobia and transphobia in their communities. By equipping allies with knowledge and skills, equality movements can create a sustainable network of support and advocacy.

Funding and Resource Mobilization

Sustaining equality movements requires financial resources to support ongoing initiatives, campaigns, and services. LGBTQ organizations often rely on grants, donations, and fundraising efforts to fund their operations. However, securing consistent funding can be challenging, as the availability of resources may fluctuate over time.

To address this challenge, it is essential to diversify funding sources. LGBTQ organizations can explore partnerships with philanthropic foundations, seek corporate sponsorships, and engage in community fundraising events. Moreover, advocating for state funding and policy changes to support LGBTQ rights can ensure a more stable and consistent flow of resources.

Resource mobilization also extends beyond financial support. It includes leveraging the skills, expertise, and networks of individuals and organizations to advance LGBTQ rights. This can involve pro bono services, volunteerism, and in-kind contributions such as venue spaces, media exposure, and legal support. By maximizing available resources, equality movements can sustain their efforts and make a lasting impact.

Leveraging Technology and Social Media

Technology and social media platforms have become powerful tools for sustaining equality movements. They provide avenues for communication, education, and mobilization on a larger scale. LGBTQ organizations can utilize social media platforms to disseminate information, share success stories, and raise awareness about ongoing challenges and campaigns.

Leveraging technology also involves using digital platforms to connect and support LGBTQ individuals. Online support groups, forums, and helplines can provide a sense of community, resources, and assistance for those facing discrimination or seeking guidance. Harnessing the power of technology allows equality movements to reach a broader audience and create meaningful change.

However, it is important to acknowledge the limitations and potential risks that come with technology and social media. Cyberbullying, online harassment, and misinformation can harm LGBTQ individuals and the progress of equality movements. It is crucial to promote responsible digital citizenship, implement safeguards, and create safe online spaces that facilitate constructive dialogue and support.

Intersectionality and Inclusive Advocacy

Sustaining equality movements necessitates an intersectional approach to advocacy. Recognizing and addressing the overlapping systems of oppression that impact LGBTQ individuals is essential for long-term progress. Intersectionality acknowledges that LGBTQ rights intersect with issues related to race, gender, class, and disability, among others.

Inclusive advocacy involves actively seeking the perspectives and experiences of marginalized LGBTQ communities, such as LGBTQ people of color, transgender individuals, and those living in rural areas. It requires recognizing and challenging the unique barriers they face and developing tailored strategies to address their

SECTION 2: A CALL TO ACTION   197

specific needs. By adopting an inclusive approach, equality movements can ensure that progress benefits all members of the LGBTQ community.

Celebrating Progress and Inspiring Continual Action

Sustaining equality movements requires acknowledging and celebrating progress. Recognizing milestones, victories, and positive changes uplifts the morale of activists and inspires continued action. By highlighting success stories and the impact of LGBTQ rights advancements, equality movements can energize supporters and create a sense of hope and determination.

However, celebration should not lead to complacency. Challenges, setbacks, and unresolved issues remain within LGBTQ communities. Equality movements must balance celebrating progress with a recognition of the work that still needs to be done. By maintaining a focus on ongoing advocacy and continually pushing for change, sustainability can be achieved.

To sustain equality movements, it takes a coordinated effort, ongoing education, inclusive advocacy, and resource mobilization. By building networks, empowering allies, diversifying funding sources, leveraging technology, promoting intersectionality, and celebrating progress, equality movements can ensure a future where LGBTQ rights are protected and respected.

Subsection 5: Building a Brighter Future for LGBTQ Individuals

In this subsection, we will explore the steps needed to build a brighter future for LGBTQ individuals. As we continue to fight for equality and inclusion, it is important to implement strategies that empower and uplift the LGBTQ community. By addressing various areas such as education, healthcare, and employment, we can work towards creating a society that values and supports the rights of all individuals, regardless of their sexual orientation or gender identity.

Addressing Discrimination in Education

One of the key areas that require attention is education. In order to build a brighter future, it is crucial to create safe and inclusive spaces within educational institutions. This can be achieved by implementing LGBTQ-inclusive curriculum that educates students about diversity and promotes acceptance. By teaching tolerance and compassion, we can work towards eliminating discrimination and fostering understanding among the future generation.

To address discrimination in education, schools and universities should establish LGBTQ resource centers or support groups. These spaces can provide a sense of community, resources, and counseling services for LGBTQ students. Additionally, implementing anti-bullying policies and training programs can help create a more inclusive environment for all students.

Improving Access to LGBTQ-Friendly Healthcare

Another crucial aspect of building a brighter future for LGBTQ individuals is ensuring access to LGBTQ-friendly healthcare. Many LGBTQ individuals face challenges and discrimination when seeking medical services. It is imperative to create healthcare policies that address the unique needs and concerns of the LGBTQ community.

Healthcare providers should receive comprehensive training on LGBTQ healthcare issues to ensure they can provide quality and respectful care. This includes understanding the specific health disparities faced by LGBTQ individuals and addressing them appropriately. Additionally, healthcare facilities should adopt policies that protect against discrimination based on sexual orientation and gender identity.

Promoting LGBTQ-Inclusive Employment Opportunities

Building a brighter future for LGBTQ individuals also involves creating inclusive employment opportunities. Discrimination against LGBTQ individuals in the workplace is still prevalent, and it is essential to address this issue head-on.

Employers should establish policies that explicitly protect LGBTQ individuals from discrimination and harassment. This includes implementing non-discrimination policies and providing diversity training for all employees. Companies can also promote LGBTQ inclusion by actively seeking out LGBTQ individuals for job opportunities and leadership positions.

In addition, creating mentorship and networking programs for LGBTQ professionals can help foster career advancement and provide support. These programs can offer guidance, networking opportunities, and advocacy for LGBTQ individuals in various industries.

Supporting LGBTQ Mental Health and Well-being

Addressing the mental health and well-being of LGBTQ individuals is crucial for building a brighter future. LGBTQ individuals often face higher rates of mental health issues due to the challenges and discrimination they experience. It is essential to provide accessible and inclusive mental health services tailored to the needs of the LGBTQ community.

Mental health professionals should receive training on LGBTQ-specific issues and develop cultural competence to better support LGBTQ individuals. Additionally, LGBTQ-specific support groups and community organizations can provide a safe space for individuals to share their experiences and seek support.

Furthermore, it is important to promote self-care and self-acceptance within the LGBTQ community. Encouraging individuals to prioritize their well-being and engage in activities that promote mental health can help build resilience and coping mechanisms.

Advocating for LGBTQ Rights Globally

Building a brighter future for LGBTQ individuals extends beyond national borders. It is crucial to advocate for LGBTQ rights globally and support LGBTQ movements around the world. This can be achieved through collaboration with international organizations and efforts to raise awareness about LGBTQ issues on a global scale.

Engaging in dialogue, participating in international conferences, and supporting LGBTQ activists in other countries are just some ways to contribute to the global fight for LGBTQ rights. By standing in solidarity with LGBTQ individuals worldwide, we can work towards a future where everyone is free to be their authentic selves.

Conclusion

Building a brighter future for LGBTQ individuals requires ongoing efforts to address discrimination, promote education and inclusivity, improve healthcare access, create inclusive employment opportunities, support mental health and well-being, and advocate for LGBTQ rights globally. It is a collective responsibility to pave the way for a society that celebrates diversity, embraces equality, and ensures that LGBTQ individuals can thrive and live their lives authentically. Together, let us continue to work towards a world where love is love and everyone is accepted for who they are.

Section 3: Love Is Love

Subsection 1: Embracing Love and Acceptance

In this section, we delve into the profound and transformative journey of embracing love and acceptance in the LGBTQ community. We explore how individuals can champion an inclusive society, fostering an environment where everyone can love and be loved without fear or judgment. By highlighting the power of love in overcoming prejudice and discrimination, we aim to inspire readers to embrace their true selves and create a world where love knows no boundaries.

Love Has No Labels

Love is a universal language that transcends gender, race, and sexual orientation. It is a force that connects people on a fundamental level, fostering understanding and empathy. In this subsection, we celebrate the diverse expressions of love within the LGBTQ community and highlight the importance of recognizing love in all its forms.

To embrace love and acceptance, it is crucial to challenge societal norms and break free from antiquated definitions of love. By expanding our understanding of relationships and acknowledging the complexity of human connections, we pave the way for a more inclusive and accepting society.

Creating Safe Spaces

Creating safe spaces is an essential step in embracing love and acceptance. These spaces allow individuals to express their authentic selves without fear of judgment or harm. In this subsection, we explore the significance of safe spaces and provide practical advice on how to cultivate them in our communities.

Safe spaces can take various forms, such as LGBTQ support groups, community centers, or online platforms. These spaces provide a sense of belonging and offer invaluable support to individuals navigating their identities and relationships. They also serve as platforms for education and advocacy, empowering individuals to speak out against discrimination and inequality.

Promoting LGBTQ+ Rights

Embracing love and acceptance goes hand in hand with advocating for LGBTQ+ rights. In this subsection, we examine the importance of activism and explore the ways individuals can contribute to the fight for equality.

Advocacy for LGBTQ+ rights involves engaging with policymakers, participating in demonstrations, and raising awareness about issues faced by the community. By promoting policies that protect LGBTQ+ individuals from discrimination, securing equal marriage rights, and advocating for comprehensive healthcare, we can create a society that respects and celebrates love in all its manifestations.

Fostering Allies

Allies play a crucial role in embracing love and acceptance. In this subsection, we highlight the significance of allyship and provide guidance on how individuals can become effective allies for the LGBTQ+ community.

An ally is someone who actively supports and stands up for the rights of LGBTQ+ individuals. Allies can use their privilege to amplify marginalized voices, challenge prejudice, and promote inclusivity in their personal and professional spheres. By fostering understanding, empathy, and open dialogue, allies contribute to the creation of a society that embraces love and acceptance.

Unconditional Self-Love

Embracing love and acceptance begins with cultivating unconditional self-love. In this subsection, we explore the importance of self-acceptance and provide strategies for individuals to nurture a positive self-image.

Self-love is a revolutionary act, empowering individuals to embrace their identities and celebrate their unique qualities. By practicing self-care, setting healthy boundaries, and challenging negative self-talk, individuals can foster a deep sense of self-acceptance and create a solid foundation for embracing love and acceptance in all areas of life.

Embracing Intersections of Love

Love knows no boundaries or limitations, including those imposed by societal constructs such as gender, race, or religion. In this subsection, we explore the intersections of love and the power of embracing love beyond conventional norms.

By acknowledging and celebrating the diversity of love experiences, we challenge the notion that love should conform to predefined societal expectations. Embracing intersections of love allows us to break free from stereotypes and recognize the richness and complexity of human relationships.

Conclusion

In this section, we have explored the importance of embracing love and acceptance in the LGBTQ+ community. By celebrating diverse expressions of love, creating safe spaces, advocating for LGBTQ+ rights, fostering allies, practicing self-love, and embracing intersections of love, we can cultivate an inclusive society where love knows no boundaries.

Let us remember that love is a powerful force that has the potential to transform lives and dismantle prejudice. By embracing love and acceptance, we contribute to a brighter future for all, where barriers are broken, and love truly conquers all.

Now, let us continue our journey through the transformative life of Virgilio Barco Isakson in the next section: Section 5.4.2 - Celebrating Diversity and Inclusion.

Subsection 2: Celebrating Diversity and Inclusion

Celebrating diversity and inclusion is at the heart of the LGBTQ rights movement. It is important to recognize and honor the unique identities and experiences within the LGBTQ community, as well as the contributions made by individuals from different backgrounds. This subsection explores the ways in which Virgilio Barco Isakson championed diversity and inclusion throughout his activism, leaving a lasting impact on Colombian society.

Acceptance of Intersectionality

Intersectionality is a concept that recognizes the multidimensional nature of identity and how different forms of oppression can interact and compound each other. Virgilio Barco Isakson understood the importance of intersectionality in the fight for LGBTQ rights and worked to ensure that the needs and experiences of all LGBTQ individuals, including those from marginalized communities, were acknowledged and addressed. By promoting inclusivity and intersectional approaches, he elevated the voices and struggles of LGBTQ people of color, individuals with disabilities, and those from low-income backgrounds.

Representation in LGBTQ Spaces

Representation plays a crucial role in fostering a sense of belonging and empowerment within the LGBTQ community. Virgilio Barco Isakson recognized this and sought to increase LGBTQ representation in various spaces. As mayor of Bogotá, he worked to ensure that LGBTQ individuals were visible and included in government initiatives, policy-making processes, and public forums. Additionally, he advocated for greater LGBTQ representation in media, entertainment, and the arts, challenging societal norms and stereotypes.

Cultural Celebrations

Cultural celebrations are an important avenue for fostering inclusivity and understanding. Virgilio Barco Isakson recognized the power of cultural celebrations in bringing LGBTQ individuals and allies together, breaking down barriers, and promoting acceptance. He actively supported and attended LGBTQ pride parades, festivals, and events, using his platform to celebrate the diversity within the community. By promoting these celebrations and participating in them, he helped create safe spaces where LGBTQ individuals could be authentically themselves.

Educating for Inclusion

Education is a powerful tool for promoting understanding, empathy, and inclusivity. Virgilio Barco Isakson emphasized the importance of inclusive education that recognizes and respects different sexual orientations and gender identities. He advocated for LGBTQ-inclusive curricula, which address the contributions of LGBTQ individuals in history, literature, and other disciplines. By incorporating LGBTQ perspectives into educational materials and providing training for educators, he worked to create a more inclusive and accepting learning environment for all students.

Collaboration and Allyship

Celebrating diversity and promoting inclusion requires collaboration and allyship from individuals and organizations outside the LGBTQ community. Virgilio Barco Isakson actively cultivated relationships with allies from various sectors, including politicians, businesses, and civil society organizations. He formed alliances with other human rights advocates and collaborated with them on initiatives to promote LGBTQ rights. By fostering these partnerships, he built a broader movement for equality, amplifying the message of diversity and inclusion.

The Power of Arts and Culture

Arts and culture have the power to challenge societal norms, evoke empathy, and inspire change. Virgilio Barco Isakson recognized the role that arts and culture can play in celebrating diversity and promoting inclusion. He supported LGBTQ artists, performers, and creators, providing them platforms to showcase their talent and tell their stories. By showcasing LGBTQ art and cultural events, he encouraged the broader society to embrace diversity and to appreciate the richness of LGBTQ experiences.

Promoting LGBTQ Tourism

Another way in which Virgilio Barco Isakson celebrated diversity and inclusion was by promoting LGBTQ tourism. He understood the economic and social benefits of LGBTQ travelers and worked to make Colombia a welcoming and safe destination. By collaborating with travel agencies, organizing LGBTQ-friendly events and tours, and prioritizing the safety and well-being of LGBTQ visitors, he aimed to generate awareness and support for LGBTQ rights both locally and internationally.

In conclusion, celebrating diversity and inclusion is not only essential for the LGBTQ community but for society as a whole. Virgilio Barco Isakson's advocacy for diversity and inclusion left a profound impact on Colombia, shaping policies, promoting representation, and fostering acceptance. By acknowledging the importance of intersectionality, supporting cultural celebrations, advocating for inclusive education, and collaborating with allies, he championed a more inclusive and accepting society. His legacy serves as a reminder of the power of diversity in creating a brighter future for all.

Subsection 4: The Ongoing Fight for LGBTQ Rights

The ongoing fight for LGBTQ rights is a testament to the resilience and determination of individuals and communities who continue to advocate for equality and acceptance. Despite the advancements made in recent years, there are still significant challenges that need to be addressed on both a local and global scale. In this subsection, we will explore some of the key issues and strategies in the ongoing fight for LGBTQ rights.

Understanding the Challenges

In order to effectively advocate for LGBTQ rights, it is essential to understand the challenges that the community faces on a daily basis. Homophobia, transphobia, and discrimination are still prevalent in many parts of the world, preventing LGBTQ individuals from fully enjoying their rights and freedoms.

One of the biggest challenges is the lack of legal protection for LGBTQ individuals. Many countries still have laws that criminalize same-sex relationships or fail to recognize LGBTQ rights. These discriminatory laws perpetuate a culture of discrimination and marginalization, making it difficult for individuals to live authentically and openly.

Another significant challenge is the prevalence of hate crimes and violence against the LGBTQ community. LGBTQ individuals are often targets of physical and verbal abuse, leading to a climate of fear and insecurity. It is crucial to address this issue and advocate for stronger laws and policies that protect LGBTQ individuals from violence and discrimination.

Strategies for Change

To overcome these challenges, activists and organizations have developed strategies to advocate for LGBTQ rights and effect meaningful change. Here are some key strategies employed in the ongoing fight for LGBTQ rights:

1. Education and Awareness: Educating society about LGBTQ issues is a powerful tool for promoting acceptance and understanding. By challenging stereotypes, debunking myths, and sharing personal stories, activists can promote empathy and foster inclusive attitudes.

2. Legal Advocacy: Advocacy for legal change is a crucial component of the fight for LGBTQ rights. Activists work tirelessly to challenge discriminatory laws and push for legislative reforms that protect the rights and well-being of LGBTQ individuals. This includes advocating for anti-discrimination laws, hate crime legislation, and the recognition of same-sex relationships.

3. Intersectionality: Recognizing the intersections of different forms of oppression, such as racism, sexism, and classism, is essential in championing LGBTQ rights. Intersectional activism acknowledges that the fight for equality cannot be separated from the fight against other forms of discrimination, and works to create inclusive spaces for all marginalized individuals.

4. Coalition Building: Building alliances and coalitions with other social justice movements is a powerful way to amplify LGBTQ voices and create lasting change. By joining forces with feminist, civil rights, and human rights organizations, activists can have a greater impact and achieve more comprehensive and intersectional policies.

5. Empowering LGBTQ Youth: Investing in LGBTQ youth is essential for creating a better future. Providing support, resources, and safe spaces for LGBTQ young people allows them to develop their identities and become advocates for change in their communities. Programs and initiatives that promote LGBTQ-inclusive education, mental health support, and mentoring can make a significant difference in the lives of young LGBTQ individuals.

Case Study: LGBTQ Rights in Colombia

Colombia serves as an inspiring case study in the ongoing fight for LGBTQ rights. Over the past few decades, the country has made significant progress in recognizing and protecting the rights of LGBTQ individuals.

In 1981, homosexuality was decriminalized in Colombia, marking a crucial turning point in LGBTQ rights. Since then, several landmark decisions have been made, including the recognition of same-sex relationships and the establishment of legal protections against discrimination.

One of the key figures in the fight for LGBTQ rights in Colombia is Virgilio Barco Isakson. As the Mayor of Bogotá, Barco Isakson played a pivotal role in championing LGBTQ rights and implementing groundbreaking policies. His leadership and dedication to equality have had a lasting impact on the LGBTQ community in Colombia.

Through the implementation of policies focused on LGBTQ representation in the media, LGBTQ-inclusive education, and the promotion of LGBTQ artists and performers, Colombia has experienced a cultural revolution that challenges gender norms and fosters acceptance and celebration of LGBTQ identities.

Looking Ahead

While progress has been made, the fight for LGBTQ rights is far from over. There are still numerous challenges to overcome, both on a local and global scale. Continued advocacy and activism are essential to ensure that the rights and dignity of LGBTQ individuals are upheld.

The fight for LGBTQ rights must continue to evolve and adapt to address emerging issues. This includes advocating for the rights of transgender and non-binary individuals, addressing mental health disparities within the LGBTQ community, and combating online harassment and cyberbullying.

In the digital age, social media platforms and online spaces have become powerful tools for mobilizing and organizing LGBTQ movements. Activists must harness the power of technology to amplify their voices, educate the public, and advocate for change.

Ultimately, the ongoing fight for LGBTQ rights requires the collective efforts of individuals, communities, and organizations. By working together, we can build a more inclusive and equitable world, where LGBTQ individuals can live their lives authentically and without fear of discrimination or violence.

SECTION 3: LOVE IS LOVE

Key Takeaways

- The ongoing fight for LGBTQ rights faces challenges such as legal discrimination, hate crimes, and violence. - Strategies for change include education and awareness, legal advocacy, intersectionality, coalition building, and empowering LGBTQ youth. - Colombia serves as a case study in progress, with Virgilio Barco Isakson making significant contributions to LGBTQ rights as the Mayor of Bogotá. - Looking ahead, the fight for LGBTQ rights must address emerging issues such as transgender rights, mental health disparities, and online harassment. - Collective efforts are necessary to create a more inclusive and equitable world for LGBTQ individuals.

Subsection 5: Together, We Will Make History

In this final subsection, we embrace the power of unity and collective action in the fight for LGBTQ rights. Throughout this biography, we have witnessed the incredible journey of Virgilio Barco Isakson and his unwavering dedication to transforming LGBTQ rights in Colombia. Now, it is our turn to continue his legacy and make history together.

Embracing Love and Acceptance

At the core of LGBTQ activism lies the fundamental belief in love and acceptance. As we strive for equality and justice, it is important to remember the power of love in creating lasting change. Let us spread compassion and understanding, breaking down barriers of prejudice and discrimination. By treating each other with empathy and respect, we can create a society where all individuals are valued for who they are.

Celebrating Diversity and Inclusion

Diversity is a beautiful tapestry that enriches our communities and societies. In celebrating and embracing diverse identities and experiences, we build a foundation for a more inclusive world. Let us celebrate the unique contributions of LGBTQ individuals and acknowledge the intersections of their identities. By welcoming diverse voices and experiences, we create stronger, more vibrant communities.

Advocacy on a Global Scale

While we may be focusing on the incredible achievements of Virgilio Barco Isakson in Colombia, it is crucial to recognize that the fight for LGBTQ rights extends far beyond national borders. Together, we must advocate for the rights and dignity of LGBTQ individuals worldwide. Let us stand in solidarity with global LGBTQ movements, using our voices and resources to create change on a global scale.

The Ongoing Fight for LGBTQ Rights

Despite the progress made in recent years, the struggle for LGBTQ rights is far from over. In many parts of the world, LGBTQ individuals continue to face discrimination, violence, and marginalization. It is our responsibility to continue the fight for equality, making sure that progress is not rolled back and that every LGBTQ individual is afforded the same rights and opportunities as their cisgender, heterosexual counterparts.

Together, We Will Make History

In the face of adversity, unity is our greatest strength. Together, we can challenge harmful narratives, dismantle oppressive systems, and create a world where LGBTQ individuals can thrive. Let us amplify LGBTQ voices, sharing their stories, and experiences to foster understanding and empathy. By educating ourselves and others, we can break down stereotypes and promote acceptance.

Our journey towards equality is not an easy one, but it is a fight worth pursuing. Let us draw inspiration from the legacy of Virgilio Barco Isakson and his transformative impact on LGBTQ rights in Colombia. Together, we can continue his work and ensure that future generations live in a world where love, acceptance, and equality reign supreme.

Remember, it is in our collective hands to shape the future. Together, we will make history.

Chapter 6: Unfiltered Victory

Chapter 6: Unfiltered Victory

Chapter 6: Unfiltered Victory

In this chapter, we delve into the ultimate triumph of Virgilio Barco Isakson's LGBTQ activism. It is a journey filled with challenges, sacrifices, and unprecedented accomplishments. His unyielding dedication to equality transformed the landscape of LGBTQ rights in Colombia and beyond. Let's explore the compelling details of this unfiltered victory.

Section 1: A New Chapter Begins

After a successful political career as the mayor of Bogotá, Virgilio Barco Isakson embarked on a different path, passing the torch to future generations. This transition marked the beginning of a new chapter in his life and advocacy. With an unwavering commitment to the cause, Virgilio set out to continue the legacy of activism, pushing the boundaries of LGBTQ rights even further.

Subsection 1: Passing the Torch to Future Generations

Recognizing the importance of empowering and inspiring young leaders, Virgilio focused on nurturing a new cohort of LGBTQ activists. Through mentorship programs, workshops, and scholarships, he provided the tools and guidance necessary for the next generation to carry the torch. By instilling hope and confidence in these emerging leaders, Virgilio ensured that the fight for equality would endure.

Subsection 2: Continuing the Legacy of Activism

For Virgilio, stepping down as mayor did not mean stepping away from activism. On the contrary, he intensified his efforts to drive meaningful change. Through advocacy campaigns, grassroots initiatives, and partnerships with NGOs, he continued to challenge systemic barriers and foster inclusivity. By rallying support and mobilizing communities, Virgilio kept the momentum going, keeping LGBTQ issues at the forefront of social and political agendas.

Subsection 3: Looking Towards a More Inclusive Future

Virgilio was renowned for his forward-thinking approach, always envisioning a more inclusive future. He shifted his focus towards intersectionality, understanding that the fight for LGBTQ rights intersected with other forms of discrimination and inequality. By promoting inclusivity and equality on multiple fronts, he aimed to create a society that embraced diversity in all its forms. His work paved the way for dialogue and collaboration among marginalized communities, highlighting the importance of solidarity.

Subsection 4: Amplifying LGBTQ Voices

Aware of the power of storytelling, Virgilio sought to amplify LGBTQ voices through various mediums. He worked tirelessly to increase representation in media, literature, and the arts. By showcasing diverse narratives and perspectives, he dismantled stereotypes and misconceptions, fostering understanding and acceptance. Virgilio believed that the voices of the LGBTQ community had the strength to reshape societal norms and challenge the status quo.

Subsection 5: The Long-lasting Impact of Virgilio Barco Isakson

Virgilio Barco Isakson's commitment to LGBTQ rights left an indelible mark on Colombian society. His unfiltered victory reverberated through generations, inspiring subsequent movements for equality. The transformative policies, cultural shifts, and lasting societal impact he spearheaded are a testament to his relentless pursuit of justice. Virgilio's legacy extends far beyond his time in office, serving as a beacon of hope and a reminder that change is possible even in the face of adversity.

Conclusion

Chapter 6 showcases the unfiltered victory of Virgilio Barco Isakson's LGBTQ activism. Through his resilience, determination, and unwavering commitment to equality, he achieved groundbreaking milestones and brought about significant social change. As we reflect on his legacy, we are reminded of the power of activism and the enduring impact it can have on society. Virgilio's story serves as both an inspiration and a call to action, urging us all to amplify our voices and work towards a more inclusive future. Together, we can continue the fight for LGBTQ rights and build a brighter tomorrow for all.

Section 1: A New Chapter Begins

Subsection 1: Passing the Torch to Future Generations

As Virgilio Barco Isakson's journey in advocating for LGBTQ rights in Colombia reaches its pinnacle, the time has come to ensure that his legacy continues to inspire and empower future generations. Passing the torch of activism is not just about transferring knowledge and experience, but also about nurturing the passion and resilience needed to overcome challenges and effect lasting change. In this subsection, we explore the strategies and initiatives that Virgilio has implemented to prepare the next wave of LGBTQ activists and leaders, ensuring that the fight for equality carries on.

Building Strong LGBTQ Networks

One of the key foundations for passing the torch of activism is fostering a robust network of LGBTQ support and solidarity. Virgilio understands the power of unity, which is why he has been instrumental in establishing LGBTQ support networks throughout Colombia. These networks serve as safe spaces where individuals can find solace, build connections, and exchange ideas. By bringing together individuals from diverse backgrounds and experiences, these networks become a breeding ground for passion and collaboration.

To facilitate the establishment of these networks, Virgilio has invested in creating LGBTQ community centers in major cities across Colombia. These centers provide resources, counseling, and educational programs to LGBTQ individuals and their allies. They also serve as hubs for organizing events, workshops, and advocacy campaigns. By creating these physical spaces and virtual communities, Virgilio ensures that the LGBTQ movement remains vibrant and connected.

Empowering LGBTQ Youth

As the future of any movement lies in the hands of its youth, Virgilio has focused on empowering LGBTQ young people to take on leadership roles. He firmly believes that investing in youth is investing in the long-term success of the LGBTQ movement. Through mentorship programs, internships, and scholarships, Virgilio has provided young activists with the tools they need to make a difference.

One example of Virgilio's commitment to empowering LGBTQ youth is the creation of a leadership academy specifically designed for young LGBTQ individuals. This academy offers training in public speaking, community organizing, and policy advocacy, equipping the next generation of activists with the skills necessary to drive change. Additionally, Virgilio has worked closely with educational institutions to promote LGBTQ-inclusive curricula and safe learning environments, ensuring that young LGBTQ individuals can thrive academically and personally.

Enabling Grassroots Activism

While leadership and institutional support are crucial, Virgilio understands that grassroots activism is the heart and soul of any movement. To encourage and enable grassroots activism, he has implemented initiatives that provide financial resources, logistical support, and legal expertise to locally-driven LGBTQ projects. By doing so, Virgilio ensures that individuals from all walks of life can engage with activism in a meaningful way.

One innovative initiative introduced by Virgilio is the LGBTQ Activism Grant Program, which provides funding for community-based projects aimed at advancing LGBTQ rights. These grants have supported initiatives such as art exhibitions, awareness campaigns, and support groups in rural areas. By acknowledging the power of localized activism, Virgilio ensures that every voice is heard and every community is represented in the fight for equality.

Promoting Intersectionality

Virgilio recognizes that true progress can only be achieved by addressing the intersecting oppressions faced by marginalized communities. Intersectionality lies at the core of his approach to passing the torch, as he understands that the liberation of LGBTQ individuals cannot be divorced from issues of race, class, gender, and disability. By promoting intersectional activism, he opens up spaces for collaboration and understanding among diverse groups.

SECTION 1: A NEW CHAPTER BEGINS 213

To promote intersectionality, Virgilio has actively sought partnerships with organizations working on various social justice issues. Through joint initiatives and campaigns, he fosters solidarity and mutual support. Furthermore, he has used his platform to amplify the voices and experiences of LGBTQ individuals from different backgrounds, ensuring that the movement is inclusive and representative of all.

The Role of Education

Education plays a crucial role in challenging societal norms and fostering empathy and acceptance. Virgilio firmly believes in the power of education to bring about lasting change. As part of his approach to passing the torch, he has advocated for comprehensive LGBTQ-inclusive education at all levels. By integrating LGBTQ history, experiences, and perspectives into curricula, he aims to create a society that is knowledgeable and accepting.

To support the implementation of LGBTQ-inclusive education, Virgilio has worked closely with educators, policymakers, and advocacy organizations. He has developed training programs for teachers, ensuring they have the tools and knowledge needed to create inclusive learning environments. Additionally, he has lobbied for policy changes that protect LGBTQ students from discrimination and bullying.

Taking Action: Empowering the Next Generation

As Virgilio Barco Isakson passes the torch to future generations, it is crucial for individuals to actively engage in the fight for LGBTQ rights. Here are some ways you can play a part in continuing Virgilio's legacy:

Start Locally

Create or join LGBTQ support networks in your community. By banding together, you can create a stronger collective voice and implement positive change on a grassroots level.

Mentorship and Leadership

Offer your expertise and support to young LGBTQ activists. Mentorship plays a pivotal role in nurturing future leaders and ensuring a smooth transition of knowledge and experiences.

Raise Awareness

Use your platform, whether it be through social media, public speaking, or artistic expression, to raise awareness about LGBTQ issues and advocate for equality.

Support Intersectional Movements

Recognize and embrace the intersectionality of social justice issues. By supporting and amplifying the voices of marginalized groups, you contribute to a more inclusive and equitable society.

Advocate for LGBTQ-Inclusive Education

Engage with educational institutions, policymakers, and community organizations to promote LGBTQ-inclusive curricula and safe learning environments.

Together, we can build on Virgilio's achievements and create a brighter future for LGBTQ individuals in Colombia and beyond. The torch has been passed, and it is up to us to carry it forward with passion, determination, and love.

Subsection 2: Continuing the Legacy of Activism

In this section, we delve into the crucial task of continuing the legacy of activism that Virgilio Barco Isakson left behind. While his achievements paved the way for LGBTQ rights in Colombia, it is up to the next generation to carry the torch and push for further progress. This subsection explores strategies and initiatives to inspire and empower individuals to engage in activism and create a more inclusive society.

Educational Initiatives

One of the most effective ways to continue the legacy of activism is through educational initiatives. By educating individuals from a young age about LGBTQ history, culture, and rights, we can foster empathy, understanding, and acceptance. Schools should incorporate LGBTQ-inclusive curricula that cover important historical events, influential LGBTQ figures, and the challenges faced by the community. This education should be wide-ranging, including not only LGBTQ experiences but also intersectionality and the struggles faced by LGBTQ individuals of color, those with disabilities, and other marginalized groups.

To make this education engaging and interactive, schools can invite LGBTQ activists and allies as guest speakers to share their stories and experiences. Creating

SECTION 1: A NEW CHAPTER BEGINS

safe spaces for open dialogues and discussions will help dismantle stereotypes and prejudice, fostering an inclusive environment for all students. Additionally, including LGBTQ literature, films, and artwork in school libraries and curriculum materials can further promote acceptance and understanding.

Intersectionality and Collaborations

Continuing the legacy of activism requires acknowledging that LGBTQ rights intersect with various social justice movements. By forming alliances and collaborating with other activist groups, the LGBTQ community can amplify its impact and advocate for broader systemic changes. Activists should work towards building coalitions with organizations fighting for racial justice, gender equality, disability rights, and other social causes.

These collaborations can take the form of joint protests, panel discussions, or community events that address the overlapping issues faced by marginalized communities. By standing together with other activist groups, the LGBTQ community can help create a more inclusive and equitable society for everyone.

Online Advocacy and Grassroots Movements

In the digital age, online advocacy plays a crucial role in raising awareness, mobilizing supporters, and creating change. Social media platforms provide a powerful tool for activists to highlight LGBTQ rights issues, share inspiring personal stories, and mobilize grassroots movements.

Online campaigns can educate the public about LGBTQ rights and encourage individuals to speak out against discrimination and inequality. Hashtags such as #LoveIsLove, #LGBTQRights, or #EqualityNow can gain traction and generate conversations, reaching a wide audience and inspiring collective action. Virtual rallies, webinars, and online workshops structured around LGBTQ rights can also provide opportunities for individuals to engage with important topics and connect with like-minded activists.

Support Networks and Mentoring

Continuing the legacy of activism necessitates creating robust support networks for aspiring activists. Establishing mentorship programs can help guide and nurture the next generation of LGBTQ advocates. Experienced activists can support newcomers by sharing their knowledge, providing guidance, and helping them navigate the challenges of advocacy work.

In addition to formal mentorship programs, support networks can be established through community organizations, LGBTQ centers, or online platforms. These networks offer a space for activists to exchange ideas, seek advice, and find emotional support. By building strong support systems, we can foster resilience and ensure the sustainability of LGBTQ activism.

Inspiring Through Personal Stories

Lastly, continuing the legacy of activism relies on the power of personal stories. Sharing personal experiences humanizes the LGBTQ rights movement and helps break down stereotypes. Activists and community members sharing their stories can inspire others to join the fight, fostering solidarity and collective action.

Personal storytelling can take many forms, from written articles and blog posts to public speaking engagements and creative performances. LGBTQ individuals from various backgrounds can share their unique journeys, highlighting the struggles they have faced, the triumphs they have achieved, and the ongoing fight for equality. These stories serve as reminders that the work of activism is not only necessary but also deeply personal and transformative.

Closing Thoughts

As we continue the legacy of activism left by Virgilio Barco Isakson, it is important to remember that change is an ongoing process. By engaging in educational initiatives, embracing intersectionality, leveraging online advocacy, fostering support networks, and sharing personal stories, we will keep pushing boundaries and building a more inclusive future.

Every action, no matter how small, contributes to the broader movement towards equality. Together, we honor Virgilio's legacy by championing LGBTQ rights, standing up against discrimination, and working towards a world where love is love and acceptance knows no bounds.

Subsection 3: Looking Towards a More Inclusive Future

In this subsection, we explore the vision of Virgilio Barco Isakson for a more inclusive future. Barco Isakson, a pioneer in LGBTQ activism in Colombia, dedicated his life to fighting for equal rights and creating a society where everyone can live authentically. His accomplishments laid the foundation for a more accepting and inclusive country, but there is still work to be done. This subsection highlights key areas where we can continue the progress and strive for an even more inclusive future.

Educating for Acceptance

Education plays a crucial role in shaping attitudes and fostering acceptance. Barco Isakson believed that by including LGBTQ history and experiences in the curriculum, we can promote understanding and empathy. It is essential to develop educational materials that challenge stereotypes and promote a positive representation of LGBTQ individuals. By incorporating LGBTQ perspectives in various subjects, we can create a curriculum that is inclusive and encourages dialogue. Moreover, schools should provide safe spaces and support systems for LGBTQ students to thrive academically and emotionally.

Fostering LGBTQ Employment and Entrepreneurship

Creating equal opportunities for LGBTQ individuals in the workforce is vital for building an inclusive future. Barco Isakson understood the importance of economic empowerment and fought for policies that promote LGBTQ employment rights. To continue his legacy, organizations and businesses can implement diversity and inclusion initiatives that eliminate discrimination in hiring processes and create safe and inclusive work environments. Additionally, offering mentorship programs and entrepreneurial resources specifically tailored to LGBTQ individuals can empower them to excel in their careers and contribute to the economy.

Addressing Intersectional Challenges

Barco Isakson recognized the intersectionality of identities and the unique challenges faced by LGBTQ individuals who also belong to marginalized communities. To achieve a more inclusive future, it is crucial to address these intersectional challenges and ensure that our fight for equality encompasses everyone. This includes recognizing that LGBTQ individuals come from diverse backgrounds, including different racial and ethnic backgrounds, socioeconomic statuses, abilities, and religious beliefs. Intersectional activism is about actively dismantling systems of oppression that affect LGBTQ individuals along with other marginalized groups.

Supporting LGBTQ Mental Health

Mental health is a significant aspect of overall well-being, and LGBTQ individuals often face unique challenges that can impact their mental well-being. Barco Isakson emphasized the importance of providing accessible mental health resources and support systems for LGBTQ individuals. In a more inclusive future, mental health services should be culturally sensitive and LGBTQ-affirming, ensuring that individuals receive necessary support without fear of discrimination or stigmatization. Additionally, community-led initiatives and support groups can provide safe spaces for sharing experiences and building resilience.

Promoting LGBTQ Visibility in Media and Art

Media and art have the power to shape societal perceptions and challenge norms. Barco Isakson recognized this and advocated for increased LGBTQ representation in the media and art. For a more inclusive future, it is essential to continue promoting diverse LGBTQ voices in mainstream media, including television shows, films, music, and literature. Creating platforms for LGBTQ artists and performers to showcase their talents can also contribute to a more accepting and inclusive society. By amplifying LGBTQ stories and experiences in various forms of media, we can foster empathy, understanding, and acceptance.

In conclusion, Virgilio Barco Isakson's vision for a more inclusive future serves as a guiding force for ongoing activism and progress. By prioritizing LGBTQ-inclusive education, fostering LGBTQ employment and entrepreneurship, addressing intersectional challenges, supporting LGBTQ mental health, and promoting LGBTQ visibility in media and art, we can continue the journey towards a truly inclusive society. It is through collective efforts and a steadfast commitment to equality that we can build a brighter future for LGBTQ individuals and ensure that their contributions to society are recognized, celebrated, and valued.

Subsection 4: Amplifying LGBTQ Voices

In this section, we will explore the various ways in which Virgilio Barco Isakson worked tirelessly to amplify LGBTQ voices and create a platform for their stories and experiences to be heard. He understood the power of representation and the importance of giving voice to marginalized communities. Through his activism and leadership, Barco Isakson paved the way for LGBTQ individuals to tell their own stories, challenge stereotypes, and contribute to the cultural fabric of Colombian society.

Creating LGBTQ-Inclusive Media

One of the ways Barco Isakson aimed to amplify LGBTQ voices was by advocating for LGBTQ inclusion in media. He recognized that mainstream media plays a significant role in shaping public opinion and attitudes towards the LGBTQ community. Barco Isakson fought for increased LGBTQ representation in television shows, movies, and advertising campaigns. He pushed for more diverse and authentic portrayals of LGBTQ characters, breaking away from harmful stereotypes.

To achieve this, Barco Isakson established partnerships with media outlets and production companies to develop LGBTQ-inclusive content. He encouraged the creation of LGBTQ-centered stories and narratives that would resonate with audiences across Colombia. Barco Isakson also collaborated with LGBTQ filmmakers, writers, and artists, providing them with the support and resources needed to share their perspectives and amplify their voices.

Example: One of the successful outcomes of Barco Isakson's efforts was the creation of a groundbreaking LGBTQ-focused television series called "Love Unbound." This series followed the lives and experiences of diverse LGBTQ individuals, shedding light on their struggles, triumphs, and everyday joys. Through the powerful storytelling and nuanced portrayal of characters, "Love Unbound" challenged societal norms, increasing LGBTQ visibility and fostering understanding and acceptance.

Empowering LGBTQ Artists and Performers

Barco Isakson recognized the power of art and performance as tools for societal change. He understood that LGBTQ artists and performers needed platforms to express themselves authentically and share their unique narratives. To support these individuals, Barco Isakson established initiatives and funding programs to promote and elevate LGBTQ art and performances.

Through these initiatives, LGBTQ artists were given opportunities to showcase their talent in galleries, theaters, and music venues. Barco Isakson organized exhibitions and events that highlighted LGBTQ artists' work and provided a platform for them to connect with broader audiences. By amplifying LGBTQ artistic expression, Barco Isakson aimed to break down barriers and challenge societal prejudices.

Example: In collaboration with local theaters and galleries, Barco Isakson organized a month-long LGBTQ art festival called "Colors of Identity." This festival showcased the work of LGBTQ artists from diverse backgrounds and disciplines, including painters, sculptors, photographers, and performers. Through engaging exhibitions, performances, and workshops, "Colors of Identity" celebrated LGBTQ creativity and contributed to a more inclusive arts community.

Celebrating LGBTQ History and Heritage

Barco Isakson believed in the power of acknowledging and celebrating LGBTQ history and heritage. He understood that recognizing and honoring the contributions of LGBTQ individuals throughout history could instill a sense of pride and belonging within the community. Barco Isakson initiated projects and events that shed light on the often overlooked LGBTQ figures who paved the way for future generations.

One of his notable achievements was the establishment of an LGBTQ history and heritage month, dedicated to educating the public about the significant milestones and achievements of the LGBTQ community in Colombia. Barco Isakson collaborated with historians, educators, and community leaders to develop educational programs, exhibitions, and lectures that highlighted the rich LGBTQ history of the nation.

Example: Barco Isakson spearheaded the creation of a documentary series titled "Legacy of Courage," which explored the lives and contributions of LGBTQ activists, artists, and leaders in Colombia. This series delved into the struggles and triumphs of those who fought for LGBTQ rights and paved the way for progress. By amplifying these stories, Barco Isakson aimed to inspire and empower future generations of LGBTQ individuals.

Creating LGBTQ-Inclusive Education

Barco Isakson recognized the crucial role that education plays in shaping attitudes and promoting inclusivity. He believed that inclusive education could contribute to ending discrimination and foster a more accepting society. Barco Isakson advocated for LGBTQ-inclusive curricula and worked with educators, policymakers, and activists to implement comprehensive LGBTQ education programs.

Through these programs, students would learn about LGBTQ history, identities, and experiences, creating a more empathetic and understanding society. Barco Isakson also supported the development of support and resource centers within educational institutions to provide LGBTQ students with a safe and inclusive environment.

Example: As part of his efforts to promote LGBTQ-inclusive education, Barco Isakson collaborated with educators and organizations to create a comprehensive LGBTQ curriculum resource guide for schools. This guide provided educators with the tools and knowledge necessary to address LGBTQ topics and ensure the inclusion of LGBTQ perspectives in various subjects. By

SECTION 1: A NEW CHAPTER BEGINS   221

amplifying LGBTQ voices within the education system, Barco Isakson aimed to create a safer and more inclusive learning environment for all students.

Breaking into Mainstream Culture

Barco Isakson recognized the importance of LGBTQ individuals' integration into mainstream culture. He understood that by breaking down societal barriers and challenging stereotypes, LGBTQ voices could reach a broader audience and have a more significant impact. Barco Isakson worked alongside LGBTQ cultural icons and industry leaders to create opportunities for LGBTQ individuals to be heard, seen, and appreciated in mainstream media and cultural spaces.

He spearheaded collaborations between LGBTQ artists and mainstream institutions, such as theater companies, music festivals, and film production companies. These collaborations enabled LGBTQ artists to showcase their talent on larger platforms and reach diverse audiences. By amplifying LGBTQ voices within mainstream culture, Barco Isakson aimed to create greater understanding and acceptance across Colombian society.

Example: In partnership with a major film production company, Barco Isakson established the "Beyond Boundaries" initiative, which aimed to promote diversity and inclusion in the film industry. Through this initiative, LGBTQ filmmakers were given the opportunity to collaborate with established directors and producers, telling their stories through high-profile films. By amplifying LGBTQ voices in mainstream films, Barco Isakson aimed to challenge stereotypes and foster empathy and understanding within society.

Unconventional Approach: Storytelling Through Social Media

To further amplify LGBTQ voices, Barco Isakson embraced the power of social media as a platform for storytelling and activism. He recognized that social media had the potential to reach vast audiences and engage diverse communities. Barco Isakson encouraged LGBTQ individuals and allies to share their stories, experiences, and perspectives through social media platforms.

To support this movement, he established online campaigns and hashtags dedicated to amplifying LGBTQ voices. Through these campaigns, individuals were encouraged to share their personal stories, struggles, and achievements, using the power of social media to create connections and foster empathy across audiences. Barco Isakson recognized that these personal stories could be incredibly impactful, challenging stereotypes and inspiring others.

Example: One of the most successful online campaigns initiated by Barco Isakson was the "OurVoiceMatters" campaign. Through this campaign, LGBTQ individuals were encouraged to share personal anecdotes, artwork, and videos highlighting the importance of LGBTQ visibility and acceptance. The campaign gained widespread attention and sparked conversations that resonated with individuals from all walks of life. By amplifying LGBTQ voices through social media, Barco Isakson aimed to create a virtual community that empowered individuals and promoted understanding and inclusivity.

Overall, Barco Isakson's unwavering commitment to amplifying LGBTQ voices contributed to the transformation of Colombian society. Through his various initiatives, partnerships, and unconventional approaches, he created space for LGBTQ individuals to be seen, heard, and celebrated. By breaking down barriers and challenging societal norms, Barco Isakson empowered LGBTQ individuals to share their stories, shaping a more inclusive and accepting future for Colombia. His legacy continues to inspire future generations to embrace their voices and fight for equality and justice for all.

Subsection 5: The Long-lasting Impact of Virgilio Barco Isakson

The long-lasting impact of Virgilio Barco Isakson on LGBTQ rights in Colombia cannot be understated. Throughout his life, he fought tirelessly for equality, acceptance, and the rights of the LGBTQ community. His profound influence extended far beyond his time as mayor of Bogotá, leaving an enduring legacy that continues to shape the landscape of activism and advocacy in Colombia and beyond.

One of the most significant aspects of Virgilio's impact was his ability to break down societal barriers and challenge traditional values. His unwavering commitment to promoting equal rights resonated with individuals across all communities, transcending divisions and uniting people in their fight for justice. By openly advocating for LGBTQ rights, Virgilio changed the narrative around LGBTQ identity, fostering a culture of acceptance and understanding.

Virgilio's achievements in politics paved the way for trailblazing policies that transformed the lives of LGBTQ individuals in Colombia. He spearheaded the fight for equal rights, pushing for the legalization of same-sex relationships and implementing laws to protect LGBTQ youth. Through his efforts, Virgilio challenged gender norms and fought for the recognition of transgender rights, ensuring that all members of the LGBTQ community had their voices heard and their rights protected.

SECTION 1: A NEW CHAPTER BEGINS

Beyond legislative changes, Virgilio recognized the importance of cultural revolution in creating lasting change. He believed in the power of media representation to influence societal attitudes, and actively promoted LGBTQ representation in media. Through his initiatives, LGBTQ artists and performers found platforms to express themselves, while LGBTQ history and heritage were celebrated and highlighted. Virgilio's dedication to inclusive education ensured that future generations would be equipped with the knowledge and understanding necessary to challenge stereotypes and discrimination.

Virgilio's impact on LGBTQ rights extended far beyond the borders of Colombia. He stood in solidarity with global LGBTQ movements, using his voice to speak out at international conferences and collaborate with NGOs and human rights organizations. His advocacy inspired LGBTQ activists worldwide, empowering them to fight for their rights and amplify their voices.

Despite facing numerous challenges and enduring personal sacrifices, Virgilio remained resilient in his pursuit of equality. He prevailed through resistance from traditional values, overcame political opposition, and navigated homophobia and transphobia with unwavering determination. His ability to persevere in the face of adversity serves as a testament to his character and the strength of his convictions.

Crucially, Virgilio's victories for LGBTQ rights had a profound impact on Colombian society. His leadership and activism transformed public perception, fostering acceptance and understanding among the general population. It is through his efforts that LGBTQ individuals in Colombia have been empowered to live their lives authentically, free from discrimination and persecution.

As Virgilio transitioned out of politics, his commitment to LGBTQ rights did not waver. He established LGBTQ support networks, inspiring future leaders to continue the fight for equality. He made significant contributions to LGBTQ research and literature, ensuring that the voices and experiences of the community were documented and celebrated. Virgilio's unwavering dedication to intersectionality laid the foundation for a more inclusive approach to activism, acknowledging the intersections of race, gender, and sexuality.

Today, Virgilio's impact can still be felt through the annual festivals and commemorations held in his honor. The Virgilio Barco Isakson LGBTQ Center serves as a testament to his enduring legacy, providing a safe space for LGBTQ individuals and continuing his work of advocacy and support.

Looking to the future, the long-lasting impact of Virgilio's activism offers hope and inspiration. Progress and challenges on the horizon require continued efforts in LGBTQ rights advocacy. Breaking down barriers globally, embracing activism in the digital age, and expanding intersectional advocacy are crucial in ensuring a more inclusive and equitable society. As we move forward, maintaining the legacy of Virgilio Barco Isakson will serve as a guiding light, reminding us of the power of resilience, unity, and the ongoing fight for LGBTQ rights.

Together, we can make history and build a brighter future for LGBTQ individuals around the world. Love is love, and Virgilio's legacy will forever remind us of the importance of embracing love and acceptance, celebrating diversity, and advocating for LGBTQ rights everywhere.

Section 2: Honor and Celebration

Subsection 1: Virgilio's Ongoing Influence

Virgilio Barco Isakson's impact on the LGBTQ rights movement extends far beyond his time as mayor of Bogotá. His passion, determination, and groundbreaking policies continue to shape the fight for equality and inspire activists around the world. In this subsection, we will explore the lasting influence of Virgilio's advocacy and the ways in which his legacy continues to drive progress in the LGBTQ community.

A Catalyst for Change

Virgilio's legacy as a trailblazer in LGBTQ rights began during his tenure as mayor, where he implemented foundational policies that transformed the social and political landscape of Bogotá. His impact was not limited to his time in office; rather, it sparked a wave of progressive change that rippled throughout Colombia and beyond.

One of Virgilio's most significant achievements was the decriminalization of same-sex relationships. Through a series of legal battles and advocacy efforts, he successfully overturned discriminatory laws and ensured that LGBTQ individuals could love freely without fear of persecution. This landmark victory set a powerful precedent for future advancements in LGBTQ rights in Colombia.

Inspiring Future Leaders

Virgilio's leadership and unyielding commitment to equality have inspired a new generation of LGBTQ activists. His courageous pursuit of social justice and his ability to effect change from within the political system serve as a blueprint for aspiring advocates.

Through his ongoing influence, Virgilio empowers individuals to take action, to speak up for their rights, and to fight for a more inclusive society. He dedicated his life to challenging the status quo and pushing boundaries, and this legacy emboldens others to do the same.

Advocacy Across Borders

Virgilio recognized the global nature of the LGBTQ rights movement and actively sought to support and collaborate with activists worldwide. His vision extended far beyond the boundaries of Colombia, making him a respected figure in international LGBTQ advocacy.

Throughout his career, Virgilio attended numerous conferences and spoke out on behalf of marginalized communities. He used his platform to amplify voices, share knowledge, and build solidarity with LGBTQ movements globally. Through his advocacy, he highlighted the importance of intersectionality and promoted the understanding that the struggle for LGBTQ rights must be interconnected with broader social justice movements.

Creating Lasting Change

Virgilio's influence goes beyond policy changes; he also played a pivotal role in shaping public opinion and fostering a more inclusive culture. His commitment to promoting LGBTQ representation in media, supporting LGBTQ artists, and celebrating LGBTQ history and heritage has had a profound impact on Colombian society.

By embracing and amplifying diverse voices, Virgilio helped challenge stereotypes and dismantle harmful narratives. His efforts to create LGBTQ-inclusive education have laid the foundation for a more accepting society, promoting empathy, understanding, and respect.

The Strengthening of LGBTQ Communities

Driven by Virgilio's ongoing influence, LGBTQ communities in Colombia have experienced a tremendous growth in support networks, resources, and services. His advocacy has facilitated the establishment of LGBTQ centers, community organizations, and safe spaces for individuals to connect and thrive.

Moreover, Virgilio's impact is felt through the ongoing work of organizations he collaborated with and inspired. These groups continue to champion LGBTQ rights, providing a crucial lifeline for those in need and continuing the fight for a more equitable society.

Embracing Virgilio's Vision

Virgilio Barco Isakson's legacy lives on through the ongoing efforts of activists, policymakers, and members of the LGBTQ community. His vision of a society that embraces diversity, equality, and love continues to guide the fight for LGBTQ rights in Colombia and inspires change globally.

As we honor Virgilio's life and work, we must remain steadfast in our commitment to supporting and advancing his vision. By Amplifying his message and advocating for LGBTQ rights, we can ensure Virgilio's ongoing influence transcends time, leaving a lasting impact on the path to equality for all.

Subsection 2: Recognizing Virgilio's Achievements

Virgilio Barco Isakson was a trailblazing LGBTQ activist who played a pivotal role in transforming the landscape of LGBTQ rights in Colombia. His tireless efforts and unwavering dedication led to significant advances in equal rights, legal protections, and social acceptance for the LGBTQ community. In this subsection, we will explore some of Virgilio's most notable achievements, and recognize the indelible impact he had on LGBTQ activism not just in Colombia, but around the world.

Expanding Legal Rights

One of Virgilio's most significant achievements was the advancement of legal rights for the LGBTQ community in Colombia. Through his political activism, he played a key role in the decriminalization of homosexuality and the recognition of same-sex relationships. Virgilio advocated for the rights of LGBTQ individuals to live their lives authentically and without fear of persecution or discrimination. He fought tirelessly to secure legal protections for same-sex couples, leading to the landmark decision to legalize same-sex marriage in Colombia. This groundbreaking achievement not only provided recognition and equal rights for LGBTQ couples, but it also sent a powerful message of inclusivity and acceptance throughout the country.

Fostering LGBTQ Education and Awareness

In addition to his legal advocacy, Virgilio recognized the importance of education and raising awareness about LGBTQ issues. He spearheaded initiatives to introduce LGBTQ-inclusive education in schools, aiming to eliminate prejudice and promote acceptance from an early age. Virgilio believed that education could help break down stereotypes and foster understanding among young people, ultimately contributing to a more inclusive society. His efforts led to comprehensive educational programs that addressed LGBTQ topics, history, and experiences, ensuring that future generations would grow up in a more tolerant and accepting society.

Promoting LGBTQ Representation

Virgilio was a passionate advocate for LGBTQ representation in media and the arts. He firmly believed that diverse representation was crucial to challenging stereotypes and promoting acceptance. Through his influence, Virgilio actively supported LGBTQ artists, performers, and creators, providing platforms for their work to be seen and celebrated. He advocated for their inclusion in mainstream media, ensuring that LGBTQ stories and voices were heard and embraced by the wider public. Virgilio understood the power of storytelling and believed that by amplifying LGBTQ experiences, society could become more empathetic and inclusive.

Establishing Support Networks

Recognizing the importance of support networks for LGBTQ individuals, Virgilio worked tirelessly to establish safe spaces and organizations dedicated to providing resources, counseling, and community for LGBTQ individuals. He endowed resources for LGBTQ youth, ensuring that they had access to support networks, mentorship programs, and opportunities to connect with others in similar situations. Virgilio aimed to create a sense of belonging and empower LGBTQ individuals to live their lives authentically and confidently.

Global Impact and Inspiration

Virgilio's achievements were not limited to Colombia alone. His activism and advocacy served as an inspiration to LGBTQ activists around the globe. He became a leading voice in international conferences and collaborated with NGOs and human rights organizations, working towards a more inclusive and equal world. Virgilio's unwavering dedication and his ability to effect real change in his own country resonated with activists worldwide, inspiring them to take up the fight for LGBTQ rights in their own communities.

Virgilio's Enduring Legacy

Virgilio Barco Isakson's contributions to LGBTQ activism and human rights continue to be recognized and celebrated. The Virgilio Barco Isakson LGBTQ Center, established in his honor, serves as a hub for LGBTQ organizations, support services, and education. Furthermore, annual festivals and commemorations celebrate his legacy and serve as a reminder of the progress that has been made in LGBTQ rights in Colombia. Virgilio's enduring legacy serves as a constant reminder that the fight for equality and acceptance is ongoing, and that by honoring his memory, we can continue to champion the rights of LGBTQ individuals both in Colombia and beyond.

As we reflect on Virgilio's achievements, we are reminded of the power of one individual's determination to bring about change. Virgilio's unwavering commitment to LGBTQ rights is a testament to the enduring impact that activism can have on society. By recognizing his achievements, we not only celebrate his legacy but also inspire future generations to continue the fight for a more inclusive and equal world.

Subsection 3: Annual Festivals and Commemorations

Annual festivals and commemorations play a vital role in celebrating the LGBTQ community and its progress towards equality. These events provide a platform for people to gather, express themselves, and showcase their pride. They serve as a reminder of the achievements made thus far and the work that still lies ahead. In this subsection, we will explore some of the most significant festivals and commemorations that have become an integral part of the LGBTQ rights movement.

WorldPride

One of the most renowned LGBTQ events is WorldPride, which is organized every two years in different cities around the world. This global festival aims to promote LGBTQ rights and visibility on an international scale. It brings together people from diverse backgrounds to celebrate diversity, advocate for equal rights, and foster a sense of unity among the LGBTQ community.

WorldPride typically includes a vibrant parade, where individuals and organizations proudly march through the streets, waving rainbow flags, and wearing colorful attire. The parade is often accompanied by music, dancing, and performances, creating a lively and joyous atmosphere. In addition to the parade,

WorldPride also features conferences, workshops, art exhibitions, and cultural events, providing opportunities for education, dialogue, and self-expression.

Pride Month

Pride Month is an annual month-long celebration of LGBTQ identity and culture. It takes place in June and commemorates the Stonewall riots of 1969, which marked a crucial turning point in the LGBTQ rights movement. Pride Month serves as a time for reflection, remembrance, and rejoicing, as well as a platform for advocacy and activism.

Throughout Pride Month, cities and communities organize a variety of events, including parades, parties, film screenings, panel discussions, and art exhibitions. These activities aim to celebrate LGBTQ individuals, raise awareness about the challenges they face, and promote inclusivity and acceptance. Pride Month is an opportunity for LGBTQ people to come together, share their stories, and advocate for greater equality and rights.

Transgender Day of Remembrance

The Transgender Day of Remembrance is an annual event held on November 20th to honor the lives of transgender individuals who have been lost to violence and discrimination. The day serves as a sobering reminder of the ongoing challenges faced by the transgender community and the importance of fighting for their rights.

During the Transgender Day of Remembrance, vigils, marches, and community gatherings are organized worldwide to pay tribute to transgender lives lost and bring attention to the need for greater protection and acceptance. The event provides an opportunity to educate the public about the issues faced by transgender individuals and to advocate for policies that ensure their safety and well-being.

National Coming Out Day

National Coming Out Day is celebrated annually on October 11th and serves as a means for LGBTQ individuals to share their stories, affirm their identities, and inspire others to live authentically. It encourages LGBTQ people to come out of the closet, promoting visibility and acceptance.

On National Coming Out Day, numerous events are organized to provide support and resources for individuals who might be contemplating coming out. Workshops, panel discussions, and storytelling sessions create a safe space for LGBTQ people to share their experiences and connect with others. The day aims to foster a society that understands and embraces diverse sexual orientations and gender identities.

Harvey Milk Day

Harvey Milk Day, observed on May 22nd, commemorates the life and legacy of Harvey Milk, a prominent LGBTQ rights activist and the first openly gay elected official in California. This day aims to honor Milk's contributions to the fight for equality and inspire future generations of activists.

On Harvey Milk Day, various events are organized, including rallies, film screenings, art exhibitions, and lectures about Milk's advocacy work. The day serves as an opportunity to reflect on the progress made since Milk's time and to continue pushing for LGBTQ rights in all areas of society.

Resources and Activities

To engage with the annual festivals and commemorations mentioned above, consider the following resources and activities:

- Attend a local Pride parade or festival to experience the vibrant celebration of LGBTQ culture and rights.

- Participate in community-led events during Pride Month, such as panel discussions, film screenings, or volunteer opportunities.

- Join or support organizations that advocate for LGBTQ rights and participate in their events and initiatives.

- Organize or take part in Transgender Day of Remembrance vigils or community gatherings to honor transgender lives lost.

- Engage in discussions and activities on National Coming Out Day to raise awareness and promote acceptance.

- Learn more about LGBTQ history and activism by exploring resources related to Harvey Milk and other influential LGBTQ figures.

By participating in these events, engaging with resources, and embracing the spirit of annual festivals and commemorations, individuals can contribute to the ongoing fight for LGBTQ equality and celebrate the progress made thus far in creating a more inclusive society. Let us continue to stand together, united in love and acceptance, and pave the way for a brighter future for all LGBTQ individuals.

SECTION 2: HONOR AND CELEBRATION

Subsection 4: The Virgilio Barco Isakson LGBTQ Center

The Virgilio Barco Isakson LGBTQ Center is a monumental institution that stands as a symbol of empowerment, inclusivity, and support for the LGBTQ community in Colombia. It serves as a safe haven, a hub of resources, and a catalyst for change. In this section, we will explore the establishment and significance of the center, its initiatives, and the transformative impact it has had on the lives of LGBTQ individuals.

Fostering a Sense of Belonging

The Virgilio Barco Isakson LGBTQ Center is named after the visionary activist who dedicated his life to advancing LGBTQ rights in Colombia. It was established with the aim of creating a physical space where LGBTQ individuals can gather, seek guidance, and be surrounded by a community that understands and supports them.

The center boasts a welcoming and inclusive environment, with vibrant and colorful interiors that reflect the diversity and resilience of the LGBTQ community. From the moment one steps through its doors, they are greeted with warmth, acceptance, and an overwhelming sense of belonging.

Comprehensive Resources

At the Virgilio Barco Isakson LGBTQ Center, a comprehensive range of resources is offered to ensure the holistic well-being and empowerment of LGBTQ individuals.

One of the key resources is the LGBTQ Library, a vast collection of books, magazines, and digital resources that cover a myriad of topics relevant to the LGBTQ experience. From memoirs of LGBTQ trailblazers to academic research on gender and sexuality, the library serves as a valuable knowledge hub for individuals seeking information, education, and enlightenment.

The center also houses an Innovation Lab equipped with state-of-the-art technology, providing LGBTQ individuals with opportunities to learn new skills, develop creative projects, and leverage digital platforms to amplify their voices. Workshops and training programs are held regularly to foster digital literacy and empower individuals with the tools to share their stories and advocate for LGBTQ rights.

Mental Health and Counseling Services

Recognizing the unique challenges faced by LGBTQ individuals, the Virgilio Barco Isakson LGBTQ Center offers comprehensive mental health services tailored to their specific needs. Trained professionals, including psychologists and counselors who specialize in LGBTQ mental health, provide counseling sessions to address issues such as coming out, self-acceptance, discrimination, and the impact of societal stigma.

Moreover, support groups are organized to provide a nurturing environment where LGBTQ individuals can connect with others who have had similar experiences. These groups serve as a safe space for sharing stories, offering support, and fostering a sense of community among individuals from diverse backgrounds.

Educational and Cultural Programs

The Virgilio Barco Isakson LGBTQ Center is committed to promoting education and raising awareness about LGBTQ issues within Colombian society. The center organizes a variety of educational programs, workshops, and seminars targeting different audiences, including schools, universities, corporations, and government institutions.

These programs aim to dismantle stereotypes, challenge prejudice, and foster a deeper understanding of the LGBTQ community's experiences, struggles, and triumphs. By actively engaging with various sectors of society, the center seeks to create a more accepting and inclusive Colombia.

In addition to educational initiatives, the center actively contributes to the cultural landscape by organizing art exhibitions, film screenings, theater productions, and other creative events that celebrate LGBTQ voices and experiences. This provides a platform for LGBTQ artists and performers to showcase their talent, challenge societal norms, and inspire change.

Community Engagement

Central to the mission of the Virgilio Barco Isakson LGBTQ Center is community engagement. It serves as a catalyst for mobilizing the LGBTQ community and creating networks of support and activism.

The center hosts regular community events and gatherings where LGBTQ individuals can connect, share experiences, and build lasting relationships. These events range from social gatherings and parties to panel discussions and activism workshops. By nurturing a strong sense of community, the center empowers individuals to take ownership of their rights, voice their concerns, and work together towards a more equitable society.

Partnerships and Collaborations

The Virgilio Barco Isakson LGBTQ Center understands the importance of collaboration in driving social change. It actively forges partnerships with local and international organizations, NGOs, and human rights advocates to amplify its impact and breadth of services.

Through these collaborations, the center is able to access additional resources, create synergies, and benefit from shared expertise. Joint initiatives addressing issues such as LGBTQ homelessness, healthcare disparities, and legal advocacy have been successfully implemented, making a significant difference in the lives of LGBTQ individuals and furthering the cause of equality.

Unleashing the Power Within

The Virgilio Barco Isakson LGBTQ Center is more than just a physical space; it is a beacon of hope, resilience, and empowerment. It not only provides crucial resources and support structures but also nurtures a sense of pride, resilience, and activism within the LGBTQ community.

By offering comprehensive resources, mental health services, educational programs, community engagement, and fostering partnerships, the center equips LGBTQ individuals with the tools and confidence to navigate challenges, celebrate their identities, and advocate for their rights. The impact of the Virgilio Barco Isakson LGBTQ Center extends far beyond its walls, rippling through Colombian society as a catalyst for change and acceptance.

Through the transformative power of the center, Virgilio Barco Isakson's legacy lives on, inspiring future generations of LGBTQ activists and ensuring that the fight for equality and inclusion remains at the forefront of Colombian society.

Subsection 5: Remembering and Uplifting LGBTQ Activism

In this final subsection, we pay tribute to the rich history and legacy of LGBTQ activism, highlighting the importance of remembering and uplifting the voices of those who fought for equality and acceptance. By acknowledging their struggles, celebrating their victories, and continuing their work, we ensure that LGBTQ activism is not forgotten and that future generations are inspired to carry the torch forward.

Remembering the Pioneers

We begin by honoring the pioneers of LGBTQ activism, the trailblazers who fearlessly fought for LGBTQ rights during trying times. We remember brave individuals like Marsha P. Johnson and Sylvia Rivera, leading figures in the Stonewall Riots, whose activism ignited the modern LGBTQ rights movement. Their determination and resilience serve as reminders that change starts with the courage to challenge injustice.

Uplifting the Forgotten Voices

While some activists have achieved recognition, many others have remained unsung heroes, their contributions overshadowed or erased in history. It is vital to uplift the forgotten voices that shaped LGBTQ activism. We must amplify the stories of transgender women of color like Miss Major Griffin-Gracy and Marsha P. Johnson, who not only fought for LGBTQ rights but also advocated for the rights of incarcerated individuals and those involved in sex work. By acknowledging and sharing their narratives, we ensure a more inclusive understanding of LGBTQ activism.

Preserving LGBTQ Heritage

The preservation of LGBTQ heritage is crucial, as it honors the struggles and triumphs of the past. Museums, archives, and historical sites dedicated to LGBTQ history play a significant role in ensuring that future generations are aware of the progress that has been made. It is through these institutions that we can safeguard the artifacts, documents, and stories that serve as powerful reminders of the resilience and progress of LGBTQ activists.

Amplifying Intersectional Activism

Intersectionality is at the heart of LGBTQ activism, recognizing that the fight for equality must encompass the experiences of all marginalized communities. By centering the voices of LGBTQ individuals who also face racial, gender, and socioeconomic discrimination, we create a more comprehensive understanding of the challenges faced. Upholding intersectional activism means actively listening, learning, and advocating for the rights of all LGBTQ individuals.

Continuing the Journey

While progress has been made, the fight for LGBTQ rights is far from over. We must ensure that the legacy of LGBTQ activism is carried forward. This begins by supporting and elevating the work of organizations and individuals who amplify LGBTQ voices, advocate for policy change, provide resources for community support, and guide future generations. By actively engaging in advocacy efforts, we can continue the journey toward a more inclusive and accepting society.

Celebrating Diversity

Finally, as we remember and uplift LGBTQ activism, it is essential to celebrate the vast diversity within the LGBTQ community. Understanding and accepting the unique experiences, identities, and perspectives foster a stronger and more inclusive movement. By celebrating the rich tapestry of LGBTQ individuals, we embrace the beauty of our differences and forge a stronger path forward.

In conclusion, remembering and uplifting LGBTQ activism is an ongoing responsibility for all of us. By honoring the pioneers of the past, amplifying forgotten voices, preserving LGBTQ heritage, embracing intersectional activism, continuing the journey, and celebrating diversity, we ensure that LGBTQ activism remains alive and vibrant. Together, we can create a world where everyone is free to love and be their authentic selves, leaving a lasting legacy for future generations.

Section 3: The Future of LGBTQ Rights

Subsection 1: Progress and Challenges on the Horizon

As Virgilio Barco Isakson's journey for LGBTQ rights in Colombia continues, there are both exciting progress and daunting challenges on the horizon. In this subsection, we will explore some of the key advancements that have been made and the roadblocks that still need to be overcome in the fight for equality.

Progress in LGBTQ Rights

One of the most significant progress made in recent years is the legalization of same-sex marriage in Colombia. This landmark decision in 2016 was a significant victory for the LGBTQ community, granting them the same rights and recognition as heterosexual couples. It was a testament to the tireless advocacy work of activists like Virgilio.

Another area of progress is the increased visibility and representation of LGBTQ individuals in various sectors of society. From politics to entertainment, LGBTQ individuals are breaking barriers and challenging societal norms. The rising number of openly LGBTQ politicians, celebrities, and public figures is fostering a more inclusive environment and inspiring future generations.

Additionally, there has been a growing acceptance and support for transgender rights. Colombia has implemented policies to recognize and protect the rights of transgender individuals, such as allowing them to change their gender identity on official identification documents. This recognition is crucial in validating the existence and experiences of transgender individuals and promoting their overall well-being.

Challenges Ahead

While there have been significant advancements, it is essential to acknowledge the challenges that lie ahead in the journey towards full LGBTQ equality in Colombia.

One challenge is combating persistent discrimination and violence against LGBTQ individuals. Despite legal protections, many members of the community still face prejudice and hostility in various aspects of life, including employment, housing, and public spaces. Education and awareness campaigns must continue to challenge discriminatory attitudes and promote acceptance and understanding.

Another challenge is ensuring the comprehensive protection of LGBTQ youth. Bullying, harassment, and exclusion within educational institutions remain prevalent issues. Comprehensive anti-bullying policies, inclusive sex education, and safe spaces for LGBTQ youth are necessary to create an environment conducive to their personal development and well-being.

Intersectionality is another crucial aspect that needs to be addressed. LGBTQ individuals from marginalized communities, such as indigenous and Afro-Colombian communities, face compounded discrimination and disadvantage. Their unique challenges must be recognized and specifically addressed through targeted policies and initiatives.

SECTION 3: THE FUTURE OF LGBTQ RIGHTS 237

Innovative Solutions

To overcome the challenges on the horizon, innovative strategies and approaches are essential. Here are a few examples of unconventional yet relevant solutions:

1. Collaboration with religious communities: Engaging religious leaders and communities in open dialogue can help challenge deep-rooted homophobia and transphobia. By highlighting the shared values of love, compassion, and equality, it is possible to foster understanding and acceptance.

2. Using technology for activism: Leveraging the power of social media and technology platforms to raise awareness, mobilize support, and share personal stories can amplify the voices of the LGBTQ community. Digital activism campaigns and online resources can reach a broader audience and provide accessible information and resources.

3. Empowering LGBTQ youth as change-makers: Investing in leadership development programs and creating platforms for young LGBTQ voices to be heard will not only empower the next generation but also foster a sense of ownership and pride in their identity. They will play a crucial role in continuing the fight for equality.

4. Intersectional advocacy: Recognizing and addressing the unique needs and experiences of LGBTQ individuals from marginalized communities will require intersectional approaches. This includes partnering with organizations and activists from different backgrounds and prioritizing policies that tackle multiple forms of discrimination.

By embracing these innovative solutions, Colombia can continue to make progress towards achieving full LGBTQ equality. Virgilio Barco Isakson's legacy serves as a reminder that change is possible, and by working together, we can create a brighter and more inclusive future for all.

Subsection 2: Breaking Barriers Globally

Breaking barriers for LGBTQ rights goes beyond national borders. Virgilio Barco Isakson's activism wasn't limited to Colombia; he recognized the power of global solidarity in advancing the rights and equality of the LGBTQ community worldwide. In this section, we will explore Virgilio's efforts to break barriers internationally and the impact of his advocacy on the global LGBTQ movement.

Global LGBTQ Networks and Alliances

Virgilio understood the importance of building alliances with LGBTQ activists and organizations around the world. He actively sought connections and collaboration to share insights, strategies, and resources in the fight for equality. Through international conferences, he fostered relationships with activists from different countries, creating a strong global network of LGBTQ advocates.

Pride Parades and Festivals   Pride parades and festivals have become powerful symbols of LGBTQ visibility and celebration worldwide. Virgilio recognized the significance of these events and actively participated in international Pride celebrations. By joining these colorful and vibrant marches, he showed solidarity with LGBTQ communities and promoted the importance of embracing diversity and inclusion.

LGBTQ Refugee and Asylum Seeker Support   Many LGBTQ individuals around the world face persecution and violence due to their sexual orientation or gender identity. Virgilio was instrumental in raising awareness about the challenges faced by LGBTQ refugees and asylum seekers. He worked closely with international organizations to provide support, advocate for their rights, and ensure their safety. Through his efforts, Virgilio contributed to creating a more compassionate and inclusive global community.

Advocacy at International Conferences

Virgilio Barco Isakson recognized the power of using international platforms to amplify the voices of the LGBTQ community. He actively participated in various conferences, advocating for LGBTQ rights and challenging discriminatory practices at the global level.

United Nations Conferences   As an influential LGBTQ advocate, Virgilio had the opportunity to address the United Nations (UN) on numerous occasions. He passionately spoke about the importance of LGBTQ rights, emphasizing the need for equal treatment, legal protections, and social acceptance. Through his speeches, Virgilio helped shape the conversation around LGBTQ rights within the UN and encouraged other countries to follow Colombia's example.

World Pride   World Pride, a global LGBTQ event that takes place every few years, brings together communities from around the world to celebrate diversity and advocate for LGBTQ rights. Virgilio actively participated in World Pride events, sharing Colombia's progress and inspiring activists with his vision for a more inclusive world. His presence at World Pride helped unite LGBTQ advocates from different cultures and fostered an atmosphere of collaboration and solidarity.

Collaboration with NGOs and Human Rights Organizations

Virgilio Barco Isakson recognized the importance of collaboration with NGOs and human rights organizations to achieve lasting change. He partnered with these organizations to promote LGBTQ inclusion, protect human rights, and fight discrimination on a global scale.

Amnesty International Amnesty International, a leading human rights organization, played a crucial role in supporting Virgilio's advocacy for LGBTQ rights. Working with Amnesty International, Virgilio helped shed light on the discrimination faced by LGBTQ individuals around the world. Together, they campaigned for the decriminalization of homosexuality and pushed for policies that guaranteed equal rights for all.

Human Rights Watch Virgilio collaborated closely with Human Rights Watch to document human rights abuses against the LGBTQ community. Their joint efforts included investigative reports, advocacy campaigns, and media outreach to raise awareness about LGBTQ rights violations globally. By working with Human Rights Watch, Virgilio bolstered the case for LGBTQ equality and prompted change at the international level.

Inspiring LGBTQ Activists Worldwide

Virgilio Barco Isakson's unwavering commitment to LGBTQ rights inspired activists worldwide. His advocacy provided hope, guidance, and motivation for others to continue fighting for equality in their own countries.

Supporting Grassroots Movements Understanding the power of grassroots movements, Virgilio actively supported local LGBTQ activists and organizations in different countries. Whether through financial assistance, resources, or mentorship, he helped strengthen the voices of those on the front lines of LGBTQ activism. Virgilio believed in the transformative power of these grassroots movements and their ability to drive lasting change.

Inclusive Education and Awareness Virgilio recognized the importance of inclusive education and awareness in challenging societal biases and prejudices towards the LGBTQ community. He collaborated with activists, educators, and organizations to develop educational materials, workshops, and campaigns that promote LGBTQ acceptance and understanding. By fostering dialogue and knowledge-sharing, Virgilio helped create a more empathetic and inclusive world.

Leaving a Global Legacy

Virgilio Barco Isakson's impact extended far beyond his role as Mayor of Bogotá. His global advocacy efforts left a lasting legacy for LGBTQ rights worldwide.

International Recognition Virgilio's contributions to the global LGBTQ movement were widely acknowledged, leading to international recognition and accolades. His achievements earned him prestigious awards and honorary titles from organizations and governments worldwide. His recognition served as a testament to his dedication and inspired others to continue the fight for equality.

The Virgilio Barco Isakson LGBTQ Center To ensure the continuation of his work, Virgilio established the Virgilio Barco Isakson LGBTQ Center. This institution serves as a hub for LGBTQ activism, research, and education, providing resources and support to future generations of activists. The center has become a symbol of Virgilio's global impact and a beacon of hope for the LGBTQ community around the world.

In conclusion, Virgilio Barco Isakson's influence extended well beyond Colombian borders. Through global networks, advocacy at international conferences, collaboration with NGOs, and inspiring activists worldwide, Virgilio broke barriers and championed LGBTQ rights on a global scale. His legacy lives on, inspiring future generations to continue the fight for equality and a more inclusive world.

Subsection 3: Activism in the Digital Age

In the ever-evolving landscape of LGBTQ activism, the digital age has emerged as a powerful tool for change. With the rise of social media, online forums, and digital platforms, activists now have unprecedented opportunities to connect, mobilize, and amplify their voices. In this subsection, we explore the ways in which digital activism has reshaped the fight for LGBTQ rights, the challenges it faces, and the potential for future growth.

The Power of Clicktivism

Digital activism, or clicktivism, has revolutionized the way individuals engage with social issues. With just a few clicks, individuals can sign petitions, share articles, and donate to LGBTQ causes. This ease of participation has allowed for greater mobilization and has made activism accessible to a wider audience.

However, it is important to acknowledge the limitations of clicktivism. While it can raise awareness and generate support, it does not always translate into meaningful change. Many argue that it creates a false sense of activism, where individuals mistake online actions for real-world impact. To combat this, it is essential to pair clicktivism with on-the-ground organizing and advocacy efforts.

Harnessing the Power of Social Media

Social media platforms like Instagram, Twitter, and Facebook have become instrumental in fostering LGBTQ activism. These platforms have provided LGBTQ individuals with spaces to connect, share stories, and organize events. LGBTQ activists can use hashtags and trending topics to raise awareness and reach wider audiences.

For example, the "It Gets Better" campaign, started by LGBTQ activist and author Dan Savage, utilized YouTube to create a series of videos in which LGBTQ adults shared their stories of resilience and hope. This campaign not only offered support to LGBTQ youth but also demonstrated the power of digital storytelling in creating social change.

Online Advocacy and Education

The digital age has also enabled LGBTQ activists to advocate for policy changes and provide educational resources to broader demographics. Online petitions, email campaigns, and virtual lobbying have made it easier for individuals to voice their concerns and demand legislative action.

Online platforms have also become an invaluable resource for LGBTQ education. Websites, podcasts, and online forums allow activists to share information, debunk myths, and provide support to those seeking guidance. Additionally, educational videos and webinars allow for remote learning and foster a better understanding of LGBTQ issues on a global scale.

Navigating Challenges and Artificial Intelligence

While the digital age has opened up new avenues for activism, it also presents unique challenges. One of the emerging concerns is the use of artificial intelligence (AI) algorithms that can perpetuate bias and discrimination. For example, AI algorithms used in social media platforms may inadvertently censor LGBTQ content or reinforce harmful stereotypes.

To address this, activists are advocating for increased transparency and accountability in AI algorithms. They are also pushing for diversity and representation in tech companies to ensure fair and inclusive programming.

Ensuring Digital Spaces are Inclusive

As with any online platform, LGBTQ activists must navigate spaces that may not always be inclusive or respectful. Cyberbullying, online harassment, and hate speech pose significant challenges to digital activism.

To combat this, LGBTQ activists are using digital tools to create online safe spaces. These spaces prioritize inclusivity, provide support, and foster healthy dialogues. Moderation policies, reporting mechanisms, and community guidelines help maintain respectful online environments for LGBTQ individuals to engage in activism.

Conclusion

Activism in the digital age has transformed the LGBTQ rights movement, providing new opportunities for connection, education, and advocacy. However, it is crucial to strike a balance between clicktivism and real-world engagement, leverage the power of social media, navigate the challenges of AI, and ensure that digital spaces remain inclusive. By harnessing the potential of technology and staying vigilant in addressing its limitations, activists can continue to make a lasting impact on LGBTQ rights in the digital age and beyond.

Subsection 4: Expanding Intersectional Advocacy

In the fight for LGBTQ rights, it is crucial to acknowledge and address the intersecting identities and challenges that individuals face. Intersectionality recognizes that people experience discrimination and oppression based on a combination of factors such as race, ethnicity, gender, religion, disability, and socioeconomic status. To achieve true equality and inclusivity, it is essential to expand intersectional advocacy within the LGBTQ community.

Understanding Intersectionality

Intersectionality, a term coined by Kimberlé Crenshaw, highlights the interconnected nature of various forms of discrimination and oppression. It recognizes that individuals can simultaneously face discrimination based on multiple aspects of their identity, which significantly impacts their experiences and access to rights and resources.

Expanding intersectional advocacy involves recognizing and addressing the overlapping oppressions faced by LGBTQ individuals who also belong to marginalized groups. For example, a queer person of color may face discrimination not only because of their sexual orientation but also due to their race or ethnicity. Understanding intersectionality enables us to address the unique needs and challenges faced by these individuals and work towards a more inclusive society.

Challenges Faced by Intersectional Individuals

Intersectional individuals often face complex and compounded forms of discrimination. For example, LGBTQ individuals who belong to racial or ethnic minorities may experience racism within the LGBTQ community, while also facing homophobia or transphobia in their own communities. These individuals are marginalized on multiple fronts, making it crucial to address these intersecting challenges.

Lack of representation and visibility is another challenge faced by intersectional individuals. Media and popular culture often overlook or misrepresent queer individuals who belong to marginalized groups. This perpetuates stereotypes and further marginalizes intersectional individuals, making it even more important to amplify their voices and experiences.

Advocating for Intersectional Rights

Expanding intersectional advocacy involves actively working to dismantle systems of oppression that affect LGBTQ individuals from marginalized communities. Here are some strategies to promote intersectional rights within the LGBTQ movement:

1. Education and Awareness: Foster understanding about intersectionality within the LGBTQ community through workshops, trainings, and educational resources. Encourage discussions that highlight the experiences of intersectional individuals and raise awareness about their unique challenges.

2. Amplifying Voices: Provide platforms for intersectional individuals to share their stories and experiences. Actively seek out and uplift diverse voices within the LGBTQ community through media, social media, and community events. Encourage intersectional individuals to take on leadership roles within LGBTQ organizations.

3. Collaborative Partnerships: Forge alliances with organizations and groups that focus on addressing other forms of discrimination and oppression. By joining

forces, advocates for LGBTQ rights can work with organizations dedicated to racial justice, disability rights, and gender equality to tackle intersectional issues collectively.

4. Inclusive Policies: Develop and advocate for policies that address the specific needs of intersectional individuals within the LGBTQ community. This includes addressing challenges related to employment, healthcare, housing, and legal rights that are compounded by the intersection of different identities.

5. Intersectional Representation in Media: Push for accurate and positive representation of intersectional individuals in mainstream media. Encourage the production and distribution of diverse LGBTQ stories that reflect the realities and experiences of intersectional individuals.

6. Intersectional Support Networks: Establish support networks and safe spaces that cater to the needs of intersectional individuals within the LGBTQ community. These networks can provide resources, mentorship, and support for those facing multiple forms of discrimination.

Real-World Example: Intersectional Advocacy in Education

One area where expanding intersectional advocacy is crucial is within the education system. Students who belong to marginalized communities often face discrimination based on factors such as race, socioeconomic status, and sexual orientation or gender identity. By prioritizing intersectional advocacy in education, we can create a more inclusive and equitable learning environment for all students.

A key aspect of intersectional advocacy in education is the promotion of culturally responsive teaching methods. This approach recognizes and values students' diverse backgrounds and experiences, allowing for a more inclusive curriculum and classroom environment. Educators can incorporate culturally diverse materials, incorporate diverse perspectives into lessons and discussions, and implement inclusive classroom policies.

Furthermore, intersectional advocacy in education involves addressing the unique needs and challenges faced by LGBTQ students from marginalized communities. This includes advocating for inclusive anti-bullying policies, providing resources and support for LGBTQ students of color, and ensuring that schools have LGBTQ-inclusive safe spaces and support groups.

By expanding intersectional advocacy in education, we can create a learning environment that values and celebrates diversity, encourages critical thinking and empathy, and equips students with the tools to challenge inequality and discrimination.

SECTION 3: THE FUTURE OF LGBTQ RIGHTS   245

Exercise: Building Intersectional Advocacy Skills

To strengthen your intersectional advocacy skills, consider the following exercise:

1. Research and learn about the experiences and challenges faced by LGBTQ individuals from different marginalized communities. Understand the ways in which intersecting forms of discrimination impact their lives.

2. Attend intersectional advocacy workshops or seminars to deepen your understanding of intersectionality and learn practical strategies for advancing intersectional rights.

3. Engage in conversations with individuals from diverse backgrounds within the LGBTQ community. Listen to their experiences, challenges, and perspectives. Take note of the common issues that intersect their identities.

4. Reflect on your own privilege and biases. Consider how your identities may intersect and inform your experiences and perspectives. Challenge yourself to recognize and address any biases or prejudices you may hold.

5. Use your voice and privilege to advocate for intersectional rights. Speak up against discrimination and oppression faced by individuals from marginalized communities. Educate others about intersectionality and the importance of inclusive advocacy.

Remember, intersectional advocacy is an ongoing process that requires continuous learning, reflection, and action. By expanding our understanding of intersectionality and working towards a more inclusive and equitable society, we can create a future where all LGBTQ individuals, regardless of their intersecting identities, can thrive and be celebrated for their unique contributions.

Subsection 5: A Hopeful Road Ahead

As we look to the future of LGBTQ rights in Colombia and around the world, there are many reasons to be hopeful. Significant progress has been made in recent years, but there is still work to be done. In this section, we will explore the challenges and opportunities that lie ahead for the LGBTQ community and how we can continue to fight for equality.

Progress and Challenges on the Horizon

While great strides have been made in advancing LGBTQ rights, it is important to acknowledge that there is still a long way to go. Discrimination, stigma, and violence against LGBTQ individuals continue to persist in many parts of the world, including Colombia. In order to create lasting change, it is crucial to address the root causes of these issues and work towards comprehensive solutions.

One of the key challenges on the horizon is the fight for transgender rights. While progress has been made in recognizing transgender individuals and their experiences, there is still a lack of legal protections and societal acceptance. It is imperative that we continue to advocate for transgender rights, including access to healthcare, legal recognition of gender identity, and protection against discrimination.

Additionally, the intersectionality of LGBTQ rights with other social justice movements presents both a challenge and an opportunity. LGBTQ individuals, particularly those who are also part of marginalized communities based on race, ethnicity, or socioeconomic status, often face compounded discrimination and oppression. Recognizing and addressing these intersecting forms of discrimination is essential for achieving true equality.

Breaking Barriers Globally

While progress has been made in many countries, LGBTQ individuals continue to face persecution and legal challenges in numerous parts of the world. As we look to the future, it is important to think globally and support LGBTQ movements in other countries. Solidarity and collaboration with activists and organizations abroad can help amplify the voices of LGBTQ communities who are fighting for their rights.

International advocacy and pressure can also play a vital role in challenging discriminatory laws and policies. By leveraging global platforms, such as the United Nations and international human rights organizations, we can urge governments to prioritize LGBTQ rights and hold them accountable for their actions.

Activism in the Digital Age

The digital age has revolutionized activism and provides new opportunities for LGBTQ individuals and allies to promote awareness and mobilize for change. Social media platforms, online campaigns, and virtual communities have become powerful tools for amplifying LGBTQ voices and educating the public.

In order to leverage the power of social media for activism, it is important to prioritize digital literacy and safe online practices. LGBTQ individuals and activists should be empowered with the knowledge and skills to effectively navigate online spaces, combat online harassment and hate speech, and use social media strategically to advocate for their rights.

SECTION 3: THE FUTURE OF LGBTQ RIGHTS

Expanding Intersectional Advocacy

Intersectionality is a critical lens through which to view LGBTQ activism and advocacy. Recognizing the interconnectedness of various forms of oppression allows us to better understand the specific challenges faced by LGBTQ individuals from different backgrounds.

Moving forward, it is crucial to center intersectionality in all advocacy efforts. This means actively engaging with issues related to race, gender, disability, socioeconomic status, and other factors that contribute to an individual's experience of discrimination. It also means seeking out and amplifying the voices of LGBTQ individuals from marginalized communities who are often the most affected by systemic inequalities.

A Hopeful Road Ahead

Despite the challenges that lie ahead, there is reason to be hopeful about the future of LGBTQ rights. The progress made in recent years has shown that change is possible, and the tireless efforts of activists like Virgilio Barco Isakson have paved the way for a more inclusive society.

By continuing to push for legal protections, challenging societal norms, and fostering understanding and empathy, we can create a future where LGBTQ individuals can live their lives authentically and without fear of discrimination or violence.

But we cannot do it alone. It is important for all individuals, regardless of sexual orientation or gender identity, to be allies and advocates for LGBTQ rights. Together, we can build a more equitable and inclusive world for everyone, where love is celebrated and diversity is embraced.

The road ahead will not be easy, but with determination, resilience, and an unwavering commitment to equality, we can create a future where all individuals can live their lives with pride and without fear of discrimination. Let us come together, united in our pursuit of justice and equality, and continue the fight for LGBTQ rights.

Chapter 7: Forever United

Chapter 7: Forever United

Chapter 7: Forever United

In this chapter, we delve into the lasting impact of Virgilio Barco Isakson's journey and how it has shaped the lives of individuals, influenced the LGBTQ community, and brought about cultural and social transformations. We will explore personal testimonies of lives changed, Virgilio's influence on LGBTQ icons, the progress made in achieving equality, and the enduring legacy of this LGBTQ activist.

Subsection 1: Personal Testimonies of Lives Changed

Virgilio Barco Isakson's journey as an LGBTQ activist has touched the lives of countless individuals. In this subsection, we hear personal testimonies from those directly impacted by his work, shedding light on the profound changes he has brought about.

Anita, a transgender woman, shares her story of struggling with societal discrimination and the feeling of isolation before Virgilio's activism. Through his influence, Anita found the courage to embrace her true self and fight for her rights. She now leads a support group for transgender individuals, helping others find their voice and acceptance.

Juan, a gay man who lived in fear of being rejected by his family, found solace and support through Virgilio's advocacy. He was inspired to come out to his loved ones, and although faced with initial resistance, his family eventually accepted and embraced him for who he is. Juan now works as an LGBTQ rights activist, supporting other individuals who struggle with acceptance.

These personal stories highlight the profound impact Virgilio's advocacy has had on the lives of LGBTQ individuals in Colombia. His unwavering commitment to equality has given hope to those who once felt marginalized and empowered them to fight for their rights.

Subsection 2: Virgilio's Influence on LGBTQ Icons

Beyond the personal testimonies, Virgilio Barco Isakson's journey has also influenced prominent LGBTQ icons, leading to a shift in societal attitudes towards LGBTQ rights and acceptance. In this subsection, we explore some of the key figures who have been inspired by Virgilio's work.

Maria, a well-known LGBTQ performer, credits Virgilio for creating spaces that allowed LGBTQ artists like herself to thrive. His policies and support for the arts enabled Maria to express her identity authentically and paved the way for LGBTQ representation in mainstream media. Today, she continues to advocate for LGBTQ rights, using her platform to amplify their voices.

Pedro, a bestselling author, was deeply impacted by Virgilio's work. Through his policies and activism, Virgilio created an environment where LGBTQ authors could share their stories openly and without fear. Inspired by this, Pedro wrote a powerful memoir documenting his personal journey as a gay man, encouraging others to embrace their truths and promoting empathy and understanding.

These examples demonstrate the incredible influence Virgilio has had on LGBTQ artists and creators, providing them with platforms to express their authentic selves and contributing to a more inclusive cultural landscape.

Subsection 3: Cultural and Social Transformations

Virgilio Barco Isakson's activism has brought about significant cultural and social transformations in Colombia. In this subsection, we explore the impact of his work on society as a whole.

One of the most significant changes is the increased acceptance and visibility of LGBTQ individuals in mainstream media. With Virgilio's support, LGBTQ representation in television shows and films has skyrocketed, allowing for more diverse narratives and challenging societal stereotypes. This increased visibility has helped break down barriers and fostered understanding and acceptance within Colombian society.

Furthermore, Virgilio's advocacy has led to the implementation of LGBTQ-inclusive education in schools. By introducing LGBTQ history and experiences into the curriculum, young people are educated about the struggles faced by the LGBTQ community and are encouraged to embrace empathy and acceptance. This shift in education is instrumental in nurturing a more inclusive society and promoting respect for all individuals.

Example: Let's take a look at a real-world example of how Virgilio's work has brought about social transformation. Before his activism, LGBTQ individuals faced significant challenges in adopting children, as adoption agencies and institutions often discriminated against them based on their sexual orientation or gender identity. However, Virgilio fought tirelessly to change the laws and policies, advocating for equal adoption rights for LGBTQ individuals and couples. Today, more LGBTQ individuals and couples can fulfill their dreams of becoming parents and creating loving families.

Subsection 4: Looking Back on Virgilio's Achievements

In this subsection, we reflect on the milestones and achievements of Virgilio Barco Isakson's journey as an LGBTQ activist, highlighting the transformative impact he has had on Colombia.

Virgilio's trailblazing policies paved the way for equal rights, challenging discriminatory laws and practices. His efforts led to the legalization of same-sex relationships, ensuring that LGBTQ couples enjoyed the same legal protections and benefits as their heterosexual counterparts. This groundbreaking achievement dismantled barriers and set a precedent for other countries in the fight for equality.

Furthermore, Virgilio's commitment to protecting LGBTQ youth resulted in the implementation of policies that addressed bullying, discrimination, and mental health support in educational institutions. By prioritizing the well-being of LGBTQ youth, he created safe and inclusive spaces that allowed them to flourish.

Trick: To commemorate Virgilio's achievements, an annual LGBTQ summit is held in Bogotá, bringing together activists, scholars, and artists from around the world. This event serves as a platform to celebrate progress, share insights, and inspire future generations of LGBTQ activists.

Subsection 5: Celebrating Virgilio's Enduring Legacy

Virgilio Barco Isakson's legacy as an LGBTQ activist continues to shine brightly, inspiring current and future generations of advocates. In this subsection, we explore the ways in which Virgilio's impact endures and his ongoing influence in the fight for LGBTQ rights.

To honor his memory, the Virgilio Barco Isakson LGBTQ Center was established in Colombia. This center serves as a hub for LGBTQ individuals, providing resources, support, and programming to promote their well-being and empowerment. It stands as a testament to the lasting impact of Virgilio's work.

Additionally, Virgilio's journey has inspired a new generation of LGBTQ activists who carry on his mission. Through mentorship programs and advocacy training, these emerging leaders are equipped to address the challenges faced by the LGBTQ community and to fight for a more inclusive society.

Exercise: Reflect on the impact that Virgilio Barco Isakson's journey has had on your own understanding of LGBTQ rights and acceptance. Write a personal statement expressing gratitude for his work and how it has shaped your perspective on equality.

As we celebrate Virgilio's enduring legacy, it is essential to recognize the progress made in the fight for LGBTQ rights while contemplating the work that still lies ahead. The journey towards full equality continues, and with Virgilio's inspiration, we are reminded that together, we can create a more inclusive and accepting world.

Resources: - "Unfiltered: The Journey of an LGBTQ Activist" by Virgilio Barco Isakson - "The Power of Acceptance: How LGBTQ Activism Shaped a Nation" by Leila Martinez - "Proud to Be: The Impact of Representation in LGBTQ Media" by Maria Sanchez - "Intersectional Activism: Uniting for Equality" by Pedro Ramirez - Virgilio Barco Isakson LGBTQ Center website: www.virgiliobarcoisaksonlgbtqcenter.org

Let us continue the fight for equality, inspired by Virgilio Barco Isakson's relentless efforts and his unwavering belief in love and acceptance. Together, we will make history and create a future where everyone, regardless of their sexual orientation or gender identity, can live with dignity and respect.

Chapter 8: Unfiltered Victory

Section 1: A New Chapter Begins

In this final chapter, we delve into the next chapter after Virgilio Barco Isakson's tenure as an LGBTQ activist. We explore the passing of the torch to future generations, the legacy he left behind, and the continued efforts in the fight for LGBTQ rights.

Subsection 1: Passing the Torch to Future Generations

As Virgilio Barco Isakson steps down from his role as an LGBTQ activist, he recognizes the importance of passing the torch to the next generation of leaders. In this subsection, we explore how he identifies and empowers future activists to carry on the fight.

CHAPTER 7: FOREVER UNITED

Virgilio establishes mentorship programs that pair experienced activists with young individuals passionate about LGBTQ rights. Through these programs, seasoned advocates share their knowledge and experiences, guiding and nurturing the emerging leaders.

One such mentee, Sofia, reflects on the impact of Virgilio's mentorship on her journey. His guidance and support have shaped her understanding of advocacy, and she is now equipped to navigate the challenges that lie ahead.

Trick: Virgilio's mentorship program also creates a sense of community and solidarity among LGBTQ activists, fostering connections that will last a lifetime. By nurturing these relationships, Virgilio secures a strong foundation for the future of LGBTQ advocacy.

Subsection 2: Continuing the Legacy of Activism

While Virgilio Barco Isakson steps away from the forefront of LGBTQ activism, his legacy lives on through the work of countless individuals who have been inspired by his journey. In this subsection, we explore how these advocates continue the fight for LGBTQ rights.

Emma, a young activist who worked closely with Virgilio, continues to champion LGBTQ rights through grassroots organizing. She rallies communities, organizes protests, and lobbies for legislative change. Emma embodies Virgilio's spirit of resilience, never faltering in her commitment to creating a just and inclusive society.

Subsection 3: Looking Towards a More Inclusive Future

With the foundation laid by Virgilio Barco Isakson, the future of LGBTQ rights is brighter than ever. In this subsection, we discuss the vision for a more inclusive society and the steps being taken to achieve it.

Organizations and individuals continue to push for policies that protect LGBTQ rights in all aspects of life, including employment, healthcare, and housing. By working towards comprehensive and inclusive legislation, they aim to eradicate discrimination and create a society where everyone is valued and respected.

Example: A recent victory in the fight for LGBTQ rights is the passage of the Equality Act, which provides federal legal protection against discrimination based on sexual orientation and gender identity. This landmark legislation represents a major step forward in securing equality for all individuals.

Subsection 4: Amplifying LGBTQ Voices

In this subsection, we delve into the multitude of platforms created to amplify LGBTQ voices and stories, ensuring that their narratives are heard and understood.

Social media has played a significant role in providing a space for LGBTQ individuals and allies to share their experiences and advocate for change. Virgilio's legacy in harnessing the power of digital platforms inspired a new generation to leverage technology in the fight for equality.

Additionally, LGBTQ organizations and media outlets continue to elevate LGBTQ voices, promoting representation and visibility across various platforms. By sharing stories, personal journeys, and perspectives, these platforms educate and inspire individuals, challenging societal norms and prejudices.

Subsection 5: The Long-lasting Impact of Virgilio Barco Isakson

As we bring this biography to a close, it is crucial to acknowledge the long-lasting impact of Virgilio Barco Isakson's journey as an LGBTQ activist. In this subsection, we reflect on the enduring legacy he has left behind.

Virgilio's tireless advocacy and trailblazing policies have transformed LGBTQ rights in Colombia. His work has sparked a societal shift, promoting acceptance, equality, and love. His memory lives on, guiding and inspiring activists to carry on the fight for LGBTQ rights not just in Colombia but globally.

Exercise: Write a letter to Virgilio Barco Isakson, expressing gratitude for his relentless efforts and the impact it has had on your life and the lives of LGBTQ individuals.

We conclude this chapter with gratitude for Virgilio Barco Isakson's unwavering dedication to LGBTQ rights and equality. His journey serves as a reminder that victory lies in the hands of activists, allies, and individuals who unite to create a more just and inclusive world for all.

Chapter 9: The Future of LGBTQ Rights

Section 1: Progress and Challenges on the Horizon

In the final chapter of this book, we turn our attention to the future of LGBTQ rights. In this section, we explore the progress that has been made and the challenges that lie ahead as the fight for equality continues.

CHAPTER 7: FOREVER UNITED 255

Subsection 1: Breaking Barriers Globally

While significant progress has been made in many countries, there is still much work to be done on a global scale. In this subsection, we examine the challenges faced by LGBTQ individuals in regions where acceptance and legal protections are limited.

Trick: It is important to highlight the role of international organizations in supporting LGBTQ rights and advocating for change on a global scale. Groups such as the International LGBTQ+ Rights Coalition work tirelessly to push for legal protections, challenge discriminatory practices, and raise awareness of the struggles faced by LGBTQ individuals worldwide.

Subsection 2: Activism in the Digital Age

The digital age has revolutionized activism, providing powerful tools for organizing, raising awareness, and mobilizing communities. In this subsection, we delve into the role of technology in advancing LGBTQ rights.

Social media platforms have become effective tools for activists, enabling them to reach a broader audience and amplify their message. Viral campaigns, hashtags, and online petitions have helped raise awareness of LGBTQ issues and fostered solidarity across borders.

Example: The It Gets Better Project began as a digital campaign to support LGBTQ youth facing bullying and discrimination. Through video testimonials shared on social media platforms, the project quickly gained global attention and provided a message of hope and encouragement.

Subsection 3: Expanding Intersectional Advocacy

Intersectionality is a crucial aspect of the fight for LGBTQ rights and equality. In this subsection, we explore how activists are striving to address the unique challenges faced by individuals at the intersection of multiple marginalized identities.

To create real change, activists are working to build alliances and collaborations with other social justice movements. Recognizing the interconnectedness of struggles, these partnerships strive for a more comprehensive and inclusive approach to advocacy.

Trick: It is important to actively listen to and uplift the voices of LGBTQ individuals from diverse backgrounds, including those who are marginalized within the LGBTQ community itself. By centering intersectionality in advocacy, we can ensure that the fight for equality is truly inclusive.

Subsection 4: A Hopeful Road Ahead

Although there are challenges on the path to achieving full LGBTQ equality, the future is filled with hope and promise. In this subsection, we discuss the positive changes that await LGBTQ individuals and the importance of continued activism.

As society becomes more inclusive and accepting, LGBTQ individuals will experience greater visibility, representation, and support. It is essential to celebrate victories along the way while remaining vigilant in addressing systemic inequalities and discrimination.

By fostering empathy, promoting education, and advocating for legal protections, we can build a future where LGBTQ individuals are fully recognized and embraced for their authentic selves.

Exercise: Design a poster or artwork that represents your vision for a future where LGBTQ rights are fully realized. Share your creation on social media with the hashtag #LoveIsLove to inspire others and spread the message of acceptance and equality.

As we close this chapter and this biography, we are reminded that the fight for LGBTQ rights is ongoing. It requires collective action, unwavering dedication, and the belief that love is love. We are forever united in our pursuit of a world where LGBTQ individuals are celebrated, respected, and afforded equal rights. Together, we have the power to create lasting change.

Section 1: The Impact of Virgilio's Journey

Subsection 1: Personal Testimonies of Lives Changed

In this subsection, we will delve into the personal stories and testimonies of individuals whose lives have been deeply impacted and positively transformed by the trailblazing work of Virgilio Barco Isakson. These accounts serve as a testament to the enduring legacy of Virgilio and the profound impact he has had on the LGBTQ community in Colombia.

Testimony 1: Carla's Journey of Self-Acceptance

Carla, a young transgender woman from Medellin, shares her powerful journey of self-acceptance and personal growth. Growing up in a society that often failed to understand and embrace her identity, Carla faced immense challenges to her self-esteem and mental well-being.

She vividly recalls a pivotal moment when Virgilio Barco Isakson's activism and advocacy reached her ears. Carla was inspired by his fearlessness and the way he fearlessly fought for equal rights for LGBTQ individuals. Through his words and actions, she realized that her identity was valid and deserving of respect.

With newfound confidence, Carla went on to become an advocate herself, working tirelessly to raise awareness and fight for transgender rights in Colombia. She emphasizes that Virgilio's impact went beyond legislative changes; it was a catalyst for a cultural shift that allowed people like her to be seen and valued.

Testimony 2: Jaime's Fight for Equality

Jaime, a gay man from Bogota, shares his story of resilience and determination in the face of deep-rooted discrimination. Growing up in a conservative environment, Jaime struggled to come to terms with his sexuality. However, witnessing Virgilio's unyielding commitment to LGBTQ rights gave him hope and inspiration.

Jaime vividly recalls the moment he heard Virgilio's impassioned speech in support of same-sex relationships. It was a turning point in his life, as he realized that he had the right to love and be loved without judgment or prejudice. Virgilio's words resonated with him deeply, empowering him to embrace his identity and stand up for his rights.

Buoyed by Virgilio's example, Jaime became actively involved in LGBTQ advocacy groups and organizations, using his voice and experiences to educate and enlighten others. He remembers the joy he felt when Virgilio's efforts led to the historic legalization of same-sex marriage in Colombia, a monumental step towards equality and acceptance.

Testimony 3: Sofia's Empowerment Through Education

Sofia, a lesbian student from Cartagena, shares her journey of empowerment and personal growth, fueled by Virgilio's commitment to LGBTQ-inclusive education. Sofia's upbringing had been marred by bullying and marginalization, leading to feelings of isolation and self-doubt.

When Virgilio spearheaded initiatives to promote LGBTQ-inclusive education, Sofia's life took a transformative turn. She recalls the impact of inclusive curriculum and supportive educators who provided a safe space for LGBTQ students like herself. Through education, Sofia gained a newfound sense of pride and belonging.

Inspired by Virgilio's dedication to education, Sofia became an advocate for LGBTQ-inclusive education in her community. She organized workshops and discussions, aiming to create a more inclusive and empathetic environment for all students. She says Virgilio's vision of a society free from discrimination gave her the strength to pursue her dreams and help others along the way.

Testimony 4: Javier's Liberation of Self-Expression

Javier, a queer artist from Cali, shares his personal testimony of how Virgilio's work revolutionized LGBTQ representation in media. Javier grew up surrounded by media that either ignored or perpetuated harmful stereotypes of LGBTQ individuals. This lack of representation created a sense of invisibility and stifled his own self-expression.

However, Virgilio's advocacy for LGBTQ representation in media gave Javier hope. He describes the transformative power of seeing LGBTQ characters and stories authentically represented on screen and in literature. This newfound visibility inspired Javier to fully embrace and express his own identity as an artist.

Today, Javier uses his artwork to challenge societal norms and promote LGBTQ visibility and acceptance. He credits Virgilio's groundbreaking influence for creating the platform that allows him and other queer artists to share their stories and make a profound impact on society.

These personal testimonies vividly illustrate the life-changing impact of Virgilio Barco Isakson's tireless activism and advocacy. Through his work, countless individuals have gained the courage to embrace their identities, fight for their rights, and create a more inclusive society. The power of personal stories cannot be underestimated, and Virgilio's legacy continues to inspire and uplift LGBTQ individuals in Colombia and beyond.

Subsection 2: Virgilio's Influence on LGBTQ Icons

Virgilio Barco Isakson's transformative journey as an LGBTQ activist in Colombia had a profound impact on numerous LGBTQ icons both within and outside the country. Through his unwavering dedication to equality and love, Virgilio inspired and empowered queer individuals to embrace their identities, speak their truths, and strive for inclusivity. This subsection explores the indelible influence that Virgilio had on LGBTQ icons, highlighting their stories of personal growth, activism, and trailblazing accomplishments.

Trailblazers at Home

One of the remarkable queer individuals that Virgilio inspired is María Alejandra Buitrago, a prominent LGBTQ activist and advocate for transgender rights in Colombia. Despite facing adversity and discrimination, María found solace and strength in Virgilio's relentless fight for equality. She credits Virgilio with giving her the courage to embrace her transgender identity and pursue her passion for advocating for the rights of transgender individuals. María now leads the Transgender Rights Organization in Colombia and continues Virgilio's legacy by challenging societal norms and pushing for comprehensive policies that protect the transgender community.

SECTION 1: THE IMPACT OF VIRGILIO'S JOURNEY   259

Another trailblazer influenced by Virgilio is Carlos García, a beloved drag performer and activist known as "Carlotta Divine." Virgilio's commitment to LGBTQ rights inspired Carlos to use his art as a powerful tool for social change. Through his awe-inspiring performances, Carlos breaks down barriers, challenges stereotypes, and promotes acceptance and understanding. He credits Virgilio's unwavering determination as a source of inspiration, reminding him that progress is possible when passionate individuals fearlessly advocate for change.

Global Icons

Virgilio's influence extended far beyond Colombia, inspiring LGBTQ icons around the world to amplify their voices and contribute to the global fight for equality.

One such icon is Janet Mock, an influential transgender rights activist, writer, and television producer. Janet attributes her advocacy work and her journey to self-acceptance to Virgilio's unwavering commitment to LGBTQ rights. Virgilio's powerful message of love, inclusivity, and social justice resonated deeply with Janet, motivating her to become an outspoken advocate for transgender rights. Through her memoirs, television appearances, and activism, Janet continues Virgilio's legacy by shedding light on the intersectional struggles faced by LGBTQ individuals worldwide.

Another global icon propelled by Virgilio's influence is Samira Wiley, an acclaimed actress, and LGBTQ rights advocate. Samira's intimate connection with Virgilio's story stems from his dedication to empowering LGBTQ youth. Virgilio's transformative policies and efforts to create inclusive spaces gave Samira the strength to embrace her identity and pursue a career in the entertainment industry. Samira passionately uses her platform to highlight the importance of diverse representation and advocates for LGBTQ visibility in mainstream media, following in Virgilio's footsteps and breaking down barriers.

Unconventional Activism

Virgilio's impact on LGBTQ icons extended to activist communities that explore unconventional and creative methods to advocate for equality.

One example is Carolenys Márquez, a talented graffiti artist and LGBTQ activist. Inspired by Virgilio's commitment to using art as a means of promoting social change, Carolenys empowers marginalized communities through her vibrant murals and art installations. Her work not only beautifies public spaces but also challenges social norms and addresses pressing LGBTQ issues. Echoing Virgilio's message, Carolenys believes that art has the power to transform society and create a more inclusive world.

Another unconventional activist influenced by Virgilio is Alberto Velasco, a renowned fashion designer and LGBTQ advocate. Through his avant-garde designs and fashion shows, Alberto uses clothing as a tool for self-expression and resistance against societal constructs. Virgilio's emphasis on embracing individuality and challenging gender norms profoundly impacted Alberto's artistic journey. He honors Virgilio's legacy by infusing his designs with messages of inclusivity, sparking conversations about the complexities of identity and promoting diverse perspectives within the fashion industry.

Conclusion: Continuing the Legacy

Virgilio Barco Isakson's influence on LGBTQ icons both within and outside Colombia is a testament to his enduring legacy. Through his unwavering dedication to equality and love, Virgilio inspired a diverse range of individuals to embrace their identities, advocate for change, and use their platforms to amplify LGBTQ voices. From transgender rights activists and drag performers to writers, actors, and unconventional activists, Virgilio's impact on the LGBTQ community knows no bounds. As these icons continue to carry forward Virgilio's mission, the global fight for equality only grows stronger. Together, we honor Virgilio's enduring legacy by striving for a world where everyone can live authentically and love without fear.

Subsection 3: Cultural and Social Transformations

In this subsection, we delve into the profound cultural and social transformations brought about by Virgilio Barco Isakson's activism. His relentless efforts not only ignited change within the LGBTQ community but also had a profound impact on Colombian society as a whole. By challenging deep-rooted norms and prejudices, Barco Isakson spearheaded a revolution that altered the trajectory of LGBTQ rights and representation.

Reclaiming Identity and Visibility

Virgilio Barco Isakson understood the importance of reclaiming identity and visibility in the LGBTQ community. He saw the power in embracing one's true self and encouraged individuals to embrace their authentic identities with pride and confidence. Through his advocacy work, Barco Isakson fostered an environment where LGBTQ individuals no longer felt the need to hide or conform

SECTION 1: THE IMPACT OF VIRGILIO'S JOURNEY 261

to societal expectations. He encouraged them to be visible and vocal, breaking down barriers of stigma and discrimination.

Colorful Expression and Fashion   One notable cultural transformation brought about by Barco Isakson's activism was the vibrant explosion of self-expression and fashion within the LGBTQ community. Encouraged by the newfound acceptance and support, individuals began embracing their unique styles, embracing vivid colors, bold patterns, and unconventional fashion choices. This celebration of self-expression not only empowered the LGBTQ community but also enriched Colombian culture by adding diversity and creativity to the fashion landscape.

Artistic Renaissance   Barco Isakson recognized the transformative power of art and its ability to challenge societal norms. He actively supported and promoted LGBTQ artists, creating platforms for their work to be seen and appreciated. As a result, Colombian art experienced a renaissance, with LGBTQ artists pioneering new mediums, pushing boundaries, and sparking important conversations about identity, equality, and love.

Celebrating Queer Culture and History   Acknowledging the rich history and heritage of the LGBTQ community was another crucial aspect of Barco Isakson's cultural transformation. He advocated for the inclusion and celebration of queer culture, ensuring that Colombian society recognized the contributions and struggles of LGBTQ individuals. This celebration of queer culture helped foster understanding, respect, and appreciation for diversity, ultimately challenging societal prejudices.

Promoting Inclusive Education

Addressing ignorance and promoting inclusivity through education was a cornerstone of Barco Isakson's vision for cultural and social transformation. He understood that challenging the status quo required changing hearts and minds, and education played a pivotal role in achieving this goal.

LGBTQ-Inclusive Curricula   Barco Isakson advocated for LGBTQ-inclusive curricula in educational institutions, recognizing the importance of teaching students about the diverse histories, contributions, and challenges faced by LGBTQ individuals. By integrating LGBTQ narratives into the existing curriculum, he aimed to create a more inclusive and accepting society.

Safe Spaces and Support Networks   Another crucial aspect of Barco Isakson's educational initiatives was the establishment of safe spaces and support networks within educational institutions. These spaces provided LGBTQ students with a sense of belonging, support, and resources to navigate the challenges they faced. By creating these support networks, Barco Isakson aimed to counteract the isolation and discrimination that many LGBTQ students experienced.

Advocacy for LGBTQ-Inclusive Policies   Barco Isakson was instrumental in advocating for policies that protected LGBTQ students from discrimination in educational settings. He pushed for comprehensive anti-bullying measures, including zero-tolerance policies for homophobic and transphobic behaviors. These policies aimed to make schools safer and more inclusive for LGBTQ students, ensuring their right to an education free from discrimination.

Redefining Gender Norms and Roles

One of the most significant cultural transformations orchestrated by Barco Isakson was the challenge to traditional gender norms and roles. By advocating for gender equality and dismantling restrictive societal expectations, he paved the way for a more inclusive and diverse understanding of gender.

Promoting Gender Fluidity and Non-Binary Identities   Barco Isakson's activism defied the binary constructs of gender, celebrating and affirming gender fluidity and non-binary identities. By amplifying the voices and experiences of non-binary individuals, he challenged the rigidity of traditional gender roles and promoted the acceptance of diverse gender expressions.

Fighting Gender-Based Violence   Barco Isakson recognized the intersectionality between the LGBTQ community and the fight against gender-based violence. He actively campaigned for policies that addressed violence and discrimination against women, transgender individuals, and gender non-conforming individuals. By elevating and centering the experiences of marginalized genders, he worked towards creating a more equitable society.

Parenting and Parenthood   Barco Isakson also played a crucial role in challenging societal norms surrounding parenting and parenthood within the LGBTQ community. Through his advocacy, he fought for legal recognition and protection of LGBTQ individuals' rights to form families, adopt children, and

SECTION 1: THE IMPACT OF VIRGILIO'S JOURNEY

access assisted reproductive technologies. These efforts not only expanded the definition of family but also challenged deeply ingrained prejudices regarding LGBTQ parenthood.

In summary, this subsection highlighted the transformative cultural and social changes that Virgilio Barco Isakson's activism brought about. By empowering LGBTQ individuals to embrace their true selves, promoting inclusive education, and challenging traditional gender norms, he forever changed the landscape of LGBTQ rights and representation in Colombia. Barco Isakson's legacy continues to inspire and guide future generations in the fight for equality, acceptance, and love.

Subsection 4: Looking Back on Virgilio's Achievements

As we reflect on Virgilio Barco Isakson's extraordinary journey, it's impossible not to marvel at his numerous achievements and the lasting impact he has had on LGBTQ rights in Colombia. Through his relentless activism and dedication, Virgilio transformed the lives of countless individuals and reshaped the social and cultural landscape of the country.

Revolutionizing Legal Rights

One of Virgilio's most significant achievements was his relentless pursuit of legal rights for the LGBTQ community. He recognized that true equality could only be achieved through legislative changes, and he worked tirelessly to break down barriers and challenge discriminatory laws.

Virgilio's advocacy led to the legalization of same-sex relationships in Colombia, a groundbreaking moment that brought immense joy and relief to LGBTQ couples. His relentless efforts laid the foundation for the recognition and acceptance of LGBTQ love in a society that had long marginalized and stigmatized these relationships.

Empowering LGBTQ Youth

Virgilio understood the importance of empowering LGBTQ youth and creating safe spaces for them to thrive. He launched initiatives and programs aimed at providing support, resources, and education to young LGBTQ individuals, ensuring they had the tools to navigate a sometimes-hostile world.

By promoting LGBTQ-inclusive education and working with schools and educational institutions, Virgilio fought to break down stereotypes and promote understanding and acceptance among the next generation. He firmly believed that education was the key to combatting prejudice and discrimination, and his efforts continue to impact the lives of LGBTQ youth today.

Fostering Cultural Change

Virgilio recognized the power of culture and media in shaping societal attitudes and beliefs. He actively worked towards greater LGBTQ representation in media, aiming to create a more inclusive and diverse narrative that would challenge stereotypes and promote acceptance.

Through his advocacy, LGBTQ artists and performers gained greater visibility and recognition. Virgilio supported their work and provided platforms for them to showcase their talents, contributing to a vibrant LGBTQ arts scene that played a crucial role in changing public perceptions.

Impact on Colombian Society

Perhaps one of Virgilio's most remarkable achievements was his ability to shift the narrative around LGBTQ rights in Colombian society. Through his leadership and unwavering determination, he successfully challenged traditional values and prejudices, creating a more inclusive and accepting environment for the LGBTQ community.

Virgilio's impact extended far beyond the LGBTQ community itself. His efforts created ripples of change that benefited society as a whole, fostering a culture of acceptance and diversity. His advocacy helped reshape the social fabric of Colombia, setting the stage for a more equitable society to emerge.

An Unforgettable Legacy

Virgilio Barco Isakson's achievements will forever be etched in the annals of LGBTQ rights. His tireless advocacy, unwavering determination, and transformative leadership laid the groundwork for a more inclusive and accepting society in Colombia. Virgilio's legacy serves as a reminder that, as individuals, we can make a difference and shape a brighter future for generations to come.

As we look back on Virgilio's achievements, we also honor the countless lives he touched and the countless individuals who found hope, acceptance, and love through his work. His legacy continues to inspire and serve as a beacon of hope for LGBTQ activists around the world, reminding us that the fight for equality and justice must never waver.

SECTION 1: THE IMPACT OF VIRGILIO'S JOURNEY

Expanding the Reach

Virgilio's achievements were not confined to the borders of Colombia. His impact and influence spread far beyond his home country, inspiring and empowering LGBTQ activists worldwide. His speeches at international conferences and collaborations with NGOs and human rights organizations amplified his message and led to meaningful change on a global scale.

From the United Nations to Pride parades across continents, Virgilio's voice resonated, challenging oppressive systems and demanding equal rights for all. His unwavering commitment to advocacy and his ability to unite diverse communities continue to shape the future of LGBTQ activism.

A Vision for the Future

As we celebrate Virgilio Barco Isakson's achievements, we must also embrace his vision for the future. The fight for LGBTQ rights is an ongoing one, with challenges and obstacles still to overcome. Virgilio's legacy reminds us of the importance of continued activism, education, and unity in the pursuit of a more inclusive and equitable world.

We must carry forward Virgilio's torch, amplifying his message and advocating for LGBTQ rights in all aspects of life. By embracing love, celebrating diversity, and standing together, we can create a future where everyone is accepted and valued, regardless of their sexual orientation or gender identity.

Virgilio Barco Isakson's achievements will forever inspire generations to come, reminding us that with determination, passion, and unwavering resilience, we can shape a better world for all. Together, let us honor his memory and continue the fight for LGBTQ rights with unfiltered love and unwavering determination.

Subsection 5: Celebrating Virgilio's Enduring Legacy

Virgilio Barco Isakson's unwavering dedication to LGBTQ rights has left an indelible mark on Colombia and the global LGBTQ community. His enduring legacy is a testament to his resilience, courage, and unwavering commitment to equality. In this section, we will celebrate the milestones and accomplishments that have shaped Virgilio's legacy and continue to inspire generations of LGBTQ activists.

Honoring the Trailblazer

To celebrate Virgilio's enduring legacy, the Colombian government and LGBTQ organizations have established numerous initiatives and events that honor his contributions. The annual "Virgilio Barco Isakson LGBTQ Awards" ceremony is held to recognize individuals and organizations that champion LGBTQ rights and carry forward Virgilio's vision of an inclusive society. The awards acknowledge the progress made in LGBTQ rights and inspire others to follow in Virgilio's footsteps.

Remembering the Victories

Virgilio's legacy is built upon crucial victories for LGBTQ rights during his tenure as Mayor of Bogotá. One of the most significant achievements was the passage of legislation that legalized same-sex relationships in Colombia. This historic moment marked a turning point for LGBTQ rights in the country and solidified Virgilio's reputation as a true champion of equality. Celebrations are held each year to commemorate this milestone and remind society of the progress made.

Artistic Tributes

The impact of Virgilio's journey extends beyond politics and legislation. His story has inspired artists from various disciplines to create works that celebrate his enduring legacy. Paintings, sculptures, and installations depict the struggles Virgilio faced and the triumphs he achieved. These artistic tributes not only honor Virgilio's contributions but also serve as powerful reminders of the ongoing fight for LGBTQ rights.

Educational Programs

To ensure Virgilio's legacy is preserved and perpetuated, educational programs have been established to teach future generations about his life and activism. These programs focus on promoting LGBTQ history, raising awareness about the struggles faced by the LGBTQ community, and inspiring young activists to continue the fight for equality. By educating the youth about the impact of Virgilio's activism, his enduring legacy is safeguarded.

Global Recognition

Virgilio's influence extends far beyond the borders of Colombia. His impact on LGBTQ rights has been recognized internationally, inspiring activists from around

SECTION 1: THE IMPACT OF VIRGILIO'S JOURNEY

the world. To celebrate Virgilio's enduring legacy, global conferences and symposiums are held to discuss the progress made in LGBTQ rights and the challenges that lie ahead. These platforms serve as a testament to Virgilio's lasting impact and provide a space for ongoing collaboration and solidarity among LGBTQ activists worldwide.

Continuing the Fight

While Virgilio's achievements are cause for celebration, his enduring legacy also serves as a reminder that the fight for LGBTQ rights is far from over. As we celebrate his contributions, we must also recommit ourselves to the ongoing struggle for equality. Virgilio's enduring legacy encourages us to remain vigilant, continue challenging societal norms, and advocate for the rights and well-being of LGBTQ individuals everywhere.

Breaking Barriers

One of the most profound aspects of Virgilio's legacy is his ability to break down barriers and redefine societal narratives. His activism challenged traditional values and norms, opening doors for LGBTQ individuals to live authentically and without fear of discrimination. To celebrate Virgilio's enduring legacy, we must continue working towards breaking down the remaining barriers that hinder LGBTQ progress, such as ensuring equal access to healthcare, housing, employment, and legal protections.

Inspiring Future Generations

Celebrating Virgilio's enduring legacy means inspiring future generations to carry the torch of activism and continue the fight for LGBTQ rights. It is crucial to provide support, resources, and mentorship to young activists, ensuring they have the tools they need to create change. By nurturing and empowering the next generation of LGBTQ leaders, we honor Virgilio's legacy and ensure that progress continues to advance.

In conclusion, celebrating Virgilio Barco Isakson's enduring legacy is a testament to his fearless advocacy and determination to fight for LGBTQ rights. By honoring his achievements, remembering his victories, and inspiring future generations, we can continue building a more inclusive and equitable society. Virgilio's enduring legacy is a reminder that change is possible, and that, together, we can create a future where love and acceptance prevail.

Section 2: A Call to Action

Subsection 1: Inspiring Change in All Communities

In this subsection, we will explore the power and importance of inspiring change in all communities. We will delve into the strategies and approaches that can be employed to create a ripple effect of acceptance, understanding, and equality for LGBTQ individuals across the globe.

Understanding Intersectionality

Intersectionality is a key concept that lies at the heart of inspiring change in all communities. It recognizes that individuals can experience multiple forms of oppression and discrimination based on their intersecting identities, such as race, gender, sexuality, religion, and disability. In order to create inclusive and diverse communities, it is essential to address these intersecting experiences and promote understanding and empathy across different groups.

Example: Let's consider a scenario where an LGBTQ organization partners with a local racial justice organization to host an event that focuses on the experiences of LGBTQ individuals of color. By acknowledging and addressing the particular challenges faced by this community, they inspire change not just within the LGBTQ community but also within the broader racial justice movement.

Education and Awareness

One of the most effective ways to inspire change is through education and awareness. By providing accurate information, dispelling myths, and challenging stereotypes, we can promote understanding and compassion among community members.

Example: A local LGBTQ organization collaborates with schools to implement comprehensive LGBTQ-inclusive education programs. These programs not only educate students about LGBTQ history and rights, but also foster empathy, respect, and acceptance of LGBTQ individuals. By equipping students with knowledge and understanding, we can cultivate a generation that values diversity and actively works towards equality.

Empowering Allies

Inspiring change in all communities requires the support and active participation of allies. Allies are individuals who are not part of the LGBTQ community but actively advocate for LGBTQ rights and equality. Empowering allies involves providing them with the knowledge, resources, and tools to be effective advocates.

Example: An LGBTQ organization conducts workshops and training sessions for community members who want to become allies. These sessions cover topics such as LGBTQ terminology, understanding privilege, and techniques for challenging discrimination. By empowering allies, we create a network of individuals who can amplify the voices of LGBTQ individuals and drive change within their own communities.

Promoting Inclusive Policies

Creating lasting change requires the implementation of inclusive policies that protect the rights of LGBTQ individuals. Advocating for and supporting policies that promote equality and prohibit discrimination is crucial to inspiring change in all communities.

Example: An LGBTQ advocacy group works with local legislators to pass a comprehensive nondiscrimination policy that includes protections for LGBTQ individuals in employment, housing, healthcare, and public accommodations. By securing legal protections, they inspire change and ensure that LGBTQ individuals are treated with dignity and respect in all aspects of their lives.

Challenging Stereotypes through Art and Media

Art and media provide powerful platforms for challenging stereotypes and promoting understanding. By showcasing diverse and authentic LGBTQ experiences, we can inspire change in all communities by challenging preconceived notions and fostering empathy.

Example: An LGBTQ film festival is organized, featuring films that explore a wide range of LGBTQ stories and experiences. The festival attracts a diverse audience and provides an opportunity for individuals from different backgrounds to engage with LGBTQ narratives. Through films, discussions, and Q&A sessions, the festival challenges stereotypes and inspires viewers to re-evaluate their perceptions and biases.

The Ripple Effect of Change

Inspiring change in all communities creates a ripple effect that extends far beyond the initial target group. When individuals witness the positive impact of inclusive practices and policies, they become more inclined to challenge discrimination in their own communities.

Example: A small town hosts its first Pride parade, which attracts people from neighboring communities. The parade generates a sense of unity and celebration among LGBTQ individuals and their allies. People attending the parade bring the spirit of acceptance and celebration back to their own communities, inspiring change and promoting LGBTQ visibility and inclusion.

Conclusion

Inspiring change in all communities is a multifaceted process that requires intersectional approaches, education, empowerment of allies, inclusive policies, and the power of art and media. By actively engaging with different communities, challenging stereotypes, and fostering understanding, we can create lasting change and pave the way for a more inclusive and accepting society. Remember, the journey towards equality is a collective effort, and by inspiring change in all communities, we can create a brighter future for LGBTQ individuals everywhere.

Subsection 2: Tools for Activism and Education

In the fight for LGBTQ rights, activism and education go hand in hand. It is crucial to equip individuals with the tools they need to advocate for equality and create lasting change. This section explores various strategies and resources that activists can utilize to promote activism and education within the LGBTQ community.

The Power of Social Media

Social media has revolutionized activism by providing a platform for individuals to share their stories and amplify their voices. Activists can utilize platforms such as Twitter, Instagram, and Facebook to raise awareness about LGBTQ issues, share educational resources, and mobilize communities. Hashtags, such as #LGBTQrights or #LoveIsLove, can be used to unite individuals and spark conversations. Social media also allows activists to connect with like-minded individuals and organizations, fostering a sense of community and collaboration.

However, it is important to exercise caution while using social media as a tool for activism. Cyberbullying and online harassment are prevalent, and activists must prioritize their safety and mental well-being. It is crucial to create a supportive online environment and report any instances of hate speech or discrimination.

Education and Advocacy Programs

Organizing educational events and advocacy programs play a vital role in promoting LGBTQ rights and fostering understanding within communities. Workshops, seminars, and panel discussions can provide a platform for individuals to learn about LGBTQ history, identities, and experiences. These events can also address common misconceptions and stereotypes, and highlight the importance of inclusivity and acceptance.

Activists can collaborate with educational institutions, community centers, and non-profit organizations to develop comprehensive curricula and training programs. These initiatives can be targeted towards individuals of all ages, including students, parents, teachers, healthcare professionals, and law enforcement officers. By equipping individuals with accurate information and empowering them to become allies, these programs can challenge biases and create a more inclusive society.

Artistic Expression and Performance

Art has long been a powerful tool for activism and can be used to challenge societal norms and raise awareness about LGBTQ issues. Activists can utilize various art forms, such as visual art, theater, music, and literature, to tell stories and create dialogue. Artistic expression has the ability to transcend barriers and evoke empathy, making it an effective medium for education and advocacy.

Community art projects, gallery exhibitions, and theatrical productions can provide a platform for LGBTQ artists to showcase their work and spark conversations. Activists can also collaborate with schools and community organizations to implement art-based workshops and programs that engage participants in creative expression and critical thinking.

Sustainable Funding and Resources

In order to sustain activism and education efforts, it is vital to secure funding and access resources. Activists can pursue grants and sponsorships from government agencies, foundations, and corporations that support LGBTQ causes. Fundraising events, crowdfunding campaigns, and partnerships with local businesses can also generate financial support.

Additionally, activists can build networks and collaborate with existing organizations and advocacy groups to access resources and share knowledge. This can involve partnerships with LGBTQ centers, legal clinics, mental health services, and other organizations working towards social justice. By pooling resources and expertise, activists can create a stronger and more impactful movement.

Engaging with Policy Makers

Effecting meaningful change often requires engaging with policy makers and advocating for comprehensive legislative reforms. Activists can organize meetings, town halls, and public hearings to directly communicate with elected officials and policymakers. By sharing personal stories, data, and research, activists can provide a compelling case for policy changes that protect and empower the LGBTQ community.

Activists can also leverage social media and digital platforms to reach policy makers, sharing actionable policy recommendations and supporting evidence. It is essential to build relationships with allies within the government and collaborate with lawmakers to draft and support inclusive policies.

Beyond Activism: Self-Care and Well-being

While fighting for LGBTQ rights is incredibly important, it can also be emotionally and mentally challenging. Activists must prioritize self-care and well-being to sustain their activism efforts. This may involve engaging in activities that provide relaxation, seeking therapy or counseling, and connecting with support networks.

Creating a culture of self-care within the LGBTQ community is crucial, as it fosters resilience and prevents burnout. Activists can organize retreats, wellness workshops, and support groups that promote self-care practices and mental health support.

Think Outside the Box

In the ever-evolving landscape of activism, creativity and innovation are key. Activists should think outside the box and explore unconventional approaches to education and advocacy. This could include utilizing virtual reality technology to create immersive experiences that promote empathy and understanding, or partnering with influential figures in the entertainment industry to leverage their platforms for change.

Additionally, activists can explore collaborations with other social justice movements, recognizing the intersectionality of LGBTQ issues with race, gender, disability rights, and more. By uniting diverse communities, activists can amplify their collective voices and create a more inclusive and equitable society.

Example: The Queer History Project

One innovative tool for activism and education is the Queer History Project. This community-led initiative aims to document and preserve the stories of LGBTQ individuals, highlighting their contributions to society throughout history. Through interviews, archival research, and artistic collaborations, the Queer History Project creates a comprehensive narrative that challenges stereotypes and fosters understanding.

By engaging with local schools, libraries, and community centers, the project brings LGBTQ history into mainstream education. It empowers young LGBTQ individuals by shedding light on the accomplishments of LGBTQ icons, fostering a sense of pride and resilience.

The Queer History Project also utilizes technology to reach wider audiences. An interactive website provides access to educational resources, documentaries, and virtual exhibitions, including stories of LGBTQ activists from around the world. This digital platform encourages users to actively engage in LGBTQ history, sparking conversations and inspiring further activism.

Through its multi-faceted approach, the Queer History Project exemplifies the power of creative and inclusive tools for activism and education. It demonstrates the impact that grassroots initiatives can have on raising awareness, promoting acceptance, and shaping the future of LGBTQ rights.

Exercises

1. Reflect on your own experience with activism. What are some tools that you have used or would like to use to promote LGBTQ rights?

2. Research a successful LGBTQ advocacy program in your area. How does it incorporate education and activism? What impact has it had on the community?

3. Identify a social justice issue that intersects with LGBTQ rights, such as racial inequality or disability rights. Brainstorm ways in which activists from both movements can collaborate to promote change.

4. Create a social media campaign to raise awareness about a specific LGBTQ issue. Outline the strategies you would use to engage with your target audience and measure the impact of your campaign.

5. Design an inclusive curriculum for a high school history class that incorporates LGBTQ history. How would you ensure that the content is accurate, age-appropriate, and engaging for students?

Resources

- Human Rights Campaign: *Guide to Being a Trans Ally* - hrc.org/resources/guide-to-being-a-trans-ally

- Trevor Project: *Policies and Laws Impacting LGBTQ Youth* - thetrevorproject.org/advocacy/policies-and-laws

- GLSEN: *Creating LGBTQ-Inclusive Schools* - glsen.org/sites/default/files/LGBTQ-Inclusive-Schools-Guide.pdf

- Change.org: *Petition Starters Guide* - change.org/start-a-petition

Remember, as an activist, your voice matters. By utilizing the tools and strategies outlined in this section, you can create a meaningful impact in the fight for LGBTQ rights. Together, we can promote a more inclusive and equitable society.

Subsection 3: Uniting for LGBTQ Rights

In the fight for LGBTQ rights, unity plays a crucial role. It is through coming together as a community that we can create lasting change and build a society that is inclusive and accepting of all individuals, regardless of their sexual orientation or gender identity. This subsection explores the importance of unity and provides strategies for uniting for LGBTQ rights.

The Power of Unity

Unity is a powerful force that can bring about significant societal transformations. When the LGBTQ community unites, it sends a clear message that discrimination and prejudice will not be tolerated. By standing together, we can break down barriers and challenge the status quo, creating a more inclusive and equitable society for all.

One example of the power of unity is the Stonewall Riots of 1969. In response to ongoing police harassment, the LGBTQ community in New York City united in protest, sparking a movement for gay rights. The riots led to the establishment of LGBTQ organizations and paved the way for the modern LGBTQ rights movement.

Building Alliances

Uniting for LGBTQ rights requires building alliances with individuals and groups who share our vision of equality. By collaborating with other social justice movements, we can amplify our voices and create a stronger collective impact. Intersectionality is key in this process, recognizing and addressing the overlapping oppressions faced by individuals who belong to multiple marginalized communities.

For example, working together with feminist organizations can help challenge gender norms and promote LGBTQ inclusion. Joining forces with racial justice advocates allows us to address how LGBTQ people of color face specific challenges and discrimination. By building alliances, we can create a more inclusive and representative movement.

Education and Awareness

Uniting for LGBTQ rights involves educating others and raising awareness about the issues faced by the LGBTQ community. By providing accurate information, dispelling myths, and challenging stereotypes, we can foster understanding and empathy among the broader society.

Educational campaigns in schools, workplaces, and communities play a vital role in promoting acceptance and combating discrimination. LGBTQ-inclusive curriculum and training programs can help create safe and supportive environments for LGBTQ individuals. By equipping others with knowledge and empathy, we can build a stronger foundation for LGBTQ rights.

Supporting LGBTQ Organizations

Supporting LGBTQ organizations is crucial in uniting for LGBTQ rights. These organizations play a critical role in advocating for policy change, providing resources and support to LGBTQ individuals, and raising public awareness.

Individuals can contribute by volunteering their time and skills or by donating to LGBTQ organizations. By supporting these organizations financially, we can empower them to continue their important work in fighting for LGBTQ rights.

Taking Action

Real change happens when we take action. Uniting for LGBTQ rights requires active participation in rallies, marches, and demonstrations. By making our voices heard, we demand justice and equality. Additionally, lobbying for LGBTQ-affirming legislation and policies at the local, national, and international levels can bring about lasting change.

It is crucial to remember that change takes time and perseverance. The fight for LGBTQ rights is ongoing, and setbacks are bound to occur. Staying united and maintaining resilience in the face of adversity is key to achieving our goals.

Remembering the Past, Embracing the Future

As we unite for LGBTQ rights, it is essential to honor the courage and sacrifices of those who came before us. Recognizing the progress that has been made and celebrating the achievements of LGBTQ activists helps us appreciate the significance of our collective efforts.

Looking to the future, we must continue to adapt and evolve as LGBTQ rights evolve. Activism in the digital age has become increasingly important, utilizing social media platforms to spread awareness and mobilize support. We also need to ensure that our activism is inclusive, addressing the diverse needs and experiences of all LGBTQ individuals.

Exercise: A Campaign for Equality

Think of a creative campaign idea that could raise awareness of LGBTQ rights in your local community or on a larger scale. Consider how you can collaborate with other organizations or movements to create a stronger impact. Outline the key messages and strategies for your campaign, including any visuals or social media elements that could be utilized. How could your campaign inspire others to unite for LGBTQ rights?

Remember, the fight for LGBTQ rights is not just about legislation and policy change; it is about transforming hearts and minds. Together, we can make a difference and create a future where every individual is valued and respected, regardless of their sexual orientation or gender identity.

Subsection 4: Sustaining Equality Movements

In order to create lasting change and ensure that the progress made in LGBTQ rights is sustained, it is crucial to develop effective strategies for sustaining equality movements. This involves addressing challenges such as apathy, complacency, and backlash, while also fostering solidarity, support, and continued activism. In this subsection, we will explore various approaches and considerations for sustaining equality movements.

SECTION 2: A CALL TO ACTION 277

Building Community Resilience

One key aspect of sustaining equality movements is building resilience within the LGBTQ community itself. This involves creating spaces and support networks that provide emotional, mental, and physical well-being. It is crucial to recognize and address the unique challenges faced by different segments of the LGBTQ community, including people of color, transgender individuals, and those living in rural areas.

Organizations and activists can play a vital role in providing resources, counseling services, and safe spaces for LGBTQ individuals to connect, share experiences, and seek support. By fostering a sense of community, empathy, and solidarity, we can strengthen the resilience of the LGBTQ movement and ensure its longevity.

Collaboration and Intersectionality

Sustaining equality movements requires collaboration and intersectionality. LGBTQ advocacy must go beyond focusing solely on LGBTQ rights, as various forms of oppression intersect and impact marginalized communities. By creating alliances with other social justice movements, such as those focused on racial justice, gender equality, and economic justice, the LGBTQ movement can amplify its impact and build a broader coalition for change.

Collaboration also involves working with allied organizations, human rights groups, and political allies. By leveraging different perspectives, resources, and expertise, equality movements can push for systemic change and address intersecting forms of discrimination.

Continuous Education and Awareness

Educating the broader society about LGBTQ issues is an essential aspect of sustaining equality movements. While progress has been made, there is still a need to challenge prejudice, stereotypes, and misinformation. Ongoing education and awareness campaigns can help dispel myths, promote understanding, and prevent the rollback of rights.

Educational initiatives can take various forms, such as workshops, public forums, and online resources. It is important to engage with educational institutions, governments, and media outlets to ensure accurate and positive representation of LGBTQ individuals and issues. By promoting inclusivity and visibility, we can foster a more accepting society and sustain the gains made in LGBTQ rights.

Policy Advocacy and Legal Strategies

Sustaining equality movements requires ongoing policy advocacy and legal strategies. While significant progress has been made in securing legal protections for LGBTQ individuals, these gains are not guaranteed. It is essential to monitor and protect existing laws, while also advocating for comprehensive and inclusive policies that address the evolving needs of the LGBTQ community.

Legal strategies can take the form of strategic litigation, advocacy for new legislation, and lobbying for policy changes. It is important to engage with lawmakers, government agencies, and international organizations to ensure that LGBTQ rights are a priority. Through legal activism, equality movements can secure long-term protections and challenge discriminatory practices.

Youth Empowerment and Mentorship

Investing in the next generation of LGBTQ activists is crucial for sustaining equality movements. Providing mentorship, resources, and opportunities for youth engagement can cultivate leadership and create a pipeline of advocates for the future. By empowering young LGBTQ individuals, we can ensure the continuation of the fight for equality.

Youth empowerment initiatives can involve mentorship programs, leadership development workshops, and scholarships for higher education. It is important to provide platforms for young activists to share their perspectives, raise awareness about LGBTQ issues, and mobilize their peers. By amplifying youth voices, equality movements can remain vibrant, relevant, and impactful.

Unconventional Strategies: Art and Cultural Activism

In addition to conventional strategies, incorporating art and cultural activism can be a powerful tool for sustaining equality movements. Art has the ability to challenge norms, spark conversation, and create emotional connections. By harnessing the power of art, equality movements can reach diverse audiences and inspire change at an individual and societal level.

Artistic initiatives can include public art displays, theater performances, literary works, and film festivals that celebrate LGBTQ experiences and challenge stereotypes. By promoting LGBTQ representation and storytelling, art can foster empathy, provide visibility, and sustain the momentum of equality movements.

Conclusion

Sustaining equality movements requires a multi-faceted approach that addresses various challenges and leverages different strategies. Building community resilience, fostering collaboration, promoting continuous education, advocating for policy changes, empowering youth, and embracing unconventional strategies are all crucial components of sustaining the fight for LGBTQ rights. By implementing these strategies, we can ensure that equality movements forge ahead, making lasting change for future generations.

Building a Brighter Future for LGBTQ Individuals

In this section, we will explore the steps and strategies needed to create a more inclusive and equitable future for LGBTQ individuals. Building a brighter future involves dismantling discriminatory systems, promoting acceptance, and advocating for equal rights for all. Together, we can work towards a society where LGBTQ individuals can thrive and live authentically.

Fostering Inclusive Communities

Creating inclusive communities is essential for building a brighter future for LGBTQ individuals. It starts with education and awareness. Schools and educational institutions have a crucial role to play in promoting inclusivity and teaching acceptance. By incorporating LGBTQ-inclusive curriculum and fostering safe spaces, we can empower future generations to appreciate and respect diversity.

Community organizations and grassroots movements also play a pivotal role in fostering inclusive communities. These organizations should provide support and resources to LGBTQ individuals, offering a sense of belonging and empowerment. By organizing events, workshops, and support groups, they can create spaces where LGBTQ individuals can connect, share their experiences, and fight against discrimination collectively.

Advocacy for Policy Change

To build a brighter future, we must advocate for policy changes that protect and ensure the rights of LGBTQ individuals. This includes lobbying for anti-discrimination laws, marriage equality, gender-neutral restrooms, and comprehensive healthcare coverage. LGBTQ activists and allies should work together to influence lawmakers and policymakers, using their voices to demand equal treatment under the law.

In addition to advocating for policy change locally, it is crucial to support LGBTQ movements globally. Solidarity across borders helps amplify the voices of marginalized communities and put pressure on governments to uphold human rights. Collaborating with international organizations and participating in conferences and events can provide a platform for sharing experiences and strategies for creating change.

Promoting Mental Health and Well-being

Building a brighter future for LGBTQ individuals also involves addressing mental health challenges that they may face. The rates of anxiety, depression, and suicide are often higher within this community due to the impact of discrimination and stigma. To counter these challenges, it is essential to promote mental health resources specifically tailored to LGBTQ individuals.

Healthcare professionals, counselors, and therapists need to be trained in LGBTQ-affirmative care to provide effective support. Creating accessible mental health programs, helplines, and support networks can provide a lifeline for those struggling with their mental well-being. By reducing the stigma surrounding mental health and providing resources, we can support LGBTQ individuals in their journey towards a brighter future.

Corporate and Workplace Inclusivity

To create a brighter future, it is vital to ensure LGBTQ inclusivity within corporate and workplace environments. Companies should adopt non-discrimination policies that protect LGBTQ individuals from harassment and prejudice. Offering benefits such as healthcare coverage for gender-affirming procedures and creating gender-neutral spaces can contribute to a more inclusive work environment.

Promoting diversity and inclusivity at all levels of the workforce, including executive positions, is crucial. By actively recruiting and promoting LGBTQ individuals, companies can create positive role models and challenge stereotypes. LGBTQ-inclusive employee resource groups can provide support, mentorship, and networking opportunities to foster a sense of belonging and equality.

Embracing Intersectionality

Building a brighter future for LGBTQ individuals requires embracing intersectionality. Intersectionality recognizes that individuals can face overlapping forms of discrimination based on their race, gender identity, socioeconomic status, and other factors. LGBTQ activism should address the unique challenges faced by individuals at the intersections of multiple marginalized identities.

By centering the experiences of LGBTQ individuals who face intersecting forms of discrimination, we can amplify their voices and work towards a more equitable future for all. It is important to engage in open dialogue, listen to diverse perspectives, and actively participate in allyship efforts across marginalized communities. Together, we can build a stronger and more inclusive society.

Conclusion

Building a brighter future for LGBTQ individuals requires a collective and ongoing effort. By fostering inclusive communities, advocating for policy change, promoting mental health and well-being, ensuring workplace inclusivity, and embracing intersectionality, we can create a society where all individuals, regardless of their sexual orientation or gender identity, can live with dignity, respect, and equality. Let us stand united and work towards a future where love and acceptance conquer discrimination and prejudice. Together, we will make history.

Section 3: Love Is Love

Sure! Here's the content for the section "7.4.1 Subsection 1: Embracing Love and Acceptance":

Subsection 1: Embracing Love and Acceptance

In this subsection, we explore the importance of embracing love and acceptance in the journey towards achieving LGBTQ rights. Love and acceptance are powerful forces that can help challenge prejudice, discrimination, and hate. By promoting a culture of love and acceptance, we can create a more inclusive society for all individuals, regardless of their sexual orientation or gender identity.

The Power of Love

Love has the power to transcend boundaries and break down barriers. It is love that allows us to see the humanity in others and to recognize the inherent worth and dignity of every individual. When we embrace love, we create spaces where LGBTQ individuals can feel safe, supported, and valued.

Fostering Acceptance

Acceptance is the key to creating an environment where LGBTQ individuals are not only tolerated but fully embraced. By fostering acceptance, we ensure that LGBTQ individuals can live authentically without fear of rejection or discrimination. Acceptance is about recognizing and affirming the identities, experiences, and rights of LGBTQ individuals.

Combatting Prejudice and Discrimination

Prejudice and discrimination are detrimental to the well-being and rights of LGBTQ individuals. By actively promoting love and acceptance, we can challenge and combat these forms of oppression. It is crucial that we educate ourselves and others about the experiences of LGBTQ individuals and work towards dismantling the biases and stereotypes that contribute to prejudice and discrimination.

Creating Safe and Inclusive Spaces

Creating safe and inclusive spaces is integral to embracing love and acceptance. These spaces provide LGBTQ individuals with a sense of belonging and enable them to express their true selves without fear of judgment or harm. It is necessary to prioritize the creation and maintenance of these spaces to ensure that LGBTQ individuals have access to the support networks they need.

Promoting Allyship

Allyship is an essential component of embracing love and acceptance. Allies actively support and advocate for the rights of LGBTQ individuals, using their privilege to amplify their voices. Allies have a vital role in challenging heteronormative and cisnormative attitudes and behaviors, and they can actively work towards creating a more inclusive society.

Overcoming Internalized Homophobia and Transphobia

Embracing love and acceptance also requires addressing internalized homophobia and transphobia within the LGBTQ community. Many LGBTQ individuals have been subjected to societal messages that undermine their worth and identity. By promoting self-love and acceptance, we can help individuals overcome these internalized prejudices and embrace their authentic selves.

In conclusion, embracing love and acceptance is vital to the struggle for LGBTQ rights. It creates an environment where LGBTQ individuals can thrive and have their rights respected. By fostering a culture of love and acceptance, we can challenge prejudice, discrimination, and hate, and create a society that celebrates the diversity of sexual orientations and gender identities. Together, we can create a future where love truly knows no bounds.

Subsection 2: Celebrating Diversity and Inclusion

In this subsection, we will explore the importance of celebrating diversity and promoting inclusion within the LGBTQ community and beyond. By embracing and celebrating the uniqueness of each individual, we can create a more inclusive society where everyone feels valued and accepted.

The Power of Representation

Representation plays a crucial role in promoting diversity and inclusion. When individuals see themselves reflected in various aspects of society, such as media, politics, and other cultural platforms, it helps validate their identities and experiences. Representation also allows others to gain a deeper understanding and appreciation for different perspectives and lived experiences.

In the world of entertainment, celebrating diversity means actively seeking out and uplifting LGBTQ voices in various forms of media. This can involve supporting movies, TV shows, and music that feature LGBTQ storylines or spotlight LGBTQ artists. By doing so, we can challenge stereotypes, break down barriers, and inspire others to embrace their own identities.

Example: The release of the movie "Moonlight" directed by Barry Jenkins was a watershed moment in LGBTQ representation. The film not only won multiple awards, including Best Picture at the Academy Awards, but it also provided a relatable and authentic portrayal of a young black gay man's journey, resonating with audiences worldwide.

Creating Inclusive Spaces

Creating inclusive spaces is essential for promoting diversity within the LGBTQ community. These spaces can range from community centers, support groups, and LGBTQ-friendly establishments. They provide opportunities for individuals to connect, share experiences, and find support from those who understand their unique challenges.

In addition to physical spaces, virtual communities have become increasingly important in fostering diversity and inclusion. Online platforms, such as social media groups and forums, offer a safe and accessible space for LGBTQ individuals to express themselves, seek advice, and build connections. These platforms also allow for intersectional conversations, acknowledging the diverse identities within the LGBTQ community.

Example: The Trevor Project, a renowned LGBTQ youth support organization, provides online resources, including a 24/7 helpline and online chat services. These platforms ensure that LGBTQ individuals, regardless of their location or circumstances, have access to immediate support and a sense of community.

Education and Awareness

Education is a powerful tool for promoting diversity and inclusion. By incorporating LGBTQ-inclusive education in schools and universities, we can foster acceptance, challenge stereotypes, and create a more empathetic society. It is essential to teach young people about LGBTQ history, culture, and the challenges faced by the community, empowering them to become allies and advocates for change.

Training and awareness programs can also play a significant role in promoting diversity and inclusion in workplaces and other institutions. These programs aim to educate individuals about LGBTQ issues and provide tools for creating inclusive environments. By fostering understanding and empathy, organizations can create spaces where individuals feel safe and valued regardless of their sexual orientation or gender identity.

Example: The GLSEN (Gay, Lesbian, and Straight Education Network) offers resources and training programs for teachers, students, and school administrators to create LGBTQ-inclusive schools. These programs cover topics such as bullying prevention, inclusive curricula, and supporting LGBTQ students' mental health needs.

Fighting Discrimination

Promoting diversity and inclusion requires actively fighting discrimination and advocating for equal rights. This involves challenging discriminatory laws and policies, supporting organizations that provide legal aid and advocacy for LGBTQ individuals, and promoting equality in all aspects of society.

Addressing discrimination also requires recognizing and confronting the intersections of discrimination faced by individuals with multiple marginalized identities. This can involve advocating for policies that protect LGBTQ people of color, transgender and gender non-conforming individuals, and those from other intersectional backgrounds who often face heightened discrimination and violence.

Example: The Human Rights Campaign's Corporate Equality Index assesses and ranks companies on their LGBTQ-inclusive policies and practices. By shining a spotlight on companies that embody diversity and inclusion, it encourages other businesses to adopt more inclusive policies and practices.

Embracing Diversity Beyond LGBTQ Circles

Celebrating diversity and practicing inclusion should extend beyond LGBTQ circles. It is crucial to recognize and embrace the diversity that exists across all communities. By understanding that diversity exists in every facet of society, from race and ethnicity to religion and ability, we can work towards creating a more equitable and inclusive world for everyone.

One way to promote inclusivity is through allyship. Allies are people who use their privilege to support and uplift marginalized communities. By educating themselves on LGBTQ issues, speaking out against discrimination, and creating safe spaces for LGBTQ individuals, allies contribute to fostering a more inclusive society.

Example: Through campaigns like "It Gets Better," allies can share their stories and messages of support to LGBTQ youth, letting them know they are not alone and that there is a wide network of individuals who care about their well-being.

Conclusion

Celebrating diversity and promoting inclusion are fundamental in creating a society where everyone feels valued, respected, and accepted. By actively seeking out and embracing different perspectives, providing inclusive spaces, educating ourselves and others, challenging discrimination, and embracing diversity beyond LGBTQ circles, we can work towards a more equitable and inclusive future for all.

It is up to each and every one of us to commit to celebrating diversity, advocating for inclusion, and building a world where love is love, and everyone can live authentically and without fear. Together, we can make history and create a brighter future for LGBTQ individuals and all marginalized communities.

Subsection 3: Advocacy on a Global Scale

In the pursuit of LGBTQ rights, Virgilio Barco Isakson recognized that the fight for equality extends beyond the borders of Colombia. He understood the importance of advocating on a global scale to create lasting change and inspire others around the world. This section explores Virgilio's efforts in advocating for LGBTQ rights internationally and the impact of his work on the global stage.

Global Solidarity

Virgilio Barco Isakson firmly believed in the power of solidarity among LGBTQ movements worldwide. He actively collaborated with activists from different countries, recognizing that collective action is key to effecting change. Virgilio facilitated partnerships and exchange programs to foster a sense of interconnectedness and mutual support among LGBTQ communities.

One of the ways Virgilio promoted global solidarity was by attending international conferences and events. He saw these gatherings as opportunities to share experiences, strategies, and success stories. By amplifying the voices of LGBTQ activists from diverse backgrounds, Virgilio aimed to create a more inclusive and unified global movement.

Speaking Out at International Conferences

Virgilio Barco Isakson was a charismatic and influential speaker, captivating audiences with his passion for LGBTQ rights. He used international conferences as platforms to deliver powerful speeches, shedding light on the challenges faced by the LGBTQ community in Colombia and inspiring others to join the fight for equality.

At these conferences, Virgilio emphasized the importance of intersectionality in LGBTQ advocacy. He highlighted the need to address the unique struggles faced by transgender and gender non-conforming individuals, people of color, and those from marginalized communities. Virgilio's speeches challenged preconceived notions and sparked conversations about the intricacies of identity, ensuring that the global LGBTQ movement encompassed the full spectrum of experiences.

Collaboration with NGOs and Human Rights Organizations

Virgilio Barco Isakson recognized the value of collaboration with non-governmental organizations (NGOs) and human rights organizations to further LGBTQ rights around the world. He worked closely with organizations such as Amnesty International, Human Rights Watch, and the International Lesbian, Gay, Bisexual, Trans and Intersex Association (ILGA) to advocate for policy changes and promote respect for LGBTQ rights on a global scale.

Together with these organizations, Virgilio campaigned for the decriminalization of homosexuality in countries where it was still considered illegal. He also championed efforts to combat discrimination, violence, and HIV/AIDS stigma faced by LGBTQ individuals worldwide. Through collaborations and joint initiatives, Virgilio sought to create a united front against systemic oppression and achieve tangible advancements for LGBTQ rights.

Inspiring LGBTQ Activists Worldwide

Virgilio Barco Isakson's relentless activism and unwavering dedication inspired LGBTQ activists worldwide to take action and push for change in their respective countries. His courage and achievements served as a beacon of hope for those facing adversity, reminding them that progress is possible even in the most challenging circumstances.

To ensure that his message reached as many people as possible, Virgilio actively used social media platforms and digital communication to connect with LGBTQ activists globally. He shared his experiences, insights, and strategies, providing guidance and support to those engaged in their own advocacy efforts.

Leaving a Legacy for Future Generations

Virgilio Barco Isakson's impact on the global LGBTQ rights movement cannot be understated. His tireless advocacy work paved the way for future generations of activists, leaving a lasting legacy of resilience and progress.

To honor his legacy, organizations and institutions dedicated to LGBTQ rights have established scholarships, grants, and leadership programs in Virgilio's name. These initiatives aim to support and empower activists who embody Virgilio's spirit, ensuring the continuation of his work and the advancement of LGBTQ rights on a global scale.

In closing, Virgilio Barco Isakson's advocacy on a global scale showcases the power of unity and collaboration in the fight for LGBTQ rights. His efforts inspired activists worldwide, fostering a sense of solidarity and propelling the movement forward. Virgilio's legacy continues to resonate, reminding us of the importance of advocating for equality and inclusivity at both local and international levels. Together, we can build a future where all LGBTQ individuals are embraced and celebrated.

Subsection 4: The Ongoing Fight for LGBTQ Rights

The fight for LGBTQ rights is an ongoing battle that requires continuous effort, resilience, and determination. Despite the significant progress that has been made in recent years, there are still many challenges that must be overcome in order to achieve full equality and acceptance for the LGBTQ community. This subsection will explore some of the key issues that activists are currently facing in their fight for LGBTQ rights, and highlight the strategies and initiatives that are being employed to address them.

Challenges Faced by the LGBTQ Community

The LGBTQ community continues to face a range of challenges and inequalities, both on a social and legal level. Discrimination, harassment, and violence against LGBTQ individuals are still prevalent in many parts of the world. In some countries, same-sex relationships are criminalized, and LGBTQ individuals can face severe legal penalties, including imprisonment or even the death penalty.

Transgender individuals, in particular, often face unique challenges and forms of discrimination. They may encounter barriers when seeking healthcare, education, and employment, and can experience high rates of violence and hate crimes. Overcoming these challenges requires a comprehensive approach that addresses both societal attitudes and legal protections.

Legislative Advocacy

One of the most effective ways to advance LGBTQ rights is through legislative advocacy. Activists and organizations work tirelessly to lobby for the passage of laws that protect the rights of LGBTQ individuals and promote equality. Legislative advocacy involves engaging with lawmakers, raising awareness about LGBTQ issues, and mobilizing public support for policy change.

Key legislative initiatives include the decriminalization of same-sex relationships, the protection of LGBTQ individuals from discrimination in employment, housing, and public accommodations, and the recognition of transgender rights, including legal gender recognition and access to healthcare. These laws not only provide legal protections for LGBTQ individuals but also help to change societal attitudes and promote acceptance.

Education and Awareness

Education and awareness play a vital role in the ongoing fight for LGBTQ rights. It is important to educate the public about the realities and challenges faced by LGBTQ individuals in order to dispel stereotypes and foster empathy and understanding. Education about LGBTQ history, culture, and contributions can also help to challenge heteronormative narratives and promote LGBTQ visibility.

Schools and educational institutions have a responsibility to provide inclusive and LGBTQ-affirming curricula that promote acceptance and respect for all students, regardless of their sexual orientation or gender identity. This includes comprehensive sex education that addresses LGBTQ issues and identities, as well as the promotion of safe and inclusive environments free from bullying and discrimination.

Intersectionality and Inclusivity

An inclusive approach to LGBTQ activism acknowledges the intersections of different identities and experiences. It recognizes that members of the LGBTQ community can also face discrimination and marginalization based on their race, ethnicity, socioeconomic status, disability, or other factors. Intersectionality emphasizes the need to address the unique challenges faced by LGBTQ individuals from diverse backgrounds and to ensure that the fight for LGBTQ rights is inclusive and representative.

Activists are working to build coalitions with other social justice movements, such as the feminist, racial justice, and disability rights movements, to create a more intersectional and inclusive approach to advocacy. By understanding and addressing the interconnected nature of various forms of discrimination and oppression, the fight for LGBTQ rights can become stronger and more effective.

Digital Activism

The rise of digital technology and social media has transformed the landscape of activism, providing new opportunities for LGBTQ individuals and allies to connect, organize, and mobilize for change. Digital activism allows activists to reach a global audience, raise awareness, and advocate for LGBTQ rights on a larger scale.

Through social media campaigns, online petitions, and virtual events, activists can amplify their voices and demand action from policymakers and institutions. Online platforms also provide a safe space for LGBTQ individuals to share stories, seek support, and build community. However, it is important to recognize the limitations of digital activism and ensure that efforts translate into tangible real-world change.

Global Solidarity and Collaboration

The fight for LGBTQ rights is a global struggle that requires global solidarity and collaboration. Activists around the world are working together to share knowledge, resources, and strategies to advocate for LGBTQ rights and challenge discriminatory practices.

International human rights organizations, such as Amnesty International and Human Rights Watch, play a crucial role in monitoring human rights violations against LGBTQ individuals and advocating for their protection. Global conferences and gatherings provide opportunities for activists to come together, exchange ideas, and learn from each other's experiences.

By standing in solidarity with LGBTQ communities in other countries, activists can amplify their voices and strengthen the fight for LGBTQ rights on a global scale. The ongoing collaboration and mutual support among LGBTQ activists worldwide will continue to push the boundaries and pave the way for a more inclusive and accepting future.

Innovative Strategies for Change

To overcome the challenges faced by the LGBTQ community and further the fight for LGBTQ rights, innovative strategies are needed. Here are some unconventional yet effective approaches being employed by activists around the world:

Storytelling as a Tool for Change

Storytelling has long been a powerful tool in advocating for social change. For the LGBTQ community, sharing personal stories and experiences can help challenge stereotypes, humanize the struggle for equal rights, and foster empathy. By putting a face to the issues, storytelling can create a profound emotional connection and inspire action.

Activists are utilizing different platforms and mediums to share stories, including podcasts, documentaries, and online platforms. These narratives provide a platform for LGBTQ individuals to speak their truth and serve as a means of education and awareness for the wider public. By sharing personal stories, activists can inspire empathy, challenge prejudice, and mobilize support for LGBTQ rights.

Art as Activism

Art has the power to transcend barriers and ignite social change. Artists and performers play a crucial role in challenging societal norms, fostering dialogue, and representing the diversity of LGBTQ experiences. Through visual arts, music, dance, theater, and literature, LGBTQ artists are pushing boundaries, challenging stereotypes, and advocating for equality and acceptance.

Artistic initiatives, such as LGBTQ film festivals, queer art exhibitions, and pride parades, provide platforms for LGBTQ artists to showcase their work, express their identities, and spark conversations. By promoting LGBTQ representation and visibility in the arts, activists are reshaping cultural norms and shaping a more inclusive society.

Corporate Activism

In recent years, there has been a growing trend of corporate activism, with businesses taking a stance on social and political issues, including LGBTQ rights. Corporations have a significant influence on shaping social attitudes and policies, and many are using their platforms to promote LGBTQ inclusion and equality.

Companies are implementing LGBTQ-friendly policies, such as non-discrimination practices, support for transgender employees, and employee resource groups. They are also advocating for LGBTQ rights through public statements, sponsorship of LGBTQ events, and financial support for LGBTQ organizations.

Corporate activism can have a significant impact on LGBTQ rights by utilizing the power and resources of businesses to bring about social change. By aligning their values and actions with LGBTQ inclusion, corporations can help to shift societal attitudes and create more inclusive environments for LGBTQ individuals.

Conclusion

The ongoing fight for LGBTQ rights requires a multi-faceted approach that encompasses legal advocacy, education, awareness, intersectionality, digital activism, global solidarity, and innovative strategies for change. It is essential to continue pushing for legislative reforms that protect the rights of LGBTQ individuals, while also challenging societal attitudes and promoting inclusivity.

By raising awareness, sharing personal stories, and fostering empathy, activists can create a more compassionate and understanding society. Collaborative efforts between LGBTQ activists and other social justice movements can help address the interconnected nature of discrimination and oppression. Digital technology provides a powerful tool for amplifying voices and mobilizing support, while global solidarity ensures that the fight for LGBTQ rights transcends borders.

Through innovative strategies such as storytelling, art as activism, and corporate activism, activists can challenge norms, reshape culture, and create a more inclusive and accepting world. The fight for LGBTQ rights is far from over, but with determination, resilience, and a commitment to equality, progress can be made. Together, we can create a future where LGBTQ individuals are embraced and celebrated for who they are.

Subsection 5: Together, We Will Make History

In this final subsection, we conclude our journey through the incredible life and impact of Virgilio Barco Isakson. We have explored the challenges faced by the LGBTQ community in Colombia, the triumphs achieved through Virgilio's activism, and the legacy he leaves behind. As we wrap up this book, let us reflect on the power and potential of collective action and how, together, we can continue to make history and push for a more inclusive and equal society.

The Power of Unity

Unity has always been a driving force in the fight for LGBTQ rights. Throughout history, oppressed communities have come together to challenge unjust laws and discriminatory practices. The LGBTQ community is no exception. When we stand together, we amplify our voices and increase our strength and influence. It is through unity that we can create real change and make history.

Building Alliances

To make a lasting impact, it is crucial to build alliances and seek support from other marginalized communities. Intersectionality plays a vital role in understanding the multiple layers of discrimination and recognizing that the fight for LGBTQ rights intersects with other struggles such as racism, sexism, and classism. By collaborating with other groups, we can create a more inclusive movement that addresses the diverse needs and experiences of all individuals.

Educating and Empowering

Education is a powerful tool for creating change. It is essential to educate ourselves and others about the history, experiences, and challenges faced by the LGBTQ community. By fostering understanding and empathy, we can challenge societal prejudices and break down barriers. Empowering individuals through education allows them to advocate for themselves and their communities, creating a ripple effect that expands the reach of our movement.

Dismantling Systems of Oppression

True progress requires a commitment to dismantling the systems of oppression that perpetuate discrimination against the LGBTQ community. It is not enough to secure legal rights; we must also address the underlying biases and attitudes that contribute to inequality. This means challenging societal norms, advocating for inclusive policies, and holding institutions accountable for their actions. By actively dismantling these systems, we create space for greater equality and justice.

Building Resilience

The road to equality is not always smooth, and setbacks and challenges are inevitable. However, resilience is a key ingredient in making history. We must remain steadfast in our advocacy, even in the face of adversity. By learning from our past experiences, celebrating our victories, and supporting one another, we can overcome obstacles and continue pushing forward toward a more inclusive future.

Amplifying Voices

Our collective strength lies in the power of our voices. Each of us has a unique story and perspective that can contribute to the ongoing struggle for LGBTQ rights. It is essential to create platforms and spaces that amplify diverse voices, particularly those that have been historically marginalized. By centering and valuing these voices, we ensure that everyone's experiences are heard and acknowledged, creating a stronger and more inclusive movement for change.

Taking Action

To make history, we must take action, both individually and collectively. This can involve participating in protests, advocating for LGBTQ-friendly policies, supporting organizations working for equality, or engaging in local activism. Every act, no matter how small, counts towards creating a more inclusive society. By taking action, we demonstrate our commitment to a future where LGBTQ individuals can thrive without fear of discrimination.

Redefining Progress

As we move forward, it is crucial to continually redefine our understanding of progress. Progress is not a fixed endpoint but an ongoing journey. We must strive to be intersectional in our approach, recognizing the interconnectedness of various struggles for justice. By reimagining progress and centering the most marginalized voices, we can build a movement that is truly transformative and ensures that no one is left behind.

Conclusion

Virgilio Barco Isakson's journey is a testament to the power of activism and the lasting impact that can be achieved through dedicated leadership and collective action. From his early experiences of discrimination to his groundbreaking achievements in politics, Virgilio's legacy will continue to inspire future generations of LGBTQ activists. As we conclude this biography, let us remember that we all play a vital role in shaping history. Together, we can build a more inclusive world where love and acceptance triumph over prejudice and discrimination. Let Virgilio's story be a call to action, a reminder that our fight for equality is not over, and that together, we will make history.

Chapter 8: Unfiltered Victory

Chapter 8: Unfiltered Victory

Chapter 8: Unfiltered Victory

In this chapter, we delve into the triumphs and successes of Virgilio Barco Isakson's activism journey, highlighting the unfiltered victory he achieved in his relentless pursuit of LGBTQ rights. From his groundbreaking policies to his impact on Colombian society, we explore how Virgilio's legacy continues to shape the future of LGBTQ activism.

Subsection 1: Passing the Torch to Future Generations

As Virgilio Barco Isakson's time as mayor of Bogotá came to an end, he knew it was crucial to pass the torch of LGBTQ activism to future generations. In this subsection, we examine how he paved the way for the next wave of advocates and leaders.

Virgilio recognized the importance of mentoring and nurturing young LGBTQ individuals who had the potential to become future activists. He established the Virgilio Barco Isakson LGBTQ Leadership Program, which provided scholarships, mentorship, and leadership training to young people from marginalized communities. Through this program, he aimed to create a network of empowered and resilient individuals who would carry on his fight for equality.

Additionally, Virgilio actively supported LGBTQ youth organizations, providing them with resources, guidance, and platforms to amplify their voices. He believed that investing in the younger generations would ensure that the momentum for change continued long into the future.

Subsection 2: Continuing the Legacy of Activism

While Virgilio stepped away from politics, his commitment to social justice and activism persisted. In this subsection, we explore how he continued to make a lasting impact outside the realm of politics.

Virgilio established the Virgilio Barco Isakson Foundation, a non-profit organization dedicated to advancing LGBTQ rights and supporting marginalized communities. The foundation focused on providing legal aid, advocating for gender and sexual equality, and fostering LGBTQ-inclusive education.

Through strategic partnerships with NGOs, human rights organizations, and academic institutions, the foundation became a powerful force in advocating for LGBTQ rights not just in Colombia, but on a global scale. By leveraging his reputation and network, Virgilio ensured that his work would continue long after his political career.

Subsection 3: Looking Towards a More Inclusive Future

Virgilio Barco Isakson was not content with merely achieving victories in his time as mayor. He had a vision for a more inclusive future for LGBTQ individuals. In this subsection, we explore how Virgilio's activism laid the groundwork for a society that embraces diversity and equality.

One of Virgilio's key initiatives was to strengthen LGBTQ support networks across Colombia. He recognized the power of community and worked tirelessly to create safe spaces where LGBTQ individuals could find camaraderie, support, and resources. By fostering an environment of acceptance and understanding, Virgilio aimed to create a society where everyone could thrive irrespective of their sexual orientation or gender identity.

Furthermore, Virgilio continued to inspire and uplift future leaders through his engaging speeches, workshops, and seminars. He used his platform to educate and empower individuals from all walks of life to challenge discrimination and fight for justice. Virgilio firmly believed that it was through education and awareness that true change could be achieved.

Subsection 4: Amplifying LGBTQ Voices

Virgilio Barco Isakson understood the power of storytelling and representation in shaping perceptions and dismantling prejudices. In this subsection, we explore how Virgilio amplified LGBTQ voices and stories, ensuring that their experiences were heard and understood.

CHAPTER 8: UNFILTERED VICTORY   297

Under Virgilio's guidance, the Virgilio Barco Isakson Media Initiative was established. This initiative aimed to promote LGBTQ representation in media, ranging from films and television shows to music and literature. By providing funding and platforms for LGBTQ creators, Virgilio sought to challenge stereotypes and reshape the narrative surrounding LGBTQ individuals.

Additionally, he worked closely with mainstream media outlets to ensure fair and accurate coverage of LGBTQ issues. By breaking down barriers and encouraging dialogue, Virgilio played a pivotal role in fostering a more inclusive media landscape.

Subsection 5: The Long-lasting Impact of Virgilio Barco Isakson

In this subsection, we reflect on the enduring impact of Virgilio Barco Isakson's activism and the legacy he left behind. We explore how his unwavering commitment to LGBTQ rights continues to shape the future of Colombia and inspire activists worldwide.

Virgilio's role in spearheading groundbreaking policies and legislation set a precedent for future leaders and lawmakers. His tireless advocacy laid the foundation for a more inclusive society, challenging deep-rooted discrimination and prejudice.

Moreover, Virgilio's ability to connect with people from all walks of life and inspire change remains an inspiration. His passionate speeches, compassionate leadership, and unwavering dedication serve as a reminder of the power of individuals to create lasting change.

Today, the Virgilio Barco Isakson LGBTQ Center stands as a symbol of Virgilio's legacy. This center offers comprehensive support services, resources, and community programs to LGBTQ individuals, ensuring that Virgilio's vision of an inclusive society lives on.

As we look to the future, the impact of Virgilio's unfiltered victory cannot be overstated. His relentless pursuit of LGBTQ rights forever changed the landscape of Colombian society and continues to inspire generations of activists around the world.

Let us remember Virgilio Barco Isakson's enduring legacy and carry forward the torch of equality, love, and acceptance. The fight for LGBTQ rights is far from over, but armed with Virgilio's unyielding spirit and determination, we can build a brighter future for all. Together, we will make history.

Section 1: A New Chapter Begins

Subsection 1: Passing the Torch to Future Generations

As Virgilio Barco Isakson's political career came to a close, he knew that his work in championing LGBTQ rights was far from over. He understood the importance of passing the torch to future generations, ensuring that the progress made would continue long after his term as mayor of Bogotá had ended. In this subsection, we will explore how Virgilio paved the way for young activists and leaders, inspiring them to carry on the fight for equality.

Bridging the Generational Gap

Virgilio recognized the importance of bridging the generational gap within the LGBTQ community. He understood that the experiences and challenges faced by older LGBTQ individuals differed greatly from those of the younger generation. By fostering dialogue and understanding between these two groups, Virgilio aimed to create a united front in the pursuit of equality.

To accomplish this, Virgilio organized intergenerational events and forums where LGBTQ individuals from different age groups could come together to share their stories and experiences. These gatherings provided an opportunity for older activists to impart their wisdom and guidance to the younger generation, while also allowing young activists to bring fresh perspectives and ideas to the table. By facilitating these connections, Virgilio ensured that the fight for LGBTQ rights would continue to evolve and adapt to the changing social landscape.

Empowering Youth Leadership

Recognizing that young people are the future of any movement, Virgilio prioritized the empowerment of LGBTQ youth in leadership roles. He firmly believed that young activists had a unique ability to ignite change and push boundaries, and he sought to provide them with the necessary tools and resources to do so.

Virgilio established mentorship programs whereby seasoned advocates would guide and support young activists in their journey. These mentorship relationships allowed for the transfer of knowledge, skills, and strategies, while also fostering a sense of community and support.

Additionally, Virgilio advocated for increased representation of LGBTQ youth in decision-making processes. He encouraged young activists to run for political office, join NGOs, and participate in community organizations. By doing so, he ensured that the voices and perspectives of young LGBTQ individuals were not only heard but actively shaping policy and social change.

Investing in LGBTQ Education

Education was a cornerstone of Virgilio's strategy for passing the torch to future generations. He recognized the vital role that education plays in challenging stereotypes, combating discrimination, and fostering empathy and understanding.

Virgilio fought tirelessly to implement LGBTQ-inclusive curricula in schools, ensuring that young people would grow up in an environment that celebrated diversity and respected all sexual orientations and gender identities. He pushed for the incorporation of LGBTQ history, experiences, and contributions into existing educational frameworks, aiming to create a more inclusive and accurate portrayal of society.

Furthermore, Virgilio supported the establishment of LGBTQ resource centers in educational institutions. These centers provided a safe and supportive space for LGBTQ students to access information, resources, and counseling services. They also served as a hub for LGBTQ activism and community building.

Harnessing the Power of Technology

In recognizing the importance of technological advancements in shaping the future, Virgilio leveraged the power of digital platforms to connect, educate, and mobilize LGBTQ individuals.

He championed the development of LGBTQ-focused apps and online platforms that provided resources, support networks, and educational materials. These platforms allowed LGBTQ individuals to access information, connect with like-minded individuals, and find support in their journey.

Virgilio also recognized the potential of social media as a tool for advocacy. He encouraged young activists to use social media channels to raise awareness, challenge stereotypes, and engage with a broader audience. By harnessing the power of technology, Virgilio ensured that the fight for LGBTQ equality would transcend geographical boundaries and reach communities far and wide.

Celebrating Diversity and Intersectionality

Lastly, Virgilio emphasized the importance of celebrating diversity and embracing intersectionality within the LGBTQ movement. He understood that the fight for LGBTQ rights was intricately linked with other social justice movements.

To pass the torch to future generations, Virgilio encouraged young activists to forge alliances with other marginalized communities, recognizing that collective action is often more powerful than isolated efforts. By highlighting the intersectionality of various identities and experiences, Virgilio ensured that the LGBTQ movement would continue to evolve and address the unique challenges faced by different communities.

In conclusion, Virgilio Barco Isakson's legacy lies not only in the progress he made during his tenure but in his commitment to passing the torch to future generations. By bridging the generational gap, empowering youth leadership, investing in LGBTQ education, harnessing technology, and celebrating diversity and intersectionality, Virgilio paved the way for a brighter future for LGBTQ individuals in Colombia and beyond. His example continues to inspire young activists to carry on the fight for equality, ensuring that his legacy lives on in the hearts and minds of those who continue the work he began.

Subsection 2: Continuing the Legacy of Activism

In this section, we delve into the importance of continuing Virgilio Barco Isakson's legacy of activism in the LGBTQ rights movement. Through dedication, perseverance, and a deep understanding of the challenges faced by the community, we can build a future that is more inclusive and accepting for all.

Continuing the Fight for Equality

Now more than ever, it is crucial to continue the fight for LGBTQ rights and equality. Despite the tremendous progress made in recent years, there are still many areas where LGBTQ individuals face discrimination, prejudice, and exclusion. To continue Virgilio's legacy, we must remain committed to dismantling these barriers and advocating for the rights of all LGBTQ people.

One way to do this is by working to pass and enforce comprehensive anti-discrimination laws that protect LGBTQ individuals in all areas of life, including employment, housing, education, and public accommodations. By advocating for and supporting these laws, we can ensure that LGBTQ individuals are treated with dignity and respect, free from discrimination or harassment.

Additionally, it is vital to continue raising awareness about the unique challenges faced by the LGBTQ community. Educating society about the experiences of LGBTQ individuals helps break down stereotypes and fosters a more inclusive and accepting society. By engaging in dialogues, organizing events, and participating in educational campaigns, we can continue to promote empathy, understanding, and acceptance.

Building Alliances and Coalitions

Building alliances and coalitions is another critical aspect of continuing Virgilio's legacy of activism. By working together, we can amplify our collective voices and create meaningful change. It is essential to develop connections and partnerships with other social justice movements, recognizing that the fight for LGBTQ rights intersects with other struggles for justice, such as racial equality, gender equality, and immigrant rights.

Through collaborations with other advocacy groups and organizations, we can broaden our impact and work towards a more comprehensive vision of social justice. By joining forces, we can address the systemic issues that contribute to inequality and discrimination, creating a more just and equitable society for all.

Youth Empowerment and Mentorship

One crucial aspect of continuing the legacy of activism is empowering and mentoring LGBTQ youth. By offering support, guidance, and resources, we can nurture the next generation of activists and leaders who will carry forward the fight for LGBTQ rights.

Establishing mentorship programs and support networks is an effective way to provide LGBTQ youth with the tools they need to navigate the challenges they may face. By sharing our experiences, wisdom, and advice, we can inspire and empower LGBTQ youth to create change within their communities and beyond.

Furthermore, creating safe spaces and inclusive environments is crucial for the emotional and psychological well-being of LGBTQ youth. By establishing LGBTQ community centers, support groups, and educational programs, we can provide a nurturing space for personal growth, self-acceptance, and empowerment.

Using Technology for Advocacy

In today's digital age, technology plays a crucial role in activism and advocacy. To continue Virgilio's legacy, we must embrace the power of technology to raise awareness, mobilize communities, and effect change.

Social media platforms, such as Twitter, Facebook, and Instagram, offer immense opportunities for LGBTQ activists to connect, share stories, and organize campaigns. By leveraging these platforms, we can reach a global audience, challenge stereotypes, and promote positive narratives surrounding LGBTQ individuals.

Online petitions, crowdfunding platforms, and digital advocacy tools provide avenues for fundraising and resources to support LGBTQ organizations and initiatives. Through these platforms, we can unite people from diverse backgrounds and geographical locations to support and advance LGBTQ rights.

However, we must also be mindful of the potential pitfalls of technology. Online harassment, hate speech, and the spread of misinformation are prevalent challenges in the digital realm. To effectively navigate these issues, we must prioritize digital literacy and create safe online spaces that foster dialogue, respect, and inclusivity.

Arts and Media as Vehicles for Change

Another powerful way to continue Virgilio's legacy is through arts and media. Throughout history, art and media have played a pivotal role in challenging social norms and fostering social change. By promoting LGBTQ representation and narratives in various forms of art, including literature, film, music, and visual arts, we can promote visibility, empathy, and understanding.

Supporting LGBTQ artists and performers is crucial for both their artistic development and the broader LGBTQ rights movement. By attending LGBTQ-focused arts events, purchasing LGBTQ-created artwork, and supporting LGBTQ musicians, we not only celebrate their talents but also contribute to the visibility and cultural validation of the LGBTQ community.

Moreover, integrating LGBTQ stories and perspectives into mainstream media is imperative to challenge the prevailing heteronormative narratives. By advocating for LGBTQ representation in television, movies, and literature, we can shape public discourse and challenge societal norms, fostering a more inclusive and accepting society.

Redefining Activism for the Future

As we continue Virgilio's legacy, it is essential to acknowledge that activism evolves with time. The challenges facing the LGBTQ community today may differ from those faced in the past. Therefore, our approach to activism must adapt and respond to the changing landscape.

Recognizing the interconnections between different social justice movements and promoting intersectional approaches is crucial. By acknowledging the unique experiences and challenges faced by LGBTQ individuals who are also members of marginalized communities, we can fight for justice on all fronts.

SECTION 1: A NEW CHAPTER BEGINS

In addition, we must remain vigilant against any attempts to roll back the rights and protections gained through years of activism. This requires active participation in political processes, lobbying for LGBTQ-friendly policies, and supporting LGBTQ candidates for office.

The future of LGBTQ activism lies in our unwavering commitment to fighting for equality, justice, and acceptance. By continuing Virgilio's legacy, we not only honor the progress made but also create a more inclusive and affirming world for future generations of LGBTQ individuals. Together, we have the power to make history and ensure that love truly triumphs.

Subsection 3: Looking Towards a More Inclusive Future

As we reflect on the incredible journey of Virgilio Barco Isakson and the transformative impact he had on LGBTQ rights in Colombia, we must also turn our attention to the future. The fight for equality and inclusion is an ongoing battle, and it is crucial that we continue to push for progress and work towards a more inclusive future for all.

1. Embracing Intersectionality:

One key aspect of moving towards a more inclusive future is acknowledging the intersectionality of identities and experiences. We must recognize that individuals can face discrimination and marginalization not only based on their sexual orientation or gender identity, but also due to their race, ethnicity, socioeconomic status, disability, and other factors. It is essential that we advocate for the rights and well-being of all individuals at the intersections of multiple identities, ensuring that no one is left behind.

2. Education and Awareness:

Education plays a vital role in promoting inclusivity and breaking down stereotypes and prejudices. It is crucial to foster a curriculum that is inclusive of LGBTQ history, contributions, and perspectives. By teaching our children and young people about the diverse experiences of LGBTQ individuals, we can challenge heteronormativity and create a more accepting society. Moreover, incorporating LGBTQ-inclusive sex education in schools can promote healthy relationships, consent, and respect for all sexual orientations and gender identities.

3. Promoting LGBTQ Representation:

Representation matters. In order to create a more inclusive future, we need to ensure that LGBTQ individuals are represented in all aspects of society, including media, politics, and leadership positions. This requires actively promoting and supporting LGBTQ voices, stories, and talents. By amplifying these narratives, we can challenge stereotypes, inspire others, and pave the way for greater inclusion.

4. Healthcare and Mental Health:

Access to inclusive healthcare and mental health services is crucial for LGBTQ individuals. It is essential for medical professionals to be trained in LGBTQ-inclusive care, allowing them to provide appropriate and respectful treatment. Additionally, mental health support services that specifically cater to the needs of LGBTQ individuals must be readily available. By addressing the unique challenges that LGBTQ individuals face in accessing healthcare and mental health services, we can promote overall well-being and improve the quality of life for all.

5. Advocacy and Legislation:

Advocacy remains a vital tool in the fight for equality and inclusion. Continued grassroots efforts, community organizing, and lobbying for LGBTQ-friendly legislation can bring about significant change. It is crucial to push for comprehensive anti-discrimination laws that protect LGBTQ individuals in all aspects of life, including employment, housing, education, and healthcare. Additionally, advocating for the rights of transgender and non-binary individuals, such as legal recognition of gender identity and access to gender-affirming healthcare, is a crucial step towards a more inclusive future.

6. Allyship and Support:

In the journey towards a more inclusive future, allies play a vital role. It is important for individuals and organizations to actively stand in solidarity with the LGBTQ community and provide support. This can be achieved through education, creating safe spaces, listening to and amplifying LGBTQ voices, and challenging homophobia, biphobia, and transphobia whenever and wherever it is encountered. True and effective allyship requires ongoing education, self-reflection, and a commitment to learning and growing.

Looking towards a more inclusive future requires the collective effort of individuals, communities, and institutions. We must continue to push for progress, challenge systemic barriers, and amplify the voices of those who have been marginalized. By embracing intersectionality, promoting education, advocating for legislation, and fostering allyship, we can create a society where all individuals, regardless of their sexual orientation or gender identity, are celebrated, respected, and given equal opportunities to thrive.

As we honor the enduring legacy of Virgilio Barco Isakson, let us remember that the work is never done. Together, we can build a brighter future for LGBTQ individuals and create a society where love is love, and everyone can live their lives authentically and unapologetically. Together, we will make history.

Subsection 4: Amplifying LGBTQ Voices

In this section, we will explore the importance of amplifying LGBTQ voices and the various ways in which we can achieve this. By giving a platform to marginalized communities within the LGBTQ spectrum, we can create space for their stories, experiences, and perspectives to be heard and validated. Let's dive into the strategies and initiatives that can help us amplify LGBTQ voices.

Visibility and Representation

One of the crucial aspects of amplifying LGBTQ voices is increasing visibility and representation in all areas of society. This includes media, politics, academia, and the arts. When LGBTQ individuals see themselves reflected in these spaces, it can have a profound impact on their self-esteem and sense of belonging.

To achieve greater visibility and representation, it is essential to support and promote LGBTQ creators, artists, and performers. This can be done through initiatives such as LGBTQ film festivals, art exhibitions, and theater productions that showcase the work of LGBTQ individuals. Additionally, media outlets should strive to include diverse LGBTQ voices, stories, and experiences in their programming and editorial content.

Educational Initiatives

Education is another powerful tool for amplifying LGBTQ voices and fostering understanding and acceptance. Introducing LGBTQ-inclusive curricula in schools and universities can play a significant role in dispelling stereotypes, combating discrimination, and creating a more inclusive society.

Educational initiatives should focus on teaching LGBTQ history, exploring LGBTQ contributions in various fields, and promoting LGBTQ literature, art, and culture. By incorporating LGBTQ perspectives into the academic curriculum and providing resources for educators, we can help amplify LGBTQ voices and empower future generations to celebrate diversity.

Community Engagement

Amplifying LGBTQ voices within the community is crucial to creating an inclusive and supportive environment. Community engagement initiatives, such as LGBTQ support groups, workshops, and events, provide platforms for individuals to connect, share their stories, and have their voices heard.

These initiatives can also serve as catalysts for change by raising awareness about the challenges faced by LGBTQ individuals and advocating for their rights. By actively engaging with LGBTQ communities and amplifying their voices, we can foster empathy, understanding, and social change.

Intersectionality and Allyship

Amplifying LGBTQ voices should also involve an intersectional approach that recognizes the unique struggles and experiences of individuals with multiple marginalized identities. It is important to uplift and support LGBTQ individuals who are also part of other marginalized communities, such as people of color, individuals with disabilities, and those from low-income backgrounds.

Allyship plays a crucial role in amplifying LGBTQ voices. Allies can use their privilege and platform to uplift and advocate for the rights of LGBTQ individuals. This can be done through speaking out against discrimination, supporting LGBTQ-led initiatives, and actively listening to and amplifying LGBTQ voices.

Online Activism and Social Media

In the digital age, online activism and social media platforms offer powerful avenues for amplifying LGBTQ voices. Hashtag campaigns, online petitions, blogs, podcasts, and YouTube channels created by LGBTQ individuals contribute to raising awareness and promoting inclusive narratives.

Social media platforms provide opportunities for individuals to share their stories, connect with others, and build supportive online communities. Additionally, online resources and platforms dedicated to LGBTQ issues, such as forums and educational websites, help amplify LGBTQ voices by providing vital information and support.

Unconventional Means of Amplifying LGBTQ Voices

Beyond traditional strategies, we can explore unconventional means of amplifying LGBTQ voices. This may include organizing LGBTQ-themed events, such as inclusive sports tournaments, music festivals, or even LGBTQ-led entrepreneurial initiatives that provide economic empowerment.

Another way to amplify LGBTQ voices is through performances and artistic expressions. This can include spoken word poetry, drag shows, and theatrical productions that shed light on LGBTQ experiences and challenges.

By thinking creatively and innovatively, we can continue to find new and unique ways to amplify LGBTQ voices and make a lasting impact on society.

In conclusion, amplifying LGBTQ voices is essential for creating a more inclusive and accepting society. Through visibility and representation, educational initiatives, community engagement, intersectionality and allyship, online activism and social media, and unconventional means, we can ensure that LGBTQ narratives are heard and celebrated. By amplifying LGBTQ voices, we can pave the way for a future where everyone's story is valued and respected.

Subsection 5: The Long-lasting Impact of Virgilio Barco Isakson

Virgilio Barco Isakson, the renowned LGBTQ activist from Colombia, has left a remarkable and enduring impact on the fight for equality and acceptance. His tireless advocacy, trailblazing policies, and cultural revolution have transformed not only Colombia's LGBTQ rights movement but also served as an inspiration worldwide.

One of the key legacies of Virgilio Barco Isakson is his pioneering work in the realm of trailblazing policies. During his tenure as mayor of Bogotá, he implemented groundbreaking measures that aimed to promote equal rights and protections for the LGBTQ community. For instance, he played a pivotal role in legalizing same-sex relationships, which was a significant milestone in Colombian history. This landmark achievement not only granted LGBTQ individuals the right to love freely but also paved the way for subsequent advancements in LGBTQ rights.

Furthermore, Virgilio Barco Isakson recognized the importance of safeguarding the well-being of LGBTQ youth. Under his leadership, the protection of LGBTQ youth became a top priority, and he spearheaded initiatives to combat discrimination, bullying, and violence in schools and communities. By championing inclusive education and fostering LGBTQ support networks, Virgilio created spaces where young LGBTQ individuals felt embraced and celebrated for who they are.

In addition to his policies, Virgilio Barco Isakson made significant strides in challenging and redefining societal gender norms. He recognized that true equality and acceptance required breaking free from the confines of traditional gender roles. Through his initiatives, he empowered individuals to express themselves authentically, regardless of societal expectations. This move towards embracing gender diversity has had a profound impact on Colombian society, fostering a more inclusive and accepting environment for all.

Virgilio's impact extended beyond policies alone. He recognized the power of media and culture to shape perceptions and challenge stereotypes. To this end, he actively promoted LGBTQ representation in the media, aiming to reduce stigma and increase visibility. Through his support of LGBTQ artists, writers, and performers, he helped create a vibrant and diverse cultural landscape that celebrated LGBTQ experiences and history. The increased representation and visibility of the community in mainstream culture not only contributed to a more inclusive society but also provided crucial role models and inspiration to LGBTQ individuals.

Moreover, Virgilio Barco Isakson understood the importance of solidarity and collaboration in achieving global LGBTQ equality. He actively engaged with international conferences and partnered with NGOs and human rights organizations to expand the reach and impact of his advocacy. Through his efforts, he connected with LGBTQ activists worldwide, sharing experiences, and strategies, and inspiring others to continue the fight for equality. Virgilio's global impact cannot be understated, as his advocacy efforts have reverberated far beyond Colombia's borders.

As we reflect on Virgilio Barco Isakson's accomplishments, we must also acknowledge the challenges he faced and the personal sacrifices he made. His journey was not without opposition, as he encountered resistance from conservative entities and endured media backlash and public scrutiny. However, his unwavering resilience and determination fueled his success in pushing the boundaries and actualizing meaningful change. Virgilio's ability to navigate through homophobia and transphobia with grace and strength serves as an inspiration for future LGBTQ activists.

The long-lasting impact of Virgilio Barco Isakson is evident in the crucial victories his activism has achieved. LGBTQ rights in Colombia have experienced significant advancements, leading to a transformative shift in societal attitudes. His achievements have created a domino effect, influencing public opinion, policies, and legislation that have improved the lives of countless LGBTQ individuals. Furthermore, his emphasis on empowering LGBTQ youth has nurtured a new generation of activists, ensuring that the fight for equality continues to thrive.

The legacy of Virgilio Barco Isakson lives on through various means. His ongoing influence can be observed through LGBTQ support networks that he established, providing resources, guidance, and empowerment to individuals seeking to make a difference. Additionally, his contributions to LGBTQ research and literature have expanded knowledge and understanding of LGBTQ experiences, paving the way for more informed activism and policymaking. Virgilio's advocacy for intersectionality has amplified the voices and experiences of marginalized communities within the LGBTQ movement, reinforcing the notion that all struggles for equality are interconnected.

To honor Virgilios's memory and uplift LGBTQ activism, annual festivals and commemorations have been established to celebrate his achievements. These events serve as reminders of the progress made and the work that still lies ahead. The Virgilio Barco Isakson LGBTQ Center, a beacon of support and inclusivity, stands as a testament to his enduring legacy and commitment to the cause.

Looking to the future, Virgilio Barco Isakson's impact on LGBTQ rights continues to shape the trajectory of the movement. His work paved the way for progress and served as an inspiration for future activists. As the world enters the digital age, new avenues for activism have emerged, and the fight for equality has become more globalized than ever before. The continued expansion of LGBTQ rights, breaking barriers globally, and tackling issues of intersectionality will be critical in achieving full equality.

In conclusion, Virgilio Barco Isakson's long-lasting impact on LGBTQ rights in Colombia and beyond cannot be overstated. His trailblazing policies, cultural revolution, and unwavering activism have transformed societal perceptions and advanced the fight for equality. His dedication to the cause serves as a call to action, inspiring change in all communities and motivating individuals to continue the work towards a more inclusive and accepting world. Together, we will make history and create a future where love is love, and all individuals are celebrated and accepted for who they are.

Section 2: Honor and Celebration

Subsection 1: Virgilio's Ongoing Influence

Virgilio Barco Isakson's impact on LGBTQ rights in Colombia has been profound and continues to be felt today. His tireless activism and pioneering policies have left an indelible mark on the country, inspiring generations of activists and transforming the lives of LGBTQ individuals. In this subsection, we will explore the ongoing influence of Virgilio Barco Isakson and how his legacy continues to shape the fight for equality.

Championing LGBTQ Rights

Virgilio Barco Isakson's unwavering commitment to LGBTQ rights laid the foundation for progress and set a precedent for future activists. His trailblazing policies challenged societal norms and paved the way for greater acceptance and inclusivity. One of his most significant achievements was the fight for equal rights, demanding that LGBTQ individuals be treated with dignity and respect under the law.

Problem: Legal Recognition Before Virgilio's influence, LGBTQ individuals faced legal discrimination and were denied basic rights. They were often denied access to housing, education, healthcare, and employment opportunities due to their sexual orientation or gender identity. Virgilio addressed this problem by pushing for legal recognition of same-sex relationships.

Solution: Legalizing Same-Sex Marriage Virgilio's visionary leadership resulted in the legalization of same-sex marriage in Colombia. He understood that denying LGBTQ couples the right to marry was a clear violation of their human rights. Through legal reforms and a strategic campaign, Virgilio successfully challenged societal norms and ensured that love knows no gender.

Example: Celebrating Love and Inclusion The impact of legalizing same-sex marriage extended far beyond legal rights. It fostered a sense of love and inclusivity within Colombian society. LGBTQ couples were finally able to publicly express their love and affirm their commitment in front of their families, friends, and the entire nation. This not only affirmed the dignity and worth of LGBTQ individuals but also sent a powerful message to society about acceptance and equality.

Resources: LGBTQ Legal Organizations To continue Virgilio's legacy, LGBTQ legal organizations play a pivotal role in advocating for the ongoing legal recognition of same-sex marriage and other LGBTQ rights. These organizations provide legal support, resources, and education to ensure that LGBTQ individuals can exercise their rights fully.

Inspiring Social Change

Virgilio Barco Isakson's influence extends far beyond legal reforms. His vision of a more inclusive and accepting society inspired cultural and social transformations, challenging prevailing attitudes and prejudices. He recognized the importance of representation, education, and celebration in fostering a society where LGBTQ individuals are embraced for who they are.

Problem: Lack of LGBTQ Representation Historically, LGBTQ individuals have been underrepresented or mischaracterized in mainstream media, perpetuating harmful stereotypes and limiting visibility. Virgilio recognized the need to address this problem and promote positive LGBTQ representation.

Solution: Promoting LGBTQ Representation in Media Virgilio actively encouraged the inclusion of LGBTQ characters in television, film, and other forms of media. By collaborating with media organizations, he sought to break down stereotypes and provide accurate and nuanced portrayals of LGBTQ individuals. This not only fostered empathy and understanding but also empowered LGBTQ individuals by giving them role models to look up to.

Example: LGBTQ Characters in Popular TV Shows One of the most significant milestones in LGBTQ representation was the inclusion of LGBTQ characters in popular TV shows. By depicting LGBTQ individuals in meaningful and authentic storylines, these shows helped to challenge prejudices and change public perception. This increased visibility has not only helped to humanize LGBTQ experiences but also paved the way for important conversations about acceptance and equality.

Resources: LGBTQ Media Advocacy To maintain the progress made in LGBTQ representation, media advocacy organizations play a critical role. These organizations work to challenge harmful narratives, ensure accurate and inclusive portrayals, and hold media outlets accountable for representing LGBTQ individuals authentically.

Empowering LGBTQ Youth

An essential aspect of Virgilio Barco Isakson's legacy is his commitment to empowering LGBTQ youth. Recognizing the unique challenges faced by young LGBTQ individuals, Virgilio advocated for supportive environments, inclusive education, and mentorship programs to ensure that the next generation has the tools to continue the fight for equality.

Problem: LGBTQ Youth Bullying and Discrimination LGBTQ youth often face heightened levels of bullying, discrimination, and mental health challenges. Virgilio understood the urgent need to address these issues and create safe spaces for LGBTQ youth to thrive.

Solution: LGBTQ-Inclusive Education Virgilio championed LGBTQ-inclusive education to challenge stereotypes, promote acceptance, and create an inclusive learning environment for all students. By integrating LGBTQ history, experiences, and perspectives into the curriculum, educators can foster empathy, dismantle prejudice, and provide a supportive space for LGBTQ youth.

Example: LGBTQ Supportive Schools Inclusive schools provide a range of supports for LGBTQ youth, including gay-straight alliances, LGBTQ-affirming policies, and comprehensive anti-bullying programs. These initiatives help create a positive and inclusive culture, empowering LGBTQ students to be proud of who they are.

Resources: LGBTQ Youth Support Organizations To ensure the well-being and empowerment of LGBTQ youth, support organizations are crucial. These organizations provide resources, counseling services, mentorship opportunities, and safe spaces where LGBTQ youth can connect and find support.

Creating Change Beyond Borders

Virgilio Barco Isakson's impact extended beyond Colombia's borders. He recognized the importance of international solidarity and collaboration in advancing LGBTQ rights globally. His engagement with international conferences, NGOs, and human rights organizations helped amplify Colombia's progress and inspire LGBTQ activists worldwide.

Problem: Limited LGBTQ Rights Globally While progress has been made in many countries, LGBTQ individuals continue to face discrimination, violence, and legal challenges worldwide. Virgilio understood that tackling these issues required global solidarity and cooperation.

Solution: Speaking Out at International Conferences Virgilio regularly participated in international conferences, where he shared Colombia's experiences and successes in LGBTQ rights. By taking the stage and addressing global audiences, he contributed to the global dialogue on LGBTQ rights, inspiring other nations to follow suit.

Example: United Nations General Assembly Address Virgilio's powerful address to the United Nations General Assembly highlighted the progress made in Colombia and called on the global community to embrace LGBTQ rights. His speech resonated with leaders from around the world, fostering conversations on global LGBTQ equality and spurring action in countries still grappling with discrimination.

SECTION 2: HONOR AND CELEBRATION 313

Resources: Global LGBTQ Networks   Virgilio's ongoing influence in the global LGBTQ rights movement is supported by international networks and alliances. These organizations work collaboratively to advocate for LGBTQ rights, support local activists, and share best practices from around the world.

In conclusion, Virgilio Barco Isakson's ongoing influence is evident in the legislative, cultural, and social advancements made in LGBTQ rights in Colombia. His commitment to equality, inclusivity, and empowerment continues to inspire activists, leaders, and individuals worldwide. By championing LGBTQ rights, promoting positive representation, supporting LGBTQ youth, and engaging globally, Virgilio has left an enduring legacy that serves as a guiding light for the future of LGBTQ activism. Together, we will march forward, building a brighter and more inclusive future for all LGBTQ individuals.

Subsection 2: Recognizing Virgilio's Achievements

Virgilio Barco Isakson's tireless dedication and unwavering commitment to LGBTQ rights have left an indelible mark on Colombian society. Throughout his lifetime, he spearheaded numerous initiatives and achieved remarkable milestones that have transformed the lives of LGBTQ individuals. In this subsection, we will explore some of Virgilio's most significant accomplishments and the impact they have had on the LGBTQ community in Colombia and beyond.

The Battle for Equal Rights

Virgilio Barco Isakson recognized the importance of equal rights for all individuals, regardless of their sexual orientation or gender identity. One of his most notable achievements was the introduction and successful passage of legislation aimed at safeguarding the rights of LGBTQ individuals. He championed the Equality Act, which protected LGBTQ individuals from discrimination in employment, housing, education, and public services.

To ensure the sustainability of these rights and to prevent discriminatory practices, Virgilio implemented strict penalties for individuals or institutions found guilty of discrimination against LGBTQ individuals. Moreover, he actively advocated for the inclusion of LGBTQ rights in the Colombian Constitution, cementing their legal protection and recognition.

Legalizing Same-Sex Relationships

Virgilio Barco Isakson played a pivotal role in the legalization of same-sex relationships in Colombia. He understood the fundamental importance of love and commitment, regardless of gender, and worked tirelessly to dismantle the barriers faced by LGBTQ couples.

Under his leadership, the Colombian government passed a landmark bill legalizing same-sex marriage, making Colombia one of the first countries in Latin America to do so. This momentous achievement allowed LGBTQ couples to enjoy the same legal rights and protections as their heterosexual counterparts, fostering a more inclusive and accepting society.

Protecting LGBTQ Youth

Recognizing the vulnerability of LGBTQ youth and the need for comprehensive support systems, Virgilio Barco Isakson initiated and implemented several programs aimed at safeguarding the well-being of LGBTQ young people. He established LGBTQ youth centers across the country, providing a safe and nurturing environment where young individuals could seek guidance, support, and mentorship.

Additionally, Virgilio partnered with educational institutions to develop inclusive curricula that fostered understanding and acceptance of LGBTQ individuals. Through comprehensive sex education programs, he aimed to prevent discrimination, bullying, and the marginalization of LGBTQ students, ensuring their full participation in academic settings and beyond.

Challenging Gender Norms

Virgilio Barco Isakson recognized the importance of challenging gender norms and promoting gender equality within society. He firmly believed that everyone should have the freedom to express their gender identity authentically and without fear of discrimination.

To challenge traditional gender norms, Virgilio introduced policies that promoted gender diversity and inclusion. He actively encouraged the participation of LGBTQ individuals in traditionally gender-segregated sectors, such as politics, academia, and business, breaking down barriers and creating opportunities for all.

Recognizing Transgender Rights

Virgilio Barco Isakson was a trailblazer in advocating for the rights of transgender individuals in Colombia. Understanding the unique struggles and discrimination faced by the transgender community, he tirelessly fought to ensure their legal recognition and protection.

Under his leadership, legislation was enacted to simplify and streamline the legal recognition of gender identity for transgender individuals. Virgilio also spearheaded initiatives to ensure access to quality healthcare, mental health support, and social services for the transgender community. By amplifying their voices and addressing their specific needs, he sought to empower transgender individuals and create a society that embraces their diversity.

Honoring Virgilio's Legacy

To honor Virgilio Barco Isakson's incredible contributions to LGBTQ rights, Colombia celebrates his legacy annually with Virgilio Barco Isakson Day. On this day, people gather to commemorate his achievements and reflect on the progress made in advancing LGBTQ rights.

In addition to the annual commemoration, the government, in collaboration with LGBTQ organizations, established the Virgilio Barco Isakson LGBTQ Center. This center serves as a hub for LGBTQ community engagement, providing resources, support, and educational programs to further advance LGBTQ rights. It stands as a testament to Virgilio's enduring legacy and a symbol of hope for continued progress in achieving equality.

The Future of LGBTQ Rights

Although Virgilio Barco Isakson's contributions have made significant strides in advancing LGBTQ rights in Colombia, there is still work to be done. The fight for equality continues, and it is now in the hands of the next generation to carry forward Virgilio's torch.

To sustain and expand LGBTQ rights, it is vital to foster ongoing dialogue and raise awareness about the challenges that LGBTQ individuals face. By promoting allyship, education, and inclusivity, we can work towards a future where LGBTQ individuals are afforded the same rights, dignity, and respect as all members of society.

Remember, recognizing Virgilio's achievements is not only a tribute to his dedication but also a call to action for us all. Together, we can continue to build a society where love, acceptance, and equality prevail.

Note: This content is intended to provide background information, inspiration, and examples for a LGBTQ activist biography. Any names, characters, organizations, places, or events mentioned are purely fictional and do not intend to represent any actual individual or organization. This content should be adapted and modified as necessary to fit the context and purpose of the biography.

Subsection 3: Annual Festivals and Commemorations

In this vibrant subsection, we delve into the colorful world of annual festivals and commemorations that celebrate LGBTQ pride, identity, and the accomplishments of Virgilio Barco Isakson. These events not only provide an opportunity for the LGBTQ community to come together, but also serve as powerful platforms for advocacy, education, and cultural exchange. Get ready to immerse yourself in the energy and excitement of these remarkable gatherings!

Festival of Colors: A Joyful Celebration

One of the most anticipated events in the LGBTQ calendar is the Festival of Colors. Inspired by the traditional Hindu festival of Holi, this vibrant celebration takes place annually in the heart of Bogotá. It brings together people from all walks of life to embrace diversity, love, and acceptance.

During the festival, the streets come alive with a riot of colors as participants joyfully throw powdered pigments at each other, creating a mesmerizing kaleidoscope of hues. This act symbolizes the breaking down of barriers and the blending of different identities into a unified whole. The Festival of Colors serves as a visual spectacle that celebrates the LGBTQ community's resilience and pride.

Barco Pride Parade: Embracing Unity

The Barco Pride Parade is an exuberant extravaganza that takes place annually in cities across Colombia. Thousands of LGBTQ individuals and allies flood the streets, adorned in vibrant costumes and waving rainbow banners. This march serves as a powerful statement of unity, defiance, and solidarity.

The parade route is lined with cheering crowds, as supporters from diverse backgrounds come together to witness the celebration and demonstrate their unwavering support for LGBTQ rights. Floats, music, and dance troupes add to the infectious energy, creating an unforgettable experience for all who participate. The Barco Pride Parade is a testament to the progress made in LGBTQ rights and an inspiring call for continued advocacy.

Legacy Ball: Honoring the Past, Inspiring the Future

The Legacy Ball is an elegant and poignant event that pays tribute to the progress achieved by the LGBTQ community under the leadership of Virgilio Barco Isakson. This gala affair brings together activists, leaders, and allies to commemorate the milestones and victories in the fight for LGBTQ rights.

During the Legacy Ball, inspiring speeches and performances highlight the importance of continued activism and create a sense of shared purpose among attendees. Funds raised during the event contribute to LGBTQ initiatives, ensuring that Virgilio's legacy lives on. The Legacy Ball serves as a reminder of the challenges overcome and motivates current and future generations to carry the torch of equality forward.

Artivism Festival: Celebrating the Power of Expression

The Artivism Festival is a unique and innovative celebration that combines the worlds of art and activism. This annual event showcases the work of LGBTQ artists and performers and explores the intersection of creativity and social change.

Participants have the opportunity to attend art exhibitions, film screenings, spoken word performances, and theatrical productions that push boundaries and challenge societal norms. Through their creative expressions, artists aim to inspire dialogue, challenge stereotypes, and foster greater understanding and acceptance.

The Artivism Festival serves as a powerful platform for LGBTQ artists to share their stories, explore their identities, and celebrate the transformative power of culture. It encourages individuals to be unapologetically themselves and to use their creativity to advocate for change.

Resource Fair: Connecting the Community

In addition to the vibrant festivities, an annual Resource Fair is held to provide vital information and support to the LGBTQ community. This event brings together NGOs, community organizations, and social services to create a space where individuals can access resources related to mental health, legal support, healthcare, employment, and education.

The Resource Fair facilitates networking and collaboration among different stakeholders, fostering a spirit of community and collective action. Attendees have the opportunity to engage directly with service providers, learn about available resources, and build connections within the LGBTQ network.

By creating a safe and inclusive environment, the Resource Fair empowers individuals to access the support they need to navigate the challenges they may face. It exemplifies the spirit of compassion and unity that defines the LGBTQ community.

Conclusion

The annual festivals and commemorations outlined in this subsection are more than mere celebrations—they are powerful catalysts for change and unity. From the vibrant colors of the Festival of Colors to the captivating performances of the Artivism Festival, these events serve as platforms for advocacy, education, and community building.

They honor the enduring legacy of Virgilio Barco Isakson, reminding us all of the progress made in LGBTQ rights and motivating us to continue the fight for equality. Through these festivals and commemorations, we celebrate diversity, embrace love and acceptance, and work towards a future where everyone, regardless of their sexual orientation or gender identity, can live authentically and with pride. The spirit of Virgilio Barco Isakson lives on in these annual gatherings, ensuring that his vision of a more inclusive and equal society endures.

Subsection 4: The Virgilio Barco Isakson LGBTQ Center

The Virgilio Barco Isakson LGBTQ Center is a visionary institution that carries on the legacy of Virgilio Barco Isakson by providing support, resources, and a safe space for the LGBTQ community in Colombia. Located in the heart of Bogotá, this center aims to empower and celebrate diversity, while advocating for the rights and well-being of LGBTQ individuals.

A Place of Support and Community

At the Virgilio Barco Isakson LGBTQ Center, individuals can find a community that understands their unique experiences and challenges. The center offers various support services, including counseling, support groups, and legal assistance, ensuring that LGBTQ individuals have the resources they need to navigate the complexities of their lives.

Promoting Education and Awareness

A key focus of the Virgilio Barco Isakson LGBTQ Center is education and awareness. Through workshops, seminars, and educational programs, the center strives to increase understanding and acceptance of LGBTQ issues among the broader society. By fostering dialogue and breaking down stereotypes, the center aims to create a more inclusive and tolerant Colombia.

Arts and Culture as Vehicles for Change

The Virgilio Barco Isakson LGBTQ Center recognizes the power of art and culture as tools for social change. The center hosts art exhibitions, film screenings, and performances that showcase LGBTQ perspectives and celebrate queer artists. These events not only provide a platform for LGBTQ voices but also challenge societal norms and open up new possibilities for self-expression.

Forging Alliances and Collaborations

To achieve its mission, the Virgilio Barco Isakson LGBTQ Center actively collaborates with other organizations, government agencies, and NGOs. By forging alliances, the center strengthens its advocacy efforts and amplifies its impact. These partnerships allow for the development of joint initiatives and the sharing of resources, ultimately benefiting the LGBTQ community as a whole.

Creating Safe Spaces

One of the primary goals of the Virgilio Barco Isakson LGBTQ Center is to create safe and inclusive spaces where LGBTQ individuals can be themselves without fear of discrimination or violence. The center provides a physical space where individuals can gather, find support, and build connections with like-minded individuals. Additionally, the center works with local businesses, schools, and institutions to promote LGBTQ-friendly environments throughout the country.

Breaking Barriers through Research and Advocacy

The Virgilio Barco Isakson LGBTQ Center recognizes the importance of research in advancing LGBTQ rights. The center conducts studies, collects data, and publishes reports on various aspects of LGBTQ life in Colombia. This research not only serves as a foundation for policy advocacy but also sheds light on the challenges faced by the community. Through evidence-based advocacy, the center strives to dismantle systemic barriers and promote equality.

Empowering Future LGBTQ Leaders

The Virgilio Barco Isakson LGBTQ Center is committed to nurturing and empowering the next generation of LGBTQ leaders. The center offers leadership development programs, mentorship opportunities, and scholarships to LGBTQ youth, providing them with the skills, knowledge, and support needed to make a positive impact in their communities. By investing in the future leaders, the center ensures the sustainability of the LGBTQ rights movement.

Challenging Gender Norms

An important aspect of the Virgilio Barco Isakson LGBTQ Center's work is challenging gender norms and promoting gender diversity. The center advocates for the recognition and affirmation of individuals who do not conform to traditional gender roles. Through awareness campaigns, policy advocacy, and education, the center aims to create a society where all gender identities and expressions are respected and celebrated.

Supporting Health and Well-being

The Virgilio Barco Isakson LGBTQ Center recognizes that the health and well-being of LGBTQ individuals are essential for leading fulfilling lives. The center provides access to healthcare services, facilitates support networks and workshops on LGBTQ-specific health issues, and raises awareness about mental health challenges faced by the community. By addressing these unique health needs, the center ensures that LGBTQ individuals can thrive and live their lives to the fullest.

Beyond Borders: International Collaboration

The Virgilio Barco Isakson LGBTQ Center understands that LGBTQ rights are not confined to national boundaries. The center actively collaborates with international LGBTQ organizations, participating in conferences, sharing best practices, and advocating for global LGBTQ rights. By engaging in international dialogues, the center contributes to the global fight for equality and enriches its understanding of LGBTQ issues on a broader scale.

In conclusion, the Virgilio Barco Isakson LGBTQ Center is a beacon of hope and support for LGBTQ individuals in Colombia. By providing a safe space, promoting education, fostering arts and culture, and advocating for equality, the center continues to pave the way for a more inclusive and accepting society. The legacy of Virgilio Barco Isakson lives on through this center, inspiring future generations of LGBTQ activists and ensuring that the fight for LGBTQ rights remains strong.

Subsection 5: Remembering and Uplifting LGBTQ Activism

In this final subsection, we honor the remarkable legacy of Virgilio Barco Isakson and explore the ways in which LGBTQ activism continues to thrive and make a difference around the world. Through remembrance, education, and support, we ensure that the progress achieved by Virgilio and countless other activists is preserved and propelled forward.

Remembering Virgilio's Courage

Virgilio Barco Isakson's unwavering courage and determination continue to inspire LGBTQ activists globally. We remember his tenacity, resilience, and trailblazing accomplishments that elevated the LGBTQ community in Colombia and beyond. As we reflect on his journey, we recognize the importance of celebrating and preserving that spirit for generations to come.

Commemorating the Achievements

To keep Virgilio's achievements alive, we commemorate his groundbreaking accomplishments annually through festivals, events, and exhibitions. These gatherings provide a platform to celebrate our progress, foster a sense of community, and raise awareness about the ongoing challenges faced by the LGBTQ community. By acknowledging our past, we ignite a sense of pride and motivation to continue striving for equality.

The Virgilio Barco Isakson LGBTQ Center

In honor of Virgilio's legacy, the Virgilio Barco Isakson LGBTQ Center stands as a beacon of hope and empowerment. This center serves as a safe space for LGBTQ individuals and provides essential support, resources, and services to the community. It offers counseling, educational programs, legal assistance, and a hub for activism, ensuring that the fight for LGBTQ rights endures.

Preserving History and Amplifying Voices

Preserving LGBTQ history is crucial in understanding our collective journey and the progress made. Through archives, documentaries, and educational initiatives, we ensure that the stories and experiences of LGBTQ activists are shared and celebrated. By amplifying their voices, we inspire future generations to embrace their identity, fight for equality, and challenge the status quo.

Empowering the Next Generation

One of the key components of uplifting LGBTQ activism is empowering and supporting the next generation of activists. Providing mentorship programs, scholarships, and leadership training helps young individuals discover their potential and develop the skills necessary to advance the LGBTQ rights movement. By investing in their growth, we ensure a sustainable future for LGBTQ activism.

Fostering Intersectional Advocacy

In the spirit of Virgilio's commitment to justice, we recognize that LGBTQ rights intersect with other social justice movements. Uplifting LGBTQ activism means fostering an understanding of the interconnected nature of struggles against racism, poverty, sexism, ableism, and other forms of oppression. By championing intersectional advocacy, we create a more inclusive and equitable movement for all.

Future Collaboration and Partnerships

Looking ahead, the future of LGBTQ activism lies in collaboration and partnerships. Building alliances with other social justice movements, organizations, and individuals allows us to amplify our message and effect meaningful change on a wider scale. By leveraging collective power, we can break down barriers and create a world where LGBTQ individuals can live free from discrimination and prejudice.

A Call to Action

As we conclude this book, we call upon all individuals, regardless of sexual orientation or gender identity, to stand in solidarity with LGBTQ individuals worldwide. We must actively challenge intolerance, promote understanding, and fight for equality. Each and every one of us has a role to play in uplifting LGBTQ activism, whether it is through education, advocacy, support, or simply amplifying their voices. Together, we can create a future where love truly knows no boundaries.

Let us remember Virgilio Barco Isakson's undeniable impact, celebrate the progress we have made, and strive to build a world where LGBTQ rights are fully realized. The journey towards equality continues, and it is up to each of us to ensure that it is a journey marked by unity, resilience, and unyielding support. Together, we will make history.

SECTION 2: HONOR AND CELEBRATION

Exercises

1. Research and identify another LGBTQ activist who made a significant impact in their country or region. Write a short biography highlighting their achievements and contributions to the LGBTQ rights movement.

2. Conduct an interview with a local LGBTQ organization, exploring the challenges they face in their community and the strategies they employ to effect change. Reflect on the interview and discuss ways in which you can support their cause.

3. Prepare a presentation or workshop on the importance of intersectionality in LGBTQ activism. Discuss how different forms of discrimination intersect and how addressing these intersections can lead to more inclusive and effective advocacy.

4. Take part in a community event or festival that celebrates LGBTQ culture and history. Reflect on your experience and discuss the impact of such events on the visibility and acceptance of the LGBTQ community.

5. Research the LGBTQ rights situation in a country where LGBTQ individuals face significant challenges. Write a report outlining the main obstacles and propose strategies for change based on the successes of activists like Virgilio Barco Isakson.

Resources

- **The Virgilio Barco Isakson LGBTQ Center:** Visit their website (www.virgiliobarcoisaksoncenter.org) to learn more about the center and the services they offer.

- **LGBTQ History Month:** Explore resources and educational materials on LGBTQ history and activism at www.lgbthistorymonth.com.

- **Amnesty International:** Stay updated on global LGBTQ rights issues and campaigns by visiting www.amnesty.org.

- **Human Rights Campaign:** Access resources, reports, and advocacy tools at www.hrc.org to support and uplift LGBTQ activism.

- **OutRight Action International:** Learn about international LGBTQ rights movements and get involved at www.outrightinternational.org.

Section 3: The Future of LGBTQ Rights

Subsection 1: Progress and Challenges on the Horizon

In this subsection, we will discuss the progress that has been made in the fight for LGBTQ rights and the challenges that still lie ahead. We will explore the advancements in legislation and societal acceptance, as well as the persistent barriers that prevent full equality for the LGBTQ community. Through a comprehensive examination of the current landscape, we can better understand the path forward and the work that still needs to be done.

Advancements in Legislation

In recent years, there have been significant advancements in legislation that protect and support the LGBTQ community. Many countries have recognized same-sex marriage and granted LGBTQ individuals the same legal rights and protections as their heterosexual counterparts. These legislative changes have been instrumental in promoting equality and challenging societal norms.

For example, in Colombia, the landmark ruling by the Constitutional Court in 2016 legalized same-sex marriage, granting LGBTQ couples the right to marry and enjoy the legal benefits and responsibilities that come with it. This decision was a significant milestone in the fight for equality and demonstrated a shift towards a more inclusive society.

Other countries have also made progress in legislating LGBTQ rights. Ireland, for instance, became the first country to legalize same-sex marriage through a popular vote in 2015. This represented a historic moment of validation, acceptance, and celebration for the LGBTQ community.

Despite these advancements, challenges persist in many regions. In some countries, LGBTQ individuals still face discrimination and violence, and their rights are not fully protected by the law. It is crucial to continue advocating for legislative changes that ensure equal rights for all individuals, regardless of their sexual orientation or gender identity.

Societal Acceptance and Challenges

Alongside legislative progress, there has been a notable shift in societal acceptance of the LGBTQ community. Attitudes towards LGBTQ individuals have evolved, with increased visibility and representation in media, arts, and culture contributing to a broader understanding and acceptance of diverse sexual orientations and gender identities.

One significant challenge, however, is the persistence of deeply ingrained biases and prejudices. Homophobia and transphobia still exist, and LGBTQ individuals often face discrimination, harassment, and violence in their daily lives. Structural barriers, such as limited access to healthcare, employment discrimination, and lack of inclusive education, hinder the progress toward full equality.

Education and awareness play a fundamental role in challenging these prejudices and building a more inclusive society. By promoting LGBTQ-inclusive education and fostering dialogue, we can dismantle stigmas and stereotypes, paving the way for greater acceptance and understanding.

Intersectionality and Advocacy

An essential aspect of the future of LGBTQ rights lies in embracing intersectionality. Many individuals within the LGBTQ community also face discrimination and marginalization due to their race, ethnicity, socioeconomic status, or disability. It is crucial to address these intersecting identities and fight for justice and equality for all.

Intersectionality acknowledges the interconnected nature of social identities and experiences and recognizes that a person's lived experiences are shaped by multiple factors. By advocating for the rights of LGBTQ individuals and acknowledging their intersecting identities, we can build a more inclusive and equitable movement.

Advocacy, both on national and international levels, is vital for advancing LGBTQ rights. Collaborating with non-governmental organizations, human rights organizations, and global LGBTQ movements can amplify voices and create meaningful change. Using social media platforms and the power of technology, activists can mobilize and reach wider audiences, raising awareness and challenging discriminatory practices.

The Role of Allies

Allies have played and will continue to play a crucial role in the fight for LGBTQ rights. Having individuals from outside the community stand alongside LGBTQ individuals amplifies the message of equality and helps create a more inclusive society.

By educating themselves, challenging their biases, and actively supporting LGBTQ individuals and causes, allies can contribute to pushing the boundaries of acceptance. It is essential for allies to use their privilege to uplift marginalized voices and advocate for change within their own communities.

A Holistic Approach to LGBTQ Rights

To continue making progress and overcoming challenges, a holistic approach to LGBTQ rights is necessary. This approach involves addressing not only legal and societal barriers but also focusing on mental health support, healthcare access, and combating the disproportionate rates of homelessness and violence faced by LGBTQ individuals.

Investment in mental health resources is paramount, as members of the LGBTQ community often experience higher rates of anxiety, depression, and suicide. By providing accessible and LGBTQ-inclusive mental health services, we can support individuals in their journey towards self-acceptance, resilience, and overall well-being.

Additionally, healthcare systems must strive to be inclusive and affirming spaces for LGBTQ individuals. This means eliminating discriminatory practices, training healthcare providers on LGBTQ cultural competency, and ensuring LGBTQ-specific healthcare needs are addressed.

Preventing and addressing homelessness within the LGBTQ community is another critical area of focus. Many LGBTQ youth are disproportionately affected by homelessness due to family rejection or lack of support. Investing in programs and resources that offer safe housing and support services can significantly impact the lives of these individuals.

The Vision for the Future

Looking ahead, the future of LGBTQ rights holds promise and potential. By continuing to advocate for equality, challenging societal norms, and addressing intersectionality, we can create a world where all individuals can thrive, regardless of their sexual orientation or gender identity.

Education, legislation, and societal acceptance must go hand in hand to achieve lasting change. By actively supporting LGBTQ rights, celebrating diversity, and recognizing the ongoing importance of inclusivity and representation, we can build a brighter future for LGBTQ individuals worldwide.

Let us remain united in the fight for equality, confident that together, we can make history. Love is love, and love will continue to be the guiding force that propels us forward.

Subsection 2: Breaking Barriers Globally

In the journey to transform LGBTQ rights in Colombia, Virgilio Barco Isakson's impact extended far beyond national boundaries. His unwavering commitment to

SECTION 3: THE FUTURE OF LGBTQ RIGHTS

equality and acceptance resonated with individuals and communities across the globe, inspiring a global movement for LGBTQ rights. This section explores the ways in which Virgilio broke barriers globally, leaving an indelible mark on the fight for equality worldwide.

Fostering Global Relationships

Virgilio Barco Isakson understood the importance of fostering relationships with LGBTQ activists and organizations worldwide. He recognized that the fight for equality transcends borders and that true change requires collaboration and solidarity on an international level. Through active participation in global LGBTQ conferences, forums, and events, Virgilio built bridges and formed alliances with activists from diverse backgrounds.

One of the key aspects of breaking barriers globally was Virgilio's commitment to learning from the experiences of LGBTQ activists in other countries. He actively engaged with leaders and organizers in the United States, Canada, Europe, and Latin America to understand their strategies, challenges, and successes. This exchange of knowledge and ideas helped shape his approach to LGBTQ activism in Colombia and contributed to the global movement for equality.

Advocating for Global Change

Virgilio Barco Isakson used his platform and influence to advocate for global change in policies and attitudes towards LGBTQ individuals. He recognized that addressing discrimination and prejudice requires systemic change at both national and international levels. Through his speeches, interviews, and public campaigns, Virgilio urged world leaders to prioritize LGBTQ rights as a fundamental aspect of human rights.

One of the groundbreaking initiatives Virgilio championed was the International LGBTQ Rights Charter. This comprehensive document outlined the essential rights and protections that LGBTQ individuals should enjoy globally. Virgilio spearheaded an international coalition of activists, diplomats, and NGOs to advocate for the adoption of this charter by the United Nations, aiming to provide a framework for LGBTQ rights across the globe.

Educating and Empowering

Breaking barriers globally also meant educating and empowering LGBTQ individuals in countries where discrimination and violence against them were prevalent. Virgilio recognized that access to information, resources, and support systems could make a significant difference for individuals living in hostile environments. He collaborated with international organizations to establish LGBTQ support networks, providing vital information, counseling, and guidance to those in need.

Virgilio also focused on empowering LGBTQ youth globally. He believed that by nurturing the next generation of activists, real change could be achieved. With this in mind, he initiated mentorship programs, scholarships, and leadership workshops to empower young LGBTQ individuals to become catalysts for change in their communities.

Driving Global Policy Change

Virgilio's influence extended to driving global policy change through collaboration with international human rights organizations and non-governmental organizations (NGOs). He actively worked alongside these entities to advocate for LGBTQ rights in countries where legal frameworks lagged behind. Through diplomatic channels and strategic partnerships, Virgilio contributed to the repeal of discriminatory laws and the introduction of legislation protecting LGBTQ individuals.

One of the exemplary cases of Virgilio's impact was his involvement in the decriminalization of homosexuality in several countries. By leveraging his connections and expertise, he supported local activists and provided them with the tools and resources necessary to challenge existing laws and push for legislative change. This collaborative approach not only helped dismantle discriminatory legislation but also inspired LGBTQ activists globally to fight for their rights.

Transforming Attitudes and Perceptions

Breaking barriers globally also meant challenging deep-seated attitudes and perceptions towards LGBTQ individuals. Virgilio recognized that legal protections alone were insufficient to bring about lasting change. Cultural and social transformation was equally critical for building a more inclusive world.

To promote understanding and empathy, Virgilio actively supported and funded initiatives that aimed to increase LGBTQ representation in media and popular culture globally. Through supporting LGBTQ artists, performers, and filmmakers, he sought to shift societal attitudes by showcasing the authentic and diverse experiences of LGBTQ individuals. By amplifying their voices, Virgilio contributed to a more nuanced understanding and acceptance of LGBTQ identities.

SECTION 3: THE FUTURE OF LGBTQ RIGHTS

A Call to Action

Breaking barriers globally requires collective action from individuals, communities, and nations. Virgilio Barco Isakson's legacy serves as a reminder that the struggle for LGBTQ rights is a shared responsibility. Each and every one of us has a role to play in creating a more inclusive and accepting world.

As we reflect on Virgilio's journey, we are called to be agents of change in our own communities. It starts with educating ourselves and others, challenging prejudice and discrimination wherever we encounter them. By advocating for LGBTQ rights, supporting local and international organizations, and amplifying LGBTQ voices, we can continue the work that Virgilio started—breaking barriers, fostering equality, and shaping a brighter future for LGBTQ individuals worldwide.

Subsection 3: Activism in the Digital Age

In the ever-evolving landscape of activism, the digital age has opened up a new realm of possibilities for the LGBTQ community. Technology has become a powerful tool that has revolutionized the way activists communicate, organize, and advocate for LGBTQ rights. With social media platforms, online campaigns, and digital resources at their fingertips, activists now have unprecedented reach and impact. This subsection explores the different ways in which activism has embraced the digital age and leveraged its potential for creating change.

The Role of Social Media

Social media has emerged as a key catalyst for LGBTQ activism. Platforms like Twitter, Facebook, and Instagram have provided a space for individuals to connect, share their stories, and raise awareness about LGBTQ issues. Activists can now reach a global audience instantaneously, allowing them to disseminate information, mobilize supporters, and challenge discriminatory narratives.

Hashtags have become a powerful tool in galvanizing support and generating dialogue. Campaigns like #LoveIsLove, #TransRightsAreHumanRights, and #ProudToBe have sparked conversations and created a sense of community across borders. Activists use these hashtags to share personal experiences, amplify voices, and advocate for policy changes. The widespread use of hashtags also allows for the identification and mobilization of allies, fostering a sense of solidarity and support.

Online Campaigns and Petitions

The digital age has revolutionized the way campaigns are conducted. Online platforms provide space for activists to launch virtual campaigns, create compelling content, and engage a broader audience. Petition websites like Change.org and Avaaz have made it easier than ever to collect signatures and garner support for LGBTQ causes. Through these platforms, activists can create petitions targeting policy changes, discriminatory practices, and human rights violations. These petitions have proven to be effective in raising public awareness and putting pressure on decision-makers.

One example is the successful petition calling for the repeal of discriminatory laws in a particular country. Through a coordinated online campaign, activists were able to collect hundreds of thousands of signatures and present them to the government. This led to a public discourse on LGBTQ rights, creating a momentum that ultimately resulted in the repeal of the laws.

Online Activism and Cybersecurity

While the digital age offers new opportunities for activism, it also presents challenges related to cybersecurity and privacy. Activists must navigate the complexities of online spaces that can expose them to surveillance, hacking, and harassment. Governments and anti-LGBTQ groups have been known to target activists through cyberattacks and online harassment campaigns.

To address these challenges, there has been an increased focus on digital security and encryption tools. Activists are encouraged to use secure communication channels, such as encrypted messaging apps, to protect their identities and information. Training programs and resources are available to educate activists on cybersecurity best practices, ensuring their safety in the digital realm.

Virtual Protests and Digital Activism

The digital age has also witnessed the rise of virtual protests and digital activism. In situations where physical protests may be unsafe or restricted, activists have turned to online platforms to express their dissent and continue advocating for LGBTQ rights. Virtual protests allow individuals to participate from the comfort and safety of their own homes while still making a powerful statement.

Digital activism takes various forms, including online petitions, email campaigns, and tweetstorms. Activists mobilize their online networks to flood decision-makers with messages, creating a visible and vocal presence. Online

SECTION 3: THE FUTURE OF LGBTQ RIGHTS

activism allows individuals who may otherwise be limited by geographical, economic, or accessibility constraints to actively participate in the movement.

Online Education and Resources

The digital age has significantly expanded access to education and resources for LGBTQ individuals and allies. Online platforms and websites provide a wealth of information on LGBTQ rights, history, and support networks. Educational resources, such as webinars, podcasts, and online courses, facilitate learning and create spaces for dialogue.

Online support networks and forums allow individuals to connect with others who share similar experiences and challenges. LGBTQ individuals in remote or conservative areas can find a sense of community and support through these digital spaces. Online resources also empower individuals to become advocates within their own communities, equipped with knowledge and tools to challenge discrimination and educate others.

The Potential for Online Allyship

The digital age has made it easier for allies to show support for the LGBTQ community. Individuals can share educational resources, uplifting stories, and messages of solidarity with a global audience. Allies can use their social media platforms to amplify LGBTQ voices and challenge homophobic and transphobic narratives.

Online allyship can also take the form of financial support. Crowdfunding platforms allow individuals to financially contribute to LGBTQ organizations and projects, providing vital resources to sustain their work. With just a few clicks, allies can make a tangible difference and be part of the movement for LGBTQ rights.

Challenges and Ethical Considerations

While the use of technology and the digital space has brought significant progress for LGBTQ activism, it is crucial to acknowledge and address some of the challenges and ethical considerations that arise. The digital divide, limited internet access, and disparities in technological literacy can hinder marginalized communities' participation in online activism. It is important for activists to actively work towards inclusivity and bridge these gaps.

Additionally, activists must navigate algorithmic biases and misinformation that can perpetuate discrimination and hinder progress. Critical digital literacy skills are necessary to analyze and challenge the narratives presented online. Addressing these challenges requires a commitment to ongoing education, dialogue, and collaboration within the LGBTQ community and with allies.

Conclusion

Activism in the digital age has revolutionized the LGBTQ movement, providing new avenues for widespread communication, mobilization, and advocacy. Social media platforms, online campaigns, and digital resources have transformed the way activists connect, organize, and influence change. However, it is crucial to approach digital activism with awareness and caution, addressing cybersecurity concerns and being mindful of the challenges and ethical considerations involved. By harnessing the power of the digital age, the LGBTQ community can continue to break barriers, inspire change, and fight for a more inclusive future.

Subsection 4: Expanding Intersectional Advocacy

In the fight for LGBTQ rights, it is crucial to recognize the importance of intersectionality. Intersectionality acknowledges that individuals can experience multiple forms of discrimination and oppression simultaneously, based on their overlapping identities such as race, gender, class, and sexuality. Expanding intersectional advocacy ensures that the LGBTQ rights movement is inclusive and addresses the needs of all marginalized communities.

Understanding Intersectionality

Intersectionality is a concept that was first introduced by Kimberlé Crenshaw, a prominent legal scholar and civil rights advocate. It highlights the ways in which social categorizations like race, gender, and class intersect to create unique experiences of discrimination and privilege. For example, a black transgender woman may face discrimination and violence not only because of her gender identity but also because of her race.

To expand intersectional advocacy, it is important to understand the interconnected systems of power and oppression that impact individuals from different marginalized communities. By recognizing the complexities of these intersecting identities, we can create more inclusive strategies and policies that address the specific challenges faced by different groups within the LGBTQ community.

Breaking Down Barriers

Expanding intersectional advocacy involves breaking down barriers that prevent marginalized LGBTQ individuals from accessing their full rights and opportunities. This can be achieved through various means, including:

1. Policy Reform: Advocating for policies that address the unique needs of intersecting identities, such as anti-discrimination laws that protect LGBTQ people of color, immigrants, and individuals with disabilities.

2. Education and Awareness: Promoting education and awareness about intersectionality to foster understanding and empathy within the LGBTQ community and beyond. This can be done through workshops, conferences, and media campaigns.

3. Collaboration and Allyship: Building alliances between different marginalized communities and uplifting diverse voices. This involves actively engaging with leaders and organizations from various social justice movements, such as racial justice, immigrant rights, and disability rights.

4. Resource Allocation: Ensuring that resources and funding are distributed equitably to support programs and initiatives that address the needs of intersectional communities. This includes investing in mental health support, healthcare services, and educational opportunities for marginalized LGBTQ individuals.

5. Representation and Visibility: Amplifying the voices and experiences of intersectional LGBTQ individuals in media, arts, and culture. This can be achieved by supporting LGBTQ artists, filmmakers, and writers from diverse backgrounds, and showcasing their work in mainstream platforms.

Challenges and Innovations

Expanding intersectional advocacy does come with its own set of challenges. Some key challenges include:

1. Lack of Awareness: Many individuals within the LGBTQ community may not fully understand or acknowledge the importance of intersectionality. Educating and raising awareness about intersectionality is crucial in overcoming this challenge.

2. Resistance and Backlash: Intersectional advocacy may face resistance from individuals and groups who do not see the relevance or value of taking an intersectional approach. Addressing this resistance requires ongoing dialogue, education, and exposure to diverse perspectives.

3. Resource Constraints: Intersectional advocacy requires resources, including funding, personnel, and time. Limited resources can hinder efforts to fully

implement intersectional strategies. Finding innovative ways to secure resources and collaborate with other organizations can help overcome this challenge.

Innovation plays a critical role in expanding intersectional advocacy. Some innovative approaches include:

1. Technology for Inclusion: Using technology, such as social media platforms and mobile applications, to facilitate connections and provide resources for intersectional communities. This can help amplify marginalized voices and address specific needs.

2. Grassroots Organizing: Mobilizing community-led initiatives that focus on local issues and specific intersectional challenges. Grassroots organizations often have a better understanding of community needs and can develop tailored solutions.

3. Intersectional Research: Conducting research that focuses on the experiences of marginalized LGBTQ individuals. This research can help inform policies and programs, ensuring they are inclusive and address the specific needs of various intersecting identities.

Case Study: The Transgender Law Center

The Transgender Law Center is an example of an organization that demonstrates the power of expanding intersectional advocacy. The organization, based in the United States, focuses on advocating for the rights of transgender and gender nonconforming individuals.

The Transgender Law Center recognizes the importance of intersectionality and actively works to address the unique challenges faced by transgender individuals from different backgrounds. They collaborate with organizations serving communities of color, incarcerated individuals, immigrants, and individuals with disabilities to create comprehensive and inclusive policies and programs.

Through their advocacy work, the Transgender Law Center has been successful in pushing for legislation that protects the rights of transgender individuals. They have also provided crucial legal support, resources, and community-building opportunities to transgender people from diverse backgrounds.

Conclusion

Expanding intersectional advocacy within the LGBTQ rights movement is essential to ensure that the most marginalized individuals within the community are included and supported. By understanding intersectionality, breaking down barriers, addressing challenges, and implementing innovative strategies, we can build a more inclusive and equitable society for all LGBTQ individuals. Through ongoing efforts, collaboration, and a commitment to intersectionality, we can create lasting change and continue the fight for equality.

Subsection 5: A Hopeful Road Ahead

As we look ahead to the future of LGBTQ rights in Colombia and beyond, we find ourselves standing at the intersection of progress and challenges. The fight for equality and acceptance is an ongoing battle, but with every victory comes the hope for a brighter and more inclusive future. In this final section of Virgilio Barco Isakson's biography, we explore the path that lies ahead for LGBTQ activism and the potential for continued change and transformation.

Progress and Challenges on the Horizon

While significant progress has been made in recent years, particularly in legal advancements and social attitudes towards the LGBTQ community, it is important to acknowledge that there are still challenges to be faced. The road ahead may not always be smooth, but with determination and resilience, we can overcome these obstacles and continue to shape a society that is truly accepting and inclusive.

One of the primary challenges that LGBTQ activists will need to address is the persistent presence of discrimination and prejudice. Despite advancements in laws and policies, discrimination against LGBTQ individuals continues to exist in various forms, whether it be in the workplace, healthcare system, or educational institutions. Therefore, a continued effort to educate and raise awareness about LGBTQ rights is crucial in order to combat these deeply ingrained biases and promote a culture of understanding and acceptance.

Another challenge lies in the intersectionality of LGBTQ identities. It is important to recognize that individuals within the LGBTQ community may also face discrimination based on their race, ethnicity, socioeconomic status, or disability. In the pursuit of equality, it is essential to address these intersecting forms of discrimination and work towards an inclusive movement that uplifts and supports individuals from all backgrounds.

Breaking Barriers Globally

While Virgilio Barco Isakson's impact on LGBTQ rights in Colombia is undeniable, the fight for equality extends far beyond national borders. The road ahead involves breaking barriers globally and supporting LGBTQ movements worldwide.

International solidarity plays a crucial role in advancing LGBTQ rights globally. By sharing experiences, knowledge, and resources, activists from different countries can collaborate and learn from one another's successes and challenges. Support for LGBTQ individuals in countries with limited rights and protections becomes even more critical, as their voices often go unheard. Advocacy efforts must extend beyond national borders to ensure that no one is left behind in the pursuit of equality.

Activism in the Digital Age

In an increasingly connected world, the power of social media and digital platforms cannot be underestimated. The road ahead for LGBTQ activism involves harnessing the potential of these platforms to spread awareness, mobilize communities, and create impactful change.

Social media has proven to be a catalyst for social movements, providing a platform for marginalized voices to be heard. The LGBTQ community can leverage these platforms to share stories, educate the public, advocate for policy change, and build supportive networks. Creating meaningful and engaging online content can be a powerful tool for challenging stereotypes, dispelling myths, and fostering understanding.

However, it is essential to recognize the limitations and dangers of digital activism. Online spaces can become breeding grounds for hate speech and harassment, and misinformation can easily spread. Activists must remain vigilant in creating safe and inclusive online environments, while also ensuring that their efforts span beyond the digital realm to create tangible change in the real world.

Expanding Intersectional Advocacy

As the LGBTQ movement continues to evolve, the importance of intersectional advocacy becomes increasingly evident. Intersectionality recognizes that various forms of oppression are interconnected and intersect with one another. Moving forward, it is crucial that LGBTQ activism embraces intersectionality, recognizing the unique challenges faced by individuals with multiple marginalized identities.

Expanding intersectional advocacy involves creating space for dialogue and collaboration between different social justice movements, such as feminist, racial justice, and disability rights movements. By acknowledging the interconnected nature of these movements, activists can forge alliances and work towards a more holistic and inclusive approach to social change.

A Hopeful Road Ahead

In conclusion, the road ahead for LGBTQ activism in Colombia and around the world is filled with challenges but also brimming with hope. Through continued education, advocacy, and resilience, we can overcome discrimination and prejudice, transform societal attitudes, and build a future where LGBTQ individuals are embraced for who they are.

The fight for LGBTQ rights requires not only the dedication of activists but also the support of allies from all walks of life. It is a collective effort that requires empathy, compassion, and an unwavering commitment to equality.

As we celebrate the enduring legacy of Virgilio Barco Isakson, we honor his contributions to the LGBTQ movement and the transformative impact he made in Colombia. By following in his footsteps and building upon his achievements, we can create a world where love is love, acceptance is universal, and equality is a reality for all. Together, we will continue to make history and pave the way for a brighter, more inclusive future.

Index

-doubt, 5, 7, 108, 174, 257

ability, 13, 45, 69, 72, 76, 78, 82, 83, 93, 96–98, 106, 107, 112, 159, 160, 165, 168, 188, 222–224, 227, 239, 261, 264, 265, 267, 271, 278, 285, 297, 298, 308
ableism, 193, 322
absence, 38
abuse, 20, 38, 99, 109, 122, 205
academia, 139, 152, 153, 192, 305, 314
academic, 85, 122, 139, 152, 164, 231, 296, 305, 314
academy, 212
acceptance, 3, 5, 7, 9–11, 13–16, 21, 26, 30, 32, 37, 38, 40–43, 45, 47, 50–53, 55, 58, 60, 62, 63, 65–72, 74, 75, 77, 78, 85, 91, 92, 94, 95, 100, 101, 105, 108, 115, 116, 120–122, 124, 126, 129, 130, 136, 139, 145, 146, 149, 150, 152, 156–160, 163–165, 167, 168, 171–177, 179, 181, 187–191, 193, 197, 199–208, 210, 213–218, 221–224, 226–234, 236, 237, 240, 246, 249–252, 254–259, 261–264, 267, 268, 271, 273, 275, 279, 281–284, 288–290, 294, 296, 297, 301, 303, 305, 307, 309–311, 314–318, 324–328, 335, 337
access, 5, 18, 34, 38, 39, 43, 44, 47, 48, 56, 62, 67, 99, 117, 120, 123, 127, 160, 163, 169, 175, 198, 199, 227, 233, 243, 246, 263, 267, 271, 273, 282, 288, 299, 304, 310, 315, 317, 320, 325–327, 331
accessibility, 51, 331
acclaim, 180
accomplishment, 131, 141
accountability, 242
achievement, 86, 173, 182, 226, 251, 307, 314
act, 47, 119, 125, 201, 293, 316
action, 12, 21, 23, 24, 42–44, 46, 53, 72, 76, 77, 80, 100, 113, 114, 134, 150, 160, 162, 165, 166, 170, 171, 186,

189, 193, 195, 197, 207, 211, 216, 224, 241, 245, 256, 275, 286, 287, 289, 290, 292–294, 300, 309, 312, 315, 317, 329

activism, 1–3, 5, 7–13, 15, 17, 19–24, 26–31, 33, 34, 39, 41, 43, 47, 48, 54, 63, 65, 70, 71, 74, 77, 83–86, 91, 94, 101, 105–108, 111–114, 116, 119, 121, 124, 131, 138–145, 151, 153–156, 158–160, 162–165, 167–181, 183, 185, 186, 188–192, 202, 205–207, 209–212, 214–218, 221–223, 226–229, 232–235, 237, 239–242, 246, 247, 249, 250, 253, 255, 256, 258–263, 265–267, 270–273, 276, 278, 281, 287, 289, 291–297, 299–303, 306–309, 313, 317, 321, 322, 327, 329–332, 335–337

activist, 1–4, 6, 11, 12, 16, 17, 19, 22, 26, 28, 31, 82, 84, 91, 92, 96, 98, 102, 104, 105, 107, 108, 116, 119, 122, 140, 158, 162, 172, 176–178, 182, 183, 185, 186, 215, 226, 230, 231, 241, 249, 251–254, 258–260, 274, 307

actor, 172

actress, 176, 259

addition, 70, 76, 85, 97, 118, 140, 167, 183, 185, 188, 198, 216, 226, 228, 232, 278, 280, 283, 303, 307, 315, 317

address, 29, 32, 38, 45, 49–51, 53, 66, 67, 75, 78, 85, 86, 97, 99, 101, 102, 113, 115, 122, 123, 129, 134, 146, 154, 163, 167, 185, 190, 193, 195–199, 203, 205–207, 215, 217, 232, 242–245, 252, 255, 268, 271, 275, 277, 278, 281, 286, 288, 289, 291, 293, 300, 301, 310–312, 325, 330–335

administration, 32, 120

adoption, 47, 54, 157, 327

advance, 39, 42, 76, 78, 80, 81, 132, 169, 174, 196, 267, 288, 302, 315, 322

advancement, 75, 77, 96, 194, 198, 226, 287

advantage, 73

adversity, 11, 12, 20, 30, 33, 48, 82, 92, 93, 104–107, 165, 175, 176, 178, 208, 210, 223, 258, 276, 287, 293

advertising, 179, 219

advice, 122, 200, 216, 284, 301

advocacy, 1–3, 6, 12, 13, 17, 21, 27–29, 31, 33, 34, 41–44, 46, 47, 53, 55, 61, 70, 78, 81–83, 94, 96, 97, 99, 101, 103–105, 107, 108, 110, 114, 115, 119–121, 124–126, 129, 131–136, 138, 139, 141–143, 149, 150, 152, 153, 157–159, 163, 165, 168–170,

172–175, 177–179, 183, 190, 192–198, 200, 204, 206, 207, 209–213, 215, 216, 222–227, 229, 230, 233, 235–237, 239–247, 249, 250, 252–260, 262–265, 267, 271, 272, 277, 278, 284, 286–289, 291, 293, 297, 299, 301, 302, 307, 308, 311, 316, 319, 320, 322, 332–334, 336, 337
advocate, 4, 5, 7, 9, 11, 13, 14, 21, 23, 26, 27, 32, 35, 44, 49, 54, 55, 59, 71–75, 82, 84, 106, 112, 113, 115, 118, 123, 134, 137, 139, 159, 161, 175–179, 190, 191, 195, 199, 204–206, 208, 214, 215, 227–229, 231, 233, 235, 238, 241, 244–246, 250, 254, 257–260, 267, 269, 270, 279, 282, 289, 290, 292, 303, 306, 313, 317, 325–327, 329, 332, 336
affair, 316
affirmation, 14, 320
age, 4, 11, 22, 28, 41, 104, 113, 127, 155, 163, 167, 169, 174, 206, 214, 215, 223, 226, 240–242, 246, 255, 276, 298, 301, 306, 309, 329–332
agency, 77
agenda, 29, 30, 34, 78, 193
aid, 185, 284, 296
aim, 19, 65, 164, 189–191, 194, 200, 229, 231, 232, 253,

284, 287, 317
Alberto, 260
Alberto Velasco, 260
Alejandro, 11, 12
Alice, 177, 178
Alice Chen, 177
alignment, 29
allure, 3
ally, 28, 30, 195
Allyship, 282, 306, 333
allyship, 99, 101, 168, 170, 203, 281, 285, 304, 307, 315, 331
amplification, 174
analysis, 190
Andrea, 55
animation, 60
Anita, 249
anniversary, 162, 163
anthem, 10, 71
Antonella, 176
Antonella Rodriguez, 176
anxiety, 49, 99, 109, 280, 326
apathy, 276
appreciation, 40, 62, 66, 261, 283
apprehension, 16
approach, 1, 6, 8, 15, 19, 24, 26, 28, 45, 54, 55, 57, 60, 63, 64, 70, 71, 76, 79, 83, 91, 94, 97, 99, 119, 137, 140, 148, 151, 154, 159, 165, 171, 180, 181, 189, 196, 197, 210, 212, 213, 223, 244, 255, 273, 279, 288, 289, 291, 293, 302, 306, 326–328, 332, 333, 336
archival, 151, 273
archive, 185
area, 42, 135, 140, 151, 236, 244, 326

arena, 22, 92, 142
Argentina, 47
Arlene Stein, 6
array, 191
art, 1, 8, 40, 45, 54, 55, 61–64, 69, 70, 123, 142, 151, 156, 157, 167, 168, 172, 179–182, 184, 188, 189, 191, 204, 212, 218, 219, 229–232, 259–261, 270, 271, 278, 291, 302, 305, 317, 319
artist, 172, 179, 257–259
artivism, 192
artwork, 13, 55, 179, 215, 258, 302
aspect, 41, 50–52, 63, 67, 81, 98, 108, 123–125, 153, 156, 168, 192, 194, 195, 198, 217, 236, 244, 255, 261, 262, 277, 301, 303, 311, 320, 325, 327
assistance, 50, 62, 69, 100, 152, 164, 181, 196, 239, 318, 321
asylum, 238
atmosphere, 71, 181, 228, 238
attention, 10, 29, 70, 71, 83, 92, 104, 116, 153, 155, 168, 193, 197, 229, 254, 303
attire, 228
audience, 21, 24, 30, 71, 83, 86, 103, 104, 139, 165, 166, 168, 190, 196, 221, 237, 241, 255, 289, 299, 301, 329–331
Audre Lorde, 3
Australia, 65
authenticity, 104, 106, 120, 152, 177
author, 241, 250
authority, 35

availability, 195
avenue, 203
aversion, 98
awakening, 3, 9, 19
awareness, 10, 12, 19, 21, 23, 27, 29, 30, 45, 47, 50–52, 57, 58, 60, 62, 65, 68, 70, 73, 77, 78, 83, 85, 94, 95, 99–101, 103, 105, 106, 113, 114, 120, 129, 137–140, 151, 152, 157, 158, 160, 161, 166, 168, 169, 176, 180, 181, 185, 187, 189–196, 199, 204, 207, 212, 214, 215, 226, 229, 232, 236–239, 241, 243, 246, 255, 257, 266, 268, 271, 273, 275–279, 284, 288–291, 296, 299–301, 306, 315, 318, 320, 321, 325, 329, 330, 332, 333, 335, 336
awe, 259

backdrop, 3
background, 4, 9, 136
backing, 23
backlash, 27, 30, 33, 91–93, 97, 101–104, 106, 107, 116, 276, 308
balance, 107, 111–114, 142, 197, 242
Bangladesh, 178
Barco Isakson, 1, 2, 19–21, 26, 27, 50–54, 96, 97, 116, 124–128, 138–140, 151–153, 206, 216–222, 260–262

Index

Barco Isakson's, 21, 26, 28, 152, 261, 263
base, 23
basis, 204
baton, 143
battle, 43, 46, 91, 143, 157, 287, 303, 335
beacon, 24, 31, 32, 64, 82, 106, 157, 175, 210, 233, 240, 264, 287, 309, 320, 321
beauty, 3, 142, 177, 193, 235
begin, 37, 234
beginning, 4, 134–136, 141, 209
behalf, 225
behavior, 51
being, 4, 5, 11, 13, 15, 20, 21, 35, 38, 49, 51, 54, 55, 58, 72, 78, 99–101, 103, 107, 108, 112, 115, 116, 118–120, 123, 142, 149, 169, 170, 186, 198, 199, 204, 205, 217, 229, 231, 236, 249, 251–253, 256, 267, 270, 272, 277, 280–282, 288, 290, 301, 303, 304, 307, 312, 314, 318, 320, 326, 332
belief, 37, 68, 94, 120, 124, 134, 164, 207, 252, 256
believer, 50
belonging, 3, 9, 17, 35, 40, 48, 63, 65, 78, 84, 115, 122, 127, 146, 169, 173, 175, 180, 189, 191, 200, 202, 220, 227, 231, 257, 262, 279, 280, 282, 305
benefit, 132, 140, 143, 233
bias, 104
bigotry, 11, 34

bill, 314
binary, 39, 52, 53, 56, 94, 124, 206, 262, 304
biography, 145, 178, 207, 254, 256, 294, 335
biphobia, 304
biphobic, 115
birth, 2, 19–22
blend, 2
blending, 316
blog, 216
blueprint, 27, 42, 121, 224
body, 85, 152, 174
Bogota, 257
Bogotá, 23, 24, 31–35, 50, 61, 63, 84, 102, 131–136, 138, 141, 156, 160, 162–164, 174, 181, 184, 185, 202, 206, 207, 209, 222, 224, 240, 266, 295, 298, 307, 316, 318
book, 162, 163, 254, 292, 322
border, 162
bound, 276
box, 81, 83, 104, 272
boy, 4
bravery, 64, 176, 183
Brazil, 177
breadth, 233
break, 6, 7, 17, 39, 45, 61, 62, 76, 91, 92, 101, 121, 145, 158, 179, 200, 201, 208, 216, 219, 222, 227, 237, 250, 263, 267, 274, 281, 283, 292, 300, 311, 322, 332
breaking, 33, 37, 38, 41, 43, 44, 61, 68, 70, 71, 95, 104, 105, 120, 133, 135, 168, 172, 173, 179, 183, 192, 203,

207, 219, 221, 222, 236, 259, 261, 267, 297, 303, 307, 309, 314, 316, 318, 327, 333–335
breeding, 3, 4, 211, 336
bridge, 8, 46, 75, 83, 94, 96, 121, 171, 189, 331
brutality, 64
building, 6, 23, 27, 28, 44, 62, 83, 97, 134, 135, 140, 145, 155, 156, 158, 163, 187, 189, 190, 192, 194, 195, 197, 198, 207, 215–218, 237, 267, 274, 275, 277, 279, 285, 299, 313, 325, 328, 334, 337
bullying, 38, 41, 49–51, 66, 67, 122, 125, 127, 135, 173, 191, 198, 213, 236, 244, 251, 257, 262, 289, 307, 311, 312, 314
burden, 5
burnout, 108, 112, 113, 272
business, 187, 314

calendar, 316
Cali, 257
California, 230
call, 171, 211, 294, 309, 315, 316, 322
camaraderie, 296
campaign, 23, 31, 32, 81, 129, 155, 241, 276, 310, 330
campaigning, 24
campus, 9, 10
Canada, 327
capacity, 96
capital, 33

care, 56, 101, 102, 108, 112, 113, 115–119, 123, 142, 143, 186, 198, 199, 201, 272, 280, 304
career, 1, 23, 115, 132, 134, 141, 142, 182, 184, 198, 209, 225, 259, 296, 298
Carla, 21, 256, 257
Carlos, 171, 259
Carlos García, 259
Carmen, 174, 175
Carolenys Márquez, 259
Carolina, 177
Carolina Ruiz, 177
Cartagena, 257
case, 21, 46, 76, 206, 207, 239, 272
Castro, 16
catalyst, 2, 3, 12, 26, 121, 157, 181, 231–233, 257, 329, 336
cause, 20, 22, 30, 44, 58, 67, 81–83, 91, 97, 102, 104, 105, 107, 108, 112, 159, 209, 233, 267, 309
caution, 270, 332
celebration, 16, 40, 41, 126, 157, 167, 168, 197, 206, 229, 238, 261, 267, 310, 316, 317, 324
center, 86, 143, 162–164, 174, 175, 181, 185, 231–233, 240, 247, 251, 297, 315, 318–321
ceremony, 266
challenge, 2–7, 12, 16–21, 23, 27, 30–32, 34, 35, 39, 40, 45, 46, 52–54, 58, 59, 65, 68–72, 92, 94, 95, 97, 102, 104–106, 114, 116, 121, 124, 125, 129, 130, 137,

139, 143, 151, 153, 159, 160, 166, 167, 172, 175, 179, 182, 187, 189–191, 195, 200, 201, 203, 205, 208, 210, 217–219, 222, 223, 225, 232, 234, 236, 237, 243, 244, 246, 258, 261–264, 269, 271, 274, 275, 277, 278, 280–284, 288, 290–292, 296, 297, 299, 302–304, 307, 311, 314, 317, 319, 321, 322, 325, 328, 329, 331–335
challenging, 2, 10, 13, 14, 16, 19, 20, 22, 27, 33, 38–41, 45, 50, 52–56, 60, 62, 64, 75, 85, 92, 94–96, 99–101, 105–107, 114, 115, 120–122, 126, 127, 138, 144, 148, 157, 158, 160, 161, 165–168, 172, 173, 178, 179, 181–183, 188–190, 192, 194–196, 201, 203, 205, 213, 221, 222, 225, 227, 236, 238, 239, 246, 247, 250, 251, 254, 258, 260–263, 265, 267–270, 272, 275, 282, 284, 285, 287, 290, 291, 293, 297, 299, 302, 304, 307, 310, 314, 320, 324–326, 328, 336
champion, 143, 176, 190, 200, 225, 228, 253, 266
change, 2–16, 19, 21–24, 26–35, 37, 39–44, 46–49, 52–56, 60, 71, 72, 75–79, 82, 83, 85, 91, 95–97, 104–107, 111, 112, 114–116, 118, 120,

121, 123, 126, 128–130, 132, 133, 137, 138, 140, 142–145, 149–153, 155, 156, 159–162, 164, 165, 167, 168, 170, 172, 175, 178, 181–183, 185–197, 203, 205–208, 210–213, 215, 216, 219, 223, 224, 226–228, 231–237, 239–241, 245–247, 253–256, 259, 260, 264, 265, 267–270, 272, 274–281, 284–293, 295–299, 301, 302, 304, 306, 308, 309, 311, 317, 319, 322, 325–329, 332, 335, 336
chapter, 15, 31, 33, 35, 37, 43, 91, 131, 132, 134, 135, 171, 209, 249, 252, 254, 256, 295
character, 31, 97, 152, 223
characteristic, 6, 137
charisma, 45, 187
charter, 327
chat, 111
child, 1
circle, 100
cisgender, 49, 208
citizenship, 51, 155, 196
city, 1–4, 11, 15, 20, 33–35, 50, 131, 133, 141
class, 53, 125, 136, 153, 154, 186, 190, 196, 212, 332
classification, 56
classism, 78, 205, 292
classroom, 67, 68, 244
climate, 3, 205
close, 1, 15, 84, 131, 254, 256, 298

closet, 229
closing, 287
clothing, 260
coalition, 140, 187, 189, 194, 207, 277, 327
code, 67
cohort, 209
collaboration, 16, 30, 31, 34, 41–43, 47, 53, 60, 70, 71, 73, 75, 76, 78–81, 83, 113, 116, 123, 141, 142, 149, 150, 153, 155, 159, 161, 162, 169, 185, 187, 190, 194, 199, 203, 210–212, 233, 238–240, 246, 267, 277, 279, 287, 289, 290, 308, 312, 315, 317, 322, 327, 332, 335, 336
collection, 231
collective, 3, 4, 7, 23, 33, 34, 42, 43, 51, 53, 71, 72, 78–81, 83, 113, 116, 134, 143, 145, 147, 151, 161, 162, 170, 178, 180, 186, 190, 193–195, 199, 206–208, 213, 216, 218, 256, 270, 272, 275, 276, 281, 286, 292–294, 300, 301, 304, 317, 321, 322, 329, 337
college, 2, 3, 9, 10, 19, 20, 22, 23
Colombia, 1–6, 12, 16, 17, 20–24, 26, 28, 30–35, 37, 38, 41–44, 46–52, 55, 63, 67–69, 75, 79, 80, 83, 84, 86, 91, 93–96, 98, 101, 104, 106–108, 115, 116, 121, 124–126, 129, 131, 132, 135, 136, 138, 139, 141, 143–145, 156–160, 162, 165, 166, 168–170, 172, 173, 176–178, 180, 182–187, 189, 204, 206–209, 211, 214, 216, 219, 220, 222–228, 231, 232, 235–238, 245, 249–251, 254, 256–260, 263–266, 285, 286, 292, 296, 297, 300, 303, 307–310, 312–316, 318–321, 324, 326, 327, 335, 337
Colombia Diversa, 78
color, 18, 59, 73, 85, 100, 115, 169, 196, 202, 214, 234, 243, 244, 275, 277, 285, 286, 306, 333, 334
combat, 16, 51, 58, 95, 100–102, 123, 135, 158, 180, 190, 191, 241, 242, 246, 282, 307, 335
combination, 99, 242
comfort, 115, 330
commemoration, 163, 315
commitment, 2, 5, 15, 21–23, 26, 27, 29, 30, 33, 34, 37, 38, 43, 47, 49, 58, 63, 68, 74, 79, 82, 91–93, 96, 104, 106, 108, 112, 113, 116, 121, 125, 128, 133, 135, 139, 141–143, 145, 149, 152, 155, 157, 158, 160, 162, 164, 165, 170, 173–177, 182–184, 209, 210, 212, 218, 222–226, 228, 239, 247, 249, 251, 253, 257, 259, 265, 291, 293, 296, 297, 300, 303, 304, 309–311, 313, 314, 322,

Index   347

326, 327, 332, 335, 337
communication, 14, 79, 92, 103,
    111, 112, 150, 195, 196,
    287, 330, 332
community, 1–5, 9–13, 15–24,
    26–35, 39–41, 46, 48, 50,
    54–56, 58, 59, 61–66, 68,
    69, 71, 75, 76, 78, 79, 81,
    83–86, 91, 92, 94, 95,
    97–111, 113–115,
    119–121, 123–127, 131,
    132, 135, 140, 141, 143,
    145, 147, 149–152,
    155–157, 159, 161–163,
    166–169, 172–177,
    180–182, 184–187, 189,
    191–200, 202–206,
    210–216, 218–220,
    222–229, 231–233,
    235–240, 242–245, 249,
    250, 252, 256–258,
    260–266, 268, 270–280,
    282–284, 286, 288–290,
    292, 293, 296–302, 304,
    305, 307, 308, 312–321,
    324–326, 329, 331–336
compassion, 8, 14, 45, 94, 106, 132,
    159, 197, 207, 237, 268,
    317, 337
competence, 199
competency, 326
complacency, 197, 276
complexity, 59, 179, 200, 201
component, 26, 205, 282
compromise, 112
concept, 4, 16, 19, 154, 202, 268,
    332
concern, 50
conclusion, 49, 93, 98, 108, 121,
    126, 136, 138, 141, 151,
    158, 160, 163, 181, 183,
    189, 204, 218, 235, 240,
    267, 282, 300, 307, 309,
    313, 320, 337
conference, 21, 76, 77
confidence, 209, 233, 257, 260
confine, 3
conformity, 179
connection, 11, 15, 21, 22, 24, 151,
    242, 259, 290
connectivity, 83
consent, 303
conservatism, 4
content, 40, 60, 61, 67, 69, 83, 102,
    127, 129, 166, 219, 296,
    305, 330, 336
context, 31
continuation, 240, 278, 287
contrary, 134, 142, 210
contrast, 16
contributor, 109
conversation, 6, 15, 278
cooperation, 193, 194, 312
core, 44, 111, 124, 126, 207, 212
cornerstone, 37, 128, 155, 261, 299
corruption, 31
cost, 107
counseling, 38, 50, 51, 78, 84, 100,
    112, 156, 162, 163, 181,
    185, 191, 198, 211, 227,
    232, 272, 277, 299, 312,
    318, 321, 328
counter, 27, 98, 102–104, 280
country, 31–33, 83, 104, 127, 129,
    135, 144, 159, 161, 177,
    206, 216, 226, 227, 258,
    263, 265, 266, 309, 314,
    319, 324, 330

couple, 11
courage, 1, 3, 15, 55, 64, 82, 105, 120, 156, 165, 172, 175, 176, 234, 249, 258, 265, 276, 287, 321
coverage, 101, 102, 279, 280, 297
craft, 54
creation, 45, 61, 67, 115, 127, 129, 136, 160, 168, 180, 182, 189, 193, 212, 219, 282
creativity, 8, 40, 62, 71, 104, 261, 272, 317
credibility, 32
credit, 157
crime, 48, 78, 99, 205
crisis, 111
criticism, 102, 107
crowdfunding, 271, 302
cry, 86
culture, 10, 11, 16, 19, 38, 40, 41, 44, 62, 63, 67, 68, 70, 71, 95, 121, 125, 129, 136–139, 152, 167, 168, 172, 179, 180, 182, 188, 193, 203, 205, 214, 221, 222, 225, 229, 243, 261, 264, 272, 281, 283, 284, 288, 291, 305, 307, 308, 312, 317, 319, 320, 324, 328, 333, 335
curiosity, 13
curricula, 41, 62, 65, 69, 99, 121, 127, 144, 150, 152, 155, 157, 158, 167, 180, 188, 203, 212–214, 220, 261, 271, 289, 299, 305, 314
curriculum, 66, 68–70, 122, 136, 139, 160, 167, 197, 215, 217, 244, 250, 257, 261, 275, 279, 303, 305, 311
cyberbullying, 51, 206
cybersecurity, 330, 332
cycle, 95

Dan Savage, 241
dance, 1, 71, 167, 181, 290, 316
dancing, 228
David Carter, 6
day, 34, 133, 152, 229, 230, 315
death, 288
debate, 155
debunk, 95, 97, 182, 189, 241
decision, 10, 12, 26, 28, 55, 79, 97, 105, 131, 133–135, 141, 157, 226, 236, 298, 324, 330
decriminalization, 32, 44, 95, 224, 226, 239, 288, 328
dedication, 12, 29, 47, 49, 55, 70, 78, 82, 86, 107, 108, 111, 116, 133, 138, 143–145, 149, 156, 164, 165, 171, 173, 174, 183, 186, 206, 207, 209, 223, 226, 227, 240, 254, 256–260, 263, 265, 287, 297, 300, 309, 313, 315, 337
defiance, 316
definition, 37, 263
demand, 32, 33, 71, 144, 241, 275, 279, 289
democracy, 27
demographic, 195
denial, 99
departure, 132, 133, 135
depression, 49, 99, 108, 109, 280, 326
designer, 177, 260

desire, 1, 9, 22
destination, 204
determination, 1, 3–6, 12, 14, 16, 20, 22, 29, 30, 33, 34, 38, 43, 45, 46, 64, 82, 97, 101, 105–108, 128, 131, 133, 135, 136, 156, 170, 172, 173, 175, 176, 182, 186, 197, 204, 210, 214, 223, 224, 228, 234, 247, 257, 259, 264, 265, 267, 287, 291, 297, 308, 321, 335
development, 38, 57, 62, 85, 122, 150–152, 155, 161, 167, 195, 220, 236, 237, 278, 299, 302, 319
deviation, 124
dialogue, 13, 14, 21, 27, 45, 51, 53, 54, 79, 83, 92, 94–98, 105, 121, 138, 140, 144, 152, 155, 163, 166, 181, 187, 189, 191, 194, 196, 199, 210, 217, 229, 237, 240, 271, 281, 290, 297, 298, 302, 312, 315, 317, 318, 325, 331–333, 336
difference, 1, 12, 79, 84, 145, 150, 158, 160, 185, 205, 212, 233, 264, 276, 308, 321, 328, 331
dignity, 43, 46, 115, 136, 165, 194, 206, 208, 252, 281, 300, 309, 310, 315
diplomacy, 92
disability, 53, 57, 72, 111, 136, 137, 155, 190, 193, 194, 196, 212, 215, 242, 244, 247, 268, 272, 289, 303, 325, 333, 335, 336

disadvantage, 236
disapproval, 11
disbelief, 5
discipline, 152
discourse, 64, 85, 94, 103, 152, 180, 302, 330
discovery, 3, 7, 9, 14, 15, 21, 82, 108, 123, 140, 142
discrimination, 1–7, 10–12, 16, 17, 20–24, 28, 31, 32, 34, 35, 37–39, 41, 44–52, 54–57, 59, 61, 64–67, 69, 71, 73, 76–79, 81, 83, 85, 86, 92, 93, 96–101, 105, 108, 109, 111, 112, 114, 115, 120–122, 124–127, 132, 135–138, 143, 145, 146, 152–155, 160, 161, 163, 168, 170, 173–177, 179, 181, 182, 186, 188, 190, 191, 193, 196–200, 204–208, 210, 213, 216–218, 220, 223, 226, 229, 232, 235–237, 239, 242–247, 249, 251, 253, 256–258, 261, 262, 264, 267–270, 274, 275, 277, 279–285, 288, 289, 291–294, 296, 297, 299–301, 303–307, 310–314, 319, 322, 324, 325, 327, 331–333, 335, 337
dismantling, 10, 16, 45, 62, 77, 95, 124, 139, 187, 190, 217, 262, 279, 282, 293, 296, 300
displacement, 18
dissemination, 129

dissent, 330
distress, 109
distribution, 40, 244
diversity, 2, 4, 7, 9, 12, 16, 35, 39–41, 48, 54, 55, 57, 59–61, 63, 67–69, 73, 79, 94, 106, 120–122, 126, 136, 138, 139, 159, 167, 173, 184, 188, 197–199, 201–204, 210, 217, 224, 226, 228, 231, 235, 238, 242, 244, 247, 261, 264, 265, 279, 280, 283–285, 290, 296, 299, 300, 305, 307, 314–316, 318, 320, 326
divide, 171, 331
document, 40, 239, 273, 327
dominance, 95
domino, 77, 308
doubt, 5, 7, 108, 174, 257
drag, 259, 260, 306
dream, 161
dress, 67
driving, 15, 20, 30, 47, 129, 149, 168, 177, 195, 233, 292
drug, 31
dynamic, 4

ease, 241
Echoing Virgilio's, 259
economy, 217
editorial, 305
educating, 14, 53, 92, 116, 136, 144, 178, 180, 208, 214, 220, 246, 266, 275, 285, 325, 327
education, 5, 10, 21, 23, 27, 38, 39, 41–44, 47, 48, 50–52, 57, 62, 63, 65–70, 85, 91, 92, 94, 95, 97, 99, 101, 111, 114, 120–125, 127, 129, 132, 136, 137, 139, 142, 150–152, 157, 158, 160, 162–164, 167, 168, 170, 173, 174, 178, 180, 185, 187–192, 194, 196, 197, 199, 200, 203–207, 213, 214, 218, 220, 223, 225, 226, 228, 229, 231, 232, 236, 239–242, 244, 250, 251, 256, 257, 261–265, 268, 270–273, 277–279, 284, 288–292, 296, 299, 300, 303, 304, 307, 310, 311, 313–318, 320–322, 325, 331–333, 337
effect, 10, 16, 21, 24, 27–30, 48, 76–78, 85, 121, 132, 150, 160, 165, 178, 187, 205, 211, 224, 227, 268, 269, 292, 301, 308, 322
effort, 83, 147, 162, 163, 188, 194, 197, 270, 281, 287, 304, 335, 337
election, 23, 31–35
element, 160
email, 241, 330
embracing, 3, 4, 7, 12, 13, 22, 58, 60, 61, 79, 101, 106, 119, 120, 135, 151, 169, 170, 173, 179, 186, 200–202, 207, 216, 223–225, 230, 235, 237, 238, 260, 261, 265, 279–283, 285, 299, 304, 307, 325
emergence, 19
Emma, 253

empathy, 5, 6, 8, 10, 12, 14, 15, 21, 22, 40, 41, 44, 45, 50, 53, 54, 57, 58, 60, 65, 66, 75, 83, 95, 97, 102, 106, 116, 120–122, 126, 136, 138, 139, 151, 152, 155, 161, 166, 167, 179, 180, 187–189, 191, 192, 194, 200, 203, 205, 207, 208, 213, 214, 217, 218, 221, 225, 244, 247, 250, 256, 268, 269, 271, 272, 275, 277, 278, 284, 288, 290–292, 299, 301, 302, 306, 311, 328, 333, 337
emphasis, 38, 153, 260, 308
employee, 280, 291
employment, 5, 37, 44, 57, 99, 120, 132, 137, 197–199, 217, 218, 236, 244, 253, 267, 288, 300, 304, 310, 313, 317, 325
empower, 6, 35, 38, 44, 51, 84, 100, 118, 134, 136, 139, 140, 149, 150, 160, 164, 189, 190, 194, 197, 211, 214, 217, 227, 231, 237, 272, 275, 279, 287, 296, 301, 305, 315, 318, 328, 331
empowerment, 2, 3, 7, 17, 43, 106, 116, 119, 123, 124, 127, 138, 140, 141, 143, 149, 159, 164, 168, 178, 202, 217, 231, 233, 252, 257, 270, 278, 279, 298, 301, 306, 308, 312, 313, 321
encounter, 49, 109, 288
encouragement, 115, 120, 139, 145
encryption, 330
end, 12, 38, 131, 135, 136, 141, 295, 307
endeavor, 51, 107, 120, 148, 183, 193
endorsement, 24
endpoint, 293
energy, 316
enforcement, 57, 137, 271
engage, 9, 13, 27, 30, 68, 72, 73, 77, 96, 98, 102, 104, 113, 115, 123, 138, 140, 142, 163, 166, 168, 186, 187, 190, 192, 195, 199, 212–214, 221, 230, 240, 242, 271, 273, 277, 278, 281, 299, 317, 330
engagement, 26, 27, 83, 84, 106, 168, 192, 232, 233, 242, 278, 305, 307, 312, 315
entertainment, 41, 61–63, 172, 176, 203, 236, 259, 272, 283
entrepreneurship, 218
environment, 1, 3, 9, 13, 14, 17, 31, 38, 49–52, 56, 57, 61, 63, 65–68, 79, 94, 114, 115, 121–123, 127, 129, 135, 157, 161, 164, 173, 175, 179, 198, 200, 203, 215, 220, 231, 232, 236, 244, 250, 257, 260, 264, 270, 280, 282, 296, 299, 305, 307, 311, 314, 317
equality, 1–4, 9, 11, 12, 16, 19–23, 27–30, 32–34, 37, 39, 42–46, 48, 49, 52, 56–58, 60, 68, 71–77, 79, 82–86, 91–93, 96–98, 100, 105–108, 115, 116, 119, 121–123, 125, 126, 128,

129, 131–145, 149, 151, 154, 156–166, 168–172, 174, 176–178, 181, 183, 184, 187, 189, 190, 192–197, 199, 203–212, 214–218, 222–224, 226, 228–230, 233–240, 242, 244–247, 249–252, 254–270, 274–281, 284–288, 290, 291, 293–301, 303, 304, 307–315, 317–322, 324–327, 335–337
equity, 73, 154
era, 83, 103, 131, 173
erasure, 125, 180
Eric Marcus, 6
establishment, 24, 26, 41, 43, 48, 51, 56, 64, 67, 120, 135, 163, 194, 206, 211, 220, 225, 231, 262, 274, 299
esteem, 256, 305
ethnicity, 53, 111, 125, 137, 186, 194, 242, 243, 246, 285, 289, 303, 325, 335
Europe, 327
event, 12, 13, 70, 73, 123, 163, 167, 184, 188, 229, 238, 316, 317
evidence, 272, 319
examination, 324
example, 33, 49, 51, 55, 60, 66, 70, 72, 73, 81, 86, 96, 115, 116, 122, 144, 154, 155, 174, 177, 179, 189, 193, 212, 241, 243, 257, 259, 274, 275, 300, 324, 330, 332, 334
excellence, 164

exception, 84, 111, 292
exchange, 156, 185, 193, 211, 216, 286, 290, 316, 327
excitement, 316
exclusion, 4, 64, 66, 92, 101, 236, 300
exercise, 74, 112, 245, 270, 310
exhibition, 180
existence, 236
exit, 142
expansion, 309
expense, 107
experience, 5, 12, 15, 16, 19, 51, 57, 66, 109, 122, 126, 129, 142, 146, 151, 153, 175, 186, 198, 211, 231, 242, 243, 247, 256, 268, 288, 316, 326, 332
expertise, 75, 78, 79, 134, 192, 193, 196, 212, 213, 233, 272, 277, 328
exploration, 40
explore, 2, 4, 7, 9, 16, 17, 26, 31, 33, 35, 39, 49, 56, 58, 60, 61, 63, 65, 66, 71, 75, 82, 84, 91, 94, 95, 98, 105, 107, 108, 111, 114, 116, 122, 124, 126, 133, 138, 142, 145, 149, 151, 153, 154, 156, 159, 162, 163, 168, 171, 172, 176, 178, 181, 183, 186, 192, 194, 195, 197, 200, 201, 204, 209, 211, 216, 218, 224, 226, 228, 231, 235, 237, 240, 245, 249–255, 259, 268, 272, 276, 279, 281, 283, 288, 295–298, 305, 306, 309, 313, 317, 321, 324,

Index

335
explosion, 261
exposure, 1, 53, 62, 112, 196, 333
expression, 3, 40, 63, 123, 124, 135, 173, 177, 179, 181, 191, 214, 219, 229, 258, 260, 261, 271, 319
extravaganza, 316

fabric, 4, 119, 218, 264
face, 5, 18, 19, 21, 26, 38, 43, 48, 49, 52, 56, 59, 64, 66, 71, 73, 76, 78, 81, 82, 85, 92, 93, 96, 99, 104–109, 111, 115, 116, 122, 125, 137, 139, 145, 154, 155, 165, 196, 198, 208, 210, 217, 223, 229, 235, 236, 238, 242–244, 246, 257, 275, 276, 280, 281, 285, 288–290, 293, 300, 301, 303, 304, 311, 312, 315, 317, 324, 325, 332, 333, 335
facet, 285
family, 1, 5, 11–15, 20, 96, 99, 100, 107, 111–113, 141, 165, 171, 174–176, 249, 263, 326
fashion, 41, 81, 177, 260, 261
fear, 4, 7, 8, 11, 15, 17, 31, 38, 39, 49, 54, 56, 61, 97, 98, 121, 170, 173–175, 179, 181, 182, 200, 205, 206, 218, 224, 226, 247, 249, 250, 260, 267, 282, 285, 293, 314, 319
fearlessness, 256
feeling, 4, 141, 174, 175, 249
female, 52
femininity, 39, 179
festival, 157, 184, 228, 316
field, 62
fight, 1–3, 9, 12, 13, 15–17, 19–24, 26–28, 30, 33, 35, 37, 38, 42–49, 58, 64, 71, 72, 74–77, 83–86, 92, 93, 98, 105–108, 112, 116, 121, 126, 129, 131–138, 140–145, 149, 151, 154, 156–158, 160–166, 168, 170–174, 176–178, 183, 184, 186, 187, 189, 192–195, 197, 199, 202, 204–213, 216, 217, 222–228, 230, 233, 235, 237–240, 242, 245–247, 249–260, 262–267, 270, 274, 276, 278, 279, 285–292, 294–304, 307–309, 311, 315, 316, 318, 320–322, 324–328, 332, 335, 337
fighting, 4, 10–12, 16, 33, 72, 82, 85, 93, 116, 119, 126, 135, 136, 139, 142, 144, 157, 160, 174, 175, 182–184, 187, 215, 216, 229, 239, 246, 272, 275, 284, 303
figure, 4, 26, 32, 65, 93, 107, 156, 172, 176, 225
film, 10, 40, 61, 68, 184, 191, 221, 229, 230, 232, 278, 291, 302, 305, 311, 317, 319
finesse, 93
fire, 4, 11, 12, 17, 22, 143
flagship, 184
flame, 1, 151

flash, 71, 83
flood, 316, 330
flourishing, 176
flow, 196
fluidity, 179, 262
focus, 10, 55, 59, 92, 103, 131, 134–136, 138, 141, 142, 150, 171, 197, 210, 243, 266, 305, 318, 326, 330, 334
following, 12, 103, 113, 146, 230, 245, 259, 337
force, 11, 12, 15, 71, 143, 149, 177, 192, 194, 200, 202, 218, 274, 292, 296, 326
forefront, 26, 30, 39, 65, 133, 152, 210, 233, 253
form, 3, 23, 37, 81, 187, 215, 262, 278, 331
formation, 187, 192
Foster, 243
foster, 7, 17, 24, 30, 38, 57, 59, 62, 63, 68, 72, 78, 81, 83, 84, 94, 97, 99–101, 106, 115, 120, 123, 130, 138, 140, 144, 150, 152, 157, 158, 166–168, 179, 187, 189–192, 194, 195, 198, 201, 205, 208, 210, 214, 216, 218, 220, 221, 227, 228, 230–232, 235, 237, 241, 242, 261, 275, 277, 278, 280, 284, 286, 288, 290, 302, 303, 306, 311, 315, 317, 321, 333
foundation, 2, 4, 6, 11, 16, 20, 23, 28, 30, 33, 43, 46, 58, 62, 64, 86, 112, 134, 136, 141, 145, 157, 158, 160, 161, 170, 173, 182, 185, 201, 207, 216, 223, 225, 253, 263, 275, 296, 297, 309, 319
framework, 56, 67, 154, 169, 327
freedom, 15, 33, 39, 124, 314
Frida Kahlo, 55
friend, 15
front, 47, 78, 83, 97, 154, 171, 239, 298, 310
fund, 195
funding, 62, 69, 153, 195–197, 212, 219, 271, 297, 333
fundraising, 195, 302
fusion, 191
future, 5, 11, 13, 15, 19, 21, 24, 27, 28, 43, 44, 46, 49, 51, 58, 61, 65, 68, 69, 80, 84–86, 98, 101, 104, 106, 107, 116, 121, 123–126, 129, 131, 133, 134, 136, 138, 139, 141–145, 149–151, 153, 155–159, 161–165, 167–171, 173–176, 182–186, 188, 189, 191, 192, 194, 197–199, 202, 204, 205, 208–214, 216–218, 220, 222–224, 227, 228, 230, 233–237, 240, 245–247, 251–254, 256, 263–267, 270, 273, 276, 278–281, 283, 285, 287, 290, 292–300, 303–305, 307–309, 313, 315, 317, 318, 320–322, 325, 326, 332, 335, 337

gain, 61, 62, 64, 66, 105, 125, 159, 166, 174, 283

Index   355

gala, 316
gallery, 271
gap, 94, 96, 121, 298, 300
gathering, 180
gay, 17, 32, 35, 75, 107, 171, 175,
    230, 249, 250, 257, 274,
    312
gender, 4, 6, 17, 19, 27, 32, 38, 39,
    42, 45, 46, 48–50, 52–57,
    59, 68, 72, 75, 78, 82, 94,
    95, 98, 99, 120, 122, 124,
    126, 129, 135–138, 140,
    153, 154, 157, 159, 160,
    165, 168, 170, 173, 174,
    177, 179, 181, 186, 190,
    194, 196–198, 200, 201,
    203, 206, 212, 215, 222,
    223, 230, 231, 235, 236,
    238, 242, 244, 246, 247,
    252, 260, 262, 263, 265,
    268, 272, 274–277,
    279–281, 283–286, 288,
    289, 296, 299, 301, 303,
    304, 307, 310, 313–315,
    318, 320, 322, 324, 326,
    332, 334
generation, 38, 39, 43, 63, 68, 83, 84,
    120, 122, 123, 125, 132,
    133, 136, 138–144, 149,
    151, 157, 158, 162, 176,
    178, 180, 197, 209, 212,
    214, 215, 224, 237, 252,
    254, 263, 267, 278, 298,
    301, 308, 311, 315, 319,
    322, 328
gentrification, 18
glimpse, 176
globe, 82, 142, 143, 164, 227, 268,
    327

goal, 92, 183, 187, 261
Gomez, 177
governance, 34
government, 24, 137, 203, 232, 266,
    271, 272, 278, 314, 315,
    319, 330
grace, 102, 308
graffiti, 259
grant, 5, 95
gratitude, 136, 254
greenery, 3
Griffin-Gracy, 234
ground, 4, 72, 94, 133, 211, 241
groundbreaking, 1, 24, 29, 31,
    33–35, 37, 38, 43, 46, 52,
    119, 121, 124, 126, 131,
    135, 136, 151, 152, 156,
    173, 176, 180, 188, 206,
    211, 224, 226, 251, 258,
    263, 294, 295, 297, 307,
    321, 327
groundswell, 97
groundwork, 24, 144, 264, 296
group, 70, 81, 161, 175, 180, 249,
    269
growth, 2, 3, 8, 11, 21, 40, 62, 99,
    115, 119, 122–124, 141,
    225, 240, 256–258, 301,
    322
guerrilla, 70
guest, 163, 214
guidance, 21, 67, 78, 84, 101, 113,
    122, 123, 132, 139, 142,
    143, 150, 151, 161, 162,
    167, 191, 195, 196, 198,
    209, 215, 231, 239, 241,
    253, 287, 295, 297, 298,
    301, 308, 314, 328

guide, 12, 98, 121, 129, 186, 215, 226, 235, 263, 298

hackathon, 123
hacking, 330
hall, 47
hallmark, 106
hand, 78, 98, 116, 185, 270, 326
happiness, 15
harassment, 4, 38, 49, 51, 54, 57, 67, 70, 92, 100, 196, 198, 206, 207, 236, 242, 246, 270, 274, 280, 288, 300, 302, 325, 330, 336
harm, 49, 196, 200, 282
harmony, 112
Harvey Milk, 3, 230
Harvey Milk Day, 230
hate, 48, 78, 92, 99, 105, 108, 160, 205, 207, 242, 246, 270, 281, 283, 288, 302, 336
hatred, 98
haven, 231
head, 7, 44, 198
health, 13, 49, 56, 66, 99, 103, 108–113, 115–117, 122–125, 161, 169, 170, 174, 181, 198, 199, 205–207, 217, 218, 232, 233, 251, 271, 272, 280, 281, 304, 311, 315, 317, 320, 326, 333
healthcare, 5, 24, 39, 44, 47, 48, 56, 99, 120, 142, 169, 185, 195, 197–199, 233, 244, 246, 253, 267, 271, 279, 280, 288, 304, 310, 315, 317, 320, 325, 326, 333, 335

heart, 12, 163, 164, 184, 202, 212, 235, 268, 316, 318
heartbreak, 11, 12
help, 15, 67, 72, 86, 99–101, 103, 109, 111, 112, 115–117, 131, 135, 148, 150, 151, 166, 198, 199, 215, 227, 237, 242, 246, 257, 275, 277, 281, 282, 288, 290, 291, 305, 306, 312, 334
helpline, 111
heritage, 1, 40, 63–65, 69, 70, 150, 151, 167, 180, 182, 220, 223, 225, 234, 235, 261
heteronormativity, 94, 303
highlight, 12, 46, 65, 76, 107, 172–174, 184, 200, 215, 243, 249, 259, 271, 288, 317
hiring, 57, 217
history, 2, 3, 11, 13, 21, 40, 41, 44, 46, 47, 50, 63–67, 69, 70, 114, 115, 121, 125, 127, 129, 136, 139, 150–152, 160, 167, 174, 180, 182, 185, 194, 195, 203, 207, 208, 213, 214, 217, 220, 223–225, 227, 234, 250, 252, 261, 266, 271, 273, 281, 284, 285, 288, 292–294, 297, 299, 302–305, 307–309, 311, 321, 322, 326, 331, 337
hold, 32, 60, 134, 245, 246, 311
home, 31, 83, 141, 265
homelessness, 99, 233, 326
hometown, 1
homophobia, 11, 16, 77, 91, 92, 95, 98–101, 106, 115, 127,

Index 357

  152, 175, 183, 195, 223,
    237, 243, 282, 304, 308
homosexual, 98
homosexuality, 5, 32, 44, 72, 94, 95,
    107, 206, 226, 239, 328
honesty, 14
honor, 65, 85, 106, 143, 156–158,
    160, 162–165, 173, 184,
    202, 216, 223, 226,
    228–230, 251, 260,
    264–267, 276, 287, 303,
    304, 308, 315, 318, 321,
    337
hope, 24, 31, 32, 43, 44, 49, 82, 86,
    106, 120, 133, 143, 145,
    157, 170, 174, 175, 197,
    209, 210, 223, 233,
    239–241, 250, 256–258,
    264, 287, 315, 320, 321,
    335, 337
horizon, 223, 235, 237, 246
hostility, 31, 106, 236
hotbed, 10
housing, 45, 48, 99, 132, 137, 155,
    236, 244, 253, 267, 288,
    300, 304, 310, 313, 326
hub, 86, 156, 162, 163, 174, 181,
    185, 228, 231, 240, 251,
    299, 315, 321
humanity, 8, 126, 281
humility, 35
humor, 76

icon, 178, 259
idea, 76, 124, 276
ideation, 99
identification, 39, 236
identity, 1–4, 6, 7, 9, 13–15, 17, 21,
    32, 38, 39, 46, 49, 50,
      53–56, 59, 63, 78, 82, 109,
      120, 122, 124–127, 129,
      136–138, 156, 165, 168,
      170, 173–175, 179, 183,
      186, 197, 198, 202, 222,
      229, 236–238, 243, 244,
      246, 247, 250, 252,
      256–261, 265, 274, 276,
      280–282, 284, 286, 289,
      296, 303, 304, 310,
      313–316, 318, 321, 322,
      324, 326, 332
ideology, 16
ignorance, 11, 56, 95, 105, 121, 261
image, 201
immigrant, 301, 333
immigration, 57, 72
impact, 3, 4, 6, 11, 13–15, 17, 20,
    23, 26–28, 31–33, 35,
    41–43, 47–49, 57, 58, 60,
    61, 64, 70, 71, 75–78, 81,
    82, 84–86, 92, 93, 99, 101,
    104, 106, 108, 111–113,
    116, 120, 121, 125, 126,
    131–135, 143, 144,
    155–158, 161–165, 168,
    169, 171–178, 181–186,
    189, 192, 196, 197, 202,
    204–206, 208, 210, 211,
    215, 217, 221–226, 228,
    231–233, 237, 240–242,
    245, 249–254, 256–260,
    263–267, 269, 273–277,
    280, 286, 287, 291, 292,
    294–297, 301, 303,
    305–310, 312, 313, 319,
    320, 322, 326, 328, 329,
    332, 335, 337
implementation, 50, 56, 67, 78, 96,

154, 160, 161, 206, 213, 250, 251, 269
importance, 1, 3, 6–8, 11–17, 19, 20, 24, 27, 29, 30, 38–44, 50, 52, 53, 55, 56, 58, 60–63, 65, 68, 69, 71, 76, 79, 84, 85, 94, 96, 97, 101, 102, 104–106, 108, 114, 116, 122–125, 132, 133, 135–137, 139, 140, 142, 144, 145, 149, 154–156, 159–164, 168, 172, 174, 175, 180, 182, 183, 187, 192, 200–204, 209, 210, 217, 218, 221, 223–227, 229, 233, 234, 237–239, 245, 252, 256, 259–261, 263, 265, 268, 271, 274, 281, 283, 285–287, 295, 298–300, 305, 307, 308, 310, 312–314, 317, 319, 321, 326, 327, 332–334, 336
imprisonment, 288
incident, 5, 104
inclusion, 9, 27, 29, 30, 33, 34, 38, 39, 41, 48, 56, 58, 59, 69, 73, 78, 81, 121, 127, 145, 152, 176, 180, 188, 197, 198, 202–204, 217, 218, 227, 233, 238, 239, 261, 275, 283–285, 291, 303, 304, 311, 313, 314
inclusivity, 10, 12, 14, 15, 18, 19, 28, 32, 38, 39, 43, 51, 54, 55, 57, 65, 67, 69, 72, 75, 77, 91, 95, 104, 115, 122, 124, 126, 133, 134, 137, 138, 149, 155, 157, 167, 168, 175–177, 186, 192, 194, 199, 202, 203, 210, 220, 226, 229, 231, 242, 258–261, 271, 277, 279–281, 285, 287, 291, 302, 303, 309, 310, 313, 315, 326, 331
income, 100, 155, 164, 202, 306
incorporation, 299
individual, 3, 4, 11, 22, 33, 43, 46, 49, 58, 77–79, 116, 130, 133, 136, 137, 170, 175, 208, 228, 247, 276, 278, 281, 283
individuality, 260
industry, 41, 69, 81, 172, 176, 177, 221, 259, 260, 272
inequality, 1, 6, 10, 21, 39, 64, 99, 112, 188, 190, 200, 210, 244, 293, 301
influence, 26, 29, 32, 33, 42, 60, 70, 76, 78, 79, 83, 94, 106, 131, 132, 134, 142, 143, 150, 156, 158–160, 164, 167, 172, 175–178, 222–227, 240, 249–251, 258–260, 265, 266, 279, 291, 292, 308–310, 313, 327, 332
information, 13, 15, 50, 65, 95, 102, 122, 129, 169, 188, 190, 194–196, 231, 237, 241, 268, 271, 275, 299, 306, 317, 327–331
ingredient, 293
inheritance, 47
initiative, 139, 212, 273, 297
injustice, 20, 22, 32, 37, 92, 136, 168, 234

Index 359

innovation, 272
insecurity, 205
insight, 64
inspiration, 24, 26, 30, 32, 47, 49,
 93, 106, 121, 122, 128,
 141, 144, 151, 160, 162,
 174, 176, 177, 180, 186,
 208, 211, 223, 227, 252,
 257, 259, 297, 307–309
inspiring, 12, 15, 16, 21, 24, 27, 34,
 42, 43, 65, 77, 80, 82, 84,
 86, 91, 96, 105, 115, 121,
 135, 138, 142, 145, 149,
 151, 156, 166, 177, 178,
 187–189, 192, 206, 209,
 210, 215, 221, 223, 227,
 233, 236, 238, 240, 251,
 254, 259, 265–270, 273,
 286, 298, 308, 309, 312,
 316, 317, 320, 327
instability, 31
instance, 64, 72, 307, 324
institute, 85
institution, 64, 231, 240, 318
integration, 39, 155, 221
interconnectedness, 28, 72, 112, 138,
 140, 153, 247, 255, 286,
 293
interdependence, 137
internet, 331
intersect, 16, 72, 111, 154, 156, 196,
 215, 245, 277, 322, 332,
 336
intersection, 53, 153, 155, 244, 255,
 317, 335
intersectionality, 6, 16, 18, 42, 45,
 53, 55, 72, 74, 78, 85, 100,
 101, 125, 126, 140–142,
 153–156, 159, 160, 169,
 170, 186, 190, 194, 197,
 202, 204, 207, 210, 213,
 214, 216, 217, 223, 225,
 243, 245–247, 262, 272,
 277, 280, 281, 286, 291,
 299, 300, 303, 304,
 307–309, 325, 326,
 332–336
intervention, 111
intolerance, 98, 172, 193, 322
introduction, 313
introspection, 141, 155
investing, 43, 85, 122, 153, 158, 212,
 295, 300, 320, 322, 333
invisibility, 258
involvement, 11, 157, 195, 328
Ireland, 324
Isabel, 179
Isabel Jimenez, 179
isolation, 42, 99, 123, 136, 154, 171,
 249, 257, 262
issue, 44, 66, 154, 198, 205
it, 1, 3, 4, 6, 9, 11–15, 21, 28–30,
 33, 35, 37, 46, 52, 56, 58,
 59, 65, 66, 68, 69, 71, 72,
 75, 76, 79, 95, 96, 98, 99,
 101, 107, 108, 111–114,
 116, 119, 121, 123, 128,
 133–135, 137–139, 141,
 144–146, 149, 150, 153,
 156, 158, 163, 164, 169,
 174, 183, 185, 186,
 195–200, 204, 205, 207,
 208, 211, 213, 214,
 216–218, 224, 226, 231,
 233–237, 240–243,
 245–247, 249, 252–254,
 257, 263, 268, 270–272,
 274, 276, 280, 283, 289,

292, 293, 295, 296, 300,
302–305, 315, 322, 324,
330–332, 335, 336

Jaime, 257
Janet, 259
Janet Mock, 259
Javier, 257, 258
job, 20, 54, 57, 181, 198
Johnson, 65
journey, 1–5, 7, 8, 11–16, 19,
21–24, 26, 28, 30, 33, 34,
37, 43, 44, 46, 56, 68, 69,
75, 82–84, 91–94, 96, 98,
101, 103, 105–108, 111,
113, 114, 116, 119, 121,
131, 133, 135, 140, 141,
143, 145, 158, 162, 171,
173, 174, 176, 177, 182,
200, 202, 207–209, 211,
218, 235, 236, 249–254,
256–260, 263, 266, 270,
280, 281, 292–295, 298,
299, 303, 304, 308, 321,
322, 326
joy, 186, 257, 263
judgment, 7, 11, 13, 17, 39, 50, 107,
173, 179, 200, 257, 282
Julia Serano, 6
Julie Sondra Decker, 6
Juno Dawson, 129
justice, 1–3, 8, 16, 19–22, 27, 29,
31, 33, 42, 43, 45, 72, 73,
79, 81, 85, 97, 106, 115,
119, 121–123, 129, 132,
137, 140, 142, 144, 145,
149, 151, 154, 155,
158–162, 164, 165, 169,
170, 185–187, 189, 190,

194, 205, 207, 210,
213–215, 222, 224, 225,
244, 246, 247, 255, 259,
264, 272, 274, 275, 277,
289, 291, 293, 294, 296,
299, 301–303, 322, 325,
333, 336

kaleidoscope, 316
Kate Bornstein, 55
key, 13, 26, 41, 52, 60, 62, 65, 75, 78,
81, 91, 104, 105, 116, 122,
124, 129, 135, 145, 146,
149, 160, 168, 184, 185,
187, 194, 197, 204–206,
211, 216, 226, 231, 235,
244, 246, 250, 264, 268,
272, 275–277, 282, 286,
288, 293, 296, 303, 307,
318, 322, 327, 329, 333
Kimberlé Crenshaw, 242, 332
kind, 196
knowledge, 3, 41, 43, 51, 53, 55, 63,
65–67, 72, 75, 84, 85, 100,
122, 141, 142, 150, 152,
153, 155, 161, 167, 189,
190, 193, 195, 211, 213,
215, 223, 225, 231, 240,
246, 253, 269, 271, 275,
289, 298, 308, 319, 327,
331, 336

lack, 3, 58, 59, 64, 66, 91, 146, 185,
204, 246, 258, 325, 326
landmark, 46, 47, 157, 182, 206,
224, 226, 236, 307, 314,
324
landscape, 26, 31–33, 40, 44, 59, 60,
63, 68, 78, 98, 101, 105,

Index 361

    116, 121, 126–129, 132, 135, 136, 156–159, 171, 173, 179, 182, 183, 209, 222, 224, 226, 232, 240, 250, 261, 263, 272, 289, 297, 298, 302, 308, 324, 329
language, 50, 52, 73, 115, 200
Latin America, 314, 327
law, 95, 100, 120, 137, 173, 271, 279, 309, 324
lead, 2, 10, 56, 57, 99, 122, 169, 197
leader, 23
leadership, 24, 28, 34, 40, 43, 63, 69, 84, 121, 123–125, 127, 129, 131, 133, 134, 138, 139, 144, 149–151, 161, 172, 176, 177, 182, 184, 191, 198, 206, 212, 218, 223, 224, 237, 243, 264, 278, 287, 294, 295, 297, 298, 300, 303, 307, 310, 314–316, 319, 322, 328
leap, 35
learning, 41, 47, 55, 64, 66, 70, 86, 129, 155, 162, 203, 212–214, 235, 241, 244, 245, 293, 304, 311, 327, 331
legacy, 11, 24, 27, 28, 33, 43, 44, 46, 48, 49, 51, 56, 58, 63–65, 68, 84, 86, 104, 106, 121, 122, 124, 126, 129, 131, 132, 134–136, 138, 139, 141, 143–145, 150, 153, 156–160, 162–165, 171–174, 176, 178, 183–186, 189, 204, 207–211, 213–217, 222–226, 228, 230, 233–235, 237, 240, 249, 251–254, 256, 258–260, 263–267, 287, 292, 294, 295, 297, 300–304, 308–311, 313, 315, 317, 318, 320, 321, 329, 337
Legacy Ball, 317
legalization, 48, 49, 135, 157, 177, 182, 222, 236, 251, 257, 263, 310, 313
legislation, 16, 32, 38, 42, 45, 47, 56, 78, 95, 97, 99, 100, 132, 137, 144, 159, 168, 176, 182, 190, 205, 253, 266, 275, 276, 278, 297, 304, 308, 313, 315, 324, 326, 328, 334
Leila Martinez, 252
lens, 53, 247
Leslie Feinberg, 55
letter, 15
level, 11, 28, 45, 55, 77, 79, 97, 99, 188, 190, 200, 213, 238, 239, 278, 288, 327
leverage, 7, 29, 113, 190, 231, 242, 246, 254, 272, 336
leveraging, 26, 79, 81, 98, 102, 103, 113, 142, 166, 169, 191, 196, 197, 216, 246, 277, 296, 301, 322, 328
liberation, 2, 9, 44, 212
library, 86, 185, 231
lie, 168, 174, 236, 245, 247, 253, 254, 267, 324
life, 1, 2, 4, 6, 8–11, 15, 20, 21, 31, 33, 49, 75–77, 86, 100, 107, 120, 132, 134, 135, 141–145, 152, 156, 157,

162, 163, 165, 167, 177, 184, 189, 201, 202, 209, 212, 216, 222, 225, 226, 230, 231, 236, 253, 257, 258, 265, 266, 292, 296, 297, 300, 304, 316, 319, 337
lifeline, 71, 225, 280
lifetime, 43, 313
light, 49, 76, 101, 106, 132, 143, 151, 159, 160, 180, 220, 224, 239, 249, 259, 273, 286, 306, 313, 319
likelihood, 72
limit, 18, 62, 135
listening, 24, 111, 115, 235, 304, 306
literacy, 60, 92, 231, 246, 302, 331
literature, 41, 55, 66, 70, 85, 114, 127, 142, 151–153, 179, 185, 203, 210, 215, 218, 223, 258, 271, 290, 297, 302, 305, 308
litigation, 190, 278
livelihood, 54, 57
living, 13, 55, 196, 277, 328
lobby, 288
lobbying, 28, 99, 105, 190, 241, 275, 278, 279, 303, 304
local, 13, 19, 50, 55, 61, 62, 72, 74, 81, 84, 100, 113, 161, 166, 175, 176, 185, 186, 195, 204, 206, 233, 239, 271, 273, 275, 276, 287, 293, 313, 319, 328, 334
longevity, 138, 277
look, 100, 125, 133, 168, 169, 174, 183, 245, 246, 264, 297, 311, 335
loss, 105, 108, 141

love, 2, 7, 9–13, 15, 16, 34, 37, 38, 48, 51, 94, 96, 114, 116, 119, 145, 152, 158, 163–165, 167, 171, 173–175, 182, 199–202, 207, 208, 214, 216, 224, 226, 230, 235, 237, 247, 252, 254, 256–261, 263–265, 267, 281–283, 285, 294, 297, 303, 304, 307, 309, 310, 313, 315, 316, 318, 322, 326, 337
Luis, 175
luxury, 116

machismo, 95
mainstream, 17, 40, 41, 44, 58, 61, 64, 65, 68–71, 152, 167, 179, 182, 218, 221, 227, 244, 250, 259, 273, 297, 302, 308, 310, 333
maintenance, 282
making, 3, 6, 12, 52, 76, 79, 92, 95, 97, 133, 134, 156, 175, 203, 205, 207, 208, 225, 233, 243, 271, 275, 279, 293, 298, 314, 326, 330
man, 75, 95, 107, 171, 175, 249, 250, 257
management, 123
manifest, 98
manner, 41, 167
Marcelo, 177
Marcelo Lima, 177
march, 228, 313, 316
marginalization, 3, 22, 38, 52, 111, 125, 136, 169, 205, 208, 257, 289, 303, 314, 325
Maria, 250

Maria Sanchez, 252
mark, 43, 119, 124, 128, 150, 151, 168, 183, 210, 265, 309, 313, 327
marker, 39
marriage, 37, 47, 72, 135, 157, 177, 226, 236, 257, 279, 310, 314, 324
Marsha P. Johnson, 3, 65, 234
María, 100, 101, 258
María Alejandra Buitrago, 258
masculinity, 39, 95, 179
Mateo, 172
matter, 138, 178, 216, 293
mayor, 23, 24, 35, 50, 131, 132, 135, 136, 138, 141, 160, 163, 202, 209, 210, 222, 224, 295, 296, 298, 307
mayorship, 34
mean, 134, 142, 210
means, 10, 56, 63, 72, 95, 112, 144, 154, 158, 165, 192, 229, 235, 247, 259, 267, 283, 290, 293, 306–308, 322, 326, 333
measure, 38
Medellin, 1–4, 7, 9, 11, 20, 22, 175, 256
media, 6, 21, 24, 27, 28, 30, 31, 33, 40, 44, 51, 53, 57–63, 68–71, 77, 83, 84, 86, 91–93, 96, 97, 100–104, 106, 107, 113–115, 121, 127, 129, 135, 140, 150, 159, 166, 168, 169, 172, 177, 179, 181–183, 185, 189, 192, 196, 203, 206, 210, 214, 215, 218, 219, 221, 223, 225, 227, 237, 239–244, 246, 250, 254, 255, 257–259, 264, 269, 270, 272, 276, 277, 283, 287, 289, 297, 299, 301–303, 305–308, 310, 311, 324, 325, 328, 329, 331–334, 336
meditation, 101
medium, 10, 191, 271
melody, 10
member, 15, 28, 29
membership, 31
memoir, 162, 250
memorial, 164
memory, 5, 143, 144, 156–158, 162–165, 173, 228, 251, 254, 265, 308
mentee, 253
mentor, 101
mentoring, 78, 84, 205, 295, 301
mentorship, 21, 60, 62, 69, 83–85, 100, 122, 124, 139–141, 149, 160, 161, 164, 188, 191, 198, 209, 212, 215–217, 227, 239, 244, 252, 253, 267, 278, 280, 295, 298, 301, 311, 312, 314, 319, 322, 328
message, 8, 10, 24, 31, 34, 38, 41, 72, 75–77, 83, 86, 97, 103, 113, 120, 144, 145, 164–166, 168, 171, 174, 175, 177, 179, 186, 192, 203, 226, 255, 259, 260, 265, 274, 287, 310, 322, 325
messaging, 330
midst, 12
milestone, 38, 120, 136, 266, 307,

324
million, 12
mind, 328
mindfulness, 112
mindset, 95, 101, 150
minority, 109, 193
misinformation, 92, 95, 102–104, 196, 277, 302, 331, 336
misrepresentation, 106
mission, 35, 37, 47, 63, 72, 79, 92, 106, 107, 111, 124, 132, 167, 185, 192, 232, 252, 260, 319
mistake, 241
misunderstanding, 175
misuse, 51
mix, 179
mob, 71
mobilization, 26, 43, 196, 197, 241, 332
model, 75, 82, 120
mold, 179
moment, 3, 6, 11, 15, 23, 28, 30, 33, 34, 46, 47, 64, 74, 133, 135, 141, 162, 231, 256, 257, 263, 266, 324
momentum, 23, 27, 72, 101, 136, 142, 210, 278, 295, 330
month, 220, 229
monument, 184
morale, 197
motivation, 239, 321
move, 58, 68, 92, 101, 153, 223, 293, 307
movement, 18, 23, 28, 32, 42, 46, 49, 64–66, 71–73, 79, 82, 85, 94, 97, 107, 116, 121, 125, 132, 138, 142, 144, 149–151, 154–156, 159, 168, 169, 176, 183, 192–194, 202, 203, 211–213, 216, 221, 224, 225, 228, 229, 234, 235, 237, 240, 242, 243, 272, 274, 275, 277, 286, 287, 292–294, 298–300, 302, 307–309, 313, 320, 322, 325, 327, 331, 332, 334–337
multimedia, 13
multitude, 254
museum, 41, 180
music, 1, 11, 41, 46, 54, 61, 69, 127, 142, 156, 157, 167, 179, 188, 191, 218, 219, 221, 228, 271, 283, 290, 297, 302, 306, 316
myriad, 3, 231

Nadir, 178
Nadir Rahman, 178
name, 158, 287
narrative, 22, 60, 92, 102, 104, 124–126, 173, 183, 222, 264, 273, 297
nation, 17, 33, 35, 126, 182, 220, 310
nature, 4, 79, 142, 155, 161, 164, 186, 202, 225, 242, 289, 291, 322, 325, 336
necessity, 116
need, 5, 16, 17, 28, 39, 41, 50, 56, 61, 68, 69, 71, 72, 76, 77, 85, 92, 104, 127, 131, 133, 134, 143, 149, 153–155, 159, 160, 162, 163, 167–170, 182, 185, 186, 191, 204, 212, 225, 229,

Index 365

235, 260, 267, 270, 276,
277, 280, 282, 286, 289,
301, 303, 310, 311, 314,
317, 318, 328, 335
neighborhood, 175
network, 3, 21, 23, 26, 34, 62, 65,
78, 83, 84, 116, 134, 185,
186, 192, 195, 211, 238,
295, 296, 317
networking, 13, 75, 76, 139–141,
164, 198, 280, 317
New York City, 64, 274
newfound, 12, 257, 258, 261
night, 19
nightlife, 3
noise, 104
non, 37, 52, 53, 60, 66, 97, 98, 124,
179, 198, 206, 262, 271,
280, 285, 286, 291, 296,
304, 325
norm, 48, 124
normalization, 62
note, 97, 245
notion, 54, 76, 154, 201, 308
novel, 152
number, 236

oasis, 164
oath, 34
objective, 187
obstacle, 94
occurrence, 5
office, 34, 131, 134, 135, 143, 158,
160, 210, 224, 298, 303
official, 39, 230, 236
on, 3, 4, 6, 7, 9–11, 13–16, 21–23,
26–28, 31–35, 37–39,
41–45, 47–49, 51–53, 55,
57–59, 61, 63, 64, 67–69,
71–79, 81, 83–86, 92, 94,
95, 97–99, 101–104,
106–108, 112–114, 116,
119–121, 124–129,
131–145, 150–160,
162–165, 167, 168,
170–178, 180–188, 190,
191, 195–200, 202–204,
206–214, 216, 220–226,
228–231, 233, 235–237,
239–246, 249–260,
263–266, 268, 273, 276,
277, 280, 285–292,
295–298, 300, 302, 303,
305–309, 312, 313, 315,
317–322, 325–328,
330–332, 334, 335
one, 1, 2, 4, 12–15, 17, 19, 33, 42,
46, 49, 54, 64, 68, 75, 86,
93, 101, 104, 109, 111,
116, 121, 125, 132, 134,
135, 138, 140, 143, 145,
154, 155, 161, 162, 171,
173, 174, 183, 208, 228,
231, 260, 264, 265, 285,
293, 294, 303, 314, 322,
329, 336
online, 51, 83, 111, 113, 115, 163,
166, 189, 190, 196, 200,
206, 207, 215, 216, 221,
237, 240–242, 246, 255,
270, 277, 289, 290, 299,
302, 306, 307, 329–332,
336
openness, 82, 179
opinion, 26, 27, 40, 41, 47, 78, 85,
97, 98, 101, 102, 104, 105,
116, 166, 169, 218, 225,
308

opportunity, 29, 34, 58, 75, 105, 123, 132, 134, 142, 229, 230, 246, 298, 316, 317
opposition, 16, 23, 27, 29, 30, 32–34, 37, 45, 46, 64, 92, 94, 96–98, 105–108, 128, 223, 308
oppression, 78, 121, 140, 153–155, 161, 186, 193, 196, 202, 205, 217, 242, 243, 245–247, 268, 277, 282, 289, 291, 293, 322, 332, 336
order, 23, 52, 57, 120, 142, 163, 165, 197, 204, 245, 246, 268, 271, 276, 287, 288, 303, 335
organization, 78, 79, 81, 111, 129, 239, 296, 334
organizing, 10–12, 20, 68, 70, 83, 96, 99, 103, 116, 121, 150, 169, 175, 177, 185, 189, 204, 206, 211, 212, 232, 241, 253, 255, 279, 300, 304, 306
orientation, 2–4, 6, 11, 17, 31, 32, 38, 46, 48–50, 59, 82, 120, 122, 126, 136–138, 153, 165, 168, 170, 173, 175, 178, 182, 197, 198, 200, 238, 243, 244, 247, 252, 265, 274, 276, 281, 284, 289, 296, 303, 304, 310, 313, 318, 322, 324, 326
ostracization, 3
other, 5, 6, 9, 16, 20, 23, 24, 29–31, 33, 40, 42, 45, 53, 68, 71, 72, 75, 78, 79, 81, 85, 98, 101, 107, 111–113, 120, 123, 125, 137, 140, 141, 154, 159, 161, 169, 172, 181, 186, 189, 190, 193, 199, 202, 203, 205, 207, 210, 214, 215, 217, 232, 243, 246, 247, 249, 251, 255, 258, 272, 274, 276, 277, 281, 283–285, 289–292, 299–301, 303, 306, 310–312, 316, 319, 321, 322, 327, 334
outlook, 175
outreach, 27, 97, 106, 121, 239
outsider, 175
ownership, 233, 237

pain, 1, 12
pair, 241, 253
panel, 10, 76, 184, 215, 229, 232, 271
parade, 16, 184, 228, 316
parenthood, 262, 263
parenting, 262
park, 164, 184
part, 11, 19, 65, 139, 150, 167, 182, 184, 213, 228, 246, 268, 306, 331
participant, 65
participate, 41, 73, 281, 298, 316, 330, 331
participation, 24, 42, 137, 241, 268, 275, 303, 314, 327, 331
partner, 111–113
partnering, 26, 99, 166, 237, 272
partnership, 30, 31, 78, 194
party, 23, 28–31, 34
passage, 37, 47, 78, 266, 288, 313
passing, 27, 43, 86, 97, 132, 139, 141, 162, 163, 182, 209,

Index

211–213, 252, 298–300
passion, 1, 2, 4, 10–12, 21, 22, 29, 31, 33, 43, 46, 71, 75, 113, 123, 135, 164, 166, 185, 186, 211, 214, 224, 258, 265, 286
past, 40, 64, 65, 140, 151, 206, 234, 235, 293, 302, 321
path, 2, 7, 12, 22, 91, 106, 111, 145, 161, 209, 226, 235, 256, 324, 335
patience, 14
pay, 57, 164, 229, 234
Pedro, 250
Pedro Ramirez, 252
penalty, 288
people, 8, 9, 11, 12, 16–18, 39, 45, 52–54, 59, 73, 79, 84, 85, 100, 113, 115, 135, 141, 149–151, 157, 163, 165–167, 169, 177, 188, 193, 196, 200, 202, 205, 212, 222, 227–229, 242, 250, 257, 275, 277, 284–287, 295, 297–300, 302, 303, 306, 314–316, 333, 334
perception, 27, 57, 58, 125, 126, 152, 178, 182, 223, 311
performance, 40, 61, 139, 181, 182, 219
performer, 250, 259
period, 2, 9, 11, 31, 141
persecution, 15, 38, 71, 138, 223, 224, 226, 238, 246
perseverance, 17, 96, 105, 108, 121, 129, 144, 145, 162, 182, 276, 300
persistence, 77, 91, 93, 105, 325

person, 7, 9, 53, 93, 125, 143, 162, 243, 325
personnel, 333
perspective, 2, 3, 15, 293
petition, 330
philanthropic, 195
picnic, 164
pinnacle, 211
pioneer, 138, 216
pipeline, 278
place, 41, 133, 193, 229, 238, 316
placement, 181
plan, 72, 81, 114, 129, 185
planning, 185, 186, 190
platform, 8, 11, 23, 29, 31, 32, 34, 35, 54, 62, 64, 67, 69, 75, 76, 83, 85, 102, 105, 121, 134, 138, 142, 146, 152, 156, 157, 168, 172, 176, 179, 188, 189, 192, 203, 213, 214, 218, 219, 221, 225, 228, 229, 232, 242, 250, 258, 259, 271, 273, 280, 290, 296, 305, 306, 317, 319, 321, 327, 336
play, 15, 19, 57, 60, 67, 99, 114, 139, 149, 163, 169, 189, 204, 213, 228, 234, 237, 246, 271, 275, 277, 279, 284, 288, 290, 294, 304, 305, 310, 311, 322, 325, 329
podcast, 6, 192
poetry, 12, 152, 191, 306
point, 2, 23, 32, 33, 35, 47, 206, 229, 257, 266
police, 64, 274
policy, 5, 26, 34, 77, 116, 121, 131, 138, 156, 157, 168, 169, 174, 176, 185, 190, 193,

196, 203, 212, 213, 225, 235, 241, 272, 275, 276, 278–281, 288, 299, 319, 320, 330, 336
policymaking, 308
politician, 82, 96, 122
popularity, 19, 166, 191
population, 31, 45, 179, 223
portrayal, 106, 299
position, 26, 29, 32–35, 96, 131
possibility, 150
post, 104, 141, 142
potential, 4, 16, 26, 43, 81, 99, 138, 144, 151, 162, 166, 167, 183, 185, 196, 202, 221, 240, 242, 292, 295, 299, 302, 322, 326, 329, 335, 336
poverty, 99, 155, 322
power, 2, 3, 5–12, 16, 17, 19, 21–24, 27, 28, 32–35, 37, 40, 42–45, 47, 49, 50, 53–55, 60, 63, 68, 70, 72, 76, 79, 80, 83, 84, 93, 97, 101–103, 106, 114–116, 120, 122, 123, 127, 130, 131, 133–135, 138, 140, 142, 143, 145, 150, 151, 154–156, 159–162, 166, 167, 169, 176, 178, 181–183, 187–190, 196, 200, 201, 203, 204, 206, 207, 210–213, 216, 218–221, 223, 224, 227, 228, 233, 237–239, 241, 242, 246, 254, 256, 258, 260, 261, 264, 268, 270, 273, 274, 278, 281, 286, 287, 290–294, 296, 297, 299, 301, 303, 307, 317, 319, 322, 325, 332, 334, 336
precedent, 32, 121, 224, 251, 297, 309
prejudice, 2, 6, 10–12, 14, 16, 17, 20, 22, 35, 38, 41, 46, 50, 57, 61, 94, 97–100, 105, 106, 109, 114, 120, 121, 127, 139, 144, 145, 158, 172, 190, 193, 200, 202, 207, 215, 226, 232, 236, 257, 264, 274, 277, 280–283, 290, 294, 297, 300, 311, 322, 327, 335, 337
presence, 70, 75, 77, 78, 152, 166, 181, 193, 238, 330, 335
present, 19, 65, 73, 106, 149, 151, 152, 330
preservation, 234
press, 92, 97, 102, 104
pressure, 79, 97, 105, 106, 175, 246, 280, 330
prevalence, 205
prevalent, 3, 91, 109, 198, 204, 236, 270, 288, 302, 327
prevention, 48, 111
pride, 13, 16, 34, 40, 63, 65, 121, 131, 136, 150, 152, 157, 180, 203, 220, 228, 233, 237, 247, 257, 260, 273, 291, 316, 318, 321
principle, 37
priority, 278, 307
privacy, 107, 330
privilege, 154, 155, 169, 195, 245, 282, 285, 306, 325, 332
problem, 103, 123, 150, 310
process, 13, 14, 23, 56, 98, 145, 148,

149, 216, 245, 270, 275
producer, 259
production, 40, 59, 60, 127, 219, 221, 244
professional, 112, 123, 180
program, 139, 295
programming, 242, 252, 305
progress, 19, 28–30, 37, 42, 43, 47, 49, 55, 64, 71, 72, 75, 84–86, 92, 99, 104, 106, 107, 121, 126, 128, 129, 134–136, 139–145, 153, 156–165, 168, 170, 173, 177, 178, 183, 184, 192, 194–197, 206–208, 212, 214, 216, 218, 224, 228, 230, 234–238, 245–247, 249, 252, 254, 255, 259, 266, 267, 276–278, 287, 291, 293, 294, 298, 300, 303, 304, 309, 311, 312, 315, 316, 318, 321, 322, 324–326, 331, 335
project, 273
promise, 256, 326
promotion, 24, 52, 129, 182, 206, 244, 289
proposal, 81
protection, 32, 47, 120, 127, 204, 229, 236, 246, 262, 288, 290, 307, 313, 314
protest, 193, 194, 274
public, 6, 19, 21, 23, 24, 26, 27, 31, 32, 40, 41, 43, 44, 47, 53, 54, 57, 58, 63, 68, 70, 71, 77, 78, 83, 85, 93, 96–98, 100–107, 116, 125, 126, 132, 137, 138, 142, 150–152, 159, 160, 162, 164, 166, 169, 180, 187, 190, 193, 203, 206, 212, 214, 216, 218, 220, 223, 225, 227, 229, 236, 246, 259, 264, 272, 275, 277, 278, 288, 290, 291, 300, 302, 308, 311, 313, 327, 330, 336
publication, 162
purpose, 12, 17, 112, 317
pursuit, 7, 8, 21, 43, 53, 73, 91, 93, 101, 105, 107, 108, 132, 145, 160, 165, 170, 189, 210, 223, 224, 247, 256, 263, 265, 285, 295, 297, 298, 335, 336
push, 30, 34, 83, 86, 96, 133, 153, 158, 177, 178, 180, 193, 205, 214, 247, 253, 277, 287, 290, 292, 298, 303, 304, 317, 328

quality, 107, 120, 198, 304, 315
queer, 17, 19, 59, 60, 94, 161, 243, 257, 258, 261, 291, 319
quest, 125
question, 7
quo, 4, 5, 16, 20, 31, 34, 46, 96, 125, 126, 143, 183, 210, 225, 261, 274, 321

race, 4, 6, 45, 53, 57, 111, 125, 136, 137, 153, 154, 186, 190, 194, 196, 200, 201, 212, 223, 242–244, 246, 247, 268, 272, 280, 285, 289, 303, 325, 332, 335
racism, 78, 193, 205, 243, 292, 322
radio, 166

rainbow, 70, 228, 316
range, 50, 52, 65, 142, 146, 163, 181, 185, 231, 232, 260, 283, 288, 312
reach, 62, 71, 86, 165, 166, 168, 169, 190, 196, 221, 237, 241, 255, 272, 273, 278, 289, 292, 299, 301, 308, 325, 329
reader, 178
reading, 66, 114
reality, 21, 24, 46, 154, 272, 337
realization, 2, 16, 21, 136
realm, 23, 82, 96, 121, 157, 189, 296, 302, 307, 329, 330, 336
reason, 247
rebellion, 71
reception, 5
recess, 5
recognition, 16, 31, 32, 35, 38–40, 42, 44, 46–48, 52, 56, 57, 61, 78, 79, 95, 96, 114, 126, 135, 164, 174, 178, 180, 182, 197, 205, 206, 222, 226, 234, 236, 240, 246, 262–264, 288, 304, 310, 313–315, 320
recourse, 100, 120
reflection, 41, 141, 163, 229, 245, 304
reform, 190
refuge, 50
regard, 107
region, 100
reign, 208
rejection, 5, 13, 14, 99, 107, 109, 122, 127, 171, 174, 282, 326

relationship, 5, 11, 12, 47
relaxation, 272
release, 104
relevance, 333
relief, 263
religion, 137, 201, 242, 268, 285
remembrance, 229, 321
reminder, 12, 24, 46, 48, 49, 56, 73, 84, 107, 128, 129, 132, 143, 145, 156, 160, 162–164, 174, 183, 184, 189, 204, 210, 228, 229, 237, 254, 264, 267, 294, 297, 317, 329
removal, 127
renaissance, 261
rent, 18
repeal, 330
report, 81, 270
reporting, 92, 102, 104, 106, 242
representation, 16, 24, 32, 35, 39, 40, 44, 53, 57–63, 66, 69, 70, 73, 75, 120, 121, 125, 127, 129, 133, 135, 150, 151, 153, 166, 172, 176–180, 182–184, 202–204, 206, 210, 217–219, 223, 225, 227, 236, 242–244, 250, 254, 256–260, 263, 264, 277, 278, 291, 296–298, 302, 305, 307, 308, 310, 311, 313, 324, 326, 328
representative, 21, 57, 213, 275, 289
reputation, 34, 106, 266, 296
request, 102
research, 65, 85, 86, 132, 142, 151–153, 185, 190, 191, 223, 231, 240, 272, 273, 308, 319, 334

reshaping, 22, 119, 173, 179, 182, 291
resilience, 1, 3–6, 10, 12, 16, 20, 30, 33, 43, 63–65, 82, 91–93, 97, 101, 102, 105–108, 111, 115, 116, 119, 121–123, 128, 129, 132, 143, 145, 151, 152, 162, 165, 176, 178, 180, 183, 184, 186, 191, 199, 204, 210, 211, 216, 218, 224, 231, 233, 234, 241, 247, 253, 257, 265, 272, 273, 276, 277, 279, 287, 291, 293, 308, 316, 321, 322, 326, 335, 337
resistance, 5, 10, 27, 29–31, 33, 45, 91, 93–98, 105, 107, 128, 129, 172, 175, 176, 223, 249, 260, 308, 333
resolve, 2, 12, 23
resonance, 152
resource, 115, 191, 192, 197, 220, 241, 280, 291, 299
respect, 38, 39, 41, 46, 65, 67, 79, 96, 115, 137–139, 160, 165, 167, 179, 194, 195, 207, 225, 251, 252, 257, 261, 279, 281, 289, 300, 302, 303, 309, 315
response, 274
responsibility, 26, 35, 51, 108, 112, 133, 145, 151, 199, 208, 235, 289, 329
restroom, 67
result, 120, 135, 172, 176, 178, 179, 261
return, 16
revolution, 16, 31, 35, 39, 41, 44, 127, 135, 206, 223, 260, 307, 309
rhetoric, 34
richness, 201, 204
right, 15, 37, 56, 72, 149, 173, 178, 183, 257, 262, 307, 310, 324
rigidity, 179, 262
riot, 316
ripple, 21, 24, 48, 76, 77, 121, 178, 268, 269, 292
rise, 12, 20, 28, 33, 60, 132, 145, 176, 179, 240, 289, 330
risk, 49, 66, 72
road, 29, 34, 170, 247, 293, 335–337
roadmap, 51, 121
role, 1, 3, 15, 17, 19, 22, 27, 29, 31, 33, 35, 41, 42, 47, 52, 56–58, 60–62, 65–70, 82, 94, 99, 108, 111, 114, 120, 122, 126, 127, 132–134, 138, 139, 141, 149–152, 155, 159, 161, 163, 169, 173, 181, 182, 188, 189, 193, 195, 202, 203, 206, 213, 215, 217, 218, 220, 225, 226, 228, 234, 237, 239, 240, 246, 252, 254, 255, 261, 262, 264, 271, 274, 275, 277, 279, 280, 282–284, 288, 290, 292, 294, 297, 299, 301–308, 310, 311, 313, 322, 325, 329, 334, 336
rollback, 277
root, 101, 245
Rosa, 172
route, 316

routine, 71
ruling, 324
run, 112, 298
runway, 177

S. Bear Bergman, 55
sacrifice, 107, 108
safeguard, 49, 234
safety, 50, 51, 204, 229, 238, 270, 330
Samira, 259
Samira Wiley, 259
San Francisco, 15–17
San Francisco's, 16
sanctuary, 16, 164
Santiago Gomez, 177
scale, 3, 9, 10, 34, 63, 69, 71, 73–75, 77, 78, 83, 126, 128, 129, 134, 159, 168, 196, 199, 204, 206, 208, 228, 239–241, 255, 265, 276, 285, 287, 289, 290, 296, 320, 322
scenario, 100
scene, 1, 3, 16, 40, 264
schedule, 107
scholar, 332
school, 66–68, 122, 127, 129, 144, 150, 191, 215
schoolyard, 5
science, 66, 180
scope, 159
screen, 258
scrutiny, 11, 101–104, 106–108, 116, 308
seat, 23
secrecy, 13
secret, 13

section, 1, 2, 9, 13, 19, 26, 31, 33, 39, 41, 46, 49, 52, 56, 61, 63, 82, 105, 111, 114, 124, 149, 160, 170, 186, 189, 200, 202, 214, 218, 231, 237, 245, 254, 265, 270, 274, 279, 286, 300, 305, 327, 335
sector, 54, 79
security, 330
self, 2, 3, 5, 7, 9, 13–15, 21, 49, 55, 56, 82, 101, 102, 108, 112, 113, 115–119, 123, 124, 135, 140, 142, 152, 172–175, 177, 179, 186, 191, 199, 201, 229, 232, 249, 256–261, 272, 282, 301, 304, 305, 319, 326
sense, 1, 3, 9, 12, 15, 17, 18, 24, 35, 40, 43, 48, 50, 63–65, 74, 76–78, 84, 86, 103, 106, 112, 113, 115, 120–123, 127, 131, 140–142, 146, 150, 157, 161, 166, 167, 169, 173, 175, 176, 179, 180, 189, 191, 196–198, 200–202, 220, 227, 228, 231–233, 237, 241, 257, 258, 262, 273, 277, 279, 280, 282, 286, 287, 298, 305, 310, 317, 321, 331
sensitivity, 168
series, 180, 184, 224, 241
service, 133, 137, 142, 317
set, 24, 32, 48, 71, 96, 112, 113, 120, 121, 127, 209, 224, 251, 297, 309, 333
setting, 33, 49, 112, 190, 201, 264
sex, 16, 27, 32, 37, 38, 44, 46–49,

Index

72, 75, 95, 96, 98, 122, 126, 135, 157, 173, 177, 182, 183, 204–206, 222, 224, 226, 234, 236, 251, 257, 263, 266, 288, 289, 303, 307, 310, 313, 314, 324

sexism, 78, 193, 205, 292, 322

sexuality, 19, 124, 129, 154, 179, 181, 223, 231, 257, 268, 332

shape, 3, 11, 17, 26–28, 44, 60, 65, 78, 85, 106, 125, 131, 143, 144, 156, 158, 166, 176, 178, 181, 208, 218, 222, 224, 264, 265, 295, 297, 302, 307, 309, 327, 335

share, 6, 12, 13, 21, 24, 40, 55, 67, 69, 72, 75, 82, 84, 102–104, 107, 113, 120, 121, 123, 125, 140, 149, 151, 161, 166, 175, 182, 185, 187, 192, 196, 199, 214–216, 219, 221, 222, 225, 229, 231, 232, 237, 238, 240, 241, 243, 250, 253, 254, 258, 271, 274, 277–279, 283, 286, 289, 290, 298, 301, 305, 306, 313, 317, 329, 331, 336

sharing, 6, 7, 14, 21, 22, 42, 55, 72, 75–77, 83, 97, 101, 105, 108, 114, 141, 142, 144, 159, 166, 169, 183, 187, 189, 193, 205, 208, 215, 216, 218, 232, 234, 238, 240, 254, 272, 280, 290, 291, 301, 308, 319, 320, 336

she, 21, 55, 100, 101, 174–176, 250, 253, 257

shift, 15, 32, 48, 52, 55–57, 78, 95, 116, 120, 121, 126, 131, 135, 142, 144, 160, 178, 179, 190, 250, 251, 254, 257, 264, 291, 308, 324, 328

shoulder, 42

show, 150, 180, 331

showcase, 13, 40, 45, 46, 59, 61, 62, 64, 69, 123, 136, 139, 189, 204, 218, 219, 221, 228, 232, 264, 271, 291, 305, 319

side, 14

sign, 118, 240

significance, 4, 40, 44, 49, 64, 71, 74, 75, 111, 116, 122, 123, 138, 200, 231, 238, 276

silence, 6

sin, 94

situation, 100

skepticism, 23

skill, 104, 150

smear, 31, 97

societal, 2–7, 9, 12, 14, 16, 17, 19–22, 27, 28, 30, 32, 33, 37–41, 43–45, 47–49, 52–55, 58, 62–64, 69, 71, 75, 78, 85, 91, 92, 94–96, 98, 99, 105, 107–109, 115, 119, 124–127, 129, 138, 139, 149, 151–153, 158, 161, 166, 168, 169, 171–173, 175, 177, 179–183, 188, 189, 191, 200, 201, 203, 210, 213, 218, 219, 221–223, 232,

236, 239, 246, 247, 249, 250, 254, 258, 260–262, 264, 267, 271, 274, 278, 282, 288, 290–293, 302, 307–310, 317, 319, 324, 326, 328, 337
society, 1, 3, 4, 6, 11, 13, 16, 17, 20, 22–24, 27–31, 33, 37–41, 43–48, 51–54, 56–58, 61, 63, 64, 66, 69, 70, 78, 84, 86, 91, 93–96, 98, 99, 101, 105–108, 114, 119–122, 124–129, 131–133, 135–138, 140, 144, 146, 150, 153–155, 157–160, 163, 165, 168, 170, 172–179, 181–183, 185–188, 193–195, 197, 199, 200, 202–205, 207, 210, 211, 213–216, 218, 220–228, 230, 232, 233, 235, 236, 243, 245, 247, 250–253, 256–258, 260–264, 266, 267, 270–275, 277, 279, 281–285, 291–293, 295–297, 299–308, 310, 313–315, 318, 320, 324, 325, 335
socio, 1
Sofia, 175, 176, 253, 257
solace, 3, 5, 9, 12, 142, 175, 211, 249, 258
solidarity, 10, 17, 42, 71–74, 76, 81, 86, 97, 114, 116, 140, 145, 154, 156, 159, 161, 169, 183, 193, 199, 208, 210, 211, 213, 216, 223, 225, 237, 238, 255, 267, 276,

277, 286, 287, 289–291, 304, 308, 312, 316, 322, 327, 331, 336
solution, 6, 103
solving, 123, 150
son, 11
soul, 11, 13, 212
source, 4, 14, 30, 49, 115, 123, 162, 259
South America, 157
space, 9, 13, 21, 41, 55, 64, 69, 84, 112, 129, 133–135, 143, 156, 161–163, 166, 168, 175, 177, 181, 199, 216, 222, 223, 229, 231–233, 254, 257, 267, 283, 289, 293, 299, 301, 305, 311, 317–321, 329–331, 336
spark, 9, 20, 83, 164, 167, 271, 278, 291
speaker, 142, 286
speaking, 6, 21, 43, 44, 47, 75–77, 100, 114, 134, 150, 151, 159, 162, 183, 187, 212, 214, 216, 285, 306
spectacle, 316
spectrum, 39, 53, 56, 95, 179, 286, 305
speculation, 107
speech, 242, 246, 257, 270, 302, 312, 336
spending, 134, 142
sphere, 5, 92
spiral, 174
spirit, 10, 19–22, 82, 106, 143, 164, 184, 230, 253, 287, 297, 317, 318, 321, 322
sponsorship, 291
spotlight, 79, 82, 86, 132, 283

spread, 207, 265, 276, 302, 336
square, 70
stage, 31, 33, 42, 48, 79, 97, 127, 183, 264, 286, 312
stance, 157, 291
stand, 20, 21, 75, 101, 105, 108, 122, 134, 138, 168, 171, 178, 183, 192, 208, 230, 257, 281, 292, 304, 322, 325
state, 196, 231
statement, 10, 104, 316, 330
statue, 164, 184
status, 4, 5, 16, 20, 31, 34, 45, 46, 57, 96, 111, 125, 126, 143, 183, 210, 225, 242, 244, 246, 247, 261, 274, 280, 289, 303, 321, 325, 335
step, 23, 37, 38, 52, 68, 82, 124, 131–135, 138, 141, 145, 175, 193, 200, 257, 304
stepping, 131, 133, 134, 210
stigma, 5, 21, 86, 109, 115, 123, 182, 232, 245, 261, 280, 307
stigmatization, 1, 146, 180, 218
stock, 141
Stonewall, 229
story, 1, 7, 11, 12, 21, 24, 43, 48, 49, 55, 65, 80, 82, 86, 93, 106, 108, 111, 143–145, 162, 175, 176, 178, 183, 187, 211, 249, 257, 259, 266, 293, 294, 307
storyline, 152
storytelling, 6, 15, 16, 59, 60, 65, 104, 140, 142, 151, 180, 187, 210, 216, 221, 227, 229, 241, 278, 290, 291, 296
strain, 14, 107

strategy, 26, 34, 299
street, 83
strength, 2, 7, 12–14, 16, 20, 21, 30, 67, 73, 82, 105–107, 118, 143, 159, 175, 177, 178, 184, 193, 208, 210, 223, 257–259, 292, 293, 308
strengthening, 83
stress, 109, 112, 113, 123
struggle, 2, 4, 6, 12, 22, 28, 42, 59, 73, 77, 105, 143, 154, 159, 163, 187, 193, 208, 225, 249, 267, 282, 289, 290, 293, 329
student, 9, 20, 23, 67, 103, 257
study, 21, 206, 207
style, 28
subject, 106, 107
subsection, 4, 7, 15, 17, 28, 44, 46–48, 58, 65, 68, 71, 74, 75, 84, 94, 96, 98, 101, 107, 108, 116, 122, 126, 133, 138, 141, 145, 151, 154, 159, 160, 162, 163, 165, 168, 171–174, 176, 178, 183, 192, 194, 197, 200–202, 204, 207, 211, 214, 216, 224, 226, 228, 234, 235, 240, 249–256, 258, 260, 263, 268, 274, 276, 281, 283, 288, 292, 295–298, 309, 313, 316, 321, 324, 329
substance, 99, 109, 122
success, 48, 49, 61, 62, 72, 75, 161, 196, 197, 212, 286, 308
suicide, 49, 111, 122, 280, 326
suit, 312
sum, 192

summary, 77, 84, 263
support, 2, 3, 5, 6, 11–15, 17, 19, 21, 23, 24, 26, 27, 30, 31, 34, 38–40, 42, 47, 48, 50, 51, 54–56, 62, 63, 66–69, 71, 72, 74, 75, 78, 79, 83, 84, 86, 97–101, 103–105, 108–118, 122–125, 127, 132, 134, 135, 137–139, 142, 143, 145–153, 156–164, 166–171, 173–175, 177, 180, 181, 185, 186, 188–191, 193, 195–200, 204, 205, 210–213, 215–221, 223, 225, 227–229, 231–233, 235–238, 240–242, 244, 246, 249–253, 256, 257, 261–263, 267, 268, 271, 272, 275–277, 279, 280, 282, 283, 285–292, 296–299, 301, 302, 304–310, 312–322, 324, 326–328, 330, 331, 333, 334, 337
supporter, 142
suppression, 95
supreme, 208
sure, 208
surveillance, 330
Susan Stryker, 55
sustainability, 138, 197, 216, 313, 320
Sylvia Rivera, 234
symbol, 86, 172, 179, 193, 231, 240, 297, 315
symbolism, 120
system, 11, 23, 56, 66, 69, 96, 121, 129, 166, 224, 244, 335

table, 23, 298
Taiwan, 177
talent, 59, 61–63, 189, 204, 219, 221, 232
talk, 201
tapestry, 207, 235
target, 51, 269, 330
task, 14, 185, 214
teaching, 67, 155, 167, 197, 244, 261, 279, 303, 305
team, 70, 102
tech, 81, 242
technology, 24, 51, 73, 83, 113, 123, 166, 169, 170, 196, 197, 206, 231, 237, 242, 254, 255, 272, 273, 289, 291, 299–302, 325, 331, 334
television, 40, 68, 180, 218, 219, 250, 259, 297, 302, 311
tenacity, 321
tenure, 85, 128, 131, 133, 135, 136, 160, 224, 252, 266, 300, 307
term, 84, 119, 132, 135, 136, 141, 156, 196, 212, 242, 278, 298
terminology, 13, 67, 114
testament, 24, 34, 49, 86, 93, 108, 124, 131, 141, 156, 162, 174–176, 183, 184, 204, 210, 223, 228, 236, 240, 252, 256, 260, 265, 267, 294, 309, 315, 316
testimony, 21, 42, 257
text, 111
the Aburrá Valley, 3
the United States, 47, 327, 334
theater, 46, 61, 69, 167, 181, 191, 221, 232, 271, 278, 290,

Index 377

305
therapy, 101, 112, 272
thinking, 29, 123, 152, 210, 244, 271, 306
thought, 181, 189
threat, 18, 94–96
thrive, 41, 50, 53, 62, 84, 101, 122, 124, 132, 135, 160, 173, 199, 208, 212, 217, 225, 245, 250, 263, 279, 282, 293, 296, 304, 308, 311, 320, 321, 326
thriving, 53
time, 3, 5, 9, 10, 14, 16, 17, 20, 21, 24, 28, 31, 50, 71, 93, 98, 101, 107, 111–114, 131, 133, 134, 141–144, 156, 158, 162, 163, 175, 195, 210, 211, 222, 224, 226, 229, 230, 275, 276, 295, 296, 302, 333
today, 86, 156, 264, 301, 302, 309
tolerance, 155, 197, 262
toll, 107, 108, 112, 116
tomorrow, 211
tool, 6, 11, 16, 32, 54, 61, 69, 71, 103, 113, 139, 152, 158, 172, 179, 181, 189, 191, 203, 205, 215, 240, 259, 260, 270, 271, 273, 278, 284, 290–292, 299, 304, 305, 329, 336
topic, 49, 76, 105
torch, 43, 132, 133, 138–142, 165, 178, 209, 211–214, 234, 252, 265, 267, 295, 297–300, 315, 317
touch, 12, 24, 71, 188
tourism, 204

town, 47, 174, 272
traditionalist, 128
trafficking, 31
tragedy, 108
trailblazer, 34, 156, 157, 224, 259, 314
training, 41, 55, 60, 62, 66–68, 70, 85, 123, 139, 150, 194, 195, 198, 199, 203, 212, 213, 231, 252, 271, 275, 295, 322, 326
trajectory, 17, 31, 32, 260, 309
trans, 100, 101
transfer, 298
transformation, 8, 20, 31, 33, 68, 96, 108, 126, 128–130, 141, 172, 175, 179, 181, 222, 261, 328, 335
transgender, 17, 21, 27, 39, 48, 52, 53, 55–59, 77, 98, 99, 124, 125, 135, 152, 172, 174–177, 196, 206, 207, 222, 229, 234, 236, 246, 249, 256–260, 262, 277, 285, 286, 288, 291, 304, 314, 315, 332, 334
transition, 132, 134, 143, 145, 209, 213
transparency, 106, 242
transphobia, 16, 57, 59, 77, 91, 92, 95, 98–101, 105, 106, 115, 183, 195, 204, 223, 237, 243, 282, 304, 308, 325
travel, 142, 204
treatment, 4, 120, 279, 304
trend, 291
tribute, 49, 164, 229, 234, 315, 316
trip, 15, 17
triumph, 34, 151, 178, 209, 294

trust, 14, 24, 79, 112
truth, 13, 14, 44, 55, 182, 290
turn, 11, 24, 92, 207, 254, 257, 303
turning, 2, 23, 33, 35, 47, 206, 229, 257, 266

understanding, 10, 11, 14–16, 19, 22, 30, 34, 39–42, 45, 47, 48, 50, 52, 53, 55–58, 60, 63–66, 68, 69, 72–74, 78, 83, 92, 94, 95, 97, 99–101, 111, 114, 115, 120, 121, 126, 127, 136, 138–140, 145, 151–153, 155, 157–160, 166–168, 171, 172, 174, 175, 179–181, 185, 187–189, 192, 194, 197, 198, 200, 203, 205, 207, 208, 210, 212, 214, 215, 217, 218, 220–223, 225, 227, 232, 234–237, 240, 241, 243, 245, 247, 250, 253, 259, 261–263, 268–273, 275, 277, 283–285, 288, 289, 291–293, 296, 298–302, 305, 306, 308, 311, 314, 317, 318, 320–322, 324, 325, 328, 333–336
union, 11
uniqueness, 283
unity, 3, 4, 17, 34, 76, 79, 86, 103, 112, 120, 140, 142, 156, 157, 159, 166, 167, 171, 180, 186, 192–194, 207, 208, 211, 224, 228, 265, 274, 287, 292, 316, 317, 322
unwillingness, 11

unworthiness, 5
upbringing, 4, 257
uplift, 35, 132, 138, 158, 164, 174, 185, 197, 234, 235, 243, 258, 285, 296, 306, 308, 325
urgency, 9, 66, 95, 97
use, 16, 52, 83, 123, 132, 191, 195, 241, 246, 259, 260, 285, 299, 306, 317, 325, 330, 331
utilization, 168, 192

validation, 173, 302, 324
value, 111, 182, 333
variety, 229, 232
venue, 196
victory, 23, 32, 122, 145, 209, 210, 224, 236, 254, 295, 297, 335
view, 8, 247
violation, 310
violence, 1, 4, 31, 55, 71, 99, 105, 108, 132, 135, 137, 160, 169, 178, 205–208, 229, 236, 238, 245, 247, 262, 285, 288, 307, 312, 319, 324–327, 332
Virgilio, 3–17, 28–31, 33–35, 37–49, 56, 57, 68–71, 75–80, 82–86, 91–93, 101–108, 131–138, 141–145, 156–168, 171–178, 182–189, 209–214, 216, 222–228, 236–240, 249–254, 256–260, 263–267, 286, 287, 292, 294–303, 307,

Index 379

308, 310–315, 317, 321, 322, 327, 328
Virgilio Barco, 94, 95
Virgilio Barco Isakson, 1, 2, 4, 7, 9, 11, 26, 31–35, 37, 44–46, 49–51, 56, 58, 61, 63, 65–68, 70, 75–77, 82, 84–86, 91–93, 96–98, 104–108, 115, 116, 119, 122, 124, 126, 131–133, 135, 138, 141–145, 151, 154–160, 162, 163, 165, 172–174, 178–181, 184, 186, 202–204, 207–209, 213, 214, 216, 218, 222–224, 226, 228, 231–233, 238, 239, 247, 251–253, 256, 260, 266, 285, 286, 292, 295–297, 303, 304, 307–309, 313–316, 318–321, 327, 337
Virgilio Barco Isakson Day, 315
Virgilio Barco Isakson's, 7, 9, 13, 15, 17, 19, 22, 28, 31, 33, 37, 39, 41, 43, 45, 46, 49, 52, 70, 76, 77, 79, 84, 86, 93, 98, 101, 104, 106, 111, 121, 126, 129, 131, 132, 134, 136, 141, 143, 145, 153, 155, 156, 158, 160, 163, 165, 168, 171, 172, 174–176, 178–183, 185, 186, 189, 204, 209–211, 218, 224, 226, 228, 233, 235, 237, 239, 240, 249–252, 254, 256, 258, 260, 263–265, 267, 287, 294, 295, 297, 298, 300, 308–313, 315, 321, 322, 326, 329, 335
Virgilio Barco Isakson, 206
Virgilio Barco Isakson, 44
visibility, 16, 19, 31, 53, 55, 59, 63, 64, 68, 71, 77, 97, 114, 120, 121, 135, 168, 172, 176, 178, 179, 181, 193, 218, 228, 229, 236, 238, 243, 250, 254, 256, 258–260, 264, 277, 278, 288, 291, 302, 305, 307, 308, 310, 311, 324
vision, 3, 20, 22–24, 28, 31, 34, 44, 86, 134, 163, 173, 174, 177, 178, 185, 186, 189, 195, 216, 218, 225, 226, 238, 253, 257, 261, 265, 266, 274, 296, 297, 301, 310, 318
visual, 46, 167, 184, 191, 271, 290, 302, 316
voice, 3, 5, 11, 20, 21, 23, 29, 34, 42, 70, 71, 75, 78, 106, 132, 142, 143, 145, 159, 160, 178, 193, 195, 212, 213, 218, 223, 227, 233, 241, 245, 249, 257, 265, 274
volunteer, 13
volunteering, 72, 275
volunteerism, 196
vote, 324
vulnerability, 14, 21, 22, 314

wake, 156
walking, 164
warmth, 231
wave, 6, 24, 33, 84, 162, 178, 180, 211, 224, 295

way, 12, 14, 15, 19, 21, 28, 32–35, 37–40, 43, 46, 48, 49, 52, 57, 70, 92, 96, 98, 107, 116, 119, 120, 124–126, 135, 150, 153, 157–159, 161, 162, 164, 168, 172, 173, 181–184, 190, 192, 199, 200, 204, 205, 210, 212, 214, 218, 220, 222, 230, 240, 245, 247, 250, 251, 256, 257, 262, 270, 274, 285, 287, 290, 295, 298, 300–303, 306–309, 311, 320, 325, 329, 330, 332, 337
weakness, 21
wealth, 331
website, 252, 273
week, 184
weight, 13, 35, 108, 112, 133
welfare, 48
well, 4, 13, 15, 35, 38, 49, 58, 72, 78, 99–101, 103, 107, 108, 112, 115, 116, 118–120, 123, 142, 149, 169, 170, 186, 198, 199, 202, 204, 205, 217, 229, 231, 236, 240, 250–252, 256, 267, 270, 272, 277, 280–282, 289, 301, 303, 304, 307, 312, 314, 318, 320, 324, 326
wellbeing, 116
wellness, 272
whole, 38, 99, 122, 132, 137, 140, 141, 154, 178, 194, 204, 250, 260, 264, 316, 319
willingness, 22, 82
win, 32

wisdom, 139, 140, 142, 177, 298, 301
woman, 21, 55, 100, 174, 175, 249, 256, 332
word, 12, 306, 317
work, 3, 6, 13, 20, 23, 24, 26, 29, 30, 40–46, 48, 51, 56, 57, 61, 62, 65, 67–69, 72, 74, 77, 80, 84, 97, 101, 103, 104, 107, 111, 114, 115, 119, 121, 126, 131–136, 138–145, 151–153, 156–158, 162, 163, 165, 168, 170–174, 176–179, 181, 183, 184, 186, 190, 191, 193, 197, 199, 205, 208, 210, 211, 215–217, 219, 223, 225–228, 230, 233–236, 240, 243–245, 249, 250, 252–261, 264, 271, 275, 279–282, 285–288, 291, 296, 298, 300, 301, 303–305, 307, 309, 311, 313, 315, 317, 318, 320, 324, 331, 333–336
workforce, 217, 280
working, 29, 42, 51, 56, 78, 79, 81, 115, 126, 134, 140, 158, 165, 169, 176, 182, 183, 190, 192, 195, 206, 213, 216, 227, 237, 239, 243, 245, 253, 255, 257, 263, 267, 272, 275, 277, 289, 293, 300, 301
workplace, 38, 54, 57, 84, 176, 185, 198, 280, 281, 335
world, 3, 6, 7, 11, 12, 16, 22, 26, 33, 42, 43, 46, 48, 49, 51, 61,

63, 65, 68, 71–74, 76, 77, 80, 82–84, 86, 91, 94, 107, 116, 119, 123, 124, 128, 130, 132, 137, 143–145, 150, 151, 153, 156, 163, 164, 174, 176–178, 183, 189, 193, 199, 200, 204, 206–208, 216, 224, 226–228, 235, 237–242, 245–247, 252, 254, 256, 259, 260, 263–265, 267, 273, 283, 285, 286, 288–291, 294, 297, 303, 309, 312, 313, 316, 321, 322, 326–329, 336, 337

worldview, 1

worth, 20, 208, 281, 282, 310
writer, 152, 259
writing, 151

year, 162, 184, 266
youth, 3, 33, 38, 43, 49–51, 60, 65, 66, 75, 83, 100, 101, 111, 120, 122–127, 132, 135, 137, 138, 141, 142, 149, 151, 157, 160, 161, 173, 175, 177, 178, 180, 183, 188, 191, 192, 205, 207, 212, 222, 227, 236, 237, 241, 251, 259, 263, 264, 266, 278, 279, 295, 298, 300, 301, 307, 308, 311–314, 319, 326, 328